MONEY ISSUES IN BLACK MALE FEMALE RELATIONSHIPS

GEORGE SUBIRA
BA, M. ED., ED. S.

Published by
Very Serious Business Enterprises
P.O. Box 356
Newark, New Jersey 07101
(609) 641-0776

OTHER BOOKS BY GEORGE SUBIRA

Black Folks Guide To Making Big Money In America

Black Folks Guide to Business Success

Getting Black Folk To Sell

See Back Page For Details

DEDICATIONS

This book is dedicated to three extremely important people in my life.

Lyncoln Trower - my brother. Though younger than I, he is more knowledgeable about both Black women and writing. He is
without a doubt the one who inspired the writng of this book. Though this volume is lighter in tone and spirit than what he would have written, I hope he's satisfied with my efforts.

Mrs. Airow Ophelia Hunter - my aunt. In 1964 she told her nephew to "keep on pushin" and she has been a continued source of inspiration ever since then. Wiser beyond her seventy seven years yet as enthusiastic as a teenager, she is without a doubt one of the most fascinating women I have ever or will ever meet in my life.

Marian Wheeler (August 1948 - March 1993) No one on this earth helped me through my most depressing moments as much as the best female friend that I ever had. I miss her and think about her often. Fortunately I have many tapes that I can rewind and replay in mind for the rest of my life.

HARRIS COMPUTER SERVICES

TOP QUALITY COMPUTER SERVICES
WE DELIVER

- **SCANNING MATERIALS TO DISK**

- **DESKTOP PUBLISHING**

- **MANUSCRIPTS CAMERA READIED**

WE WILL QUICKLY PREPARE YOUR MANUSCRIPT FOR PRINTING AND PRODUCTION

(LIKE WE DID THIS ONE)

CALL (215) 548-1539

FOR QUOTES AND FURTHER INFORMATION

AUTHOR'S BIOGRAPHY

George Subira considers himself primarily an educator and became a Black Studies Instructor at Seton Hall University (N.J.) at age 25. He spent five years in the Black Cultural Nationalist Movement in Los Angeles with Dr. Maulana Karenga.

George Subira was educated at California State University at Los Angeles and Rutgers University Graduate School. His first publication in 1980, *Black Folk's Guide to Making Big Money in America,* was the first practical guide on money management and income improvement written specifically for Black people.

In 1985 he authored his second book, *Black Folks Guide to Business Success.* Another ground breaking book appeared in 1988 with the publication of *Getting Black Folk to Sell,* the first and only book to discuss selling from a Black perspective. He has appeared on television (Donahue, Today, Tony Brown's Journal, BET, Sonya Freidman Show, 700 Club etc.) and radio from coast to coast. Dozens of newpapers and magazines have featured articles on Subira and his books. As *Money Issues in Black Male Female Relationships* goes to press, over 100,000 copies of Subira's previous books have been sold. He is a frequent speaker on college campuses and at Black business and professional conferences. Business concepts are explained within the context of Black history and culture.

The author was an original particapant in the first four Kwanzaa celebrations. Insight from that experience will be featured in a future publication entitled, *Kwanzaa and the Black Economy* due for release in 1995.

DAMMAH
Productions
SPEAKERS BUREAU

P·R·E·S·E·N·T·S

LECTURERS
and speakers
ARTiSTS &
SPECIAL EVENTS

DAMMAH PRODUCTIONS - Speakers Bureau
P.O. BOX 254 NEW LONDON, CT 06320   203 443 4278

TABLE OF CONTENTS

Black Women as House Slaves - Black Men as Field Slaves - House Slaves as Role Models - Black Males Rebel Against Slavery - Black Women as Carriers of White Culture to Black Community - Modern Society More Tolerant of Black Women - Black Males and Females Tastes and Preference as an Indicator of Values.

Confusion over definition of manhood - David Walker, Nat Turner - Non-Offensive Black male role models-Native American Heroes - The 1960's - Today's False Enemies - Why the Perpetual Anger - Womanhood and Manhood Differences - The Rappers Fantacy - White Man's Reality

Early Money Consciousness - Work for Whites - Spend All of Your money - Buy from Whites - Play Together but Not Work Together -Grades over Creativity-Television Orientation to Money - School Orientation to Money - Peer and Sibling Orientation to Money.

Early Interaction - Tide Turns on Young Black Men-Younger Sisters- Black Males at Home - the Bomb Drops- Money's Role in Feminine "Maturity" - Girls Devaluing Themselves - Young Black Men Respond - Puppy Love - Learning Not To Commit - the Athletic, Music, Party Time and Bullying Routes - Drug Dealing

INTERESTED IN HAVING GEORGE SUBIRA SPEAK AT YOUR CONFERENCE CONVENTION OR SEMINAR?

FIVE OCCASIONS WHEN GEORGE SUBIRA IS A VALUABLE SPEAKER.

For KWANZAA Programs. I n 1966, George Subira attended the very first Kwanzaa celebration in Los Angeles. Maulana Karenga put him in charge of setting up the second Kwanzaa celebration in December of 1967. No one in the country, except Dr. Karenga, is in a better position to discuss this holiday from its inception to its development and relevance today. Kwanzaa has an economic significance today and this is covered in Subira's Presentation.

For Black Business Programs. George Subira's three books on Black business have sold well over 100,000 copies. Many hundreds of African Americans can trace their inspiration to go into business or their success in business to the information provided in these books or Subira's workshops.

For Black History Programs. In keeping with the theme of Black Economic Development, a special presentation has been developed that traces Black people's efforts at nation building. *A History of Economic Struggle and Development* is the title to our Black History Month lecture. If African Americans are to ever develop any economic control in their own communities, it is important for them to understand that much of what they are trying to do has already been accomplished by previous, poorer, "less educated" generations of Black people.

For Career Day Programs. Career day programs serve as important opportunities for students to study their options for earning a living and making a contribution to their communities. Almost always, self employment and entrepreneurship is left out as a viable option for students to consider. Yet most research shows that most successful business persons got started in sales and business at an early age. Thus African American students need to be exposed to the ideas of self employment during career day programs if they are to get the full range of their live's possibilities. George Subira has given such presentations on college campuses all over the nation.

For Discussions on Black Relationships. Subira's new book, *Money Issues in Black Male Female Relationships,* is the first one to really discuss the central role that money, careers, education, and status play in Black Relationships. Whether you agree with his views or not, Subira's perspective adds an exciting dimension to some of the tired old statements and ideas that are repeated over and over in these presentations on Black Relationships.

AKNOWLEDGEMENTS AND CREDITS

For reasons which are still not perfectly clear to me, this volume was by far the most challenging publication that I've put together. It may have never come together at all without the help of dozens of people who made generous contributions at cruical times.

Contributions were made by Louis and Doris Harris, Noah Lewis, Shirley Carmack, Airow Hunter, Theondrus Anderson, Giovonni Putty, Denise Banks, Ibn Trower, Lyncoln Trower, Seba Trower, Earl Willaims (George's Fuel Oil), Dr. George Jackson, Marilyn French Hubbard, Gwen Evans, James Davis, Maisha Hazzard, Preston Foster, Alma Jordan, Chris Daniels, Warren Jabali, Beverly Thomas, Melvin Turner, and Debora Young. A special thanks goes to Earl and Eursla Wells, Miami, Fl., Forrest Prichett, Richard Barber, George Jones and Dr. John Cosby.

Typing, computerwork and photo copying were done by Linda Mobley, Bonnie Smith, Trudy Johnson, Debbie Calland McCarthy, Walter Dillion, Cheryl Pitts Hawkins, Kathy Akins, Doris Harris, Vanessa Quarles, and Pauline Adams.

Computer work also done by Trina and Gloria Byrd of T-Byrd Computer Co., Dorothy James and Fran Sa Gatlin of The Consortium (Atlantic City), and Chester and Mechele Cauley. But the HNIC was Louis Harris.

Graphic Design, Lisa Mulkey.

Typesetting, Louis Harris

Editing work was done by Christine King, Sylvetta Snowten, Bonnie Smith, Louis Harris, and Lyncoln Trower.

Cover photo by Mike Ein of Einrosia in Pleasantville, N.J.

Cover Models, Vanessa Quarles and Glenn Umstead. Special thanks to Linda Mobley.

I hope that anyone who should have been added to this list, but for some reason was forgotten, will forgive me.

INTRODUCTION

As a writer and lecturer for the past fifteen years on the topic of Black economics, I've gained a degree of credibility and good will with a few hundred thousand readers and supporters. I value very highly these relationships of support and enthusiasm. But I am putting this supportive relationship at risk with many thousand's of readers, particularly female readers, with the publication of this book *Money Issues In Black Male/Female Relationships.* It contains statements that some might deem controversial or anti-feminist or worse. I can only hope that all who take the time to read this work will derive some positive or useful insight regardless of how many statements they find troublesome. That is after all what most of us do with all books including some religious documents.

I can certainly say that I have spent much more time and anguish studying Black women (and men) than I have in trying to understand Black economics. My "success" in articulating Black economic issues has given me the confidence to plunge ahead into this topic as well. Actually, there is a lot of similarity in this work and the others as you will hopefully see.

The Perfect Book Isn't Coming

The topic of Black male-female relationships is an emotionally charged one and each sex usually feels compelled to defend the positions and perspectives of their gender. Sometimes it doesn't take much for a loud shouting match to develop and what was suppose to be a "discussion" degenerates into another argument discouraging further attempts at a "dialogue" between the sexes. Every so often a book comes along which catches the attention of the Black reader and renews some of the issues over which Black men and women disagree. One of the complaints of these books (*For Colored Girls Who Have Considered Suicide...*, *The Color Purple, Brewster Place, Black Mans Guide To Understanding The Black Woman, Waiting To Exhale*, etc.) is that they lack "balance". It's said that the portrayal of the characters are too stereotypical; too dated; or that one gender, usually the men, are shown to be totally negative with no positive characters to " balance" the depiction of the sex. There must be at least an ounce of truth to this statement. Otherwise, it wouldn't come up as a problem so frequently. Right? Well yes and NO. Yes many people have trouble in what they see as the consistently negative portrayal of one sex or another - so there is some reality to the perception. But no, it is not necessarily a *problem* if it's necessary for the writer (or film director in the case of movies) to make their point.

A book is a statement. A film, a T.V. show, a magazine article is a statement - and in a free society, a person is usually allowed to arrange words, ideas, and characters in any way they wish to make the statement they wish to make. Besides, it is virtually impossible for an individual to write a full volume without injecting their own biases into their work. Everyone puts their experience, their research, their perspective and beliefs into their work while neglecting factors which they either are ignorant of or disbelieve. This writer and this work will be no different.

It might prove useful to at least theorize however, what a truly "balanced" book on Black male-female relationships would look like and then ask ourselves if we could truly deal with what we are asking for.

A "balanced book" on Black male-female relationships would start where we started, from Ancient Africa. Such a book would feature the research of several ancient African historians to tell us how we initially lived as a family. These historians would be both male and female and would be both African American and West African so that "balance" could be achieved. Next the book would contain the work of experts in the area of American slavery. These experts (male and female) would tell us exactly how the slave system changed the nature of the man' role, the woman's role, family unity and structure, communication, sex, the extended family, etc., etc. This would be followed by a series of historians on the Reconstruction Period, the Black Northern migration, the Depression era, Post World War II developments, etc. up to the modern day. Then after we had the historical viewpoint we would then look at economic developments since slavery. How did Black people support themselves in the last one hundred and twenty five years? Then we would have to look at the Black Church since slavery because that was the institution that joined us in marriage, counseled us during marriage, and aided us when death and separation occurred. We would most certainly have to look at the perspective of today's female religious leaders for "balance." Since art expresses a range of emotions that people cannot express in words, we would have to study Black women's art (poetry, novels, paintings, plays) from both a Black male and Black female viewpoint (for " balance") and then repeat the same process for Black male art.

Then Black sociologists, who specialize in Black family life, sex life, etc., would have their say (male and female professionals, of course for "balance"); and they would have to study both rural and urban families, Northern and Southern families, Black families that were poverty stricken, and also those who make over a hundred thousand dollars a year. Then the lawyers would talk about the criminal justice system's impact. Black doctors would talk about health's effect on families. Psychologists would reveal their insight and we would go on thru all the other institutions.   We haven't mentioned the educational systems yet. We would end up with the funeral parlor directors talking about how families fight, argue and curse as soon as someone dies and how death impacts the male-female relationships of the living survivors.

When all is done, a truly "balanced book" on Black male-female relationships would include the work of a hundred and twenty experts (at least 59 female for "balance") and would run slightly over seventeen hundred pages. Because each of these writers would be experts in their field, they would be paid accordingly- all one hundred and twenty of them. If you add the other normal costs of producing a book, this "balanced" book would probably cost somewhere between one hundred and sixty to one hundred and seventy dollars, before tax, shipping and handling charges. Now the question is this. Would the Black community buy such a wonderfully "balanced" book? And even if they bought it or it was given to them as a present, would they even read it? I, personally ,don't think so; and I don't think you do either. So no "balanced" book on male-female relations is due out any time soon. One will have to buy all the "biased" stuff that's out here on the market, or not read about it at all. The balance that you seek can only begin to come about by reading several books on the same topic. And even at that point, one must understand that there are always several realities in existence at the same time. So your truth would not necessarily be this writer's truth. But that doesn't mean that we both can't learn from each other' experiences and perceptions of "The Truth."

Pre Pouncing The Pouncers

Dr. Naim Akbar is a brilliant speaker and Black psychologist and a very popular presenter in Black professional and student gatherings all over America. He takes a firm position on the principles he stands for and does not lay all the blame of Black folks problems at the hands of White folks. Any speaker who demands that Black people must assume a certain amount of responsibility for either getting themselves into or getting themselves out of the problems that they are ensnared in, faces a certain amount of criticism from these Black audiences. Some Blacks believe racism is the only true reason behind every conceivable ill in our community. These critics wait in the audience to jump on a speaker for "misleading the people" and not "pointing the finger" where it ought to be pointed to- White America. Dr. Akbar calls these individuals "pouncers" because they are ready to pounce on you at the first opportunity. A pouncer comes to the lecture actually looking forward to pounce on the speaker. With any amount of luck, they will get the opportunity to hog the microphone, give a fifteen minute oration of their own, embarrass and upstage the main speaker and sit down to a powerful round of applause from their peers. Dr. Akbar has an exercise where he seeks to pre-pounce (preempt) and neutralize his challengers in the audience by laying out ahead of time his assumptions and awareness of relevant people and events of the day. This is done to discourage all but the most combative personality types from taking the mike during the audience participation segment of a program and pouncing on him as described above. With writers, there is not often the opportunity to ask them a question directly or pounce on them. So what book reviewers and critics, talk show hosts and others will sometimes do is run a personality or psychological profile on the writer in an attempt to explain why they feel, believe, think or write like they do. If they can discredit the writer or put an unflattering label on him, then it's supposed to take away the influence or credibility of a book, movie, or other statement that he has made. Thus, to Imamu Baracca, Spike Lee was too much of a middle class Negro to be qualified to do a movie on Malcolm X. Alice Walker must have been a manhater to have written *The Color Purple*. And Shahrazad Ali just had to have been a woman hater (and a whole lot worse) to have written her book on Black women. As I am writing this, there are certain guesses the public is making as to the background and personality of Terry McMillan based on the tone of her current best seller, *Waiting To Exhale.*

Because almost all books are in some small way (at least) autobiographical in nature, it is a natural and legitimate curiosity for a reader to want to know more about a writer who has already revealed a certain amount of himself in his writing. I have no problem with sharing up front with the reader some of the influences in my life in terms of people, situations, and experiences which helped shape the perspectives that you will find in this book. If this book sells as much as I hope and think it will, I will have my share of people ready to pounce on me. But rather than have people lie or make stuff up (which they may do, anyway), I'd prefer to shed some light on my own background, motivations, influences, etc.

I was raised in a two parent household with a strong, rather domineering father figure and a hard working mother. My mother's sensitivity made up for the most part for my fathers lack of the same. But being an early (1952) Black policeman in the racist Philadelphia police force (perhaps you have heard the name of Frank Rizzo former mayor and Police Commissioner) and working in the deadliest parts of North Philadelphia, would have a tendency to desensitize most people. The feminist movement was a good fifteen years away when I was absorbing my early impressions of gender roles and functions. Even so, I had no preconceived notions of an inferiority of girls either from a moral or intellectual point of view. And even if I had, Lydia Henry would have changed that impression quick.

Lydia was my girlfriend in either the 2nd or 3rd grade. She was fine by any one's standards and very smart. I found myself in a kind of academic competition with Lydia in elementary school because I guess, deep down, I thought it was kind of unfair for a person to be so fine and so smart when most people couldn't compete on either level. Lydia was my early proof that Black women could be both smart and attractive and I've never had a reason to think otherwise since then.

I had some good Black teachers in my school years and Mrs. Veronica Gaines stood out from them all. I thought Mrs. Gaines was the finest woman in the world. Looking back now, I really believe that Mrs. Gaines kept me from ever seeing White women as truly beautiful. As a very bright woman (a graduate of Oberlin College in the 1950's which was rare for a Black woman) and as a music teacher, she had a combination of beauty and intellect and soulful earthiness that I guess I've been looking for in women ever since.

The two people who influenced me the very most in my relationship with women however were not friends, family, teachers or girlfriends. They were singers. I have always said that Smokey Robinson and Curtis Mayfield were the main causes of my troubles with women. *Shop Around* was the 2nd record that ever came into our house, and from the very beginning I was hooked on Smokey. At 14, I had the fortune, or misfortune, depending on how you want to look at it, of falling in love. Actually, to be really truthful, it was beyond love. To say I worshiped Beverly Thomas is probably more accurate. A part of you grows up real fast at 14 when you are absolutely and fully aware that you will never ever love like this again in this lifetime. Anyway back then, *Bad Girl* was the love record of that time. That record cemented in stone, a type of neurological and emotional bond that was to exist between George Subira and Smokey Robinson's music and the feelings of intense love forever. In a supporting role with a similar effect was Curtis Mayfield and the Impressions. What these two men did in their music is very simple to explain. They basically told young Black men that it was ok to worship a Black woman if you wanted to. Don't play games with them. Tell them and show them how far you will go to win their affection. The idea was that if you went far enough, they usually reward you by giving it back. That was usually the way it worked out on the records, but real life was a different story altogether. I must have picked my heart up off the ground a half dozen times before my first marriage. I would always rinse it off, iron out the wrinkles, cracks and scratch marks and then look for somebody else to fall in love with all over again. Do not ask me how I would have dealt with girls, love, rejection, and fears without the guidance of Smokey Robinson and Curtis Mayfield. Their suggestions of letting it all hang out there got me into several emotional entanglements. Yet it was some of these same songs that also consoled me, and let me know I had plenty of company, and had nothing to be ashamed of. Looking back now it was at this point that I learned what risk and reward really were. If you can learn how to put your heart on the line, you can learn how to put your money on the line. They are two sides of the same coin. You can't hit the jackpot in love or business without taking the risks. And yes most people do lose! So what?

The next major development in my "lessons" about Black women took place in Los Angeles during the mid and late 60's. California was the place to be in the 60's if you wanted to learn and practice "Blackness." The Black Panther Party, the Black Studies movement, The first major Black urban rebellion (Watts 1965), the Black Student Union movement, the Black Olympic Boycott movement, the first national Black holiday (Kwanzaa) and the Black Cultural Nationalist movement all started in California during these times. As an activist involved in several of these developments, I wasn't being just baptized in Blackness, I was being marinated in it. I choose to affiliate with the US cultural nationalist organization headed by Maulana Karenga. I was intrigued with Karenga's intellect and ability to analyze and explain things so that anyone could understand. He has been, by far, my greatest teacher and I know I will never meet anyone like him again if I live to be a hundred years old. Seldom does a week past that I do not draw from the many lessons learned from that experience. US organization produced a systematic way of looking at the 1960's world of Blacks, Browns and Whites. It seemed to make more rational sense than any other program, religion or organization existing at that time. This "system" was called Kawaida and addressed itself to the seven areas of culture as defined by Dr. Karenga. Within that system was one area called social organization, and within social organization, there were defined roles for the newly emerging African American male and female as well as a criteria for marriage and a marriage ceremony. It was through my nationalist teachings that I learned that the role of the African American woman was to be "submissive" to her man, take care of the children and develop the social fabric of the community. The word *submissive* seemed to be fully appreciated by most of the brothers in the organization. They seemed to need it to justify attitudes, actions and treatments that they had already adopted as their mode of operation toward Black women. I on the other hand, was uncomfortable with the idea for several reasons. Was I suppose to "make" my woman submissive or was she supposed to be that way automatically or naturally? What specific actions did she have to do in order for me to know I was being submitted to? If I was just uncomfortable with the whole concept was I supposed to speak up on it or just keep my mouth shut for peer pressure reasons? I had a hard time picturing any of the women I had admired, and or loved submitting to me in ways the organization said was appropriate. Since I had always been attracted to intelligent women, somebody that could teach me something about a lot of things, how could I pretend that this intellectual equal was supposed to submit to me? Besides Smokey and Curtis said nothing about this. Maulana was the expert on Black Nationalist cultural theory. I accepted that. But Smokey and Curtis were the authorities on love and women even if their stuff didn't and hadn't worked for me yet. I was confused and it showed.

As things turned out, my reputation among my organizational brothers suffered when my lady snuck around and did some undermining things. Subira got a reputation of not being able"to control his woman". How can you fight the revolution brother, when you can't even control what goes on in your own house? My previous romantic disappointments were never this public and degrading before. This humiliation still did not cause me to adopt a macho reaction towards women. Logically, it seems that's what should have happened so that I could ensure that I wouldn't be humiliated again and to regain the lost status that I had suffered in the eyes of Karenga and everyone else in the Organization. In a way, I felt very similar to a punk that has been beaten up by a bully and still refuses to learn how to fight. For a long time, I believed that I was a weak man because I couldn't adopt a macho attitude toward sisters. I *like* being someone who has a deep respect for the equality of sisters and brothers. I must admit, however, that I was emotionally hurt often when I saw so many fine intelligent sisters buckle under to some stupid ass brother acting macho and beating his chest. I kept asking myself the same questions month after month, year after year. If I'm right and women are to be treated and respected as equals and my nationalist brothers are wrong in assuming that sisters are to walk two steps behind the man, how come the brothers have so many nice looking women while I go through so many periods of having no one at all? Maybe Smokey and Curtis were wrong; after all, their stuff hadn't worked for me in all my years of belief and faith.

My personal confusion about how to look at and treat women was a preview of what was just about to occur between Black men and women nation wide. By the early to mid seventies some of the ideology of the women's movement had found its way into the thinking of some nationalist sisters. Who would have thought that I would have hooked up with one of the primary sisters pushing things in this new direction.

Her name was Tulani Davis, a poet from Virginia. We met in the Black Studies Department at Seton Hall University where we both worked. Tulani helped me put my confidence and self image back together when my first marriage ended. Tulani was the first real intellectual woman that I formed a relationship with and it was different from anything I had experienced before. Tulani's very best friend at the time was a sister who is now the very well known writer, Ntozake Shange. One night I was invited to go to a poetry reading/play in the Village in New York. A number of sisters read poems/statements in a small dark theater concerning Black men. They were exploding out of their mouths what seemed like one thousand years of repressed frustrations in dealing with Black men. The title of the play didn't make much, if any, sense at all. It was called *For Colored Girls Who Have Considered Suicide When The Rainbow Is Enough*. It was intense. Part of me was genuinely curious to understand how frustrated these representative personalities were with Black men. But another part of me felt like twenty women were throwing snowballs at me and hitting me consistently five, six and seven times at once all over my body. I had never heard anything that intense before. At the end of the program Tulani asked me did I "like it." I really couldn't answer. This was her art and her best friend's art. I had to be tactful and considerate. But how do you "like" two hundred snow balls hitting you everywhere for no reason other than you happen to be one of the only stupid males present at this event. That play as some of you are aware, became a major milestone in Black literature. Who could have known. Little did I know then that the viewing of a play not yet complete would lead eventually to this very book. This book is, among many other things, a response to feelings I felt that night about eighteen years ago.

A Unique Perspective

This volume is about two emotional issues; Black male/female relationships which cause one set of responses and reactions in people and money, which sets off a different set of responses. There is no pretense to try to portray both male and female perspectives here because *the writer can only discuss that with which he is most familiar; the male perspective*. If a decent job is done in describing that perspective, then hopefully that will be interpreted as an overall contribution to the ongoing desire of Black men and women to understand each other. But even as the material will include many statements pertaining to gender relationships, the primary emphasis will be on economic/career/business issues.

There is the assumption that knowledgeable people wish to see the Black community build economic enterprises which will serve its people's interests. But in order for that to happen, several things must be in place. First, the Black community must have a sense of itself as a specific community in need of its own economic entities. There must also be a sense of or spirit of cooperation and a common meeting of the minds in order for this building to take place. And a strong community is almost always comprised of strong family units (ie, spouses, children and extended family members). When most of these things are not present, talk of community economic development is just that; talk.

Unfortunately, too many Black communities lack most of these things and there is often the absence of even talk about economic growth. Not only is the sense of community absent, but the building blocks of the community; individual family units; are shot to pieces in too many cases. Finally even when there is the appearance of "stable" family units, we find that the money disagreements and the money pressures are volatile enough to threaten the existence of even these units. Thus the house of cards nature of many of today's Black communities makes them unlikely to reach the maximum use of their economic potential. But change must start somewhere, and it appears that a meeting of the minds between spouses over money and its real uses and symbolic meanings is a good place to start. Although personal money management has been at least touched on in all three of my previous books, this volume is intended to hit a slightly different nail on its head.

Limitations and Disclaimers

In a further attempt "to level" with the reader, I have to state publicly that I have lost a significant amount of contact with young adults under say the age of twenty five or so. Hopefully, some will be able to relate to the issues and interpretations brought forth in this book.

Secondly, although I have had substantial interaction with Black men from the so-called ghetto, in almost all instances, we were engaged in progressive activities or legal recreational activities. I have not been around Black men in gang situations, in the army, jails, in crack houses, bars, street corners, or unemployment offices, etc. I have not seen many Black men at their most depressed, desperate moments. This is basically because I was fortunate enough to have kept on a fairly consistent road toward the more positive things in life. It was not luck that I was travelling on this road, but I am lucky that I wasn't pulled off. What this means, I guess, is that a lot of the kinds of pain that hundreds of thousands, maybe millions of Black men and women have faced and complained about is foreign to me personally. To a certain extent, I am unqualified to comment intelligently on some of the deepest misery that Black women have given Black men and Black men have given Black women when either of them are at their lowest moments. But I think what's presented here is enough for those who are serious about starting a meaningful dialogue, to begin a conversation. If Black men and women can't talk intelligently to each other about each other, why should we assume that we can talk intelligently about anything else?

BOOK SUMMARY

Ordinarily and logically one would expect that a book's summary would come at the end of the volume. Such an expectation makes perfect sense except for one small detail; the overwhelming majority of books are not read to completion. Industry experts say that less than a quarter of books purchased are read from cover to cover. For that reason this book summary is being placed here at the beginning so that you can understand easily and quickly what this authors perspective is regarding *Money Issues In Black Male/Female Relationships*.

If you find that these points of view run counter to your personal experience, please read on to the books completion so that you can see how such a different perspective was legitimately reached.

If you see that these statements mirror your life and circumstances, I again suggest that you read on. Its usually very comforting to find someone who seems to have drawn the same conclusions that we have in dealing with this thing called life.

Deep in the minds of most Black Americans lies, at the very least, a vague awareness of the terms "house Niggas" and "field Niggas". These two styles of Black workers represented different levels in the Black social order during the more than two hundred year slave experience in America. Associated with these two different places in the Black social order were two distinct mentalities. The "house Nigga" mentality is generally understood to be that way of thinking and looking at the world that most closely resembled that of the White master. It represents, generally speaking, a wholesale acceptance of the masters values as to what constitutes good and bad, beauty and ugliness etc. It is referred to as the "house mentality" because it is most characteristic of slaves who worked in the masters house. The "field Nigga" mentality was most characteristic of slaves who worked in the hot fields of the American South. The field mentality and personality was much more likely to retain the original African perspective of the world as well as harbor strong desires to rebel against the people holding Blacks in bondage.

The first point to be made in this volume is that Black women, from the beginning and for a variety of reasons were made into house slaves at a much greater frequency than were Black males. Thus it is not out of line to assume that Black people can trace a major portion of the "house" thinking that has always been part of our history, to Black Women.

Because American culture has always been about wealth and materialsim, Black women as house slaves, absorbed values that had to do with wealth and materialsim. Black female houseslaves carried a great deal of influence over the thinking of the other slaves. Not only did she work close to the master, but she was often lighter in skin color, better educated, better dressed, physically cleaner, and qualified for many more previledges than most other slaves. She was in a position to promote the masters values to the other slaves by her example; if not by instruction, and thus became a "role model" to most female field slaves as well as to many men.

It is not out of order to trace Black people's excessive imitation of the materialistic values and European lifestyle partially to the Black women serving as house slaves. Today, well over a hundred years after slavery, "a good Black man" works hard to fulfill his Black wife's dreams that too often still revolve around accumulating the same material assets as "the master." Black men today are still weighed and measured partly by how well they can compete in providing these dollars (and the things that dollars buy) for their women. And this with full knowledge that the soceity within which the Black man wages this competition is specifically set up and designed so that he is among the last to ever get the dollars.Thus it would appear that the first imbalance in the Black male female perspective on money is part of a long pattern of Black women having financial desires and expectations as overly excessive and materialistic as our oppressors. And this imbalance in her perspective is even more problematic given the no win situation that most Black men are placed in when striving to attain these dollars and possessions. Specifically Black men do not win if they *do not seek* the dollars and possessions because in that case they are deemed "lazy." And they do not win if they go after the dollars because society has specific limitations on how far the average Black man can go financially.

While the Black female house slave was developing one aspect of the American "Negro" personality, the Black man was trying to develop one also. But he was trapped again, this time being unable to develope a legitimate sense of manhood.

Black male slaves could not define and feel their sense of manhood and empowerment from their traditional source - their African customs, traditions, beliefs and practices - because those cultural traditions died. They died because American slaves were taught that such traditions were savage, unchristian, and worse (if that is possible).

The Black man could not adopt the White American definition of manhood because of peer pressure of being called an "Uncle Tom", House Nigga etc. from his fellow men and also because White America would not let him practice a form of manhood equal to that of White Males. And the Black man decided the overwhelming majority of the time not to practice the "universal" definition of manhood which was to kill your oppressor at the best opportunity or die in the attempt at doing so. In those rare instances where someone did implement this latest practice (ex. Nat Turner) they were in no way universally celebrated as being a masculine role model for other Black males to follow. Thus for his entire stay here in America, the Black man has had many, many problems that can be directly traced to his discomfort in feeling like a real man. The Black woman, the family, community safety, productive work and earning habits are just some of the major areas of Black life that have suffered because of this torturous problem.

As children, most Black people learn that all money comes from and goes back to White people. Children learn that honest money comes from working and working almost always is depicted as a form of physical labor. The average child gets little if any orientation towards supporting Black businesses or starting their own business. Kids are pushed to do well in school, often at the expense of their own creative and productive capacities. The spoken or unspoken assumption directed to Black children is that with a better education, they can get a better job with White people. With this "better job" one can then make more money from White people, which can then be paid right back to them (White people) to purchase the products that Whites produce. Living the "good life" is usually defined as having more of these products and things than the rest of your peers.

With respect to Black males and females relating to each other in the early teen years, a specific pattern is usually apparent when they reach about fourteen years old. At this age the females begin to ignore the romantic efforts of her male peers in favor of boys two or more years older than she. At this point she begins to measure her own sense of value, development, importance etc., on how much she can cause to be offered to her for her companionship with these older boys. Her image and reputation begins to be based not so much on her personal capabilities and accomplishments so much as "who her boyfriend is," and what she gets to do with that boyfriend or what she gets the boy friend to do for her. Young Black males react and respond to their loss of status in the eyes of peer age females by using certain time tested routes to gain popularity. These traditional avenues for status are sports, dancing, dressing, fighting, and music. At the same time, boys also learn that being "a good guy" does not for the most part result in getting the preferred girls. This is the most crucial period for the development of the values and coping mechanisms for both sexes. Both sexes learn directly or indirectly that money and status count for more than what their parents and teachers tell them. Some young Black males become motivated to sell drugs to make the money that will allow them to get girls and the material things that the girls now expect.

In most situations, the habits and dating patterns that males and females developed in high school, follow them into adulthood. They become good at selecting boyfriends and girlfriends but have no means of learning how to select husbands and wives. This would be especially true for the non-college bound youngsters who are obviously the overwhelming majority in the Black community.

Interracial dating amd marriage is still a less then ten percent phenomeon in the Black community. But where it does exist, Black men are at least twice as likely to cross over as Black females. In addition to the usual reasons listed for such unions, this volume tries to go deeper. Black men of substance, status or income seem to say that White women either a)accept them more for who they really are than Black women do b) better understand what costs have to be paid to be successful than Black women do c) are willing to pay a dearer cost to be their mate than Black women are willing to do and or d) make more of an effort to understand them than Black women do.

With respect to the communication process between Black men and Black women, clearly many Black women are clueless in aspects of male culture. There are specific reasons why men in general and Black men in particular are short on words. In many ways and from a very early age Black boys and men are taught that their words are worthless. They talk in their own language which is assumed to be crude (slang) until it is embraced by the larger society when it is then used in television commercials and pop culture, and is deemed acceptable. Black men are assumed to be liars or great exaggerators. Black men are known to "talk a good game" or "talk the talk" but supposedly not be able to deliver during crunch time. Talking has always been seen within the Black male culture as an indication that it is a substitute for action or accomplishment. Thus boys learned that ones image was better if he didn't draw attention to himself by talking. This principle held true in sports, academics, dating, fighting, dressing and other aspects of youth culture. Minimizing the expression of ones feelings lowered expectations adults developed for the male and the disappointment at substandard achievements by those males. A number of other aspects on communication are provided.

Committment is a concept that women somehow assume is as advantageous to males as it is to females. Nothing could be further from the truth. Committment is a restriction on freedom; the very thing the Black man has been trying to experience. Black males can not be bullied into submitting to committment. Black males still think committment is a two party decision and resent how their honesty in stating their unreadiness for commitment is seen as a sign of their immaturity. Certain social financial and other benefits come to females when they marry that point out clearly why women would want to marry in their young adult years. It has nothing to do with their presumed advanced morality or maturity. Naked self interest is much closer to the mark.

And even the brow beating lectures of one of our own brillant thinkers, Haki Madhabuti, can not change that reality.

Waiting to Exhale, the mega selling hit book, of 1992-94, was suppose to explain the plight of today's sophisticated educated, middle class, urban and suburban independent Black women. Her plight in not being able to find or attract a similarly positioned Black male was suppose to bring forth buckets of tears and sympathy from empathic supporters. But astute Black males, looking past the comedy and entertainment value of the book, could see something very different.

Black males could see that beyond a change in jobs, location and wardrobes, these sisters were merely updated sapphires. They cussed like sailors, screwed like whores, destroyed property for spite, and were largely selfish and self absorbed. Men's personal business and their own sexual exploits were put on the street like the weekly trash, for anyone to sift through as they wished. Rather than show how far Black women have come, "Exhale" reminded Black males how much sisters haven't budged. This book shows how even "the best" of today's Black women have lost their moral authority to claim any form of character superiority over Black men. If Black men are dawgs which many can't disclaim, sisters like these are truly our bitches.

When Black men and women do commit to marriage, Black men find that they are not nearly as in control of their household, even their own money, as they would have believed. Black men see themselves as working to pay everyone of significance in their lives except themselves. In many situations, where a man lives and how he lives is not of his own choice so much as it is a product of his wife's decisions. His job is to pay for her choices. But there would be a certain amount of justice and fairness if it paid Black men to be the good husbands that wives and society wish them to be. But it doesn't. If an unhappy married Black male decided to "stick it out until the children grew up", the divorce laws of this society will surely make him pay for his decision to stay committed. If he is thrifty, accumulates property, denies himself certain toys, the law and judges will make him pay should he decide that he's earned the right to be free. Basically in this soceity it pays the Black man, to be a trifling father and husband. It would be very naive to believe that Black men haven't caught on to this reality by now. Nor is it a non factor in Black men refusing to make the full commitment of marriage. Black women are rather selective when labeling their primary oppressor an oppressor. Because at crucial times, like those when she and her devoted spouse decide to call it quits, her primary oppressors(White laws, lawyers and judges) become her ally in deciding how much money and manhood they will strip away from the Black man. Do not think that this is a non factor in the hesitancy of Black men to marry.

After having said all of that however, there is still too much hype given on the Black man leaving his martial home. Brothers who have no knowledge of being fathers are treated as cruelly as known deadbeats. Fathers who sacrifice their lives are not viewed that way. Fathers whom welfare laws persuade to leave home are then faulted for following "the system." Over twenty legitimate explanations for the Black absentee father are listed in order to raise the awareness level of chronic Black male bashers.

The under representation of Black men in college and the representation of them in prison is not a mystery to those who have taken the time to understand Black men, Black women and American society. Many Black men do not have either the preparation, interest or value for   college that many Black women appear to have. The faith in being able to complete college and, belief in the benefits of having completed college are significantly lower in Black males than Black females. The role of money in college, the motivations of Black females and the mindset of Black male college athletes are examined in some detail. Prison is also looked at as a place where more than a few Black men find a home away from home.

This volume also tries to give a more accurate analysis of why today's Black woman has been given the many new opportunities in education, employment, politics and other areas. Oddly enough her own efforts played much less of a role than Black women probably would like to believe. Black male civil rights leaders (with people like Angela Davis, Ms. Rosa Parks and Fannie Lou Hamer being more the exceptions than the rule) were out front pushing for all Blacks to have more rights. Many paid the ultimate price. Black male urban rebels literally burned their messages into the minds of White America in order that they not forget the Black agenda at hand. And White females in a quarter century of feminist activity, not at all coincidentally modeled after Black civil rights organizations, did the rest. Black women's position on the "freedom train" was often in the caboose trailing behind all the more aggressive actors. The pride that todays Black women feel in their "progress" and their readiness to bash Black men suggest that they think that they were always out front and the men were always in the rear. Nothing could be further from the truth. The fact that Black women are so reluctant to give credit where credit is due (the exception being Dr. King and maybe Malcolm X since Spike Lee's movie) is but another indication to the Black man how his liberation efforts go unappreciated even by those who stood the most to gain. The clash of careers, money, power and sex between Black men and women has unlimited twists, turns, interpretations and "solutions." We address some that aren't covered in the popular mass market magazines and books.

With respect to healing the hurts and gaps that stand between Black men and women, a few things are certain. Black women are going to have to change their self righteous attitudes. Black man are going to have to come up with a manhood definition which rechannels the anger that he's now using to kill his women, children, brothers and self. It's also clear that there will be about as many solutions to relationship problems as there are couples looking for solutions. But common ingredients will likely include a greater appreciation on the part of Black women for the non-conforming nature of the Black man and a better understanding of his ego and manhood difficulties. Black men will have to realize that if they decide not to play the game according to the White man's rules and standards that they must do more than simply complain on the sidelines. They must come up with some means to meet the basic needs that families have in the twentieth and twenty first centuries. All people create and build something. Black men must arrange more coordinated efforts to build on what we've already built thus far.

Neither Black men nor women can afford to remain ignorant of money and financial management or continue to pass that ignorance down to their offspring. Slavery was primarily an economic system to benefit Whites and exploit Blacks. Our peoples continued financial ignorance continues a similar imbalance in the economy today. We have substantial resources and we have no one to blame for the degree of our poverty but ourselves. Not only must men and women better understand each other, but each needs to learn how to see the contradictions in their behaviors and statements. While we must not dwell on our mistakes, we certainly must be willing to face up to them and correct them if our relationships are to have opportunities to grow.

THE LEGACY OF BLACK FEMALE HOUSE SLAVES

Some of the conflicts between Black men and women are not only not new, but can go back as far as two hundred years for those willing to study African American history. I personally find it frustrating that many people who find history so *boring*, including African American history in many cases, are the same people who seem so perplexed in trying to understand "our problems" as a people. Understanding the factors that cause a problem to develop not only helps you to solve the problem, but should help you to tolerate and work around the problem until it *is* solved. When one understands better what one is dealing with, it reduces the tendency to single out individuals to blame for individual acts when essentially most of the acts are a part of the same historical problem. We'll take time here therefore to look at an interpretation of Black History, in an effort to understand the money and lifestyle issues and conflicts between today's Black man and woman.

House, Yard and Field Slaves

Most people who have even the slightest exposure to African American history have probably heard about "house niggas" and "field niggas". This is because there existed on most slave plantations a division of labor and in this labor pool, certain people had more responsibility, status and privilege than others. Black people who worked in the master's house usually lived under better conditions than other slaves and had access to privileges that field slaves did not enjoy. Unfortunately, this brief bit of information is all that most African Americans know, and they have no idea how this division became institutionalized in such a way that it's influence moves through our community even today.

In order to understand the house slave you have to first understand that in Southern plantation life, where people lived miles apart and even farther from city centers, plantations were very independent. Plantation owners had to provide many things for themselves. In most cases, one did not go into town to a food store, clothing store, furniture store, shoe store and all the other kinds of stores that we take for granted today. It meant that much more than field work had to be done in order for a plantation to run efficiently. Inside the master's house, cooking, house cleaning, child rearing and washing clothes easily come to mind as duties that needed to be fulfilled. But also fabric and cloth had *to be made* from the raw cotton and other materials so that clothes could made. Tablecloths, blankets, sheets, etc., had to be made by hand. This was indeed "house work", work done in the master's house.

Most of this work has been historically viewed as "women's work." Thus it should be no surprise that most house slaves were *female. This is very important to understand.* Stephen Birmingham, in his book *Certain People* (published by Little, Brown and Company, 1977), a book about Black Elites, states the following on page 32:

> " In the houses of Southern planters, the house slaves were better treated. In a real sense, they had to be, for they were entrusted with caring for children, preparing meals, running the house, caring for guests. In many households, slaves were treated almost as members of the family and, working as maids, cooks, nurses, and laundresses, the house slaves were predominantly women."

There were several reasons why a White family might feel more comfortable with a house full of Black women as opposed to Black men. First of all, the plantation was a business and the Black man, an able-bodied Black man, would be more valuable producing wealth via crop production for his master in the field, than trying to cook the evenings dinner, make candles or spinning yarn. Secondly, the Black man was a physical threat that could overpower the White people of the house, kill them, and escape. A house is supposed to be a man's castle, not his prison. For this reason alone it was best to keep the Black man out of the house. Third, the Black man was viewed as a sexual threat. The mythology that eventually was woven during slavery maintained that White women lusted for the loins of the potent Black man, whose penis size and physical stamina was said to be enough to satisfy the most fantastic sexual cravings that a White woman could possibly imagine. And the Black man, whose mental and genetic makeup were supposed to be trapped somewhere between a gorilla and the White man, was considered a savage who would likely pounce on the bones of any available White woman and ravage her. So for these reasons as well as others, not many Black men made it to the house as servants. Those Black men who did become house servants were butlers, doormen, bartenders, shoe shine boys, or coach drivers. They were usually old or injured men, or men who were either no good for field work, or who had "earned" the right to be a house slave due to some impressive loyalty and/or butt-kissing.

In between the house slaves and the field slaves was an often forgotten group of Black men called yard slaves. Yard slaves as the term suggests, were people who worked in the yard around the house. They were craftsmen who had carpentry skills, painting skills, plumbing skills and masonry and iron worker skills. These men built and repaired the barns, houses, grain storage bins, and chicken houses. They mended fences, dug the wells, trained the horses, shoed the horses, made saddles, etc. Not only did these men do it for their master, but they were often hired out to other Whites to earn money for their master.

For example, let's say that a new neighbor moved into the area and needed a new barn built, a travel wagon repaired, a well dug and his house painted. He might approach a large plantation owner and contract to use the services of some of his slaves for a week or two. After the slaves did the work, the new neighbor would pay the plantation owner for the work that the slaves did. In other words, those Whites that didn't own slaves could "rent" them on a need basis. Obviously, in most cases the plantation owner kept all the money for himself. However, history does show that sometimes masters gave slaves a portion of the money.

It is not really enough of an analysis of Black people's relationships to simply say that Black house slaves (mostly females) looked down on Black field slaves (mostly males). We must understand what caused this division to grow and become part of the division among Black people and specifically between Black men and women. When the women house slaves grew up in the house they learned the ways of White folks. They understood these ways not as merely the ways of the people who happened to be in power but as the *right* ways, the *civilized* ways, the intelligent, proper, sophisticated ways that things were done. Period. In the research for this point, again Stephen Birmingham seems to say it best and make it sound so believable. (*Certain People* p.37-38):

> "In the house, these women learned the ways and manners of Southern gentlefolk - how to set a table properly, how to arrange flowers, how to keep silver gleamingly polished, how to treat good furniture (and how to distinguish it from bad), and otherwise how to run a manor house. Because, in many wealthy Southern families, the children were taught by tutors, with the children's nurse in charge of seeing to it that they did their lessons, many of these women became self-educated, learned, at least, to read and write, which their fellow slaves in the fields had no real opportunity to do. These women learned to behave and talk, and also to think, like members of the Southern White aristocracy."

Michelle Wallace in her book, *Black Macho and the Myth of the Super Woman* (Dial Press Publisher, 1978) makes a similar point:

> "In slave narratives there can be found accounts of slaves,

particularly house slaves, who began to admire and idealize the
White skins and the lifestyles of their owners. It was the house
servant who was most feared in the planning stages of a slave
revolt, feared for her intimacy with the master's family. The
extent to which the black female slave became unable to
distinguish her own reality from the White view of that reality,
and the extent to which she leaned toward the latter, were the
measure of the beginnings of a process of psychic
deterioration."

When one understands the great measures used by Whites to stamp out aspects
of African culture (traditions that tended to be passed down in slave culture)
and the labeling of that culture as backward, savage, animalistic etc., it is rather
easy to see how Blacks, could be programmed to see the master's culture as
superior.

In all fairness to Black female house slaves, not all of them were taken
in by the supposed "advantages" of living in the house. Paula Giddings in her
heavily researched work entitled *When and Where I Enter* (William Morrow
Co. Publisher, 1984 pages 34-40), tells of several instances where Black female
house slaves either poisoned the master through his food or burned down the
house with the White family in it. The price for such a courageous act was to
be burned at the stake. Other Black female house slaves have been known to
be part of slave rebellions and escapes. Female house slaves passed
information about the master's whereabouts and his plans for the day. Other
Black women actually participated in slave rebellions, but whether they were
house or field slaves is not clear.

It was not in the interest of White folks to broadcast or document the
successful times when slaves rebelled against their authority, thus many
uprisings will never be known to us. Also, in successful instances when Black
women poisoned Whites and the Whites were assumed to have died of natural
causes, there would not have been any way for Black women to have received
proper "credit" for a job well done because nothing out of the ordinary would
have been perceived as having happened. Thus we will never know how many
heroines there were.

Michelle Wallace, who some might consider the originator of the Black
male bashing movement with her 1978 book, *Black Macho and the Myth of the
Super Woman* (Dial Press publisher) made the point about women not going
so far as to *lead* slave revolts.

"Lastly, it was the men, in all cases, who planned and/or led the
slave revolts. Although women participated, every known
slave plot or actual rebellion was the result of male initiative."

(page 22)

As much psychological and emotional liberation and satisfaction that a successful slave revolt would have created, history does not show that very many large or successful ones ever took place. Escape from slavery, however, is another matter, and our history has no greater figure of that movement than a Black woman, Harriet Tubman. Harriet Tubman made more than twenty trips back into the South, after she made good on her personal escape to the North, to help liberate over two hundred former slaves. Southern Whites placed a twenty thousand dollar dead or alive bounty on her head. In 1990 dollars, that would be close to a million dollars. Still she kept coming back to free more of her people. Legend has it that Ms. Tubman on at least one occasion cocked and pointed a gun to the head of a male slave who was beginning to chicken out on his mission to leave the master's plantation. On pointing the gun Ms. Tubman is reported to have said, "You will come with us or we will leave you here (dead), but you ain't going back!" My research shows no male equivalent to Harriet Tubman in daring or success.

Having said that, however, we must note that Ms. Tubman was but one Black woman. Regardless of the number of Black heroines we may have had, their number is small compared to the thousands of Black female house slaves who saw and judged the world through White folks' eyes, values and standards. It is tempting to harshly judge these Aunt Jemima types in the master's house, and many of them probably did things to deserve the scorn of the greater Black community . But if we are to understand ourselves and human nature better, then we should attempt to understand the dynamics of what was going on at that time and today's results from these same dynamics.

In the first place, there is a natural human tendency to respond favorably toward people who respond favorably toward you. There are mothers and fathers with favorite daughters and sons whom they treat a little special, regardless of how much they know they shouldn't. There are favorite students, prison inmates, employees and favorite soldiers who get better treatment than the rest by those who have some supervisory capacity over them. So if a White master treats someone a little "better" for reasons that only he or she may know, the eventual human response over an extended period of time is to treat that master decently, even if *one is not* necessarily caught up in the masters supposed "superiority." Thus house slaves cared more for the master simply because he placed them in a position to make them feel that they were special. And this loyalty to the master, which sickens us to some extent, would have been present regardless of whether the master was Chinese, Japanese, Indian, Russian or Greek. A student of psychology would probably agree with that. All this is to say that the sisters in the house are not to be hated for merely behaving the same way that any other people (including Black men) would probably have behaved had they gone through the same experience.

Secondly, we must examine how these Black women were viewed by the field slaves. It would be unfair not to mention at this point that in addition to the special rights and privileges that house slaves enjoyed, they were also quite often light skinned African Americans, the product of White male-Black female unions. Most of these unions were the result of some form of rape or intimidation by the White males. Some perhaps were conscious schemes by the Black women, and a few, we must concede, had a truly romantic basis. (Alex Haley's *Queen* being one example.)

The rape of Black women will not be explained here due to the assumption that every reader knows what that situation entailed. Some African American women, however, made themselves available to White men for a number of reasons. Some thought, for example, that if they could emotionally involve their masters, that their masters would, in fact, free them or at least, treat them as if they were free. This did in fact happen often enough that it made sense to some sisters to explore it as a way to obtain freedom. Some Black women wanted children who would be free. Knowing any child by another slave would be just another slave, a number of Black women sought a White father for their children on the assumption that the father might recognize his children and grant them freedom. This, in fact, did happen often; especially among the French in the Louisiana Territory. Sex is, in part, a power game, and always has been. Thus, some Black women simply wanted to take back some of the control that the masters held over them and were willing to use their bodies to do so. The moral questions which some people today might have about such behavior represents luxury that many slave women could not afford a hundred and fifty years ago.

So, house slaves were light-skinned, with straight hair (good hair), and were considered "pretty" and "lady-like". They dressed better than field slaves, took baths more often, were better fed, and healthier.

If all of these advantages, both real and perceived, did not mean anything to the regular field slave, African American history would be totally different than it is today. But that is not what happened. The field slave looked up to the house slave in most instances as being prettier, smarter, luckier and a role model to aspire to. Yes, there was distrust, and a great deal of envy which produced a form of hatred. But Black people did what we have always done, which is to wrestle with the contradictory nature of our feelings. We want something, yet run away from it; we love something while hating it at the same time; we think one thing but act in an altogether different direction. Slavery had to be full of situations like that. In his book *The Negro In the*

United States,, E. Franklin Frazier cites the story told by an ex-slave named Austin Steward. (The MacMillin Co. publishers, 1957 page 55):

> "It was about ten o'clock when the aristocratic slaves began to assemble, dressed in the cast-off finery of their master and mistress, swelling out and putting on airs in imitation of those they were forced to obey from day to day. House servants were of course, "the stars" of the party; All eyes were turned to them to see how they conducted, for they, among slaves, are what a military man would call "fugle-men". The field hands, and such of them as have generally been excluded from the dwelling of their owners, look to the house servant as a pattern of politeness and gentility. And indeed, it is often the only methods of obtaining any knowledge of the manners of what is called "genteel society"; hence, they are ever regarded as a privileged class; and are sometimes greatly envied, while others are bitterly hated."

The basic purpose of this very brief history of slavery is to drive home one major point: Black women, more than Black men, accepted at face value the so-called superiority and correctness of the European culture and lifestyle, and has pushed and driven the Black man, her mate, to obtain as much of it as he can, ever since. Many of the money issues between Black men and women today involve the man trying to please his woman who to this day defines "the good things in life" very much as today's White woman would. Before the masses of Black men decided to reclaim a part of their African heritage, values and Blackness (in the 1960's), some Black men were even proud of the Black women's role in keeping Black people focussed on White culture. *The Crisis* magazine is the official publication of the N.A.A.C.P. and for many years was edited by W.E.B. Dubois after he founded it about 1915. Look at what this magazine said as quoted by Paula Giddings in her book already cited:

> "Throughout American history colored women have played a most significant role in the development of our civilization. Because their ties with Africa were abruptly severed ... and because their greater struggle for survival compelled a speedier adaptation to a new life here, they have placed their imprint indelibly on our national life. *They are the chief repository of Anglo-Saxon culture. Some students even hold that if every White person were to disappear from the United States, it would continue culturally to be Anglo-Saxon with, of course, the softening and sophisticated touch of Africa.* The colored woman is responsible to a large degree for the rapid adaptation

of black folk to American life, *for she conveyed to the less favored male what she learned by closer association with the best that the civilized White minority had to offer.*" (Emphasis mine)

It is not to be suggested here that a large number of Black men throughout our history have not also imitated the White man, praised European culture, and swallowed whole the idea of the superiority of their values. Nor can we deny that African American women, kept alive in our culture many Africanisms for as long as they were alive. But as this research shows, as well as other materials to be cited later, Black women, or at least a significantly large, influential, group of Black women, pushed Black people to the worship of Whiteness and its accompanying materialism that we chase after to this very day.

If this idea of the Black woman representing the White materialist aspect of our history and culture is to be made more believable, we must show how the Black male represented something qualitatively different. This is easy enough to do. Throughout most of his history in America, the Black man has been the embodiment of rebellion. Only the American Indian can say he rebelled against the White man more than Black men. As has already been cited, every known slave revolt, whether successful or not, had been the plan of a Black male. Black men rebelled by killing White men and their families, by killing Black men who represented the interests of White men, and by simply escaping slavery. In many Black men's eyes, the raping of White women, on those occasions when that did actually happen (which was certainly much less than has been charged), was a statement to White America of rebellion and defiance. The means that Black men used to fight White men and their system of slavery could easily fill a book twice the size of the one you are reading now.

And White men knew that Black men were a threat to their life, which is why White men have this long history of "showing everyone whose boss". Although our history shows numerous instances of Black women being killed, cut up, and their babies being ripped from the womb, Black men were clearly more targeted. At least ninety percent of the time it was the Black male who was lynched, castrated and burned, not only because of suspected threatening acts against Whites or real acts which harmed the Whites, but to instill fear to ward off potential harmful acts to Whites. The entire purpose of the KKK was to intimidate Black people against committing the acts they suspected might come their way. There generally was not this type of action taken against Black women, not because the KKK loved or respected Black women but because there was not enough of a history of threats from or fear of Black women rebelling in the same way. Not too many Black women have been known to kill

White people and simply let the chips fall where they may.

But killing was not the Black man's chief means of rebelling against White authority and value systems. That is easy to see. The record shows that neither Fredrick Douglass, W.E.B. Dubois, Noble drew Ali, Marcus Garvey, Elijah Muhammed, Malcolm X or Louis Farrakhann *put together* have killed even *one* White person.

The Black man's chief means of rebelling against White values was and remains simply *creating his own thing, his own style.* For example, White America wanted to Christianize the slaves to make them submit to a White Jesus and the White man . Generally speaking the White man was successful in doing this. But in between all the sermons and Bible readings, Black male religious leaders used both the scripture and the church to convey the themes of liberation and develop Black leadership. Of course the Black female was not allowed to assume leadership roles in Churches. If she were allowed, she may or may not have done some of the same things. But we *know* what the men did in this situation.

Black men rebelled on the slave cargo ships, and rebelled by committing suicide rather than live as slaves. The early writings of Black men, such as the newspaper *Freedom's Journal and David Walkers Appeal* were about freedom. We rebelled by fighting for the Union army *against* the slave masters that so many of our female house slaves loved so well.

And while we were being molded and hammered into something called an American Negro, some of our brightest male minds were devising ways to return to Africa and developing a Black Nationalist philosophy. I do not know of Black female equivalents of Martin Delaney, Henry Highland Garnet, Captain Paul Cuffie, David Walker and countless others who talked about Black Nationalism and going back to Africa even before Marcus Garvey brought his ideas to America in the 1920's.

One might reasonably put forth the argument that slavery was so horrible, so controlled, so dangerous and so inhuman that people should not be held accountable for what they did or said during those times. That only when men and women have some minimal sense of freedom, education and physical distance between themselves and Whites should they be held fully accountable for their thoughts and actions. Unfortunately, when that did happen, we see the same patterns. We see the Black woman still measuring "progress" by how closely social, cultural, economic and material matters in our community approximated the existing White world. While, on the other hand, the Black man was still looking for ways to rebel against White society and create his own statements about who he was. This is not to say that the overwhelming majority of both Black men and women were not trying to imitate and be accepted by Whites, because they certainly were. But when we look at who the most influential and well-regarded Black women were, they were normally the women who were pushing for de-Africanized Black people to move closer to the White model. When we saw who *at least some* of the Black male heroes were, they were people who were creating alternatives to the White status quo and/or threatening White rules, laws, and assumptions of authority.

In all fairness again to Black women, they were not allowed to make many decisions in the male dominated organizations of the time. We don't know what they would have done had they been given the opportunity. But we do know of another problem which made their lives hell and confusing. And that was the problem of Black men's choice of what constituted the ideal mate. In far too many situations, a Black man would talk about the importance of Blackness, Self-determination, Africanness, Pan Africanism, etc., and yet chase after or go home to a woman that was light-skinned, with European features, straight hair and "ladylike" mannerisms which too often translated into being the White female personality. This caused severe problems for Black women. Do they believe the "Black rap" that Black men talk or do they believe his preference in women which they see with their own two eyes? This contradiction would come up too often to be a mere chance occurrence. This preference for very light damn-near-white women inevitably encouraged many Black women to continue along their integrationist, bourgeois path because that seemed to be what brothers positively responded to. How can you convincingly fault Black women for that? Quite frankly the only reason it probably wasn't a lot worse may very well have been because so many White men had their ropes in the trunks of their cars and were ready to deal with brothers who so much as looked at a White woman. This phenomena will be looked at in another part of this book.

Today's Environment

What impact did the early "white washing" of female house slaves have on today's interaction between Black women and men? Are patterns, complaints and problems heard between the sexes today traceable perhaps to the events previously discussed? Obviously every individual has his or her own perspective and story to tell. But I think that one can say that *generally* Black women do not drop out of school as often as males, attend college in greater numbers than males, work in more middle class White collar jobs than the males and are much less likely to resist police, participate in "riots", and own guns than Black males. In other words, to this day, Black women are still more likely to be more fully integrated into and less rebellious of the general society than her male counterpart. There are the same two major reasons for this phenomena today as those that existed two hundred years ago. First, Black women are more *interested* in blending in with White society than the Black male and thus they take more steps to move toward White people on the whole. Second, White people, male and female, feel much more comfortable around and are more tolerant and accepting of Black females. One of the latest books produced by a White liberal writer notes this point. Andrew Hacker in *Two Nations* (Ballantine Books, 1992 pages 115-116) says the following:

" But this describes only one element in the equation. Of at least equal importance are attitudes and decisions among White employers. If and when organizations feel compelled to hire more black workers, they generally prefer to take on black women rather than black men. Black women, like all women, are perceived as being less assertive and more accommodating. Thus there is the hope that black women will show less resentment or hostility, and will be less apt to present themselves as "black" in demeanor and appearance. A further concern of White employers, albeit not one openly stated, is that having black men and White women work together might lead to familiar relationships that could either be misunderstood or have some grounding in fact. In addition, black and White women tend to mingle more easily in workplace settings. This is partly because women tend to feel less tense about race. But there is also evidence that women can ignore racial lines in acknowledging common experiences, at least to a far greater extent than men are willing to do. At restaurants near their place of work, groups of black and White women can be seen enjoying lunch together. Far less frequently -if at all- does one encounter similar parties of men. Circumstances like these are not lost on employers, who may conclude that if they must have racially mixed workforces, things will go better if they consist largely of women."

Thus we have two hands washing each other just as they always have. The Black woman is constantly moving toward the White man and the White man is becoming more accepting of the Black woman. And as the White man becomes more accepting, more Black women, even those not "gifted" with the light skin, straight hair, European looks and mannerisms, become more comfortable, trusting and optimistic that maybe they too can find "acceptance" from the White man. And the beat goes on.

When one hears about "racial crimes and tensions on the rise", they usually are not talking about Black women. It must be Black men. Is today's relationship between Black and White much different than say during slavery? In a rather unique article published in the November, 1992 issue of *Essence* magazine, five White men were assembled to talk about one central issue: Why White men fear Black men. Andrew Hacker also happened to be one of the five men picked for this interview and according to this writer also made the most significant statements. On page 126 he stated:

> "At this point, organizations are much more willing to promote Black women and Asians than Black men. That's because Black men are seen as having a chip on their shoulders, the rebels, not really willing to go along with the values of XYZ, Inc., or, for that matter, Harvard University."

In this statement he is agreeing with the point of this writer. Many Black men are not interested in fitting into "the best" colleges, companies or organizations even if they were accepted. They are "rebels" because they don't agree with the values of these institutions. Perhaps it is because their greater emotional, intellectual, and creative need is to build alternative institutions. At another point in this article, Mr. Hacker is very candid about the feelings of what is probably a very significant number of White men when he talks about Willie Horton, the Black criminal figure that former president George Bush used as part of his racial scare tactics in his first presidential campaign:

> "What is there about Willie Horton, for instance, that scares us? There are a couple of things. The first is that Willie Horton, generically, is unafraid. He's not afraid of prison, he's not afraid of being beaten, he's not afraid of being shot, he's not afraid of dying. Young men who carry guns, they know they can be targets of guns too, living on the thin edge. And you're always afraid of someone who is fearless in that sense. Also, our other fear of this group of Black men is that they are so physical. Most of us who are White and middle-class are less physical today, despite all our tennis-playing. And there's a notion that they (Black men) can really hurt us physically. This is the Mike Tyson notion, you know. What could they do to us? Rip us limb from limb? In addition, what can they do to our women? And once gain, whether it's Willie Horton or Mike Tyson, somehow the Black rapist inflicts more damage than a White rapist ever could. This comes back to the physical, the potency, the strength there. And not only that, the rape - I don't know how far we want

to get into this-also has undertones of miscegenation, planting a seed, mongrelizing our "pure" race. What we're afraid of is being accosted- not politically - but by someone who wants our money. But we're also afraid that after he takes our money at knife point, he'll then take another moment and do something to us in retribution for what our people have done to his people. That's our fear of Willie Horton. That he's not just a criminal, not just a rapist, but he's part of a Black insurrection."

Rather than simply insert more quotes to support the authors point of view, it might be more intellectually honest to compare the interests, the patterns and the perspectives of Black females and males to see if they support this theme of integrationist vs rebel between the genders in our community.Let's look at several areas:

1. Education

In every country in the world the purpose of the educational system has two major functions. The first being to pass on the body of real knowledge such as that for instance that relates to Science and Mathematics. Courses in algebra, physics, chemistry, computers, statistics, etc., are fairly universal in classrooms all over the world. The second function of educational systems is to pass on the cultural values of that nation state. Thus courses like language, communications, art, history, psychology, religion, etc., are not universal in many respects but follow the cultural, religious and subjective preferences that are part of the history of that nation. To be "good" in school in the United States is to be responsive to, accepting of and knowledgeable in European values, heroes, and interpretation of facts. Young Black men and a few Black women have said in many studies of high school students that, from their point of view, a person who excels in school is *trying to be White*! That idea angers, frightens and frustrates older African Americans who would like to dismiss it as stupidity amongst a small number of non-conforming, problematic boys. In fact there is more than a little truth to the legitimacy of this feeling of whiteness. For all the B.S. that's put out on multi-cultural education, so that young people can better tolerate (not *learn* about) each other, European values are still paramount in the school system. World history is still largely European history, foreign language is still French, German or Spanish, not Swahili or Arabic. Literature is still equated with Shakespeare and his ilk and excellence in music and art refers still to Europeans of the Middle Ages. When a person has internalized much of their school work, they are learning how to be a better White person whether they are White or not. Young Black female students excel in this stuff and look forward to it much more than Black males. Black females are much more likely to take a trip to Europe with their White classmates than young Black males. Actually this is part of a long tradition also going back to slavery.

> "There were, of course, throughout the long years of slavery, many liaisons between the female house slaves and the male plantation owners or their sons. The lighter-skinned offspring of these unions were frequently acknowledged by their fathers, especially the girls, and especially the " pretty" little girls. The boys were needed for work in the fields, and were usually dispatched there as soon as they were old enough, but the pampered little girls were frequently sent to the North, or even to Europe, to be educated. The descendants of these light-skinned, well educated little girls are the *grandes* dames of Black society today." (Birmingham, Certain People, p.38)

2.Television Tastes

I don't think it would take a national poll by Time, CNN, the Gallop organization, or the Neilson ratings to say the following:

a.   There are some shows that Black men and women enjoy equally well; for example Black comedies, musical award shows, music videos, etc.

b.   Black women, however, are also very, very strong followers of the White soap operas, game shows and talk shows. The soap operas, though sprinkled with a few Blacks (whose personalities seem almost identical to the Whites on the show) appear to be completely about the problems, values and personalities of middle to upper middle class White America. Why would Black women follow these stories day after day, month after month, unless they strongly identified with the characters?   With regard to the game shows, they apparently fulfill both a female fantasy and a Black female fantasy. Namely, that someone is going to give you a great material gift *for nothing*. No sex is attached, no work is attached and no real knowledge is required in most instances. Just show up, look pretty, smile and the White man will just give it to you. Nothing, nothing is further from the Black man's reality than a game show. The Black man has never been given even what he has earned two and three times over, never mind something for free. But this reality applies to the Black woman as well. She was never given what she was due either. Yet some Black women perhaps have more faith, and confidence that maybe the day will come when the White man will shower her with free gifts *before* her Black mate will give her the *things* (as asinine as they may be) that her little heart desires.

As far as talk shows go, no person in their right mind can deny that these shows are not largely directed to the sexual concerns of White women. Yes, other topics are occasionally covered, from national politics to L.A. (black male) gangs. But for the most part, these talk shows usually deal with some problem between a White girl and her husband or boyfriend. And it is usually played out on the screen like the very same soap opera that will be on that same channel a couple of hours later. And while there are hundreds of thousands of busy Black women who work in important positions for sixty, seventy or more hours a week, it is fascinating to watch how quickly they can get into this junk if given the opportunity such as on sick days, vacation days, etc. *Probably the single biggest danger for Black men is that many Black women are actually convinced that they are learning a great deal about Black men as they study what White men do.* They mistakenly think that there is an ideology that connects us Black men with White men as they believe feminism connects many Black women with some of their White sisters. Yes, both Black men and White men suffer from being sexist, and that is an important problem in need of a solution. But it would be a mistake to think that White and Black men are alike enough to use one group in order to learn about the other.

    c.   Black men watch sports on television, a lot of basketball, football, baseball and boxing mostly. And we watch it first and foremost because we *are watching ourselves*, not White people for the most part. To watch an athletic competition on TV is to watch more Black men at one time in the public media doing something positive than at any other time. We watch it because we are *in control on the athletic field.* Although there are usually a few White men running around as referees in the ring, on the field and behind the plate telling us again what rules we've broken and how we are to be penalized (as in real life), we are still largely in control. And if we do get very angry we can express our anger even if it costs us money, which at that point we have plenty of. We watch sports because we take a game and make it an art.

We watch sports to beat the White man. It probably is not an exaggeration to say that every Black male, regardless of economic status, skin complexion, educational level etc., has had an urge to kill a White man at some point in his life. Often the White man gives us cause to have that feeling. Fortunately (or unfortunately, depending on how you look at it) ninety-nine percent of Black men will never have that experience. But through sports, many Black men live out their fantasy by watching Black men "beat" Whites in the sports. It started with Jack Johnson, the first Black heavyweight champion, in 1908, then Jesse Owens beating Hitler's "superior race", Joe Louis beating the German Max Schmelling and so forth. When the athlete is not only a champion but a proud Black man, and defiant of Whites as well, he becomes a true super star to Black males. As great as Malcolm X, Martin Luther King and Thurgood Marshall were to the cause of Black liberation and masculinity, Muhammed Ali is still the greatest living embodiment of heroism to the broadest cross section of Black males, young and old, in this century. It is no accident that when he reigned, he was the singularly most popular human being of any race or gender in the entire world. Period.

Reading Material - Books and Magazines

It's not secret that Black males read less and have less reading skill than Black females. Some educators might be quick to say that one of the major problems in finding "suitable" mates for today's Black women is the poorer education/exposure/reading levels of Black males as compared to Black females. There is some truth to this. But it is interesting to see what Black women tend to read once they master this skill called reading versus what Black males read who are supposedly retarded in this area.

Black women read material similar to the material they watch on television. The same applies to the men. Essence magazine, designed for Black women (at least certain classes of them) is wholeheartedly purchased by about one million Black women monthly, and is read by probably five times that many. Black men in significant numbers buy the publication (or at least read it) also.

Ebony and Jet magazines also sell a million or more copies per issue and likewise have a following that is probably seventy percent or more female.

Black Enterprise, a business magazine, is probably the only widely circulated Black publication that has a mostly male readership but the subscription to that magazine is only a quarter of a million and thus has many less Black readers across the board. The point here is that Black women do support Black publications and in fact probably dominate the readership of all major Black journals except one. This is good news to those who *push* the importance of education.

But once you travel outside the Black publications you will see a big difference in Black male and female readership, taste and interests.

For every single copy of, say, Esquire or GQ magazine that a Black male might read to check out what White people think is important, maybe ten or more Black women will buy Cosmopolitan, Mademoiselle or a similar magazine. They will read the stories of Danielle Steele and others like her, as well as tons and tons of Harlequin romance novels. For all the reading ability that Black women undoubtedly have over Black men, we have to ask if it is being put to use to better our racial situation or is it creating more distance between the Black man and Black woman?

Black women want to know why Black men don't communicate (more about that later), but what are we to talk about? Danielle Steel's new book? The latest issue of the Star with Oprah's new diet in it? Or the article on why married men masturbate as explained by the November issue of Cosmopolitan? Black women seemingly cannot possibly get enough of how White women act and think and it can't all be attributed to the Black man's historic fascination with Miss Ann. At the same time many Black women seem to have trouble with really wanting to understand Black history, Black men, "the struggle," etc. Its as if they sub consciously understood that if they *really understood* our true reality as a people, they couldn't in good conscience continue to dream/fantasize about White folks anymore.

This first came to my attention twenty years ago when I was a Black Studies instructor at Seton Hall University in New Jersey. I had relatively small classes so it was easy to notice who was absent from class and who was not. Over the course of a couple of months, I noticed that certain students were always absent and that they were female students. After checking the records, I learned that these students were not commuting students who needed to catch buses at precise times to make the class on time. These were students who lived on campus, less than a hundred yards from the classroom. As it turned out, these female students had decided that watching General Hospital was more important than my Black studies class. (Luke and Laura were a hot item back then). I asked other instructors to see if it was my personal teaching style that turned them off or whether these instructors were experiencing the same thing. As it turned out, female attendance was dependent on the degree of *hard coreness* of the class. I taught a history of Black Nationalism class- hard core. An African brother taught African Revolutionary Movements- hard core. We had problems. The director taught a class entitled *the Black Woman* -no problem. Another person taught *Blacks in the Media* and Black Music soft core no problem. So I have noticed Black women's reluctance to really get into Black Radical subjects for some time. In 1977 or so, I remember talking to some Black women about their impressions of Alex Haley's *Roots* T.V. program. "I haven't watched it", some said. "I've seen a little of it", others said. Why? I asked. "Well, its too depressing" they said. " Besides this is today, we have to deal with today, not what happened in Africa. We *don't know* what really happened in Africa. This is just one man's story". I swear I wanted to hit them. Not because they did anything to me personally, but because they crushed my hopes that sisters could really deal with the idea of Black men defining reality in their own terms.

Since 1980 I have been a book seller. I sell to bookstores and I sell to individuals. I sell by myself and I share experiences with other Black book sellers. If you were to take a seat in a typical Black Bookstore for an entire ten hour day, this is what you would see over and over again: You will see more males entering the store than females. You will see the brothers buying books on African history, Political Science, Black Sociology and Black Biographies (Malcolm, DuBois, Garvey etc.) When the Black women come in they will ask "Do you have any children's books?" The idea I guess is that she *already has herself together*, she doesn't need to read any "Black stuff." It's her *child* that she wants to get together with positive Black images. After children's books, Black women will ask about Poetry books, plays, novels, books on the Black church, and of course, Black women's writings. You will rarely see large numbers of Black women congregating around the hard core Black power and historical books. If you do see them, they will usually say "I need this book for a class, do you have it?" Their meaning here is simple. She would only get this book to get a grade, not to better understand herself or her people! The thing which is so very sad is that these same single parent women will go to the school board meeting one day and in a very bold, authoritative tone of voice, talk about what *the school system should be doing* to "make sure these kids have positive images and know their history". It's a sad, vicious cycle.

If Black males are to ever be respected as men and leaders,: it will not be enough to simply read Black history and study political theory. We must take action, and build things. Too many Black men read to prepare for action that they have no real intention of ever taking. I listen to some of my Afro-centric brothers and they will have you believe that you have to read-a thousand books before you are qualified to do something practical and real in the world. And to be very honest, I *don't know* what is worse, to not read and want to know about yourself, or to read everything and not do a damn thing to improve yourself. Perhaps if Black women saw a direct relationship between a brother's level of reading and his commitment to his personal and family's well being, they would pay more attention to Black books. If they saw a relationship between a brother reading and his service as a public official, community participant and institution builder, they would see the message in the Black books as powerful. If a brother's ability to manipulate White people in order to provide a decent home, transportation, clothes, food, heat and education for his family could be traced to the Black books in the Black bookstore instead of the White boys' books in the White college book store, sisters might get down right supportive and help the brothers set up a study class or two.

Summary

Black men and women, though partners and victims in many aspects of American life, have a history of seeing the materialist aspect of America differently. Thus it should follow that they would have a difference of opinion of the importance of money and the achieving of material wealth. This discrepancy in views seems to have started almost from the very beginning of slavery when select groups of Black females, often mulattos with an identity problem of their own, were able to see and somewhat understand, participate in and enjoy aspects of the wealth of White Southern aristocrats in ways that Black men rarely experienced. These female house slaves were envied by both field slaves and yard slaves of both genders. At a time when Black people were convinced of their own inferiority and White superiority, many of these women represented to the rest of the slaves the best that Black people could be. These women were admired not only for their light skin but for having successfully achieved the status of true "ladyhood" by having absorbed the maximum amount of European values that was possible under the circumstances. Some of these ladies in fact traveled to Europe to soak in more Europeanisms and thus became even more of a standard of what a Black lady could look, talk, walk and smell like if given the opportunity. Black men during this time of constant rebellion and innovation were never able to convey to themselves or their women that there was another model of womanhood that they admired more. That they could place a dark "African Queen" on a pedestal over this mulatto model never occurred to many Black men. So it was accepted over the hundreds of years that the preferred model of Black beauty and femininity was this mulatto model. And it was reinforced over that entire period by the fact that the leading Black men in all walks of life, (i.e. medicine, athletics, entertainment, the ministry, etc.) very often chose this type of woman as their permanent, lifetime mate. Today a real White woman has, to some, become an even more preferred standard of "excellence".

With the acceptance of the "cultured," almost "aristocratic", "educated" model of Black womanhood must come the assumption of the responsibility to provide a lifestyle for a person with these expectations and self concept. Thus Black men have continuously used money and titles to chase after those few Black women who seemed to fit this mold. And because many, if not most, of these types of women based their material expectations on an analysis of what her White model received as opposed to what was reasonable to expect from a Black man in America, stupid and wasteful spending habits have been part of the habits of successful Black men, Black leaders and the middle class ever since. If such waste, role playing and pretentiousness were confined only to the egos of the "talented tenth", the Black community at large would be in pretty good shape. But many members of the less talented nine tenths decided to follow the worst habits of their so called leaders and tried to out spend, out imitate and *out fool* their foolish "role models". Dr. Carter **G.** Woodson tried to bring this to the attention of the Black middle class in the 1930's when he published The *Miseducation of the Negro*. Other criticisms of the values of middle class Blacks have been made in books and movies right up to the recent *Queen* T.V. series by Alex Haley. But as I write this in 1993, mulattoism, miscegenation and materialism are still on the rise. Black music videos pump that into us daily. The tradition of Black men reveling and developing alternative ways of interpreting the world that Black people live in have not yet had the desired impact on the women in our community.

MANHOOD PROBLEMS THAT WON'T GO AWAY

The second set of issues that has to be looked at from a historical point of view and that impact greatly on Black male female relationships are those that concern the issue of manhood. Manhood is an intangible idea that is defined in many ways in many cultures even on the continent of Africa. Various African nations had specific "rights of passage" ceremonies that signaled to the entire population that a boy was now being recognized as a man. When the African was taken into slavery and to the US, those symbolic and meaningful practices were ended. The question at that point could have been, what now constituted manhood to the African Slave Man? Could a slave in fact be a true man if he is under the will and domination of another man? Who is to define what constituted a man ? The White man (the man in power) or the Black woman who has her own idea as to what makes a man? Does the Black man have the right to come up with his own definition of manhood? Is the Black woman's idea of what she thinks a man ought to be, to be taken into consideration as a defining aspect of Black manhood? These questions and many others like them have been causing trouble for the African American male ever since he has been in America. Black men want respect as men and always have. Yet society has always been structured in such a way that he had to not only question his economic, social and political status among men but to question whether he is in fact seen as a man at all. And if he is not seen as a man or treated as a man, can he continue to feel like a man? And if White people don't see him as a man, (and it is very obvious that they don't), then can his Black woman see him as a man if she sees the world so much like White people do? And if his woman does not see him as a man, does he then act more like a White man (not to actually *be* a White man) to at least be seen as a man by his woman?

I have no recollection of ever reading or hearing Black men discuss and delineate these issues in this way but I believe that they are at the very core of a lot of the confusion in the minds of all Black men. Even Black men who might claim that they have no "manhood hangups" must interact with dozens of Black men who do. And this would be a problem even if there was no such thing as homosexuality. The fact that there is such a thing as homosexuality just makes it that much more complicated to pin point an acceptable understanding of what manhood is and how the standard is to be met.

One of the first really significant series of statements involving the issue of manhood and the Black man came from *David Walkers Appeal*, published in September, 1829. David Walker was born in North Carolina in 1785 and little is known of his early life except that he obtained both his freedom and an education. He traveled widely throughout the South and saw all the aspects of slavery. He moved to Boston in the 1820s and set up a shop selling old clothes. Walker became involved in the abolition movement in Boston and talked against slavery to the mostly small crowds of "free Blacks" and sympathetic Whites. Understanding that it was the Black slave that needed to hear his message and not free people, Walker came up with an idea that he thought would put him in closer touch with his intended audience. He wrote a small book called *An Appeal to the Colored Citizens of the World*, printed it at his own expense and started his own distribution system. Most of the clothes that Walker sold were to seamen. He put his book into the pockets of these used clothes and thus his books traveled all over the South. Some of the seamen were Black and passed the book back and forth among themselves. His book caused panic and uproar among White Southerners and a price of up to ten thousand dollars was placed on his head. By June 1830 he was found dead and poisoning seemed to be the cause. What statements did David Walkers book make that caused such controversy, excitement and fear? Walker raised issues of Black manhood (Hill and Wong Publishers, 1965, New York, Page 16).

> "It is time for me to bring this article to a close. But before I close it, I must observe to my brethren that at the close of the first Revolution in this country, with Great Britain, there were but thirteen states in the union, now there are twenty-four, most of which are slave holding states, and the whites are dragging us around in chains and in handcuffs, to their new States and Territories to work their mines and farms, to enrich them and their children - and millions of them believing firmly that we being a little darker than they, were made by our Creator to be an inheritance to them and their children for ever — the same as a parcel of brutes."

> "Are we MEN I ask you, 0 my brethren! are we MEN? Did our Creator make us to be slaves to dust and ashes like ourselves? Are they not dying worms as well as we? Have they not to make their appearance before the tribunal of Heaven, to answer for the deeds done in the body, as well as we? Have we any other Master but Jesus Christ alone? Is he not their Master as well as ours? What right then, have we to obey and call any other Master, but Himself. How we could be so submissive to

a gang of men whom we cannot tell whether they are as good
as ourselves or not, I never could conceive."

In another part of his book Walker disputes comments that Thomas Jefferson made concerning slaves and again asks Black men if they are men. (Page 15).

"See how the American people treat us — have we souls in our
bodies? Are we men who have any spirits at all? I know that
there are many swellbellied fellows among us, whose greatest
object is to fill their stomachs. Such I do not mean— I am after
those who know and feel, that we are MEN, as well as other
people; to them, I say, that unless we try to refute Mr.
Jefferson's arguments respecting us, we will only establish
them."

David Walker's appeal is most significant when we understand that it is one of those rare instances when the American Black man tapped into the *universal* understanding of what a good part of manhood is all about. Because whereas each society may define and emphasize those aspects of manhood relating to specifics such as being the provider for the family, being the architect of civilization or being the servant of God, etc., one masculine requirement seems to have been a part of all nations understanding of manhood. Namely, that a man faces and eliminates his enemy, even if it costs him his life, in order that his family and his people be saved from the evil of that enemy. It is here that David Walker did not bite his tongue. And whereas many Black writers, leaders, etc. have been quick to talk about dying for freedom, few have talked about Black people *killing* for freedom. This is what made David Walker's idea of manhood worth noting. In at least three places in his book he talks about killing Whites. First, a quote from page 6:

"ear not the number and education of our enemies, against
whom we shall have to contend for our lawful right; guaranteed
to us by our maker; for why should we be afraid, when God is,
and will continue,(if we continue humble)to be on our side?
The man who would not fight under our Lord and Master
Jesus Christ, in the glorious and heavenly cause of freedom and
of God— to be delivered from the most wretched, abject and
servile slavery, that ever a people was afflicted with since the
foundation of the world, to the present day— ought to be kept
with all of his children, in slavery, or in chains, to be butchered
by his cruel enemies."

A quote from page 32 says

> "Why, what is the matter? Why, they know that their infernal deeds of cruelty will be made known to the world. Do you suppose one man of good sense and learning would submit himself, his father, mother, wife and children ' to be slaves to a wretched man like himself, who, instead of compensating him for his labors, chains, hand-cuffs and beats him and family almost to death, leaving life enough in them, however, to work for, and call him master? No! no! He would cut his devilish throat from ear to ear, and well do slave-holders know it."

Walker wonders out loud why Black man have been so slow to kill for their freedom. On page 24 he says.

> "Natural observations have taught me these things, there is a solemn awe in the hearts of the blacks, as it respects murdering men which is the reason the Whites take advantage of us. Whereas the Whites, (though they are great cowards) where they have the advantage, or think that there are any prospects of getting it, they murder all before them, in order to subject men to wretchedness and degradation under them. This is the natural result of pride and avarice."

In a sense Walker seems to be saying that perhaps the reason that Black men don't kill Whites is because they don't think their life is worth the life of the White that they would kill. On page 25 he says

> "It is just the way with black men —eight White men can frighten fifty of them; whereas if you can only get courage into the blacks, I do declare it, that one good black man can put to death six White men; and I give it as a fact, let twelve black men get well armed for battle, and they will kill and put to flight fifty Whites."

The clearest and most complete statement that David *Walker* made on dealing with your enemy is on pages 25 and 26 of his appeal.

> "If you commence, make sure work, do not trifle, for they will not trifle with you-they want us for their slaves, and think nothing of murdering us in order to subject us to that wretched condition— therefore, if there is an attempt made by us, kill or be killed. Now, I ask you, had you not rather be killed than to be a slave to a tyrant, who takes the life of your mother, wife, and dear little children? Look upon your mother, wife, and children and answer God Almighty; and believe this, that it is no more harm for you to kill a man, who is trying to kill you,

than it is for you to take a drink of water when thirsty; in fact, the man who will stand still and let another murder him, is worse than an infidel."

David Walker, as the above caption demonstrates, did not have any conflict between being a strong believer in God, indeed a Christian God, and killing his enemies. He actually thought God was on the side of the Black man (as did others who rebelled against slavery) in his fight for liberation.

It is not the purpose here to try to develop some all purpose definition of what constitutes manhood and subject Black men to that standard. What is the purpose here is to say categorically that throughout our history here in America, Black men as a group have almost universally failed to meet a major and universal standard of manhood, namely the act of attacking and killing one's enemy. There have been many reasons as to how this lack of aggression has been justified. Many slaves were converted to Christianity and believed a) that they should conform to the role of servants as explained in the bible and or b) that one Christian could not strike out against another (even though White Christians were constantly killing Black ones). Many Blacks never looked at slavery as War, therefore they saw no enemy as such. They saw only White leaders of a *system* called slavery and therefore saw no rational reason to see Whites as the enemy to kill in war conditions. Some Blacks needed the South to Secede from the union and have a civil war declared by Whites themselves against other Whites before they realized that they were in fact at war with their White masters. Evidently they felt only war justified killing and getting killed and only the White man had the "authority" to declare a war in the first place.

If we as African American people accept the universal criteria of manhood as part of our definition also, *then* Black America has produced only one truly great Black Man — universally speaking — Nat Turner. In his book entitled *A Biographical History of Blacks in America Since 1528*, Edgar A Toppin discusses Nat Turner (David McKay Company, Inc. NY 1971, Pages 431-433).

Nat Turner was born in October 1800 in Southampton County Virginia. His mother was kidnapped from Africa and never reconciled to enslavement and instilled defiance in him. His rebellious father escaped. He was a bit of a mystic at a very early age and was strongly influenced by visions and the Bible. He was very respected for his intelligent spiritual nature. He was for awhile, preaching to his fellow slaves until his visions became more intense. In May, 1828 Nat Turner heard a loud noise in the heavens and the Spirit told him he must take on Christ's yoke but to wait for a sign before slaying the enemies with their own weapons.

In February 1831, he received the sign and he plotted a revolt with four other slaves. Beginning August 21, 1831, he killed five members of the Travis family and then proceeded from house to house in the area. As he killed the Whites he freed the slaves, some of whom joined him. Working all that night and into the next day, they killed fifty five to sixty five Whites. The Turner army grew from seven people to at least Fifty. On August 22 he was beaten when attacking a house. He went into hiding and wasn't captured for six weeks. (October 30). He was hung on November 11, 1831.

It is bad enough that Black America has not praised its greatest hero to the high heavens as other people would have done their heroes. It is even worse that many Blacks hated Nat Turner for all he stood for and caused to happen. White folks killed many hundreds of innocent Blacks in their anger over the work of Nat Turner. Many Blacks were suspected of either being a part of his army or part of the forces that were hiding him for the six weeks that he was away. Whites tightened security on plantations drastically as a way of preventing a reoccurrence of this rebellion. "Free" Blacks paid a heavy price in the restrictions that were now placed on their movement as well. Black people *blamed* Nat Turner for the new pressures in their life rather than blame and strike back at the people that were actually implementing the restrictions —White folks. Thus in some ways - Nat Turner was held up as what a Black man *must not do* (hurt a few Whites which would just lead to harder times for all Blacks) rather than as a great hero to emulate and draw inspiration from. There is no other way to describe the Black mans sense of perspective on manhood than to say that it was corrupted against his own interest except that of pure survival. And while many Black men have said that there were things worse than death — such as living as a slave, many more men evidently decided that survival was better than death, even if it meant survival as history's worse treated slave.

A fair question at this point might be as follows: if the Black man rejects the heroic image of the Black warrior as put forward by David Walker and as personified by Nat Turner as the best idea of manhood, what might the proper image of outstanding Black manhood be? The pattern that we see for the projection of African American heroes is that of Black people who generally contributed to the entire nation rather than to their own people specifically. Every school child has heard of Crispus Attucks, George Washington Carver, Charles Drew, Benjamin Bannaker, etc. It is not the intention of the greater society to project strong militant Black men as leaders for Black people, and specifically Black men, to follow. It is also societies policy not to depict Black war heroes as men to admire. How curious that the only real Black war hero that Black people celebrate to this very day is Crispus Attucks, an African American who was among the first to die, not for his *own* principles against *his* oppressor but *in the cause of his oppressor* who was fighting another White nation(England) for *their* freedom. Being really objective for just a second, would you expect other people in other parts of the world to understand why a people would celebrate a man who died in order to preserve his oppressors right to continue to oppress him and his people? I don't think so. Do White institutions point out the existence of Nat Turner for African Americans to celebrate? Not hardly. All of this adds to the confusion of Black men in their search for role models.

In 1915 Dr Carter G. Woodson, founded the Association for the Study of Negro Life and History, the first ever organization designed to study the Black man. From this organization came Black History week and eventually Black History Month. But in the nearly eighty years that Black people have been studying their leaders, movements and activities, there has yet to be any recognition given to Black men who have killed their own enemies like Mr. Turner. There have been various means of recognizing Black men who have killed the *enemy* of his oppressor such as in the two world wars, The Korean War and the Viet Nam War. Black men have won many "metals of honor" killing the enemy's of his oppressor. But nothing has been done by Blacks to recognize the killing of (or victory over) their own enemies.

In the many years that Black people spent in segregated classrooms, there was ample time and opportunity for Black educators to define a pattern of manhood that would honor those Blacks that consistently rebelled against the people and the system that was oppressing them. But that is not what we see.

The pattern that we see among African Americans whose role it is to teach and project heroes to African American youth, is that they follow a pattern of "not offending White Folks." Thus even if our history were filled with people like Nat Turner and other warriors, Black teachers would not likely mention them - for fear of offending White folks. This adds to the manhood definition problem. Manhood cannot be defined in any "proper" way for fear of offending the very people whom we should be least concerned about. Black heroes and manhood is thus confined to a definition that does not make Whites "uncomfortable". As Black female school teachers outnumber Black male teachers 3, 4, 5 to one or more, we see the Black woman again, though perhaps not knowingly, the instrument of the White mans means of limiting the definition of Black heroes and Black manhood.

Contrast this against what little we have learned about the American Indian and *their* heroes. African Americans have heard of Geronimo and Cochise of the Apache Indians, Osciola among the Seminoles in Florida and

Chief Joseph among the Indians of the plains. We know of Sitting Bulls defeat of General George Custer at Little Big Horn. Thus Blacks, as ignorant as they are about the history of the Native Americans, know four times the numbers of Indians who have killed for their freedom than they know of among their own people.

It is White people not Native Americans who have made us aware of Indian heroes. And they did this not because they love Indians but because Indians forced White people to respect them unlike the case with African Americans. In San Antonio, Texas right now as I write this, there are probably some African American children visiting the Alamo in awe and admiration of Davey Crocket and Jim Bowie though they were smashed to smithereens by the Mexican General, Santa Ana (defending Mexico's land and people.) These Black children will also learn about Santa Ana before learning about Nat Turner. In simple fact our leaders, as much as we love them and are proud of them, do not stack up well against other people's heroes for one simple reason: they did not kill enough Whites to serve our people's best interests. They did not even *plan* to kill Whites even in those moments when the universal laws of manhood demanded that they should have done so.

Black leaders have shared one consistent trait for over a hundred years. They were orators supreme. If liberation were based on ones capacity *to talk* instead of acting, the Black man would be the freest man in the history of the world. Frederick Douglas, Henry Highland Garnet, Booker T. Washington, Dubois, Paul Robeson, Adam Clayton Powell, Dr. King, Stokley Carmichael, "Rap" Brown, Malcolm X, Eldridge Cleaver, etc., are all known for what they *said* as "spokesman". Not to be outdone by the men, Black women like Soujoiner Truth, Mary McCloud Bethune, Shirley Chishom, Angela Davis and Barbara Jordan were also rappers supreme. Not a single foe has been killed by any of them put together. I don't know how Sitting Bull talked or, how Osciola or Cochise talked. But their statements on the battlefield are much louder than anything Black people have said this century. Period. If you try to pry yourself out of romantic pride and judge our people on a *world* standard with other nations and cultures, then you would reach the same conclusion. If riding a BMW and living in a great condo was so great, if it was the answer to our true liberation, why do some Black men who have achieved this level of success still have so many questions about their manhood?

The 1960s Last Chance for Manhood Definition

The difference between a soldier and a criminal is that the soldier kills on the basis of an opponents military or political significance. They do not kill indiscriminately and they do not kill women and children for the most part. The 1960s was the last time the Black man was at war with America and thus was the last time a significant political statement could have been clearly made without (from *our* perspective) the overtones of simple random crime.

If you are under thirty five and an African American male or female you are probably sick and tired of hearing about the 1960s. But the 1960s was perhaps the American Black mans last chance to really assert his manhood in the same way that other men have in history. Black men could have made one Hell of a statement that would have changed American and therefore part of World History. For example, in a five year period between 1963 and 1968, five famous people out of the one hundred eighty million that made up all of America, were killed. They were President John Kennedy, Medgar Evers (state head of the Mississippi NAACP), Malcolm X, Dr. Martin Luther King and Attorney General Robert Kennedy. Most people say that just these five deaths changed the course of American History.

The Black man wanted to change the course of American history during that time in such a way as to redefine his relationship to his former master forever. His actions of legal procedures, marching, voting, sitting in and even "rioting" were measures that he used to make his case for change. And while change did come and the Black self concept did improve, the Black man *did not seek or reach the universal definition of manhood.* He did not kill his enemy. But he did go thru all the motions that temporarily made him feel free and like a real man. The Black is Beautiful theme, the long Afros, the African name changes, the Black leather jackets and power fists and calls for Black power etc. allowed some Black men to live out the fantasy of manhood. Thousands of Black men even owned loaded guns, practiced shooting and made all the right body gestures for the ever present T.V. cameras. But when the smoke from the "riots" cleared, once and for all it was proven beyond a shadow of a doubt that Black men had no interest in and/or guts for killing their enemy — the White man. The White man did not hesitate to kill Blacks however. Most of the bodies left after the riots were of Black males. Few Whites were killed by Blacks and only a few of those had any *political* significance. *Any freaky White boy such as Richard Speck, Charles Manson, Ted Bundy, your local serial killer or the* disgruntled *postal worker of recent years, killed more White people (sometimes in one day) than the entire Black movement did in an entire decade.* The White man called our bluff and found out for yet another time that we were very much bluffing. Although we put on a good show in talking militant, Black militants did not kill a single solitary member of the KKK, White Citizens Council or other racist organization during the 60's.

What could Black men in the 1960s have done in making a statement to White America about their intent to support their interests and deal with their enemies? What could have happened? Well, think about this. If five mens death supposedly changed the nation's history forever, what would one hundred more have done? If Black men could have made up a hit list of a mere 100 White men, starting with J. Edgar Hoover our most obvious enemy, we could have made a hell of a statement to White America. George Wallace, Governor Faulbus, James Eastland, Jessie Helms, KKK leaders, White police commissioners whose hands were wet with the Blood of Black men would all have made good targets. If Black men could have wiped out just a small number of representative racist leaders it would not have made up for three hundred years of slavery, but it would have given the best taste of manhood to the American Black man in nearly five hundred years.

But that is not what Black men did at all in the 1960's. Instead Black men killed maybe a hundred thousand people in Viet Nam, Cambodia and Laos, but it was the wrong place to prove manhood. And they killed many thousands in the communities where they lived. They killed a few thousand of their own relatives and finally quite a few thousand creatively killed themselves. The Black man as we have come to expect kills everyone except the people he is suppose to kill and now everyone knows it. Deep down no one believes (including the Black man himself) that the Black man has the guts or the intelligence to pursue his true historical enemy. And it effects and hammers away at his true feeling of being a man. This failure to come to terms with ones duty to fight ones true enemy has long lasting and pervasive effects on our community today.

As a result of the Black mans failure to develop his own sense of legitimate manhood, he has been displacing his real enemies with *false* enemies. If Malcolm X and the Honorable Elijah Muhammad had killed just a few of the enemy that they both said that they hated so much, maybe Malcolm would have been killed in the heat of a *real* battle like other peoples heroes as opposed to the sorry set of events we all know so well. Some of the false (or minor) enemies that the Black man has erected to take the place of his"true" enemy are as follows:

New Asian Merchants: The fact that the many small grocery stores, liquor and convenience stores in the Black community are now being run by recently arrived Asians is not a pretty picture. But Black people have had at least an entire generation to capture and control these stores themselves if they were really interested. Why get angry at someone who is willing to work longer, harder and cheaper than yourself. Black people have long looked down their noses at these types of occupations and were always concerned about getting a degree and working downtown, preferably with White folks. The Asian may not be our friend or treat us with much respect but that shouldn't make him our number one enemy either. We shouldn't rob his store, burn his store or kill him. Especially since we haven't touched our real enemy.

Jews in the Community: There are various Black scholars whom I respect that make a strong case in showing that the Jewish Community is guilty of many transgressions against the Black Community including involvement in the slave trade. I believe that there is a lot of truth in these charges. However I also know that many Jews, more so than any other White people, gave of their money, time and talent over a couple of generations to help Black Americans get a better shake in America. Did their good deeds compensate for their bad deeds? Probably not. But what I do know is that for various periods of time we shared the same hard core enemy — the KKK and similar racist groups and they helped Blacks fight these groups when nobody else cared or dared. That makes them less than my primary enemy even if the Jewish people are generally against my primary interests as a Black person. Again the theme here is that we should deal with our *primary* enemy first.

Gays in the Community: Quite frankly I don't know if Black gay people catch any more hell in the Black Community for being gay than non gay people do. But I do know that because they are different and to some people represent even more of the nonmasculine profile that Black men insecure in their manhood already experience, that they are subject to be harassed and attacked. Anyone who thinks that Black gays are Black people's enemy is a real lost soul and a dumb one at that.

Economically stable Blacks: When an African American gets to the point where they have a solid income, credit and assets, they often reach a point where they are dammed if they leave the Black Community and dammed if they stay. If they leave the community they will hear the usual charges of being an Uncle Tom, Oreo or leaving the Black Community without positive role models. If they stay, a few poor Blacks will likely become resentful of their wealth and break into their cars, vans and homes taking things that they feel wealthy Blacks are no more entitled to than themselves. It is foolish for the Black Community to turn on itself and tear down the first person or family that looks like it has just a little more than the rest. But this is typical behavior from a people who will not face their true enemy with the legitimate rages and anger that many Blacks carry around with them daily.

Why The Perpetual Anger

There's a scene played out on television every week on some type of talk show. You will first see a Black man on stage or in the audience speaking very angrily about the injustices perpetuated against Black people "for the last four hundred years". Without fail a White woman, (sometimes a White male) will pop up from the audience and say something to the effect that this Black speaker should

    a)   forget about past wrongs against his people and only deal with the events of today.

    b)   Not hold today's generation of Whites accountable for what happened a hundred years ago.

    c)   Stop using racism as an excuse for their own short comings and/or

    d)   Not judge White people as a race but as individuals because "there's good and bad in all races", etc., etc. Next, without fail that audience member will get a thunderous round of applause indicating that she has adequately spoken for the audience at large. The Black speaker is suppose to feel that his feelings are uncalled for and out of line. There is never enough time for the speaker to say completely why he feels the Black man or Black people are entitled and within their rights to be angry. And even if he were given substantial time there would still be things left unsaid or glossed over. Some aspects of Black male anger are buried so far down into the psyche of men that they can't bring it up even in moments of venting genuine anger.

But it is a very legitimate question to wonder why Black men stay so angry and its not just Whites or even non-Blacks that wonder about this. Many Black women are also puzzled as well as many Black men themselves. Here is an effort to explain why Black male anger is so pervasive and long lasting.

A)   Good Seldom Overcomes Evil

In many ways young Black boys are brought up exactly like everyone else in America. He is taught four principles which are drummed into his head daily. He is taught the difference between good and evil, he is to *do* good and *avoid* evil, he is taught that good will always over come evil and that evil will always be punished, sooner or later. Virtually every lesson he learns in his church reinforces these ideas. His parents and teachers reinforce these ideas. Every television program in the many thousands of hours that he watches reinforces the basic ideas that good will win out over bad and bad will be punished. All the movies attended, videos rented, books and even comic books read all say the same message over, over and over again.

In real life however its a very different story. There is little if any punishment dished out to the many hundreds of thousands of Whites who have perpetuated evil against Black people and particularly Black males. Good does not win out over bad in their lives. There are role reversals when it comes to Black males. So many people portrayed to him as being "good guys" become the embodiment of Satan with regard to their behavior against Black men. What Whites in America were *punished* for the evil of slavery over its better than two hundred year history? What good came to those Blacks that resisted it as best they could? How many Whites have paid a price for the active racism that they display on a daily basis? In the entire history of the American legal system there has *never* been a White man executed for the killing of a Black man. Never! Most Black men don't know that. But when they find out they wonder what that says about good always over coming evil and evil always having to pay the price for its acts. So the first major reason why Black men stay angry is because everyday he is asked to experience and understand and accept a lie. He is given a few dozen examples of good over coming evil and evil being punished. And then he is given a few dozen examples of how those principles have nothing at all to do with his own life and those in his racial family. It was that way in the past, it is his present reality and he has every reason to believe it will be that way until he dies. That means that every day that he reflects on any point of the spectrum of time that he can conceive, there are valid reasons to see the inequity of his treatment and become justifiably angry.

B)   Constant challenges To Ones Manhood

Black on Black on crime is responsible for at least twenty times more death and destruction to the Black community that all the police actions and White hate group activity in the country combined. That is a sad fact of our lives. But when White oppressors oppress and it leads to death or destruction, it still triggers an emotional response and calls the Black man's willingness to respond appropriately into question. Seldom does the Black man fight fire with fire, an eye for an eye, a death for a death. The Black mans sense of justice knows this is the way it should be. Especially when the justice system consistently allows White wrong doers to go free. Black men are always angry because every time they are tested they fail. They expect to pay no attention to that little voice inside that says if you want justice, you are going to have to take care of if yourself.

All death and destruction takes a toll on feeling human beings. But actions by police, lawyers, judges, prison authorities and other people in position to snuff out Black life do more than make the Black man feel bad, they make him feel ashamed of himself.

C)   Self Hate

Self hate is a very large area of discussion and can span the complete range of emotions from loving all things White to hating all things Black. Most readers are already familiar with various manifestations of self hate. Black boys and men are just as subject to this sickness as are the females. But in addition to the normal aspects of self hate based on race, Black males also have a form of self hate based on their gender. When the repeated tests to respond like a man present themselves to Black men, and they fail to respond however well rationalized, they begin to hate themselves as *men*. They feel like punks, whimps, "sissies" etc. They are angry at White people for having enough power and influence to make them feel this way about themselves. And just like self hate leads one to do drastic things to embrace Whiteness or reject Blackness, Black males will do ridiculous things to recapture a lost sense of masculinity. And there lies the fundamental cause of most of the violent crime in the Black community.

It is widely believed on the part of many distinguished Black thinkers that the self hate which causes many of the crimes that Black people (mostly Black males) commit against other Blacks is racially based (ie., caused by a disrespect for and hatred or shame of other Blacks). While this is absolutely part of the story, this writer thinks that a good part of these crimes are also gender based. Because the general society does a good job in preventing Black males from feeling like men, Black males develop their own ghetto-rites-of-passage-manhood-initiation processes that usually involves a criminal act. In gang activity particularly it may mean shooting certain people (never White cops it seems), robbing a bank, stealing a car or some type of risky, dangerous activity to prove that you have "heart" (guts) and have stepped over "the line". Non gang members may simply beat a person half to death to show that he is "somebody you don't mess with". In the last ten years especially, young Black men have admitted that they carry guns because it makes them feel "like a man", "powerful", "as equal as the next man." To show how valid this line of thinking is, powerfully built mature policeman with ten years of street experience now fear snotty nose fourteen year old kids because those kids now have guns bigger and more powerful then the police. Black men carrying guns and the need to express manhood *are one and the same*.

The three reasons discussed above without question contribute significantly to the ever present anger in many Black men. But it is important to also see and understand how this anger compares with the feelings of Black women who experience many of the same evils that Black men experience.

Womanhood and Manhood Differences

In the last twenty years, the lines between what is feminine and what is masculine has been getting more and more blurry. House husbands, feminism, Ms., sexist, and gender bending are just a few of the words which redefine roles between men and women.

Some roles have outlasted others. Women have for instance have challenged the notion that only men are to be the economic providers. But they have not given up the idea of men as *protectors*. Men are seen by both men and women as the ones to physically or militarily confront dangerous people, animals, situations or forces that threaten the family unit. The idea in the minds of most people is that men are still the fighters. And though society has seen the emergence of women in roles in police, fire, and the armed forces, the idea of men as protectors clearly predominates. It is for that reason that the idea of manhood is so clearly tied to fighting when fighting seems appropriate. The wisdom of men in most cultures is judged on the basis of what circumstances dictate *the necessity of fighting* not whether or not men *should ever fight*.

There are three things that push a man to a point of wanting to fight. The most obvious one is anger which can be caused by any number of factors. The second thing would be a sense of duty. There are situations where even if you are not emotionally aroused by a particular event, you feel compelled to respond. For example men drafted into the military usually have no feelings one way or the other for "the enemy". But since his country is requiring him to serve, it will be his sense of duty that makes him pull triggers and line up dead bodies, not personal feelings.

But the third and perhaps most crucial factor in determining whether a man will fight or not is how the decision *defines him as a person to himself.* Does he want to be seen as someone who can be messed over, bullied, threatened, and intimidated without the bully being concerned about a response? Or does he want to be seen as someone who will stand up for himself and make an enemy pay dearly for bringing grief to his life or the lives of his loved ones? It is possible for men to ignore their anger and rationalize walking away from a fight. Wise men seldom fight based on anger alone. Duty and responsibility tap into a higher level of motivation and rational. Men want to do the right thing and fulfilling your responsibility to whom you feel bound to serve, be it country or individual, gives more meaning to the actions (fighting) you are contemplating.

But even in situations where men can swallow their anger and excuse themselves from a commitment they see as non binding, there comes a time when they have to look inwardly at themselves. And in looking at themselves they have to make sure that they are not making a statement of cowardice by not fighting. Men have to live with themselves and like themselves whether they decide to fight or not. Thus when men fight it is sometimes due to their desperate need to maintain the self respecting image that they have always had for themselves. And if they die in the effort of maintaining that self image, then they accept that a risk and a cost that they are willing to pay. Like it or not, this is how wars are fought. And from the point of view of warriors, men fought so that women would not have to.

What causes frustrations in some Black men with regard to some Black women is that they either don't understand the males perspective or they don't agree to respect the perspective after they have understood it. These women assume that they have every right to be as angry at Whites as Black men do. And in many cases this is true. And she thinks that because she has been "strong enough" to get over her anger, then therefore Black men should be able to do like wise. If he, from her point of view, is not able to do so, then he is a hot head, immature, crazy, ego tripping etc. Black women are not and never have been as interested in going to war with White folks as Black men have. But what women don't understand is that it was never ingrained into them that it would ever be their *duty* or *responsibility* to fight. So they don't have conflicting feelings of betrayal of their responsibilities when they decide to pass on doing battle. Men *do* have these conflicting feelings and considerations. And most importantly, women have no sense of an identity loss, of being less of a woman when making the decision not to fight. On the contrary, deciding not to fight is usually considered the " lady like", " classy" decision to make. For men the situation is totally reversed. To decide not to fight a *just* fight is considered cowardly, weak, or "acting like a woman" and digs at the very core of a man's definition of himself. So women need to understand that many men can swallow their anger and walk away from a pointless confrontation just as they do. But men can not easily and in good faith walk away from a situation which calls on him to meet his responsibility as a man or challenges how he is to see himself as a man.

The Rappers Fantasy: The White Man's Reality

There are many reasons why I don't like most rap music but this is not the place to go into all the details. It is appropriate however to point out how rap supports some of the contentions of the position presented here. Many rappers appear to be gang members or ex gang members who were the very people causing young Black lives to be snuffed out, the elderly to be prisoners of their own homes and babies to be caught in cross fires between factions. These rappers look like, talk like and act like they want to be seen as tough men. Many of the lyrics to their "music" talk of guns, "fighting the power" and killing cops. In this sense rap is a prefabricated fantasy. Where are the dead cops that these gangster rappers killed when they were on the street? There are none, and never were. Instead of confronting the enemy they have killed each other and innocent Black bystanders like thousands of frustrated Black "men" before them. Ice T is the worst of the bunch. Here is a "man" who gets on national TV and admits that he's hurt (maybe even killed)brothers during his gang days. And he also says that a statement on one of his records where he talks about putting a flashlight up a woman's genitals, was "a joke". Then he puts out a record called Cop Killer and draws massive attention to himself because cops don't like the message. Ice T is no more going to kill a cop than the man in the moon. He has too much money at stake playing a tough guy in the movies and singing like a tough guy on records to actually *be* a tough guy for real. And the tough guy that he used to be wasn't the kind that Black people needed. So how in the hell can the Black Community take a guy who represents the exact opposite of everything we need to be and make him a "star" a "hero" and a "role mode". Please, I want to puke!

Meanwhile, the White man (Warner Brothers) is behind the scenes doing what they do best, paying the Black man to make a fool of himself so that he (the White man) can make even more money. The White man understands that the Black man wants very badly to be a man. So because it is now clear that he will never be one as it has been traditionally defined (confronts and fights his true enemy) the Black man has been declared safe in the same way that a toothless dog or clawless cat is safe. But the Black man doesn't realize how "safe" he is and how unthreatening he is to real men who do fight their enemies. So White people decided to allow the Black man to act out his fantasy of manhood by developing movie scripts, music videos and recording rap music which allows the Black man to do all the things he envisions in his fantasies. This might include killing cops, White landlords, politicians and judges. Because millions of Black people have this same fantasy, they become the consumers and direct millions and millions of dollars to these movies, records, stage acts, videos, etc. In the same way that a sex addict may consume pornographic movies and get a sexual orgasm without an actual sexual encounter, Black people, particularly " so called men" derive an orgasmic sense of satisfaction in seeing White cops, judges, etc. blown away on the screen without having to encounter all that would actually require. In a two hour movie White people allow the Blacks on the screen to *act* like men and the people in the seats watching to *feel* like men. Its all a show. A few Black stars and a lot of White people get a lot of money for participating in this forum for Black manhood make believe. In the 1990s White people understand that the Black man will not connect what he does or sees on the screen with the real world. That is why they feel absolutely safe in putting the shows on. We never disappoint them and they laugh all the way to the bank.

It might appear to some readers that this extended discussion on historical figures, slavery, the killing of White folks, manhood and Rap music has absolutely nothing at all to do with today's Black males and females having disagreements over money. I can appreciate that some might have that perception. However people can only produce up to their capability when they feel good about themselves, their options, judgements and vision. And what this chapter is intent on showing is that Black males have a long history of performing at less than their full capability because *their anger has gotten in the way of their ability.* And this anger is constant and justifiable based on the many ways and means that the Black man is made to feel less than a complete man. This anger is heighten and made worse because very few people who are not also Black males, understand the basis for or the legitimacy of this deep and constant anger. And whereas it may be completely pointless to expect that White people will ever understand, accept or take responsibility for this anger, it is very important for Black men and Black women to understand it. We must move forward together in developing, rather than destroying , our community and ourselves. When both parties understand the basis of the anger and frustration, it opens the door to move past it. When its clear how anger blocks the progress of the individual, the relationship, family and community, it should move couples to work on it.   Relationships where the male has a high degree of anger usually lack important things that relationships need if they are to continue; communication, commitment, stability, and adequate financial resources.   It is particularly important for Black women to understand and accept the basis for some Black male anger. Accepting it alone can be a big step in helping the male work it out of his system without feeling the need for the extreme actions that many Black males take. It is unrealistic for people to assume that the average brother can work these demons out of his system by himself ("get his self together"). This is particularly true if most of his time is spent with similarly situated Black males who are no farther along in working their demons and anger out than he is .

Of course there must be faith on the part of Black women that brothers are reachable, teachable and redeemable. There are fascinating stories of Black men purging their anger to lead productive lives. Dr. Ben Carson almost stabbed a friend to death but a well placed belt buckle broke the knife's blade before he could do damage. Today he may be the greatest Black surgeon in the world. (read *Gifted Hands, Zonderuan Publishing House* 1990). Nathan McCall also almost killed a man but is now a successful newspaper reporter and author. The mere title of his book, *Makes Me Wanna Holler,* clearly reveals his degree of pent up anger (Random House Publishers 1994).

But the purging of Black male anger is not just to help Black people in their inter - personal relationships as important as that is. It is to also help Black men rejoin the world community as a player, businessman and wheeler dealer. Black men must understand that every day men and women exchange billions of dollars in deals with people that they don't necessarily like. In fact many nations who are for all practical purposes near enemies, certainly competitors, do business together. What this means is that as angry as Black men are with White people and as much as that anger is justified, we still have to learn how to sit down with the devil, smile, and do a deal that we feel is in the best interests of our people. Every other nation has learned how to do this. Do you think the Whites of the U.S. "like" Japanese, Koreans, Chinese or Arabs as a people? Of course not. And its well known that Japanese people clearly think they are better, more intelligent and more principled than Americans. But each does business with the other and obtains more benefits for their people than if they refused to deal. Do you think for one milli second (one thousandth of a second) that Nelson Mandela "likes" DeKlerk, the former president of South Africa. Of course not. But he was able to deal with him long enough to get himself positioned as the most powerful Black man in the world as we speak. No other Black man has as much gold, military might or Nuclear weapons under his authority as President Mandela. If he had let his anger rule, he not only wouldn't be president right now, he'd probably would still be in jail. What good could he do Black South Africans and Black people if he were still there? People all over the world have said that they can't *deal* with Black Americans. Black Americans must again learn how "to deal" with the whole world in the spirit of our African ancestors who carried on international trade thousands of years ago. But we cannot do that by holding on to our anger and we cannot wait for White folks to understand our anger. We need to put that anger in our back pocket and move on. With the help of our women we can do this. At least I sure as hell hope so.

INTRODUCTION TO MONEY
THE MAKING OF A MENTALITY

It's a pretty well known fact that childhood impressions carry a tremendous impact on how individuals respond to events and circumstances in the later stages of their life. Hundreds of hours of talk show testimony has traced obesity, child abuse, sexually deviant behavior, chemical dependence and a host of other ills, to experiences that occurred in childhood. With that concept so firmly established, it would seem appropriate to look at the kinds of impressions African American children receive about money and issues surrounding money. After all, if Black males and females are to truly understand the nature of their differences on the issue of money, they should begin at the very beginning and not assume that misunderstandings only occurred after the first twenty years of their life.

This chapter will look at some of the primary influences on young people's ideas and analyze not only what types of messages they are likely to receive but also which ones they are likely *not* to receive. The four primary sources we will look at are parental actions and inactions, television images and messages, the school system and peer and sibling influence. Not all, but for certain the majority of young people's ideas (four to thirteen years old) come from some combination of these sources.

The problems with the structure and the instability of the African American family are well documented and will not be repeated here. Perhaps hundreds of thousands of Black parents are either too young, too poor, too ignorant, too chemically dependent, too sick, too abusive or too absent (or "busy") to teach their children much of anything that is nurturing to their development. This is hardly a "Black" situation per se because parents of other races are similarly situated. The over representation of African American families falling into these categories however is a fact not often challenged. We shall skip these problematic families and deal instead with the "stable" families of our community. Such families may or may not be two parent households and may or may not be on some type of government assistance. The criteria here is that the parent(s) show an interest in guiding their children, through the time and attention given to them, down the philosophical path that the parent deems acceptable for those children.

MONEY CONSCIOUSNESS

For the first four years, most of us are unaware of money's existence and couldn't care less. But sometime in our fifth and certainly by our sixth year someone has given us a nickel, dime, quarter or dollar to use as we wish. We either walk or are taken to the store and realize that with these coins we can get candy, gum, trinkets, etc. Over the next months we learn the cost of specific candies, trinkets, popcorn, potato chips and the like. This is how most of us learn about money.

Almost at the same time that we learn what money is (in terms of what you can do with it) we also become conscious of and attentive to where it comes from. In most cases it is given to us. Birthday cards, visiting grandparents, aunts and uncles, or parental gifts are the usual sources. Shortly after that, we "learn" how to ask for these little coins, usually from our parents or the other adults living in the house. As we succeed in getting what we want by merely asking, some of us may not be very discriminating and may ask   any grown person we may know. At this point many of us experience our first real conflict over money. Because whereas we have, up to that point, been receiving money because adults have given it to us and because we have specifically asked for it, our parents then tell us not to ask for it. They tell us not to beg for money, at least not to anyone outside the immediate family. At this point family traditions vary. Some families provide their children with an allowance with no strings attached at, say, eight or nine years old. Other families assign their children household duties to perform and the allowance is given based on how well or how consistently they perform these duties. Some families give an allowance based on school grades, good behavior, church attendance or other criteria. Obviously many households do not give children an allowance at all, either because they don't have the money to give, or there are too many children to provide allowances for, or maybe because they just don't believe in the idea. In any case the children take in certain lessons, messages and values from these financial transactions with the adults in their household.

Sooner or later, this child is going to have someone step forward and put forth the idea of money in exchange for work. This idea basically says to the child that if you perform certain actions for certain kinds of people, you will get paid this thing called money which you seek. Sometimes, as stated above, it will come from the parents who reward good grades or the performance of household duties. Or it could be the advice of siblings or peers that gets a child to focus on performing some "work" outside of the home for neighbors or strangers. By ten, eleven or twelve years old, many children find that they can make money by mowing lawns, raking leaves, washing cars, shoveling snow, packing groceries, caring for animals, etc. It is also at this age that they get introduced to the idea of selling things. Sometimes this selling is under the direction of an organization or institution, i.e. cookies for the girl scouts, Christmas trees for the boy scouts, candy for the school band or cakes for a church bake sale. Sometimes the youngsters will find that they have the ability to develop a regular source of money through their own business. Something like a newspaper route comes to mind. The support and encouragement of parents is crucial in determining if a child is going to sustain the ambition, initiative and discipline that it takes to "work" regularly at a particular enterprise. Some parents lead a child to focus on something that they do not do well (schoolwork) and discourage them from doing what they do well - work and serve people. It is not an easy judgement to make and both approaches can be adequately justified.

While many young people are learning by doing, many don't ever get the opportunity for a host of reasons. But all children are picking up lessons, whether they are intended or not, from their parents or older adults in the home. Some of these "lessons" are the following:

1.   **Real money, perhaps even "all" money comes from the White man.**
      This is the ultimate reality that many parents in many ways teach their children. Many parents look at their own responsibility as being that of directing their child as to *which* White man to work for, not whether or not they are to chose to do so. This is done by trying to get children to focus on certain careers, working for certain companies or associating with certain kinds of people. There is usually a lack of awareness on the part of the parents that this is what they are doing and they would certainly deny such an accusation if it was presented to them. But if you analyze exactly what they were consistently saying, implying and promoting, the reality would be there for any honest person to see.

Some parents prevent this message from being sent by constantly struggling to "make some money on the side" in their own enterprise. It could be baby sitting, fixing cars, or selling various products through a network marketing or direct sales company. It could be profiting from a hobby like "doing hair", carpentry work, selling ones own art work, jewelry or handmade dresses. This writer, being extremely pro Black business, would like for the reader to consider the following point. A parent can struggle to bring in "extra" money through their business and feel a sense of failure because that money never really amounted to much in dollars and cents. But that "failing" business could be one of the single greatest messages that a child can learn from their parents. The messages for that child to see and witness for themselves are a) never depend on one thing to always carry you through life, b) try to develop your own talents and resources for making it in life, c) never give up if you are trying to do something; hang in there even if it doesn't look like you will make it some day, d) do not depend on the White man for everything. e.)Your people have money, do business with each other when you can.

If one were to read the biographies of hundreds of successful business people, one of the main things you will find countless times in each story is that person's parents (usually their father) owned a small, sometimes struggling business that inspired that person to develop their own. Black parents should not under estimate the power of this lesson for their children. On the other hand it would be dishonest not to say that probably a like number of children are also turned off by business due to exactly the same images. They say to themselves, "I'm not going to be like my mother or father - working hard at a business that never pays any money. I am going to get a high paying job where I know how much I'm going to get paid and then enjoy life when I get home from work instead of working all the time." By talking to their children about their business, why they like it, why they do it, what they hope to accomplish with it, parents can help mold the attitudes that they would prefer their children to have. By letting the child work with you in that business, more insight and lessons are transferred.

2.   Don't save your money, don't invest your money, spend it all, all the time. There is probably not a single parent that has not told their children to save their money for a "rainy day." Everyone says that. But what do the children see every week? They see a paycheck to paycheck existence. One unpaid sick day can cause some major financial adjustment in a family that week. One unexpected but common problem can cause significant financial adjustments and disappointments. The child hears their parents complain about banks not lending Black people any money. They know that their parents do not save any money. They have to then wonder how banks ever get money to loan people if every one operated like their parents and never put money *in* the bank.

As wise as the advice of saving money appears to be, that is not what children often see. It is no wonder that their own spending habits are less than desirable when they grow up.

3.   Buy from White people when you can, Asian people or other foreigners if its convenient and Black people when its easy and cheap. Black parents are quick to talk about the importance of instilling racial pride in children. And in the 1990's there are now certain acceptable rituals that are OK to perform to help instill this pride. It's OK to buy Black dolls, wear African kente cloth, stay home on Dr. King's birthday, celebrate Kwanzaa, wear a Malcolm X hat, tee shirt, underwear, etc. But apparently spending money with Black businesses must be going a bit too far. Black parents miss the point that there are few more important statements of Black pride that their children could possibly learn than to support a Black business in the regular and normal course of daily activities.   And by not teaching their children to support Black businesses, they are in fact teaching their children a lesson that is hurting us all. They are saying that you not only get your money from White folks, but you should make sure you give it right back to them as well. Put all of it back except what you might put in the church plate. This is not to suggest that all Black businesses should be supported just because they are Black. This writer believes that quite a few Black enterprises should suspend business until they learn how to do business. But it is common knowledge that there are plenty of community enterprises that are not nurtured and supported in the way that they should be. Kids do what they see their parents do even if they are not aware of it. That parents desire to rush out to the mall to the name brand stores to buy the name brand clothes has registered with the child before they reach puberty. Parents perfectly *complete* the work that the television has initiated and unfortunately it all seems perfectly normal to both parents and children.

4.   We can play together but we can't work together.
       One of the great thrills of parenthood is to take your children out and have fun with them. We take them to sports events, amusement parks, the circuses, ice capades, community carnivals, etc. We like to see them laugh, play, enjoy their food and appreciate our efforts and dollars at making them happy. There is not enough of this going on in Black America and hopefully much more of it will take place in the years ahead. But what the nation's Black children also learn is that the same parent that is so much fun to be with under playful conditions is difficult to be around in work situations or situations involving stress.
       Helping kids with homework is a case in point. It's fair to say I think that most parents do not enjoy helping their children with their homework. (which is actually a form of teaching). They feel they should be doing "more important" things with that time even if its just relaxing. They grow impatient when their child makes a mistake or doesn't catch on or they get frustrated or embarrassed if they cannot do their child's work themselves.
       In another situation, a child may be yelled at if in the course of helping mom or dad they do the wrong thing unknowingly. A parent is often heard to say, " Go, get out of here, I'll do it myself." What children learn is that there is

the concept of individual work and individual responsibility, but the idea of *our* work and *our* responsibility is rather vague. Decorating the Christmas tree may be the only pleasant, cooperative thing (work) that parents and children look forward to in an entire year. This is sad. When Black people lived on the farm we worked together and experienced a quality of family life that the amusement parks and circuses have not replaced. Now that we are "up North"struggling to find work and keep our "individual jobs," family life in terms of lessons learned by children, working directly with their parents, has suffered. On the other hand we see Jewish , Korean, Italian and other children working *with* their parents in their businesses on a daily basis. And you know that there are a great deal more cooperative efforts that we don't see behind the scenes. As a Black youngster, we learn its hard to work with (Black) adults. The more we are convinced, the more we avoid it and the less we do it. By the time we grow up, many of us actually have little experience working with anyone in any collective enterprise. As adults we graduate from saying its hard to work with our parents to its hard to work with Black people, period. Its much easier to work with White people because we've been so programmed that they are so much smarter, better and more powerful. Our childhood memory is that our whole family did what Whites told us to do, usually without question or reservation. Why change now?

5.   Press for the grades and kill the Creativity.

As a person who has pretty seriously studied the Black experience for over a quarter century, I can tell you that part of the challenge in breaking through some of our problems as a people has to do with the cyclical nature of our problems. That is to say we might observe a problem, then come up with a "solution" to that problem but that "solution" causes a new problem very similar to the original problem that was first observed. Thus a cycle is formed. We hear about the cycle of poverty, the cycle of child abuse, etc. But there are cycles that we do not recognize that are perhaps just as dangerous. One such cycle deals with Black advancement.

If we look for Black America's greatest contribution to America, a single word, *creativity,* would probably capture it. Our creativity in music, dance, fashion, food, etc. is a major reason why America, though filled with Europeans has a culture that is different from Europe's. Black athletes for example play sports according to the same rules as others, but our creativity in those sports changes the nature of the game entirely. We create words that are eventually used all around the world. Most Black people take Black creativity for granted and don't give it particular value. But this creativity creates and sells products and produces an income for whoever is in control of the business end of the process.

This creativity has its genesis in our youthful years. As youngsters growing up in mostly Black neighborhoods and attending Black schools, churches and family gatherings, we are unaware of the so called "right" or "proper" ways to talk, eat, dress, walk, etc. We thus develop a style of our own for everything we do. When we get to school, a long process begins that many of us never recover from. This process, some call it "education", is a process where teacher's Black and White, stand up in front of the class and say in various ways that the manner is which we (Blacks) do things, see things, say and express things is improper, incorrect and wrong. It is their job as teachers to strip away all of our backward ways and replace them with the ways of White folks. The better you can do this, the "smarter" you will be. The "smarter" you are, the more money, success, happiness and respect you will have in life. You will be measured in your ability to copy Whites by a series of grades. A stands for being an excellent copier, B for good copiers and C for just average copiers. Totally lost in this system is each child's ideas about him or herself, the world in general or the subject matter being discussed. For every day a child spends in school, at least one time (but usually several times) each day that child will be told in one way or another, that what they think about a thing, person, idea, event or feeling is not important. They are expected to simply repeat what some one else says is important and relevant. Parents with the best of intentions come forward and pressure these children to get good grades, and they sometimes put even more emphasis on the repetition process than the teachers themselves. When the child would rather do another activity that allows that child to either exercise their own thoughts about a thing or develop their own creativity, they are often discouraged. Get back to the books, study and master the art of repeating back to the teacher what somebody else (usually somebody White) says or thinks about a thing. Thus, two cycles are set up. The first one starts off with the idea that Blacks are dumb and can't think well. The solution is supposed to be education. Education consists of repeating someone else's thoughts and receiving no encouragement to express your own. The result is an educated person who *still* doesn't think too much of his or her own thoughts. And they can't easily express the thoughts that they do have because that was not how they were trained or what they were being graded for. Thus, this "educated"person still comes off as sounding like a dumb person who can't think well. The second cycle that is created is that whereas Black achievement in the US is directly related to our ability to express our creativity, school (the so called answer to all our problems) is the very institution that kills our creativity by telling us that what we are doing is improper, non standard, irregular, non traditional, etc. We are best served, we are told, by copying everything we see. Copy the teacher, copy what's in the book, copy what's on television and do what every other person is doing. To copy is the very *opposite* of creativity. So while we are looking for "progress" we desert the thing that has usually served us well, our creativity. Parents assist in this process by not recognizing their children's talents, ideas and perspectives (their creativity) and pushing for the almighty school grades. Black people keep having some problems because some of our "solutions" *are part* of the problem.

Television

Television is an entertainment medium and serves that function very well. It is an advertising medium and it does that very well. It is a news medium and sometimes it provides that well through a concept called "news specials". Television's use as an educational medium however is questionable. Part of the reason it is questionable is because what constitutes real education is questionable. Right now educators are wrestling with how to include a number of ideas into the school system in ways that do not offend people. Sex education, AIDS education, education on drugs and alcohol, education on the gay lifestyle are all problematic for educators. Television is used to bring up the rear. That is, TV waits to see what the public seems to have accepted all across the country and, after some trial and error work, they bring in a watered down version of what already exists in the classroom. The rationale behind dealing with the controversial topics of sex, AIDS, drugs, etc. in school is that these issues are already being dealt with by students anyway and poor judgements are causing many to make mistakes that follow them the rest of their lives. In fact some of the mistakes cost them their lives. So the universality of the potential problem and the degree of harm a problem can produce have caused educators to think seriously about discussing things that never would have been raised in the classroom twenty years ago. Television has almost followed suit. Though not as open as some classroom discussions, television has greatly opened its eyes to the role it can play in passing on candid information about topics of an intimate nature.

This strikes me as a progressive move needed to meet the challenges of today's problems. I wonder, however, with so much flexibility in the school curriculum, why the topic of money is never dealt with seriously. And I wonder why television with its almost unlimited number of cable channels running all day and night can't also cover the topic of personal finance, career, education, business, etc. within its various coverages. Television certainly plays a role in telling you what cars, furniture, clothes and food to buy. It tells us how to be a consumer. It directs us to use Master Card, Visa and American Express cards, running up our debt. Why can't it help people, especially young people, to understand money? There are reasons for sure but they are beyond the scope of this chapter. It is enough to say that television is a provocative agent that entices watchers to buy (or in the case of youngsters, to want), without a hint of a clue as to how to pay for the products offered for sale. I can see how it serves the interests of certain businesses to keep television the way it is. But I don't really understand why certain people of influence can't use TV to educate young people about something that will eventually if not immediately concern them, every day for the rest of their lives. And certain bad judgements some young people are bound to make around the issue of money will be as troublesome or perhaps as deadly as AIDS and drugs could ever be. As a matter of fact some so called drug issues are in fact money issues in reality.

Television mixes reality and myth for the young people watching it. They see the reality of the rich and powerful being in a position to command respect and to use their wealth and influence to threaten, bribe, intimidate and force the world to move as they wish it to move. Being rich on television automatically carries the ideas of fun, fame, beauty, and power.

Sports shows emphasize the size of the winners purse, be it golf, tennis, horse racing, or auto racing. The numbers are always in the hundreds of thousands of dollars. Most young people grow up with unrealistic expectations as to what it takes to be what they see on TV.

But fantasy is in no way limited to just the sports stars. Policemen and detectives, common stars of TV shows, are never portrayed as lower middle class people just barely getting by in life. They have houses and cars that would be the envy of successful Lawyers. Are you sure Sonny in Miami Vice (Don Johnson) was able to afford a $50,000 sports car and a fast boat to live in on a policeman's salary? I always wondered what the real Miami cops thought about that. As much as I liked the Bill Cosby show, it always bothered me that this "doctor" had more time to lounge around the house than most temporary cashiers. He was always there to counsel any of his five children on anything that bothered them. His wife, supposedly a top lawyer, was also everpresent. The reality is that most baby doctors work at least seventy hours a week whether they want to or not. The same for a successful New York city based lawyer. Young people were led to believe that the Huxtables were paid well because they had merely reached *the status* of doctor and lawyer, not because they worked long and hard hours *as* doctors and lawyers. This is very unfair to the young people watching the show, particularly ones who have fathers and mothers who *are* doctors and lawyers. If these real parents are always gone, always working, are short tempered and give little attention even when they are home, guess how they appear to their real children? If Mr.

Cosby-Huxtable is also a doctor and he is always available, then their real mother or father must not love or care for them as much as Dr. Huxtable loves his kids. Real kids seldom if ever get that type of quality time from their professional parent. This to me is unnecessarily unfair to real professional parents who are pressured into being all things to everybody, yet they may still come out looking like the bad guy to their own children.

School

Some of the shortcomings of the role that school plays in educating young people about money have been explained above. But schools have a special role. Schools supposedly train people for all the occupations that America has to offer. But children typically do not know the substance of what most occupations are, how one qualifies for that career or the pay and benefits of such occupations. Children at eight, nine and certainly by eleven and twelve are already thinking about what they would like to do when they grow up. It seems almost criminal to me that schools don't help these young people to better see how they are to fit into the world. If an "at risk" group of young people have a history of finding it difficult to find an acceptable place in society, then it appears that the system would address that by educating them about the society sooner. The whole idea behind Head Start for example was to give preschool children a head start in dealing with school. If it is recognized that some people need a head start in understanding school, it shouldn't be too hard to understand that some people need a head start in understanding society and life. A good career education program would be a step in the right direction. Actually, its even prejudicial for this writer to suggest that only "at risk" children need this. There are tens of thousands of twenty two year olds (and older) of all races and income levels who have a college degree in their hands and an "area of concentration -Major" completed who still don't have much of an idea of what they want to do with their lives. Schools and "education" rate close to zero in helping children understand money or the careers that lead to money.

Peers and Siblings

Sometimes in a large family with many years spanning the ages of the children, older brothers and sisters have almost as much input into the values of younger children as the parents. Sometimes they become the role model and set the tone for what the youngsters should and should not do. Many times when young people start to go down the wrong road it is not necessarily due to what the parents have failed to do so much as it is the parents inability to overcome the influence of a new set of values and behaviors that an older son or daughter has brought into the home. They cannot break the fascination that their younger children may have for the son or daughter that is already going down the wrong street. How to handle that situation is a challenge beyond the ability of this writer to address.

Peer pressure also has a major impact on youngsters. It is difficult to say when rivalries and competition begin in children. It is not at all unusual for ten and eleven year olds to compete among their peers in the area of toys, collectibles, clothes or other items. As far back as the 1950'\s, companies would advertise a product to young people with the phrase "Be the first on your block to have ...." Such a tactic obviously promoted competition among young people to run out and buy these products. Essentially young people often get caught up in the "you are what you have syndrome" before they leave grade school. Young people want to be the first with something, or have the best of something or have more than one of something. Thus having *two* CD players may be more prestigious than having been the first with one CD or vice versa. At another point in the competition, what your family owns becomes a substitute for what one personally may own. For example, a kid whose parents own a giant screen TV, a swimming pool or a satellite dish for their cable system, might score more prestige points and popularity with his peers than someone who merely has the latest style jeans. Parents often feel bad if their children feel a sense of inferiority because of not being able to "keep up with the Joneses". Other parents get upset with their children for even wanting to compete on the basis of material possessions, even though they may have a "keep up with the Joneses" mentality themselves.

One of the things that parents can try to do to overcome peer pressure is to set up a different criteria for their children to follow. If the youngster has leadership qualities, they may be able to convert most of their peers to follow their lead. For example, lets say that a parent has convinced their child to value saving their money instead of buying every new fad. Suppose their son or daughter said to their friends, "I prefer to save my money. I now have two, three, four hundred dollars saved up." Eventually if a child gets to a point where they have truly impressed their peers with the amount of money they have saved instead of how much they have spent, they may be fully accepted on the basis of having that unique badge of honor. By being successful on his or her own terms, they may develop a healthier set of values and win friends at the same time. Besides, many if not most Black fads are neither the product of Black thought or serve our best interests. A White business person is usually the one that ends up laughing all the way to the bank. For example, Warner Brothers

Studios, not Spike Lee or Betty Shabazz, will earn most of the profits from the Malcolm X movie. Nike, not Michael Jordan, will earn most of the profits from the so called "Black fad" of wearing Air Jordan athletic Shoes. White folks have been making "Black fads" like that for us since the very beginning of fads. As a people we don't seem to get it. With fads filtering down to younger and younger children in our community, White America becomes more successful in appealing to our emotions and visions of fantasy rather than our reasoning and common sense. It is up to the adults to watch over the peer pressure that our children are exposed to and do their best to see that it doesn't get out of hand.

Summary

Young children learn the value of coin money at about the age of four but usually wait another two to three years before they consciously ask for it. Parental values and economic circumstances usually determine if the child gets a regular allowance and whether that allowance is made subject to any responsibility placed on the child. In any event children soon learn that money is directly tied to some form of work or service provided to people. Many start to do errands, provide cleaning type services or sell things to make money.

At the same time that children are having these practical lessons, they are also absorbing many other lessons about money and life through four major sources. These sources are their parents, television, school and peers and siblings. It is the collective impact of these four sources that will have a great impact on the mentality the child will develop and likely carry into adulthood.

The mentality that most Black youth collectively develop from these four sources are:

a.   That money comes by working for the White man.

b.   That you spend your money with the White man when ever you can.

c.   That money is for spending and competing with your peers on the basis of collecting things and fads.

d.   That saving and investing money is supported verbally but is not actually practiced very much by parents, siblings or peers.

e.   That as a youngster our highest priority should be to get the highest grades we can in school even at the expense of seeing a lot of our own natural creativity ignored or even discouraged. From the two powerful institutions of television and school, young children learn almost nothing useful about money or careers. Television gives them a false idea about the ease of getting money and success while enticing them to compete with their peers for toys and status. The school system while introducing children to a system of repeating back the information given to them, repeatedly ignores the value of the ideas and creativity of African American children for the most part.　In fortunate situations Black children see their parents and/or siblings struggle to make a business go and learns to work with that parent instead of just playing with the parent. This may have a positive impact on their future belief in the possibility of working with other Blacks later in life.

THE CRUCIAL ADOLESCENT YEARS

It is this writers strong belief that the most overlooked and neglected area of study in trying to understand male-female relationships is the period of the early teenage years. Therefore, to a large extent, this chapter, covering those adolescent years, is in a real sense a core area of this volume and serves as a foundation upon which many other ideas are based. The purpose of this chapter is to look at teenage behavior and attitudes and what is experienced at this stage in their lives.

The actions and reactions of the males and females continue to build on the patterns presented here and by the end of the teenage years, a new model of relating to each other is pretty much established between the sexes.

EARLY INTERACTIONS

Young boys and girls often do not show much interest in each other before reaching ten years old. Boys have a tendency to play with boys and girls do likewise. The sexes *are* different and it seems pretty obvious that each sex has to spend some time finding out what it means to be male or female before they venture out of their circle. In a large family with many brothers and sisters around the same age, I'm sure there is a more rapid development by both boys and girls to understand the opposite sex.

When boys and girls do begin to approach each other at, say, ten or eleven years old, there is a kind of honesty in their communication that may never be matched in their later years. The young people talk about the topics that you would expect young people to talk about. This might include favorite T.V. shows, records, singers, movies etc. Since school is such a dominant part of their life, they may talk about teachers, subjects, other students, and school activities like plays, games, holiday celebrations, etc. Children at this age are *usually* somewhat naive and have not yet learned how to be macho, cool, sexy, hard-to-get, sexist or any other way that gets in the way of honest communication. I think it is fair to say that there is a sense of equality between the sexes at this point that both genders accept and respect. This is not to say that there is no recognition of differences. One youngster might be aware that the other seems smarter in school or they are big or small or pretty or not so pretty, etc. And depending on dress, spending money and other clues, children may have an awareness of the fact that a neighbor or school friend's family has more or less money than their own. But I think that in the main there is a genuineness in relationships at this stage where friendship tops sexuality, and curiosity to learn about the opposite sex opens the door for sincere exchanges. The telephone becomes an object more important than the television during this period. In the privacy of his own house and safely away from the awkwardness of direct eye contact, one young man can pick up the phone and explore the mind of this recently discovered phenomenon called girls, and vice versa.

Obviously a host of factors really determine just when this situation develops. Parents can discourage such communication when they become aware that such attractions exist. Responses from peers can also nip a potential relationship in the bud in various ways. But usually, sooner or later during these preteen years, boys and girls are going to come to see each other in different ways than they had before. This relationship of equality, of honesty, of genuine curiosity and reflection has, unfortunately a short life span. It runs from about the sixth grade to the eighth grade or from about eleven years old to about fourteen years old at the max. Then all hell breaks loose.

The Tide Turns on Young Black Men

At fourteen years old, several things begin to happen to young Black men and many of them are negative. Physically, a fourteen-year-old can very well be the size of a full grown male. Thus police who may have ignored little kids walking down the street before, now see in this near adult a potential threat, a potential "suspicious looking character". He may be stopped and questioned, stopped and searched for no reason other than the fact that he is Black, a male and almost fully grown. He is to the police, "almost" the enemy. This type of treatment is *not* given to his fourteen-year-old counterpart, the developing Black woman. This fourteen-year-old male is also beginning to be followed around, with or without his knowledge, in all the major stores that he enters and again for no other reason than he is an almost grown Black male. That is all you need to be suspected of being a thief or some other criminal. Again, this is *not* usually the type of treatment that fourteen year old Black *females* receive.

In the school system, fourteen-year-olds are being asked to choose the educational track that they wish to pursue. They are asked if they intend to take college prep courses in high school or if they would prefer to study some type of vocation with the hope of immediate employment right out of high school. Perhaps they would prefer a general diploma track with standard courses, not especially useful for either college or a vocation. You must understand, however, that for several years prior to this time, the majority of the public school teachers have steadily dropped their expectations of the male students every year. Why? Because they are *Black* males and it is very common for teachers not to expect too much academically from Black males.

And since teacher expectations are one the top factors in any student doing well in school, the chances are that these fourteen year old Black males *have not* performed up to their potential. They could be in a period of *female rebellion* (which will be discussed later) as well. Chances are that the typical Black male student has little confidence that he will do well in college prep courses (his teachers haven't added to his confidence with their expectations). And if he were to move in that direction, chances are a teacher or counselor may advise him against it (remember Malcolm X's teacher discouraged him from being a lawyer and suggested he "take up" carpentry instead). So young brothers often take the less challenging of the programs offered to them and many people in the system instinctively feels they made the best move.

The Young Sisters

What about the young Black fourteen year old girl? Well the young girl has been taught by mostly female teachers her whole school life, and many if not most of them were Black if she lived in the inner city. Some of these teachers she liked and identified with. They have inspired her to consider college just by their example. Some of the teachers picked up on the admiration that the Black female students held for them and were pleased and flattered by it. Intentionally or not, the teacher more quickly recognized these young ladies hands when they went up to answer questions in class. In periods of grading, the young ladies may have more often been given the benefit of the doubt. The expectations were higher for the young girls and they responded by actually working harder and performing. Besides they weren't in *female rebellion*. So with the teachers believing a little more in the ability of the young ladies, and the young ladies believing a little more in themselves (and having grades to prove it), more choose college prep tracks.

During the course of any school year, it comes out quite clearly who the smart people are in class and who needs remedial help. It is a daily situation that students live with. But once students are made to choose a high school track, the system seems to be saying to the kids, "O.K., we are now deciding your future. Those that will be leaders, get good money and happiness in life, stand here in the college prep line, but only if you are 'qualified', or 'selected', or 'recommended'. Those of you that will be blue collar workers, periodically laid off workers, McDonalds employees or worse, you get in this line here." Of course life doesn't quite work out that way, but it's hard to tell a fourteen year old that this selection process is not an early decision that society has either approved him or her or written them off to a great extent.

Young Males on the Home Front

It is important to explain at this point what is meant by the term *female rebellion*. Many young Black men of about fourteen years old are going through a stage in their life where they are trying to understand what growing up, and what being a man really is. In far too many cases these young men do not receive enough of the proper clues from the most natural source: the biological father. The father may be absent totally and the boy is being raised in a single parent home. Or the father maybe is away most of the time, working or just out of the house. Or the father is present but constitutes a less than satisfactory role model, i.e. alcoholic, gambler, unemployed, physical abuser, drug abuser, etc. Any situation that fails to help the fourteen year old boy gain a sense of confidence and direction in his masculine growth is a potential problem. And what happens in many of these problem situations is that this adolescent develops his own sense of manhood and machoism. He may decide that part of being a man is *not* following the instructions of the women in his life. Women have consistently been telling him what to do, how to do it, and what to think all his life. You must understand that up to this point in his life he has been controlled, taught, scolded by and disciplined mostly by women. Female authority consists of his mother, grandmother(s) aunts, older sisters, and an *overwhelmingly female* teaching staff from grades one through nine. These boys are sick of being directed by women. Being directed by women not only threatens their sense of learning how to be a male but it also threatens their sense of "being grown". So in many cases the young Black male's intuition tells him "do not listen to women, women have no idea what its like to be a boy/male/man and they can't tell me how to become a man either. As a matter of fact, they seem quite intent on keeping me from growing up, period."

Thus many Black youth, especially those without fathers or older brothers, make it a point to rebel against female authority, because it instinctively gives them a greater sense of being both male and an adult. Thus from this age onward we see a more consistent pattern of boys than girls going against the status quo on purpose. And as much as this rebellion may give these rebellious males a sense of satisfaction, emotionally and egotistically, in many cases it leads them into falling deeper into the hole that society is already preparing to bury them in. It is rather ironic that at the very time that many young boys are getting interested in girls of their peer group, they are often in rebellion against older females and the domination they've had over their lives in the broader sense. It is important for the reader to appreciate this development because this contradictory set of circumstances is what makes the girlfriend that much more interesting, significant, unique and valued in the eyes of young Black males. The hormonal activity going on in the young male just raises the intensity of the feelings and sensitivities that much higher. Young boys at this age are actually biochemically unsettled and prone to do who knows what when the sexual heat gets turned up. In order to fully appreciate the points to be made later in this chapter, it is necessary to summarize what is going on in a significant number of Black males between about thirteen and fifteen years old:

A. They are beginning to be viewed as potential problems or trouble makers by the police in the community in which they reside, for no other apparent reason than that they *are* Black males; American society's usual definition of trouble maker.

B. They are now suspected as being possible thieves and or trouble makers by all store owners, most old White *women,* a significant number of younger White women and some Black women in all age groups. Again this is the case only because they are Black males.

C. They tend to be discounted and discouraged as to their educational futures and are placed on scholastic tracks that usually lead to nowhere.

D. They could very well be in some form of rebellion against authority, particularly female authority, which affects relationships both in school and at home.

E. The hormonal changes going on in the youngster along with the accompanying psychological changes, make, in many instances, for a confused young man.

All of these problems, pointed out above are going to be present without the even greater threats of teenage gangs, AIDS, dope peddlers, general poverty, health problems, etc.   The picture I'm trying to draw here is this: It is not easy being a teenager growing up in America, period.   But it is particularly hard being a Black teenager growing up in our community.   But even as we look at the situation objectively, we can't help but see that Black males particularly, are systematically singled out to receive more harassment, more avoidance, and less support. They are subject to be feared more and are assumed to be more violent and less intelligent. Does this mean Black girls have an easy time?   No! Does it mean all Black boys experience these problems? No. But by the sheer preponderance of the law of averages, the Black male is placed in a position of more stress and strain. If he happens to be a big fourteen year old, his problem is going to be worse because he'll look more like a threatening Black *man.* If he happens to be a very dark skinned young brother, his problem is going to be worse because he will be perceived as more evil, violent or dangerous because he is *so* Black. And if he looks more African than European in facial features, his problem is going to be worse because he may be perceived as more ignorant, less attractive, poorer and therefore more desperate.

If you accept that most of the above is at least partly true then you can imagine that it is no fun being a fourteen year old Black male in the ghettos of the U.S. As you struggle with your own sexual maturity, identity and direction in life, society in cohesive institutional ways is already starting to implement its struggle against you, a confused fourteen year old Black male.

The Bomb Drops

When we last looked at young boys and girls relating to each other at eleven years old, we had said that they were participating in a relationship that was mostly characterized by a sense of sincerity and equality. And it was suggested that this sweet innocence had about three years or so to run. What happens after that? Well what happens after that is all of a sudden some fourteen year old girls develop women-sized breasts and women-sized butts and women -sized legs. They start wearing make up seriously and change their hair style from girlish to womanly styles. Not all fourteen year old girls do this, but enough to significantly change the way 14 year old boys look at girls in general.

Because this fourteen year old girl has taken it upon herself to accelerate mother nature's work, she begins to look sixteen, seventeen or older and begins to attract the attention of guys in that age group who think she is of their peer group. She is flattered, praised, and proud of the new attention that she is getting, all because of her new physical development and her cosmetics. Eventually, she feels compelled to disassociate herself from that sincere fellow fourteen year old boy that was her peer and friend with whom she had so much in common. For her it is time to jump into the front seat of this seventeen or eighteen year old's car. The fourteen year old boy is devastated. Not only is he deserted by his so-called teachers and society in general, but the girlfriend he was gaining confidence in relating to has now run off with an older guy. This is upsetting to the young man in two ways. First, it causes him to lose confidence in himself as a maturing male. The message being sent to him is that *you are not mature enough* or that you *don't have what it takes* to hold on to your girl so you are being dumped. Secondly, that friend that was there to listen to your honest feelings and problems and to reassure you in some way is now gone. So both the ego and the support system is damaged. Later we will look at the typical male responses to this perceived tragedy.

Money's Role in Feminine "Maturity"

Not all fourteen year old girls walk away from their fourteen year old boyfriends to be with older guys because, frankly, some had already made the move at thirteen or even twelve. Physical maturity and "the look" is what draws the girls and boys in question to each other. Some young ladies might wait until they are fifteen, sixteen or seventeen before they decide to 'move up'. In some cases parents are keeping close tabs on their child for fear of pregnancy and sexually transmitted diseases. They would likely forbid their young daughter's association with someone they viewed as more sexually mature. Sometimes this discourages the daughter and sometimes it has the exact opposite effect and she and her new mate "sneak around". Exactly what causes these young ladies to go for the older guys? And who are the ones most likely to do it? What role does money play, if any? This writer will not suggest in this volume that he is capable or qualified to put forth the woman's/girl's viewpoint with the degree of accuracy that a female possibly can. But there is enough information from T.V. talk shows, articles in women's magazines and through personal perceptions and experiences to piece together a fairly accurate picture of what appears to be going on at least *some* of the time.

Young girls are going through many of the same pressures at home, in school and among peers as the boys. What she is not experiencing for the most part is the perception that she is dumb, dangerous, or threatening, which is the case with Black boys. Her life is less at risk walking the streets of her city than if she were a boy. She is probably not feeling forced to join a gang, carry a weapon or sell drugs like many boys are at that age. She is probably not pushed and prodded into physical fights where there is physical pain and injury like the boys are. Simply put, with all her problems and pressures, her life is still *easier*, even considering the reality of rape. Young girls of this age are looking to have their femininity affirmed and enhanced. They are breaking out of girlish habits and taking on more womanly ones. And while she is personally trying to grow, she has a peer group of other young girls that push and influence her in various directions as well. There comes a time when her personal desires and her challenges to be more of a woman meet. For example, her personal desire may be to go to a music concert and her challenge to grow up is to become more independent and less influenced by her parents idea of how she should be spending her time, and in some cases, her money. So to have a boy come by to pick her up, get her out of the house and to the concert accomplishes both goals. A fourteen year old boy will be walking, but a seventeen year old boy could very well be driving, hence, the sense of freedom and independence. If you expand on this theme, it isn't too hard to see one reason it would benefit a young girl to go out with an older guy; the older guy can take her places that the fourteen year old cannot. The car is not only a means of transportation, it is also a setting of privacy which could allow other "activity" to go on. In addition to a car, an older guy is more likely to have access to jobs and money that a fourteen or fifteen year old probably would not. Therefore money and a car become major pluses persuading the young girl to go out with the older guy. Then there is ego gratification. A young girl is aware that this guy with money and a car can choose other girls to go out with because boys like him are in demand. The fact that he has selected her is a reaffirmation of her sense of attractiveness, womanliness and maturity, or so she thinks. Essentially, while the 14 yr. old girl is being reaffirmed, the 14 yr. old boy is left behind. She feels she is winning while the younger male is feeling like he has lost. Finally, and equally important, is the amount of peer approval and envy that girls in this position generate for themselves. Although, her new boyfriend is seventeen or eighteen, this fourteen year old female's friends are still her own age. And when they find out that she has attracted this "catch", they are happy, proud, envious, or jealous of her. In any event, she is now " somebody" in the eyes of her girlfriends, not because of anything that *she* has done on her own efforts, but because of who *she has attracted as a boyfriend.* And the boyfriend is not necessarily valued for his great personality, looks, body or brains, but simply because he *has the means to make this young girl's life more exciting* than that of her girlfriends. When asked why they like a particular guy, young (and not so young) girls will usually say " he's fun to be with, he treats me good or we have a lot of fun together". Many times these phrases are just code words for "he spends *money* on me, we go places and we have a good time". Thus, the requirements for "a good relationship" from the female's point of view are not defined when she turns, twenty, she discovers them as early as fourteen and the key requirements are money, travel, and a good time.

One of the reasons I have always heard used to explain the "changing of the guard" in relationships has to do with the idea that "girls mature before boys". I've never heard an adequate definition of what constitutes "maturity". Is it physical, mental, emotional or spiritual maturity? Boys may continue to play a kid's game like basketball, but such games have gotten thousands of them full college scholarships and have made more Black men millionaires than any other activity in America. Girls may start their menstrual cycle at a young age, but by fourteen both sexes have the capacity to become parents, so I don't see much of a gap here. Emotionally you have girls that are scared of a mere spider whereas the average boy, for unfortunate reasons, finds himself taking on activities involving life and death on the streets of urban America everyday of their lives.

What is this thing called "maturity"? After thinking about possible interpretations, I can only think of one. It was brought out earlier that the nature of the relationship between two twelve or thirteen year olds seemed to be characterized by an honesty that was free of playing mental games. The fact is that these kids are usually too young to even know how to play adult courting games. Friendship and the ability to identify with each other's concerns seemed to give the relationship a meaning and a purpose free of other motives or agendas.

On the other hand, the *manipulation* of people and relationships is a game we associate more with adults. When the relationship between the older boy and younger girl is put in motion, they are not peers sharing similar concerns. They are acting as adults *manipulating*, coaxing, and persuading each other to do something to complete the agenda that each has. It appears that women learn to manipulate people (at least boys), at a younger age than boys. And many people relate the idea of being a good manipulator with being smarter, sharper, more crafty, sophisticated, etc. Thus young girls are to a degree credited with being "smart" and more "mature" for simply getting a head start in the art of human manipulation. And what these girls end up doing is repeatedly denying that they are in fact manipulating, at all, which is a key move if your intent is to be a successful manipulator. Liars and manipulators are running buddies. When you see one, you almost always see the other. Thus this "mature" young woman is learning how to be even *more* of a woman, by practicing the required skills of lying and manipulating so that the "good times"continue to roll.

Girls Devaluing Themselves

When a person uses the phrase that a young person has "lost their innocence," it has a broader meaning than that they have merely lost their virginity. It means that they are no longer innocent of the games that adults play with each other. It means they have learned how to ask for or get what they want without having to pay for it. When a person learns how to manipulate, tease, coax, and threaten, they are much more likely to be guilty of something than innocent. What is not often discussed is the price that young girls pay in the long run for these moves that they make at fourteen. If we go back to the pre-adolescent years, we see that parents instructed girls much in the same way they instructed the boys. They learned that money was to be earned through "honest work" and that you are who you are based on your education, work and personal achievements. Once a young girl sees that she can be shown a good time by boys who have money and cars, she starts to see and be seen differently. She begins to see that maybe the best, certainly the easiest, way to get what she wants is to manipulate a man, her father or her boyfriend, to get it *for* her. Her success at doing this will likely encourage her to repeat the process again and again. Eventually it may turn out that the challenge of growing up consists not of the challenge of her schoolwork, the challenge of serving her community, the challenge of finding a job, or the challenge of keeping herself fit, but rather, the challenge of getting better and better at manipulating men. She may even be unaware of it because everyone appears to be so encouraging. Her boyfriend may be glad to give whatever is requested. Her girlfriends think she is the luckiest girl in the school, and she herself feels pleased with her life. Such behavior might be viewed as a victimless crime so to speak. The real challenge for girls in this situation, from their viewpoint, is to avoid pregnancy. But what could really be happening is that the girl may be in the process of devaluing herself. She has given up the idea that her happiness and pride are to be based on her own efforts and instead has accepted the idea that a good part of who she is, is directly connected to who she dates and what that date does for her. Her personal ambition may sink and have less meaning. Marriage and children may be much more in her immediate future than college, career and contributing skills to the Black community or the greater society. She no longer feels the need to know how to make it on her own because she doesn't ever expect to be by herself or on her own again. She's confident that she knows what it takes to *get a man* and have that man give her what she wants. Her damn fingernails have, at this point , a higher priority than her schoolwork. Shopping in the mall has a higher priority than reading a Black history book. And of course, spending money is infinitely more important than saving money.

Her parents ability to influence her are reduced, not only because she is "going through that stage", but because she is no longer around the house as often to talk to. Fifteen years later, she'll be sitting at a card table, smoking a cigarette, asking her girlfriends "Why do men always look at your body and not appreciate your mind." She will have no recollection of the fact that when she first started dating at fourteen, all she had was a pretty face and a body, and she never made an attempt to impress that seventeen year old boy with her mind. She was naive and so flattered to be in his company that she never gave a thought to what the basis of the attraction was. She will also have lost sight of the fact that she has spent about a hundred times more money on her shoes, cosmetics, clothes, hair and nails than she has spent on developing this mind she assumes to be so noteworthy. She will have forgotten that her method of selecting men to date, which she started at fourteen, has been an unbroken habit of materialistic analysis right up to the present, where she sits smoking, playing cards and talking nonsense.

When you devalue yourself and don't even know it, the most disturbing moment may be when you suddenly realize how pitiful you appear to the very people you are trying to impress. Many, too many, young Black girls fall into this hole and don't even realize it.

Of course, not all fourteen year old females drop their male peers in search of older boys, but the most 'desirable' ones seem to. Desirable girls, from a high school boy's perspective, usually fit one of two criteria. Either they are so physically attractive that they represent the "best" in the class as far as beauty goes or they are not so beautiful but they give sex. This does not mean that there are no other criteria that boys use to select girls, but given the choice, they are usually going to select one of these two.

The other aspect of this situation is that it is progressive. At fifteen years old a higher percentage of girls are going with older boys than the fourteen year olds. The sixteen year olds have an even higher percentage of older boyfriends than the fifteen year olds, and so on. While this is going on , more and more young Black men learn the many ways that they fail to meet the new standards of their female friends. As can be expected, this situation merely increases the tension, the competition, the anger, and the feelings of inferiority that were already instilled by their treatment from other parts of society. Is there any wonder why young Black males feel that they just don't fit in anywhere except in groups and gangs with each other. Even the term "homeboy" could very well be interpreted as meaning " I only feel at home or at peace in the company of boys like myself who are experiencing what I am experiencing".

Young Black Men Respond

How do young men learn to deal with this most personal of rejections? It might be clear to them why the police, White society, even some teachers do not like them. They may have accepted the underlying reality of those situations. But why would a female friend just desert them for no apparent reason? What are you supposed to think about that particular girl? What of girls in general? What do you think of yourself? Is this rejection going to be a one shot deal that will pass or will this continue to happen in the future? These are just some of the questions that young men have to wrestle with as they work their way through these emotionally strained times. There is no one correct way of dealing with these rejections, thus we see many approaches used over time.

Learning From Puppy Love

Many older adults make fun of the development of and the breakup of " Puppy love". These adults try to explain to young people how unimportant the opposite sex is in that stage of their lives. As understandable as that idea might be, three things have to be kept in mind.

First, many young peoples' relationships are mirrors of themselves. That is to say, they see much of themselves through their ability to be successful in relating to the opposite sex. Success in this area provides them with a big shot of self confidence, not only with the opposite sex, but also with their same sex peers with whom they still spend most of their time. Failure with the opposite sex not only reduces their confidence, it may also make them the butt of cruel jokes around their same sex peers.

Sexual interchange during young adolescent years appears to be a significant influence in creating the self image of people who are trying very hard, to discover their self image. For a parent to say something like, "John, you shouldn't be thinking about girls at this stage. Just make sure you do your school work and chores and don't worry about the girls," is to say three things to John. It says John should remain ignorant, confused and /or fearful of girls(even as you master subjects in school that you will have little use for in the real world). It says John should remain ignorant and confused and insecure about a part of his *own personality*, which he can learn only through this interaction with girls. And it says John should be ready to suffer through jokes and unflattering comments from his male peers based on his naivete and ignorance of the opposite sex. This is too much, unnecessary pressure to place on young people who find themselves in this situation.

The second thing that parents have to understand is that while self image is being explored or pursued, coping skills are also being developed. Youngsters develop a pattern of responding to their frustrations in certain ways. These ways may involve withdrawal patterns, fits of anger and physical violence, denial of the reality, or a whole range of other responses. These coping patterns or responses form the foundation on which that person may very well react to similar situations when they become an adult. As you will see later, this makes how youngsters and parents deal with "puppy love' very important in certain key respects.

The third thing that parents have to keep in mind is that with Black boys, the breakup of puppy love maybe is the straw that breaks the camel's back. It is the rejection after all the previous rejections and rebellions discussed earlier. It is the rejection that is often the most sudden, the most unexplainable and the most *emotionally* painful . It is like getting hit on the head dozens of times by people you were already suspicious of, but then, out of nowhere, getting, hit the hardest by the one you least suspected, and for no apparent reason. This is how a significant number of young men feel during the course of their early dating years.

Learning Not To Commit

One of the single greatest complaints that Black women have about Black men is their failure to make a full commitment to the relationship. This theme is talked about so much, on so many talk shows, in so many books, and in so many personal discussions, that it is as if the mere talking about it will change the situation. But at what age do men learn not to commit? Was it as a 30 year old, or a twenty five year old? Not hardly. Almost all behaviors coming from thirty year olds have their foundation and basis in attitudes that were shaped many years prior.

When a saddened, frustrated boy, heartbroken over the loss of his girlfriend, comes to his mother, father, older brother or uncle for advice on what to do or how to feel, they are told "Look, don't worry about this girl. There are plenty other girls out there who will appreciate you the way you are. It may take time to find them, you will have to look for them, but there are *"many more fish in the sea"*. You are not advised to try to make a relationship work when you are fourteen or fifteen. You are made to think that you are foolish for feeling too deeply for someone. You are taught to "play the field". In a sense, young men are taught not to take girls seriously, relationships seriously or even to take seriously the feelings they have for a girl. And they are often taught this not by peers, but by adults who they have every reason to believe are telling them in their best interest. Part of this advice is this way because the romances of fourteen year olds, in a sense, can't be taken seriously. But the other part of this advice also is given to protect the young man from experiencing traumatic heartbreak in the future, or at least during this stage of his development. In other words, the message going out to young Black men from responsible parents/adults is this:

> "If a relationship goes bad, don't try to fix it. Move on to the
> next one. If you "play the field' and don't take any
> relationship too seriously, you will save yourself a lot of
> pain."

Thus, young Black men learn how to disengage their emotions on the instructions of the adults in their lives. Human beings are creatures of habit and habits are hard to break, especially if you have been practicing these habits for a long time and they have served you well. If you have learned at fourteen to play the field or at least not invest too much emotion in a girl, and it has spared you extreme heartbreak through your teen years and into your early twenties, how can you swallow the idea that you are such a bad guy for not fully committing when you are, say, 28? You've been in this cycle for fourteen years, and even if you wanted to change, it wouldn't be easy. Black men may very well be guilty of not committing to a relationship, but like so many other things they are supposedly guilty of, they are not the lone culprit. They just happen to be all alone when they are charged with their offense.

Just as young girls do things which devalue themselves such as de-emphasize their own talents, brains and aspirations, some young Black men unfortunately also learn to take girls (women) for granted. They learn that girls just *aren't worth* getting all upset over. Girls are not to be loved so much as to be "handled". Some young men adopt this attitude after their first painful rejection in romance. Others may adopt this attitude after a second, third, or fourth experience with rejection. And the ironic thing about these rejections is that they get increasingly expensive to experience. A fourteen year old, may have suffered pain at no financial cost, but for a nineteen year old it costs more. At nineteen, a young man buys things for his girl, takes her places, and also spends more money on himself to look more appealing. But the end results are essentially the same. In the minds of some young men, sex, instead of being a mutual opportunity to express deeply-felt romantic feelings between a man and a woman, is sometimes seen as the *required proof one needs to prove to himself that he wasn't taken for a total fool.* Fortunately for Black women and men, not all young Black men give up on women after their first few experiences with rejection. Young men take different paths to appeal to girls they like, and herein lies a big part of what the media, popular opinion and scholars miss in their understanding of Black men. But before we review some of the approaches that young men take, let us be clear about what *usually doesn't work* in getting the desirable (attractive and/or sexually active) girl.

The first thing that doesn't work is getting good grades. Grades are, according to parents, teachers and child experts, supposed to be the top priority of all students who will be competing for places in jobs and colleges in a few years. If grades are important, it doesn't register with the leading ladies in the class for the most part. Besides, grades are not necessarily public information, and unless a person told everyone what their grades were, only people who shared every class with them would know. Of course, a published honor roll would be a major public announcement, but no girl goes to that list in search of a boyfriend. The code word is sex appeal, not intellectual appeal. Based on today's Black youth's ideas about grades together with society's prejudgments of Black males, not too many brothers are going to make the honor roll anyway.

Grades will not get you the girls. The second thing that's not going to work in getting a girl is working an honest part-time, low paying job. Many young people feel embarrassed when their friends see them cleaning out the bathroom at a McDonalds or Wendys. And everyone knows the pay is minimal . A sixteen year old, unless he looks like Billy Dee Williams and can get his father's car, doesn't increase his chance of holding on to the "desirable women" by working at Mickey-Ds. A week's pay can be blown on a single night out.

The third thing that will not likely increase your sexual appeal as a fifteen year old is going to church. Churches attract people of all types. But it is likely that as a regular church goer, a young girl is absolutely convinced that sex before marriage or at a young age is a sin and a no-no. When you add in the concerns of pregnancy, abortions, AIDS, herpes, and other forms of V.D., a church girl is strictly about conversation in most instances. If a young man is on that same level, church may be a perfect place to meet a girl. Of course, there is the possibility that this nice church girl is already involved with a seventeen or eighteen year old church guy anyway, so we may be back to where we started. So then to put this in perspective what young boys learn is that by being the nice guy, you get nowhere with the girls. You can clean your room, cut the grass, wash the dishes, get straight A's, go to church and make your $3.50 an hour at Burger King, and none of that helps very much in getting you closer to settling your unsettled sexual energy or addressing your need to find a special friend of the opposite sex. As if this wasn't pressure enough, some young men even have to prove that they are neither a homosexual or a nerd or both and the *proof* is in having a girlfriend. In today's more open society where they are even teaching about gay lifestyles in the classroom, one sometimes has to take the offensive (get a girl) even if it is just to prevent being put on the defensive. This is unnecessary pressure that young men should not have to suffer through. And in response to this pressure they resort to both old and new traditions.

The Athletic Route

Athletics is a fantastic vehicle for young people, but it serves young Black men better than anyone. First, it is a tremendous vehicle to channel the anger, frustration and sexual energy that so many Black youth have stored up. Second, they develop a respectful relationship with peers, rather than the type of relationships that develop in street gangs. Then there is the influence of high school coaches who on countless occasions have acted as father figures, advisors, and disciplinarians to young boys who had no such figures at home. But most of all, sports is one major area where young Black men get a chance to reaffirm some aspect of their value. To be an athlete makes you somebody to teachers who have ignored you, and to girls who have ignored you. But for the young boy the greatest benefit may be that not only can he attract a girl, sometimes he can pick and choose from a number of girls.

Some young men try out for sports specifically because it has been a proven means of getting the most desirable girls at the school. This goes back to the original point that the girls do not necessarily appreciate boys for who they are, but as the symbols that they come to represent. Some girls have no interest in being *the state champion* in anything; they have no intention of putting out that degree of effort. But they would be very interested *in dating the state champion* of almost anything and thereby share in the rewards, popularity and experiences that come with being the state champion. Hundreds, maybe even thousands, of White and Black girls have been given scholarships by major universities in this country for no other reason than the fact that they were the girlfriends of star athletes the universities were heavily recruiting. Have you ever read about *that* anywhere? Of course not, but think about it.

The Music Route

Attendance at any concert, brings with it the wild screams of the fans. If the star is a male, total chaos has been known to break out. What lengths women will go to get close to Michael Jackson, Prince, Smokey, Luther, etc, is difficult to imagine until you've actually seen it. Women literally go crazy over recording stars. Of course this is not news to the male high school student. So one of the routes that many boys take to "get the girls" is to perform in some type of band. This is not to say that many young people don't have genuine musical interests but all musicians know about the sexual rewards that come with musical skill and popularity. Sex is a part of pop music culture, and numerous books exist that tell stories about the sexy girls who just make themselves available for the musicians after the concert. As a matter of fact non-musical associates of musicians, such as managers, sound technicians and low paid flunkies have access to much more sex than the average male of any race. A successful or popular Black male singer in high school can not only attract an attractive girl his own age, but also girls who are much older. Lacking the status of being a popular singer, such sexual opportunities would be unthinkable.

The Party Time Dance Route

Much of what sports provides for young men is provided for women through dancing. The physical activity, the fellowship with peers, the fun, the release of sexual energy and mental frustrations are all satisfied by a good three hour "dance workout". And though most girls don't have any hang-ups about dancing with other girls, most prefer to dance with males. For any number of reasons, many young men do not dance or do not dance well or do not dance often. So a guy who is a good dancer, who respects and responds to the females he dances with, is bound to get the attention of quite a few females. If in addition to dancing, he is also a stylish dresser or is up with the latest fads in hair cuts, etc., he stands to gain even more popularity, credibility and possibilities with the women. Unfortunately some of these same males have a reputation for being gay. This fact does not seem to hurt their popularity as dancing partners with girls. But it does in some instances discourage non-gay young boys from getting on the dance floor and competing with them in what they are able to do so well. An hour of watching Soul Train for example will demonstrate my point very clearly.

Bullying-Fighting-Intimidating

It is not safe in the ghetto for anyone who lives there, regardless of age or gender. Everyone feels a higher level of danger than their counterpart in the suburbs. Women are harassed, followed and frightened by some of the males who live there. Everyone in the Black community has some level of appreciation for someone who can fight because it is assumed that sooner or later that skill will be needed to defend yourself against an attack. Even in an era when guns are commonplace and anyone is capable of killing anyone else, there is still a value placed on fighting skills. Girls feel more secure around guys known for "knocking a sucka out". Some of these men have spent time in jail, become very muscular body builders, are members of a gang, carry a weapon or have some characteristic that adds to their reputation as guys you leave alone. Many girls feel "safer" being around these kinds of guys because these girls are not as likely to experience the usual harassment once it gets to be common knowledge that her boyfriend is the community bully. A significant number of young men who are not into sports, music, dancing or fashion, define themselves by their ability to command the respect, of the home boys based on their fighting abilities. Gang culture is of course a part of this. But no fighting ability can stop a bullet, thus guns flourish in our community. And what many talk shows, magazine articles and news specials fail to mention is that quite a significant number of desirable females(sexually active, and attractive) are drawn to gang member types. In fact, there are many female gangs that are linked to the male gangs. Thus many young Black men get into this life because, among other things, it helps them get girls and sex.

Drug Dealing-The Lowest Common Denominator

The number of books written to explain why young Black males are involved in the drug business would easily fill whatever room you might be sitting in right now. The most often -repeated points in most of these books are that because jobs are scarce, education is poor, the father is absent, the government intervention programs are inadequate, the money is easy, demand is high, etc., etc., drugs have been, are, and will likely be sold in the Black community. To these points most would agree. But there has been little written about young Black *girls* being causal factors in the sale of drugs in our community , whether directly or indirectly. Why is this? Is it because Black women in fact play *no significant role in the sale and use* of *drugs*? Is it because it is safer to simply point to the young Black male as the all-purpose and convenient scapegoat? Is it because White media is fearful of the public outcry and backlash at the tarnishing of the image of the Black woman? Is it because there simply has been no effort made to study the relationship between African American girls (and women) and the drug trade?

Presented here is an argument which may not win the writer any popularity contests, but which should be put forth as a reasonable explanation, in part, about what goes on in the Black community today. In looking at what young Black men will do in an effort to impress, win over, and attract a female that he finds attractive, we have thus far covered ground that is several generations old, i.e. sports, music, etc. But within the last generation, the last twenty years particularly, a new system or culture has come into existence that is today referred to as "the *drug* culture". It is more pervasive and impacts many more people and aspects of Black community life than drugs did thirty or more years ago. Up to this point there has been an assumption that all the culprits are Black males and that Black females have little or no part in this destruction except as victims of these Black males. Consider if you will the following explanation of causes and effects.

Black males, as stated earlier experience a great deal of rejection and suspicion, beginning in earnest, but not limited to, their early teenage years. These rejections can be close to home, as in the non-relationship that may exist between a biological father and his son, to the fear and panic an old suburban White lady may feel upon even being in close proximity to a young Black man.

Teachers, police, store owners, and the general public, all play a role in making a young Black man feel that unlike other children, it would be better if he were *neither* seen nor heard. Most African American young men accept the burden of this rejection, and the related prejudicial attitudes. But what they are not prepared to accept is the continual rejection of their peer age females through the entire duration of their adolescent years (fourteen to eighteen) while their emotions and bodies are biochemically craving them. Therefor, many of these young men, like young men from the beginning of time, will go through some extraordinary actions to gain the interest of the opposite sex. Those who for any number of reasons find that they cannot make a personal statement through sports, music, dancing, fashion, or even physical violence, will not suffocate their sexual desires merely because their way of getting attention doesn't fit into the normally prescribed avenues of expression. They will simply seek something else they feel fits their particular set of circumstances. And in the search for this alternative means of expression, the sale of drugs has become the consistent avenue of choice.

Certainly the primary reason a person sells drugs is to get the money. But money is a means, not an end. In selling drugs, most of the competitive disadvantages that young poor boys suffer in their competition for girls disappear. With money, the young men are able to buy the flashy clothes, the gold chains, and other jewelry (perhaps even a gold tooth!) to make their fashion statement. The money can also buy the popular toys of the day: the CD, boombox, the beeper, the mobile phone, the guns., etc. Cars are the major status symbol thus many high school drug dealers drive cars that even successful lawyers would envy. The other money, the play money, the traveling money, the entertainment money, is also now available. Money, of course, does not close the age gap that exists between a fifteen year old boy and an eighteen year old girl but just about everything else is covered.

It is at this point that young African American women play their role. They have a choice. They can turn their back on the "goodies" that the drug trade has provided for these young men, or they can jump right in and consume as much of it as they can as fast as they can and *pretend* that they don't know where the money came from. Without question, most African American women do not knowingly support the drug trade. But a significant number, a number big enough to provide the average Black male drug dealer with at least several girlfriends *are* tied in with the drug business/culture. That means that more Black women are *indirectly* tied to drug money then men are! Have you ever read *that* anywhere? The situation is similar in some ways to the charge of racism that has always existed between Blacks and Whites in this country. Blacks will say *all* Whites are racist. Whites will counter by saying they have never done a racist thing in their lives. Blacks will counter this with the idea that all Whites benefit from the exploitation of Blacks, *benefit* from having White skin and are part of the overall racist system. Similarly thousands of African American women might say that they never sold dope in their lives, never endangered children, etc. But they used the drug and gladly accepted all the gifts and benefits that they knew (or should have known) was the result of drug sales.

The point is this: people do things over and over again only because it works. Selling drugs can get you killed, but more people make money than are killed. *Making the money enables young men to attract women period*! It is a fact that throughout history having money regardless of its source, will attract women. Thus it is not out of line to say that drug sales in the Black community is a consistently effective way for young Black men to gain access to girls who under "normal conditions" (broke, without a car or clothes, etc.) would not care to associate with them. A naive reader might think, "well, any decent young man should not even want that kind of girl." The reality is that when you are young and horny and haven't had sex with *any* woman, your taste in women can be quickly and substantially compromised. Besides, the notion that only ugly, trashy women are drawn to drugs or a drug dealer is completely false. Most women are usually drawn to money. Put another way, if the sale of drugs and the possession of drug money *did not* result in a dealer's ability to attract and hold on to a significant number of desirable Black women in our community, the appeal , the power and the scale of drug sales would be quickly and greatly reduced almost overnight. Thus Black women hold some lever of control in the drug trade. In legal jargon they might be labeled as accomplices. What does all this mean? For starters it means at least three things. It means first that the supposedly hard core killer drug dealer you have been taught to instantly hate without reservation, could be just a lonely brother in need of some emotional and physical love in his life and drug sales represents his one last desperate means of trying to get that. The real violence in our community combined with the Hollywood depiction of drug dealers by both White *and* Black movie makers, have done a good job at convincing us that our sons, nephews, neighbors and school mates are not merely people gone astray but are now non-human drug dealers. We see them as animals, unfeeling savages who should be lined up and executed as fast as possible. They are in fact humans who are acting out of ignorance and desperation and who need the same sympathy in many cases as any other sick, ignorant, desperate person who is lost. The word is compassion.

Secondly, the materialism of America that causes "white collar" crime in White America is causing unending homicidal crime in the Black community. Black women must play a key role in the move away from extreme and excessive materialism. They cannot continue to ask, as does Janet Jackson, "what have you done for me lately?" They cannot continue to ask to be loved for *who they are* yet decide to "love" their mate based on *what he's got*. The excessive materialism in the Black community has both sexes contributing, but the women clearly are closer to the levers of the control. A large part of men's materialism is usually just to woo, impress and win over the women with what they believe women want. Thirdly, if we are serious about solving the drug problem (and therefore a large part of the crime problem), then we are going to have to stop pretending that Black males are 100% of the problem in our community. Black males unfortunately lack their own agenda and therefore find themselves following an agenda which is designed only to attract females. By understanding how Black females contribute to the drug problem, we will become more effective against drugs spreading. I saw something in 1991 that was very interesting, yet neither heard or read one single word about it. I know millions of other Black people saw and heard what I did, yet not a peep from anybody. In both John Singleton's *Boyz in the Hood* and Spike Lee's *Jungle Fever*, there were scenes of a Black woman (one of them was Hallie Berry, how could you not notice Hallie Berry?), offering to perform oral sex on a male in exchange for some cocaine. As a matter of fact, Spike Lee ended his film with a little girl making the same request. Why would two Black film makers make a specific effort to include the same scene, almost word for word, unless they were trying to say the same thing that s being said here now. Namely, that Black women are part of the *drug* scene and play more than one role in keeping it going. Lee and Singleton depicted these females as down and out drug addicts willing to do anything for a high. But plenty of "good girls", "professional" women, and "attractive" women do exactly what these down and out women were willing to do, and they prostitute themselves willingly. And they don't do it with just drug dealers, but with musical superstars, world famous athletes, movie stars, lawyers, businessmen, etc. It doesn't make it right that all of these acceptable people mix drugs and sex, *but it is* real. If so-called dumb fifteen and sixteen year olds know whats going on, why do full grown, mature adults pretend that they don't?

Summary

Once young boys and girls finally develop some curiosity and interest in each other, they share what appears to be a very honest and equitable relationship. This relationship appears to be based on real common concerns and opinions in the worlds of school, the home and television. Money or material concerns seem to play a rather minor role in the determination of which way the relationship is going, although there may be perceptions by either gender that one family is doing better or not as well as the other. This type of relationship seems to last about three to four years or from about *age* nine to about age thirteen or so.

At about fourteen years old, Black girls and boys start to rapidly travel in different directions. Girls develop their feminine characteristics and begin to appeal and cater to boys two or more years older. Money does not always immediately or directly cause this change in relationships, but it eventually plays a definite role. The girl at this stage is often attracted to not only the greater maturity level of the older boy, but also to his ability to provide more 'fun and entertainment', independence and time away from home than a boy her own age. Money and a car provide him with this ability. For the young girl, the quality of the relationship is at this time determined less by communication, common interests and sincerity and more by the older boy's ability to show her a good time. Again, this is largely determined by money and access to a car. At the same time that this is going on, many girls seem to become less inner-directed or self-motivated, and instead begin to measure their status, their worth and their accomplishments not on what they have personally achieved but rather on what they have been able to get older boys to do for them. There is a strong correlation between a young man's access to money and what he can do for a girl. The situation described here is a progressive one where perhaps only a small percentage of thirteen and fourteen year olds move up to older boyfriends. But for every year thereafter, a greater percentage of girls pursue older boys until, by their senior year, few boys in the school are considered mature enough for the desirable senior girls. At this point, many senior girls probably expect from a date those things that only a salaried person with their own car could provide.

At fourteen years old, young black men are beginning to experience the rejection and prejudice that will follow them to their grave. Teachers, policemen, the business community and society in general, including Black America, are plugging young boys into stereotypical roles. School failure, police harassment and or jail may already be a reality for some at this point. They are learning what it is like to be America's public enemy #1.

What adds further insult and disappointment to these societal pressures is for these Black boys to learn, sometimes rather suddenly, that they are not even good enough, old and mature enough, or wealthy enough to hold the attention of the *girls* they care about. A significant group of boys are able to win back the attention and respect of their female peers by becoming excellent in a number of traditional roles. The sports hero, the musical genius', the party-time pretty boy and the gladiator are roles that many boys use to make their statement and earn the respect of their peers, male *and* female. This is a non-financial transaction for the most part. At this stage it is still possible for some brothers to win appeal on the basis of character, talent, excellence and popularity alone.

Another segment of the Black male group can't compete because they are playing it *too straight*. Even with excellent grades, regular church attendance and model behavior at home and in the community, he still lacks the "right stuff" to entice the kind of girls that all the other guys set their standards by. Money would help his cause,, but as a mere minimum wage worker who is committed to such an array of other community activities, he will never have more than lunch money. Hopefully he will be able to get use to "dishonorable discharges" (masturbation) in high school unless he happens to luck up and maybe seduce a sophomore girl in his senior year.

Finally we get to "the loser". The loser has been told in so many ways that he is a loser' that he can't possibly count them all . He cannot compete in school work, sports, music or fighting. But he will not accept the fact that he is a loser either. He's made up his mind that he's not going to lose in life or with the girls. He has faced the more "realistic"side of life. Life is not about grades and degrees, singing and dancing, home runs or touchdowns, *its about money*. If you have money, you get everything else. So this misfit who, in addition to his other failures, may be "too ugly" " too short", "too dark" "too skinny", "too fat" or too whatever, is determined to make the money "by any means necessary". Selling dope is the easiest way to make the most amount of money in the shortest amount of time. Money is going to define his relationships with women, and he has accepted that.

Unfortunately, the entrance of money into the dating game and the advice of well meaning adults at this stage has taught many young men that you "buy" women, you don't fall in love with them. When one doesn't work out, there is the assurance that there are "more fish in the sea." Young Black dope dealers are out in the streets of urban America by the thousands. They are indeed some of the craftsmen of the drug culture. But they are not alone. They have girlfriends, more than one, usually. It was always expected that they would get to have many girlfriends once they became successful in the business. It was one of the motivating factors for getting into the business in the first place, because nothing *else* was working. Now he goes from having nothing to having everything: his own place, a nice car, jewelry, good food, clothes, toys and girls. The American dream, temporarily. But they want him dead! Who? Everybody, basically. His dope selling competitors want to rub him out. The police would like to shoot him. The corrupt judge and politicians would like to see him fry. The parents of the kids he"s hooked on the garbage would like to disembowel him.

The money trail leads us to a point where we see young Black men, young Black (or White) women, drugs, money, materialism, and sex all intertwined in a sick alliance and relationship. Society wants to break this all up. Most agree. Society says the money, the materialism and sex are okay. Do not disturb. But the drugs have to go; no question. If we kill the pusher, everyone is free, no more crime and drugs. But killing the Blackman is not the answer. Improving the relationships between Black men and women, believe it or not, is a better answer.

CHOICES AND DECISIONS IN THE DATING GAME

The previous chapter looked at certain patterns of decisions and behaviors that some young high school girls tend to make in their selection of boyfriends, and how a significant number of young men responded to those same decisions and behaviors. Over the course of the three to four years that these actions and reactions take place, patterns, habits and mind sets are being developed which develope a momentum of their own in both the girls and boys.

Graduation from or leaving high school and entering the adult world alters the day to day regimen of these young people, and they disperse into all areas of life and to all parts of the country. The most "privileged" group will probably find themselves on a college campus, possibly hundreds of miles from home. Another group may join the military and also find themselves hundreds, even thousands of miles from home. Others from the high school class may face employment in low paying jobs in the neighborhood, while the less fortunate find themselves unemployed or even in jail.

Although individuals carry with them the experiences, attitudes, preferences and habits from their early dating years, the new environments that each now experiences can drastically change these habits. Class aspirations and class-based behavior, not so important in high school, now grow in significance in determining the attitudes and behaviors of young people who are now free to find their own place in the world. Where a person finds him or herself physically located, will say a lot about the new expectations of themselves and their potential mates.

Thus people who join the army will expect that they will encounter both the demands of and the opportunities accessible to regular army personnel. If men in the army are not normally around many females, those men will accept that adjustment. If a Black woman agrees to attend an all female college away from any large city, she will normally accept the reality that she will not be around many young Black men. And if a high school grad stays in the beighborhood in which they've grown up, they understand what male and female options they have for the most part.

Class Influenced Behavior

In high school, a typical student usually tries to fit in, be accepted, be popular and feel comfortable around most of the other students. Class considerations are normally of minimal significance except for the underlying assumption that college prep students are probably going to go somewhere in life and those in vocational or general educational programs are likely to stay right there in the neighborhood. After high school however, there is a conscious effort on the part of many males and females to "grow up" and become more "sophisticated" in their behavior, tastes, associates, dress etc. It is in this drive to become "more sophisticated" (a quality assumed to be very positive) that people become more class conscious and discriminating in their behavior. A young lady who may have spoken to you in the high school hallway may now avoid eye contact altogether (and thus the expected greeting) if you do not "appear to be" a person of the class she assumes to be her own. In other words in addition to your age and the money in your pockets, your percieved "class" now becomes a factor in dating. No one is clear exactly what the word *class* means, but it's usually taken to mean some combination of income, education, vocation, "grooming", mannerisms, communication skills, personal residence and etc. Women striving to be percieved as sophisticated now try to judge the class of those brothers desiring her attention. "Street" (down to earth) language and "street" behavior is suddenly viewed as vulgar, immature and/or "unsophisticated." This is not to say that there is no validity in expecting greater maturity from a twenty year old that would distinguish him or her from a seventeen year old. But many Black women, especially those striving to be viewed as part of the Buppy class, simply take the idea to an extreme. Over time, they become very skilled at sending the message that more and more young Black men just aren't good enough for them .

Any discussion of relationships that does not take into account class status or adopted class behavior is a joke. Black people tell White people that we are no longer a monolithic people possessing one mentality. But often when we talk among ourselves we still pretend that we are. Class aspirations and expectations will begin to dictate how a person acts, what choices they make, and who they decide to associate with. Certainly these ideas have been put in their head as a result of their interactions with family, school, peers and the media . But when a person reaches the age of adulthood, he or she has real opportunity to implement their own decisions and directions to take them down the path of their choice. All this is to say that no person can say what "usually happens" with brothers and sisters relating to each other after high school without being aware of that young persons *real* expectation or idea of what part of society they belong in or aspire to. In high school you tell people "what you want to be when you grow up." After high school you begin to *act* on getting yourself where you intend to be.

Having said that, it would be nice to tell you that my analysis from here on deals with all three broad catagories of classes within our community; the so-called underclass, the working class and the lower and upper middle classes. But such an analysis is outside the scope of this book. There will be efforts made occasionally to suggest that one type of behavior or expectation might be more likely to come from one group than another. I'm sure that will spark charges of sterotypical labeling. There might be some truth to that charge but I'd rather run that risk than to continue the ridiculous practice of discussing Black folks' relationships in sweeping statements with no consideration for the numerous factors affecting a persons behavior. For example, when I look at the tremendous uproar over how Shahrazad Ali's book, The *Blackman's Guide To Understanding the Black Woman*, was received by many Black women, it was obvious that part of what happened was a *class conflict*. Middle class Black women were saying "this book is a bunch of crap because *I don't know any* Black women who act this way." Many of these women were absolutely correct, they didn't know any women who acted in ways described in the book because they had been completely out of touch with the poorer Black people like LaKeesha, Shakeesha and Takeesha in the Projects. Ms. Ali was talking about the behavior of many poor and rather desperate Black women who don't have the options that many Black middle class women enjoy. When Essence speaks about "todays Black woman" they are not talking to LaKeesha, Shekeesha and Takeesha either. These women are viewed only as *problems* our community have to deal with. When Oprah, Phil, or Sally have ladies on stage (or even in the audience) to discuss womens issues, they do not call the "Keesha" girls to express their opinions as legitimate voices representing Black women and to express their opinions. The "Keesha" girls are trotted out only to express the most heart wretching sob stories to show the greater (White) audience just how bad things can get, how stupid or malicious people can be, or how vicious the cycle of poverty is. The audience typically believes all that they hear no matter how incredible . But when Shahrazad Ali writes about these same things and the many variations of the "Keesha" women, the Black female middle class, so use to being the spokespersons for and representing Blacks in all media, become upset. They try to deny not only that the "Keesha" women have a culture of their own, but even minimize the fact that these ladies even exist in significant numbers. Ms Ali did little more than discuss the habits of some Black women who come from an economic and social class in the Black community, that middle class Blacks never want projected as representative of

Black people in America. But guess what? The Keesha class of women is *expanding*, while the Black middle class is shrinking. Given *that* reality, who should represent the Black reality in the media?

Early Dating Habits Slow to Change

For both males and females, many factors push the age at which people decide to marry, further into the future. Establishing a career becomes a major concern as never before in an era when major corporations lay off good experienced (White) employees in numbers absolutely unheard of previously. High divorce rates, sexually transmitted diseases, and the high cost of housing are just a few of the factors which cause people to put off the idea of getting married. People are either dating for longer periods of time, dating only occasionally, or they aren't dating at all. In any event, the opportunity for young men and women to reinforce their methods of seeking, impressing and choosing their dates is given even more time to solidify. There is little reason to believe that there should be any significant changes in dating rituals that have been in motion for at least three years of high school. Even if an eighteen year old female freshmen in college decides to date a male freshman, it doesn't mean that he is not suppose to have a car to travel around in and pocket money set aside for just such occasions. On the other hand the young lady may be very understanding and agree to go out with a *broke* freshman if he possesses other qualities (physical attractiveness, good communication etc).

Money does not *always* dictate the direction a relationship goes, but it's a prime factor that is often vaguely acknowledged by people who should know better. When this young lady agrees to go out with this broke freshman, she is compromising on a point that she perhaps might not compromise on with a person of a different class. Suppose, for example, this young man had an even more attractive cousin who was unemployed, had no interest in college, and was also broke. Would she, seeing this other young man heading into a different world than she, be as understanding on the issue of his depleted bank account? I can let you answer that one yourself, so you can't say it came from me.

The working girl, trapped in some low wage job, has no reason to believe that her salary can pay both for her living expenses and provide the good times she seeks. There is no reason for her to change her pattern of looking for dates who are fun to be with, funny, and the life of the party. Like other young ladies her age, she may be using a range of factors to determine her main boyfriend and money may not be a chief criterion.

Lakeesha and her sisters know all too well that love is not enough. Mothers since they were sixteen, they do not get child support from their children's fathers for any number of reasons. Trapped in the ghetto, they seldom see Black men who have been allowed to be all that they could be. Besides, even if they found such men, the men would be reluctant to assume the responsibilities and problems that come with a ready made family. Right or wrong, young men see Lakeesha's kids and assume that mama's looking for a meal ticket. She has little opportunity to prove that she wouldn't quickly accept one if one came along.

Thus, each class of young African American women is trying to make the best of their dating situation in relation to where they are and where they are trying to go. From their viewpoint, they are young (19, 23, or maybe 27 years old), and they've only got ten good years of freedom to live life as they wish without instructions from either their parents or a husband.

Common sense would dictate that you try to get as much as you can during "the best years of your life." But what exactly is it that young ladies are looking for? Who is in the best position to give it to them? What of equal value are they willing to give in return? And who has the *responsibility* of making it all happen? These are the questions that many men ask themselves all the time. Getting the right answers is difficult to put it mildly.

Dating At The Workplace

There is an old expression which says " birds of a feather flock together." Another says "it takes one to know one," while still another says "water seeks its own level". All of these old expressions lend some truth to the idea that people are most comfortable with people they consider "their own kind". What constitutes your own kind differs for different people, but clearly race, religion, age, income, education and occupation all figure into the mix some way. Because most people spend the majority of their time on their jobs and usually look and act their best on their jobs, the job might seem to be the best place to find a compatible mate. The job atmosphere creates something that both the male and female can relate to because it is so much apart of their lives. The work place is not a place that requires either party to spend money on the other, and it is "safe" in that a lady doesn't have to worry about being with a strange man, in a strange place. Objectively the work site appears to be a great place to meet that special someone. But for the upwardly mobile in corporate America at least, there is a tendency to discourage the sexes to mix work and romance. Mr. Randolph W. Cameron put a book together in 1989 called *The Minority Executives Handbook* (Warner Books N.Y., N.Y.) In it he made the following comments on page 134:

• Be selective in your choice of dating companions. Some associates have a poor reputation because of drug use or sexual promiscuity, or a "poor" attitude, or simply for incompetence or stupidity. This type of association will damage your image in a traditional corporate environment if you are a serious career person. Some people may question your judgement ability and use your social life as a valid confirmation of their doubts about you.

• Always be extremely discreet in your relationships with an associate on the job, and never display anything but professionalism while you are both on company time.

• Never assume that a company-sponsored function is an opportunity to display your affection for anyone, least of all a fellow employee. Displaying affection at a company function could spell disaster for your image at the company.

• Always be on guard for people who want to get "into your business." Chances are that they are primarily interested in getting information about you and your associate that they can use on the gossip exchange. Remember that any story, even one not originally intended to injure you, can damage your reputation.

• If you confide in someone in the company about a relationship that you have with an associate, you must assume that you will hear the story again from someone else in the company, someone you did not tell the story to. The moral of this is *don't tell anyone anything that you or your associate would not like to hear again someday, and* perhaps from someone you don't happen to want to have known your business.

There are quite a few ideas in these warnings above, so lets make sure they are plain. The first warning suggests that whereas the bad habits of either mate usually would effect the life of the opposite mate in any normal situation, the workplace has a special danger. Here your own personality and capability may be questioned and suffer if the mate you choose had a confirmed bad reputation. Regardless of the future of the relationship, one risks damage to their career and therefore their future income if they happen to get caught in this situation.

Warning number two and three suggest that one develop a   split personality on the job. They call for both individuals to be equally capable of completely separating their emotional feelings for each other from their job responsibilities *at all times*. Is this realistic? Wouldn't this put tension on the relationship and destroy the relationship over an extended period of time? Also, since most relationships do not last and often end less than peacefully, wouldn't having to work with someone that you now have bad feelings toward also hurt one's performance at work also?   Finally there is the very heavy emphasis here on the importance of *image* within the corporation. Imagery or the things specifically designed to impress, are the very things that get in the way of Black men and women getting to know and communicate, with each other honestly. If both parties have to be so concerned with their images, wouldn't they end up deceiving each other to some extent?   Some of us play a role only because we have to, to put food on our table. Others of us love playing the roles and frequently become, in our own minds, a lot like the images we consistently portray. After awhile its difficult to distinguish the real from the image.

As easily as it is to dismiss the urge to date someone on the job, it may be quite difficult to prevent in reality. There are many, many opportunities to learn about a person on the job, especially if you see them daily. They can become attracted to what they like, and they can become involved with what they are attracted to. One never knows what one will do in a situation unless or until they are tested daily. Working with someone you like is a test and it is beyond the authority of anyone to say what other people should do in this situation.

If dating is a thing that is not highly recommended, then one can assume that marriage between people at the same company is a definite No. Actually, Mr. Cameron says it depends:

> "Looking at this issue more objectively, there are obviously a
> number of young married people working in the same company
> today. As long as we are talking about low-level jobs, there is
> not much to be concerned about. However, once the couple
> attempts to move up into more senior management jobs, look
> out!" (p.138)

Cameron says that if two senior management types seek to marry they can do so, but only if one leaves the company to continue their career elsewhere because of the difficulty in maintaining separate identities on the job. Top level management doesn't want to be put in a position of having to figure out how a decision made about one spouse will effect the work, morale or cooperation of the other spouse. Management in almost any enterprise is mainly an issue of decision making. A good manager makes good decisions and a bad one, bad decisions. Thus corporate America must wonder how marriage itself would affect the decisions of other wise good decision makers. Cameron states:

"In addition, if you happen to be working closely with your spouse, there are always questions about your judgment calls, objectivity, and influence. What about the whole male versus female parity issue relative to raises, bonuses, and other fringe benefits? After all, it is common knowledge that men have traditionally received higher levels of compensation then females performing comparable work.(p.137)"

Even if a company knew that a married couple wouldn't allow their relationship to impact on their decision making, morale etc, the concern over the relationship would then be directed to the new issue of power and influence. According to Cameron one party may have their career dreams squashed in order to prevent the possibility of the couple as a unit having too much influence in the company.

"Corporations also have a way of limiting the amount of influence any one person, aside from the CEO, can have in the company. Therefore, the chance that both spouses might hold senior management jobs of significant power and influence, at the same publicly held company, is highly unlikely." (p.137)

A reading of Cameron's advice would give a lot of comfort to those who would like to see women kept in their place and would frustrate women who are looking to "have it all". What's basically being said is that if you are a low level person in a system (such as a secretary, for instance) you can fool around with upper management (or they can exploit you sexually) because you are not seen as a threat. If the heat gets too hot, a secretary can easily make a lateral move to another department, division or company. If you are a new style Black woman with every intention of getting into senior management, then you have to be super conscious of your image and curtail your social agenda at the work place. And if you happen to meet and marry a person anyway, it's unlikely both of you will make it to the senior positions.

Of course there are many places that Black men and women work that are not corporate America. But it would be a little naive and dangerous to assume that none of the ideas laid down here would not apply at all where you work.

When The Women Pursue The Men

Although I have had significant exposure to the women's movement for some time, and have made efforts to try to understand their points of view, I must confess that some things were never clear to me. One such concept which was always fuzzy was the meaning and implication of "sexual freedom". I understand that "the pill" and an increasingly sexually oriented society reduced the guilt that unmarried women use to feel after "doing it", but sexual freedom seemed to mean more than that.

One idea which seemed to be a part of female sexual freedom since the late sixties was the idea of women being able to pursue a desirable male in a more assertive manner. That women could openly and actively let a man know of her interest in him was even more openly accepted in the Black community because of the shortage of "good men". In places like Washington, D.C., Atlanta and Chicago, where large numbers of "educated" black women worked, it was supposedly ok for a sister to ask a brother for a dance, or even for his phone number. I have neither been the recipient of, witnessed or had any close acquaintances receive this type of ego boosting experience. I believe however, that even if you haven't experienced something firsthand (or had any friends who have) doesn't at all mean that it isn't happening. So let's assume that sisters are approaching men every day all over the country, with a direct interest in a friendship or a romantic or sexual relationship. The thing we want to look at in these instances are the responses of both the sisters and brothers. At issue is the widespread claim that "brothers can't handle an aggressive woman." To provide maximum clarity, it is best that an entire sequence of events be detailed in order to ensure that the points presented here are fully understood.

Situation 1.   Black women between the ages of 18-35 claim that a good Black man is hard to find. After expending a significant amount of time and effort looking for a man and making all the correct moves, let's say that a particular young lady comes up with no satisfactory date or love interest. The main problem seems to be that the desired male did not approach her, make known his interest, or follow up in any significant way after expressing initial interest. Situation 2.   Unable to continually tolerate the lack of interest shown her, and also unwilling to accept the idea that "the men just aren't out there", this particular determined Black female decides that she is going to take matters into her own hands and approach men directly. She goes back to the "proper places" and gradually perfects an approach and a conversation that she feels comfortable with. Over the course of a few months she approaches ten to twelve men. She calls them on the phone, dates a few, and even has sex one time. But after about six months, she finds no mutually satisfying relationship with a significant emotional foundation. What is the problem? According to the sisters who have tried such an approach, the problem is "brothers can't handle or feel threatened by an aggressive black woman." We also have "the brother won't commit" charge. The level of anger present in sisters who have tried unsuccessfully the direct approach is noticeably higher than the level in the normal lonely sister. In their minds they have made extra efforts, gone well beyond the call of duty, and still have nothing. Thus, in the minds of many sisters, there are more things that can be added to the long list of negative things about the Black man. The questions to be addressed are:

(a) How valid are these conclusions?

(b) What are the conclusions based on?

(c) Are we witnessing the usual tendency of the Black woman to avoid looking at herself to figure out what's not working and why?

These are important points, not merely for the purpose of reducing the frustrations of Black women, but to examine another aspect of the communication process between Black men and women. Because Black women credit themselves with being better communicators than Black men, they also assume that they have a better understanding of the entire communication process. This is often not the case.

The first thing that Black women must appreciate is that in a society where the Black man enjoys too few true freedoms, he is likely to be rather extreme in indulging in the freedoms that he does enjoy. White America does not care one bit which Black woman a Black man goes out with or marries. He is not likely to suffer one bit more from Whites for marrying Black woman A instead of Black woman B, unless of course Black woman A could easily pass for White. Therefore, when Black men choose their women, they are exercising one of the few freedoms they have. When you consider how long a relationship is "suppose" to last, and how many Black women there are to select from, it puts the Black man in the rare position of "being choosey" in a major life decision. There is an attitude in America, and its probably shared by quite a few Black women, that the Black man is not qualified enough in any area to be in a position to be choosy about anything. He shouldn't be choosey about a job, he should work wherever "they" will *let* him work. He shouldn't be choosey about his college, he should go wherever "they" will *let him in*.   He should not be choosey about his food, his apartment, his clothes, car etc. There is a sense of arrogance about a Black man, a Black man that "thinks he's somebody", when he's in a position to pick and choose. And Americans, including many Black women, have a low tolerance for a Black man who is arrogant or in a controlling situation. For those of you old enough to remember, it took Black women a lot longer to like Muhammad Ali, who bragged about how great and pretty he was, than it did for Black men. For so long, a "good Black man" was seen by Whites and many Blacks not as a proud Black man but a *humble* one. Only in the last twenty years or so has America, including many Black men and women, become comfortable with *proud* Black men. In any event there is some resentment that I think more than a few Black women bring to the table in a relationship simply because they are annoyed that Black men are in a pick and choose position, even if the men themselves are not arrogant in their nature. When you add into the situation that the Black women of today have more "education" and make about as much if not more money than the males " looking them over," it is understandably infuriating to their ego. Finally you must not leave out the always all important factor of White confirmation. By this I mean that many Black females have this idea or assumption that all privileges that anyone enjoys are or must be approved by the White man first. But sisters must face and deal with the fact that Black men have the privilege to pick and choose, and it is a privilege that didn't need to be rubber stamped by White folks. An uneducated Black male criminal just released from jail will have an easier time sharing passion (getting sex) with a love interest on his birthday let's say than a sister who makes $40,000 a year and has a masters degree. Many women are not aware of their own degree of outrage at this seemingly unfair advantage that Black men enjoy, but it is certainly there(if only at the subconscious level) every time they feel they are being "looked over."

If it's any consolation to Black women, Black men had to pay for this advantage, and pay dearly. Tens of thousands of Black men had to die or be taken out of circulation for many years to position the remaining men as they are. If Black women would want the situation turned around in their favor in terms of selection options, they might have a change of heart once they realize what it costs. The first part of the answer to question (a), then, is that what Black women think is a feeling of being threatened is often not the case. It is simply the Black man exercising his options and he simply decides *not* to select the person who has selected him. This leads to the next point: *rejection*. Rejection is a feeling that Black men are very familiar with, especially in social relationships. The male has to constantly approach the female in social settings and traditionally anything from a dance to marriage and everything in between has to be initiated by him. Because men have similar standards of beauty (a prime consideration in the selection of women), many men approach the same females. Thus many men experience rejection even if they were all "equally qualified".

Women, on the other hand, don't have much experience with this kind of rejection because they usually don't do the approaching. Women may *feel* rejected without actually *being* rejected. What's the difference you say? Alot! When you feel rejected you can play games with your head, give yourself a pep talk; and its easier to cast off the feeling because it didn't actually happen point blank. But when a male pushes his fears and doubts aside, walks right up to a female, looks her right in the eye and says can I..... and she looks him just as square in the eye and says *no*, that is *actual* rejection. You can not pretend that it did not happen. Sometimes the rejection is very public. The rejection is not only clear to you, the reject, but to witnesses and /or all of your close friends as well and many will tell you that often hurts more than the rejection itself.

When women decide that they are going to play the man's game and do the approaching, they must be prepared to receive what men receive; rejection. As a matter of fact, because men have more ladies to pick and choose from than vice versa, women can expect to be rejected more than men due to the ratio imbalance. And this would be especially true if the advancing young lady didn't meet the general criteria of "attractive". However, this seems to be a difficult thing for sisters to deal with, so they continue to play head games among themselves. They do this by not even acknowledging the rejection as ever having taken place and instead say "the brother can't deal with an aggressive woman." Women turn a rejection into a reason to down the brother and complement themselves at the same time. What is not clear is (a) if they know that is what they are doing and (b) would they admit it to anyone if they did realize they were rejected. Warren Farrell makes this point on page 154 in *Why Men Are The Way They Are*:

"Some women who believe men can't commit may feel a need to hold on to that position. As one woman confessed, "He rejected me. For a year I preferred to say, He couldn't commit. Now I'm ready to look at why." *When a woman complains about "men's fear of commitment," she may also be avoiding looking at why she was rejected"*

Later, I discuss the somewhat disturbing term *marriageble* as in a marriageable Black man. It is a term that has been easily accepted in everyday conversation, and it refers to, in many cases, a subjective judgement of a man's qualities. Many times this judgement is a negative one without a fully adequate basis. Some men are simply written off and disqualified for consideration as a potential marriage partner because they do not meet particular standards. Black men, on the other hand, have *not* setup a similar system with formal guidelines defining marriageable or unmarriageable women. I think that this is a credit to men though we don't receive such credit and its probably because many women are vein enough to believe that there is no such thing as an unmarriageable Black woman. In any event men are not without some set of standards and because of that, some women find it consistently difficult to find a date. All over the world, men value physical beauty. And in spite of what criteria is used to define beauty, many women would still fall short of the standards. Thus, if we were a society where men thought that fat was sexy, thin women would be considered unattractive and would have more problems getting dates. The point here is that it is inaccurate for women to speak in a united voice regarding "the man problem," because some women clearly have far less problems attracting men than others. Dr. Robert Staples states *in The Black Woman In America* on page 105:

"Another factor to consider is that the male shortage does not have equal effect on all Black women. The very desirable Black woman is not as likely to feel the pinch of the male shortage. In our society a female's desirability is often derived from her sex appeal, especially at the younger ages. Black women who posses less sex appeal or lack youth will be less likely to be chosen"

Thus, a woman who is attractive, young and shapely is not likely to say, "Black men can't handle aggressive sisters," because she will have her fair share (if not more) of brothers responding to her advances if she decided to take an aggressive approach. *The determining factor in the success of female aggression is not the attitudes of brothers but the physical appearance of the sisters.* There are some women who should clearly spend more time cultivating their potential beauty than categorizing the attitudes of Black men. Of course the argument here might be that men shouldn't place so much emphasis on physical beauty but rather should look beyond that and focus on the person inside. My question would be where were these same people when women drew up the long list of things which put Black men in the unmarriageable category? (See *Waiting To Exhale* for Details)

Age Differences In Dating Decisions

It was pointed out in an earlier chapter that age differences and age expectations play a heavy role in determining dating decisions. But that is not entirely true. Age is only representative of the states of minds and states of finances that people are likely to have at points in their lives.

At fifteen years old, a young female would be much more impressed with a dozen long stemmed roses and would discount her mate's passionate outpouring of a dozen "I love you's." But that same female at forty five might discount the significance of flowers from an admirer but become tearful upon having a dozen passionate "I love you's" whispered in her ear.

People want different things in their life at different times and the difficulty in relationships is one of timing. For example, many women want children early in their life (twenty to twenty five or younger). But most African American males are in college, in jail, in the Army, unemployed or underemployed at those ages, so how could they be in a position to care for an entire family when they are struggling to take care of themselves. This is not necessarily immaturity on the part of Black males at all. Nobody in their right mind would say that high school prepares you for life. Very few colleges even do that. Dealing with life prepares you for life. Its an on-the-job training type of experience. Why should a young lady expect a male to marry at twenty one? What is she prepared to do with her life besides have a baby? Why should the male's maturity level be based on the unwise decision the female is prepared to make? Most young Black females are no more prepared to make a way for themselves in life than the males are. And in those situations where "shot gun" weddings are held to smooth things over, the marriage just backfires down the road most of the time anyway. Dr. Robert Staples on page 34, makes this point in his book *The Black Family-Essays and Studies*;

>   "One other distinguishing-characteristic of the Black population
>   is the early age at which Black women give birth to their first
>   children. More than 40% of Black women have given birth at
>   least once by the time they reach 20 years of age. Estimates are
>   that only one-sixth of the Black males in that age range have
>   jobs". (Cummings, 1983). Should they marry before age 20,
>   more than 7 out of 10 such marriages fail (Cherlin, 1981)."

Black women often seek older Black men simply because older men have money and they are more likely to think in the traditional ways of doing everything for the woman. Also, these women generally have no interest in learning anything in particular from the greater experience these older men could share. Again Dr. Staples, in a much earlier work entitled *Black Masculinity,* makes the point.

>   "Considering the cost of dating, only a certain category of men
>   can and will engage in it for long periods of time. A noticeable
>   trend is toward women in their twenties and thirties dating men
>   in their late forties and early fifties. When I asked one woman,
>   a 32 year old specialist in multi-cultural education, why she
>   dated so many men in their forties, she replied: "because you
>   don't have to pick up the tab for your own dinner. They come
>   from the old school and know how to treat a woman. Besides,
>   they know if they want to date a woman 15 years their junior,
>   they have to spend money on her." These older men, of course,
>   are often at the peak of their earning power, some are recently
>   divorced and new to the dating game. Also, some men are in
>   positions where they can write off the costs of dating on expense
>   accounts or as tax deductions." (p 106-107)

Sandwiched between those young Black men who are working hard to be good boyfriend types (those that is who aren't broke, in trouble or in the service) and those older Black gentlemen who are wining and dining the younger girls with their cash and credit cards, is a third type of Black man. This type of young Black man is a told how mature, intelligent, responsible, serious and disciplined he is. But he is also very sexually frustrated because he has no lady in his life and can't seem to attract one. The reason that this type of Black man is given so many praises is due to the lifestyle he leads at such a young age.

He gets up at 6 am to go to a job that pays only seven dollars a hour, about the most that a high school grad can expect to make at twenty. At four pm he begins a second part time job which he works until seven. Four times a week (including Saturdays) he takes classes (twelve credits) at the local community college where he's working on a degree in business administration. This young man, lets call him Frank, has no car or much of a wardrobe. He is the second oldest in a family of six. No father has been present for ten years. Most of his money is used to pay for his education and the household bills as his mothers income is not enough to carry the family through. An older sister is married and gone, the other three children are younger than high school age. Frank is not a bad looking guy, doesn't smoke or do drugs. He sees girls on both of his jobs but because of the low status positions that he holds at both of them, girls don't give him much respect. Although he makes enough money to splurge on a couple of things, he can't because of his role in paying family bills and saving to meet the college expenses that will come once he transfers from community college. In all likelihood his four year college experience will also be done entirely in the evening because he can't afford to give up his day jobs. I think I could go on about Frank but I don't think I have to. Readers know a few guys like this even in todays times of screwed up values. The point here is that as good a guy as Frank is, he is still uptight. He can't get the attention of any young ladies that interest him for one major reason: lack of money. With more money he could dress better and look better to the women he encounters. With more money he could afford a decent car and the inner city insurance rates for a male under twenty five. With more money he could *look like* he was a better person to date, when in fact he would be a "worse" person. Because if Frank had more money he would not buy a car or clothes, he would move his mother and family out of the neighborhood they currently live in. If he had more money he would pay for some medical procedures that his sisters and brother don't get now because they are not on welfare. If he had more money he would quit his part time job and do more studying so he could get his grades up. In other words, Frank is either too dumb or too smart to get wrapped up into the never ending consumerism and image building traps as long as there are more important things he or his family need. Frank's sexual hormones are as active as any twenty year old males but they are a source of deep frustration rather than an ingredient in his pleasure. Frank at twenty, has as much potential to be a great father and husband, (based on his current attitudes, work ethic and sense of priorities) as a seven footer has of being a college basketball player. But unlike the seven footer,people don't notice Frank. To the people who have the most to benefit from recognizing a Frank, Black women, he is invisible. They should be recognizing Frank not only for who and what he is today but what and who he will likely be in ten years (or less).

If Black women are serious about improving their situation relative to Black men, they must do what all White athletic coaches, corporate executives, politicians and musicians do; *they must recognize potential.* If they are to be impressed with a brother's character at thirty, they ought to at least be able to recognize that character at twenty. In a culture that says it wants one thing but actually supports another, people like Frank are discouraged. When guys like Frank see ladies more attracted to the gold chains and the four hundred dollar bomber jacket of a young dope dealer than their own honest work and sacrifice, there is the urge in some to give up taking the high road in life. In America and in the Black community you are either a "somebody" or a nobody. It is hard to be seen as something in between. Potential is seldom seen and credited. Black women's level of respect among many intelligent Black men is reduced when it becomes so very obvious that they respond only to some material trinket or fad. Nor does it make a brother feel good to see that he must be a completed package, (to "already *be* what he aspires to be" according to *Waiting to Exhale*), just to merit the attention and respect of the ladies he sees. Some of these same ladies waiting for the brother to *completely* get his thing together will later have the nerve to say "I liked you the moment I saw you", or some such garbage.

Picking Boyfriends versus Picking Husbands

I believe that a major problem in the success of Black male/female relationships is that women confuse the criteria they use to select boyfriends with the ones they use to select husbands.

Boyfriends, as we see by the high school patterns, are to provide fun. A boyfriend takes you places that your own knowledge or your own money may not have allowed you to go. A boyfriend is also suppose, to be "fun to be with" which could mean any number of things. It could mean that because he's older and more experienced, that you are always learning from him and so every experience is a further adventure into adulthood and learning about life.

"Fun" could be that your boyfriend is funny. He makes you and others laugh so that during the time you are with him, your other problems don't really exist.   Your boyfriend is the kind of escape that makes alcohol or drugs unnecessary because his sense of humor takes away your depression and frustration.

"Fun" could be based on the idea that a boyfriend is "crazy".   Crazy meaning that they take risks, perhaps dangerous risks, illegal risks, and in so doing introduces his girlfriend to the very side of life that her overly protective parents and older siblings always protected her from.   This "fun" could be based on a woman witnessing and/or participating in action which step over the line ever so slightly in order that she feel the rush of the excitement which comes from doing illegal things.   Doing alcohol or drugs,   racing cars, gambling, making love in a public place or any number of crazy things could be "fun".

"Fun" could be just consuming a large portion of the common entertainment activities that saturate this country from one end to the other: dances, concerts, clubs, plays, movies, boat rides, amusement parks, museums, etc. etc. I have been in ladies' homes where they collect the ticket stubs of the events they've gone to, and the ticket stubs fill up a small fish bowl. Big Fun!

Eating is fun to everybody.   And of course there is sex, virtually everybody's definition of fun. Some people's religious or moral principles may exclude sex as part of the "fun" package. But even in the age of AIDS and other sexually transmitted diseases, sex is usually the activity which highlights the other fun experiences.

But, *fun costs* money . Not always a lot of money, but it adds up. Money is required in most cases, for a boyfriend to supply the fun that ladies of all classes look to have. The "classier" the lady, the more expensive her tastes in defining what fun is, much of the time.

The second thing that boyfriends are supposed to do is to "make her feel good."   A naive young man might assume that if you are taking a lady out and providing her the opportunity to have fun, that you are already making her feel good. But that is only partially true. In addition to the *activity* making her feel good, *you* have to make her feel good! You have to give sincere (or sincerely expressed) compliments on "her looks" (her hair, dress, makeup, nails etc). You have to integrate all the romantic moves, including flowers, wine, and music, into the evening as the situation calls for and your pockets can stand. And you have to do this in such a way that you communicate the idea that *you have no expectation of receiving anything in return*. Nothing makes a woman feel more special than getting something for nothing. Inspite of what you read or hear, the pedestal image is still good to go.

If the boyfriend has made it up to this point, he's in good shape but he could still blow it if he's not careful. The next step in making her feel good is the occasional gift. The American economy is set up so that it is stimulated by the spacing out of gift giving occasions in virtually every month. There is your Christmas - Kwanzaa gift, Valentines day gift, birthday gift, graduation or promotion gift, anniversary (of the relationship) gift, house warming gift and the occasional for no particular reason gift. Women are supposedly more romantic than men, so symbolism is important to them. We *know* they are more materialistic than men so that will work too. A smart boyfriend will check out what kind of gift profile his lady has. If she is a "its the thought that counts" sister, it means you can give a steady flow of relatively inexpensive gifts. If she is a "quality is better than quantity" sister, it means you can skip a few occasions but you are going to have to come up with something nice when you do give a gift, otherwise you will be labeled as cheap. If you have a sister that expects quality and quantity, you 'd better count your money.

Trying to be the perfect boyfriend is like trying to be the perfect Christian, Muslim, or Jew. It's an ideal that you never really reach. Many sisters are looking for their own idea of perfection. You the boyfriend, may have no real idea what that idea of perfection is. But many brothers like the challenge of being the perfect boyfriend and so they practice hard until they have it down to an art form. They are called "a lady's man" and they become very successful being somebody's boyfriend. Which brings us to our next topic - husbands.

Probably the single biggest mistake, that women in general make is to assume that the perfect boyfriend will make a perfect husband. When women say they are looking for a "good man", nothing could be more vague. A good man for what? A good man for the Dallas Cowboys, for the President's cabinet or one that makes you feel good? It is surprising when we see over and over how women complain about the husbands that made such good boyfriends.

Husbands, in most people's perspective, have to be men who have no problem assuming responsibility for whatever they might be called upon to do (within reason). And usually a person who assumes responsibility has that as one of their personality traits long before anyone is thinking of marriage. And to many "husband type" of men, it might seem an irresponsible use of time, money and total resources to try to come anywhere near being the perfect boyfriend. As a matter of fact many good husbands were probably very bad boyfriends from the stand point of the make-me-feel-good, be funny and funloving, spend money on me, act crazy behavior. Men who assume responsibility tend to think that other people should do the same, including women. So they might think that instead of their job being to make a woman happy, that the women should make themselves happy or that they should *already be happy with themselves*. A man who has to be ready to provide everything financially when needed has a difficult time respecting a woman who is ready to provide virtually nothing most of the time. Its like expecting a Mr. America or Mr. Universe to marry a woman who is lazy and obese, its not impossible but don't hold your breath. Responsible men aren't necessarily strict and serious about everything; usually just their money, energy and time, the very things they are asked to spend recklessly in order to be the life of someone's party. If all this is true, then it would appear that the so called "problem with Black men" is perhaps more due to Black womens poor understanding of and their poor judgement of the men in their lives rather than the men themselves.

In other words, people are creatures of habit and one is slow to change even when they are aware that they should. If a woman agrees to a relationship for years based on a criteria that defines *a good boyfriend*, she is very likely to be unqualified to determine what kind of person would make *a good husband* because she hasn't looked at and become familiar with those types of characteristics in men. Many men suffer ridicule after marrying these types of women. The fun loving guy is told "Why don't you grow up". The free spending guy who always spent his money on the dates, now hears his wife saying "Why are you (we) always broke? " For the professional boyfriend, relationships are still a game to him. And the risk taker eventually crosses the line and lands in jail for a long stretch of time.

What women do is *blame the men* for *being the very men* that *caused* the relationship to *come together* in the first place. They loved the men the way they were, but now all of a sudden in the marriage they don't like the way the men are because their behaviors don't lead to the new and different wants and goals that the women have. But whoever suggested that a personality could change as quickly as a woman's new wants? Men go through all kinds of changes to please women, but these habits can't be changed at the drop of a hat. If a woman wants a good husband, she shouldn't be out looking for the traditional "good boyfriend".

FALSE IMAGES CREATE ADDED PRESSURES

The next point concerns the idea that both women and men, often have false economic images of each other prior to marriage. And while that point is being explained it might also be helpful to keep in mind that these false images create a pressure and resentment that often kills the relationship before it has a chance to mature into something meaningful.

If we look at a single woman who is perhaps thirty to thirty-five years old, educated beyond the high school level, without children, and having a rather consistent and progressive work history, we are probably looking at a woman who is not exactly who she appears to be. Because when we enter this person's apartment or house we assume that it is a reflection of *her* efforts, tastes, sacrifices and purchases. Usually that is not the case in reality. Why do I say that? Lets look at the situation more closely.

Let's assume that this female started dating seriously at nineteen years old, a modest assumption. At that rate she will have been dating off and on for, say ,at least ten years if she is thirty or fifteen years if she is thirty-five. Because of cultural and societal expectations put on men, they are periodically expected to give gifts to their lady's several times a year. The favorite gift giving days are usually Valentines Day, Birthday, Christmas and very often the anniversary day of the relationship's beginning. In addition to these 3 or 4 certain holidays, there are the occasional trips to the mall where a brother purchases the impulse item, something unplanned (and often unneeded) that the lady just must have. Let's say that this happens just two times a year, again a *very* modest assumption. Finally, once a year a couple may go for a get-away vacation. And on these vacations or trips it is very common to bring back a momento to symbolize the trip. Thus a lower middle class to middle class sister who makes a decent salary herself (say twenty five thousand or more) can expect that there will be no less than six times a year that she can realistically expect to receive something tangible and significant from her man. Now if you multiply this figure by ten years, you get no less than sixty occasions for the thirty year old and ninety occasions for the thirty five year old. Of course a number of women will not have men continually for that entire period of time. On the other hand many will be dating more than one man at a time (certainly prior to the heavy impact of AIDS), and while many men will not buy a gift for all the occasions, many men will buy more than one gift for Christmas, Kwanzaa or Birthdays. If we are *conservative*, it's a good chance that an attractive and active 30 year old sister will have in her apartment at *least fifty* specific items given to her by a man. These things would include kitchen appliances, furniture, artwork, jewelery, shoes(Lord knows, shoes), dresses, sweaters, etc. Thus if you were to walk into the apartment of such a woman you might say, "wow, she really has her place looking nice, she has her act together etc." But if one were to snap their fingers and all those things purchased by men were to disappear leaving only what *she* bought with her own money, you would see something very different. What you would see would be the actual material possessions reflecting the actual lifestyle, taste, sacrifices and work efforts of the lady of the house. As a matter of fact that would not be entirely true either because women have other ways of getting things as well. When a young lady moves from her parents house to her own apartment, the parents (or parent) often try to make sure that they "get her off on the right foot." They may give the daughter significant pieces of furniture from their house or they may just go out and buy the daughter a bedroom set or some other basic items "to make the place look decent". After the parents have done all that they can, the young lady may have a *house warming* party. Ten or more ladies may come over with blankets, pots, kitchenware, bathroom items or practical gifts that fit almost anywhere. This might happen once in the person's adult life or there may be two or more housewarmings if this lady transfers for example from one city to another. The bottom line is that women are given so much stuff from so many people, for so many real and made up reasons that it seems that a very significant number of women *live a material level of comfort that is beyond their personal capacity to provide for themselves.*

When a brother meets one of these sisters, he is impressed with her home. He, you understand is still looked at as a "provider". He sees in her house the material level of comfort to which she is accustomed. He has no idea that it has been provided by a dozen or more people over a ten year period. And she is not going to tell him either. The young lady is *not* going to say "my mother gave me this, my father gave me that, my old boyfriends gave me all of these things over here, etc". She is going to pretend that she is responsible for her comfort level, and unless you know better, you, the male , are going to assume it also. Many brothers then feel intimidated because as "the provider" they have to match this level of comfort in order to feel worthy or compatible or acceptable by such a woman.

But what has not been mentioned yet is that in addition to the *tangible* material things that she has in her house, there are even more, many more *experiences* which the lady has realized that she also didn't pay for. How many women at the Super Bowl, the Kentucky Derby, the M.C. Hammer Concert, The Opera, or the Broadway Shows paid their own way? How many women eat free two or three weekends a month at some of the best restaurants in town? What percentage of Black women with a boyfriend paid their own way to Barbados, Jamaica, Cancun or Hawaii? When brothers ask a sister what she likes to do she might say "Oh I like to travel, go to shows, the Opera, concerts, etc." Of course she does, anybody would if someone else is paying! Another favorite phrase of young ladies is "I like nice things". What that usually means is "if you are going to buy me something, make sure its quality". All of us like nice things, but Black people either can't afford them or buy them anyway when they know they can't afford them. And many times when this overspending occurs, it is a brother trying to impress a lady who already seems to have so much that it gets increasingly harder to get her "something special".

Let us now switch our attention to the Black male that is the other half of this couple. This male is between thirty and forty five years old. We will assume that he has at least one child by a previous relationship and perhaps in fifty percent of the cases was married to that child's mother. If we visit his "bachelor pad" we may very well not see the latest kitchen appliances, the pretty living room decorations, the furniture, the art work etc. If he had those things in a previous marriage, in many cases he left them to his ex-wife. This is to his credit *as a person* but *he is not given credit for it*. Instead he may be seen as a person "without the necessities of life". His girlfriends may have given him gifts in the past, but no impressive objects that will last for years. I dare say that most men on most holidays receive wallets, ties, underwear, sweaters, cologne, shavers, socks and handkerchiefs. Most of these things are inexpensive, wear out quickly and do not in any significant way add to a man's image of "having his house in order." Women buy cheap gifts because: a) they make less money; b) they do not want to feel that they are *buying* a man's affections: (but its o.k. for a man to feel that way); or c) they feel that sex is a fair exchange for what they received. Society doesn't expect women to purchase fair exchange gifts. Thus, when you walk into a man's house or apartment, chances are that whatever you see there, he bought himself. Women didn't contribute much, his father and mother did not give him or buy him furniture and he had no house warming parties to suck up other freebies. A brother's comparatively empty household makes him look like a shaky character. Where is he putting his money? You guessed it - on the women. His credit card statement shows tickets for shows (for two), airline tickets (for two), hotel room and meals (always for two) as well as dresses, shoes and household items which are not in his house. He is paying eighteen percent interest on overpriced items which he doesn't even possess. Somehow his home is expected to be a showplace with plenty of liquor and food in the fridge to look good for the ladies that are shopping for a husband. Most brothers can't hang with all this weight on their shoulders. And a significant number of brothers who can pull it off do so only because they sell drugs at least part time. Many women liking the complete male package they see, pretend that they don't know what's really going on, or go along with any lie the brother tells regarding his finanical success.

The point here is this. Women (probably all women which would include sisters) usually look better and live better than what they can support on their own income. They have a false image, looking more successful than what they really are. And rather than being grateful and humble for their gifts, they often flaunt it and use them for leverage to get more. Ironically they may be *enemies* now with the very men that furnished their house or wardrobe. The women are never called on this, their character is not presented for judgement. They are just part of this sea of "good women" out there trying to find a decent man.

Brothers on the other hand suffer from being on the opposite side of the financial transactions. If he saves his money and doesn't spend it lavishly on his women, then he will be accused of not loving them and being cheap. Once you have a rep for being cheap, it goes out over the U.P.I. and Associated Press news wires and every woman in town will know about you in short order. Each one will make you spend money on them if you ever get in a position to date them.

If on the other hand you do spend money on women, then your house will reflect that and you will be seen as a nondomesticated brother who "blows" all his money on women and who "doesn't have a pot to pee in". Brothers can't win unless they make a lot of money, the last thing that America allows them to do. So once again we find that the White man sets up a model of how he allegedly functions in his social relationships, and Black women accept it as the way that they would like their relationships to function also. The Black man is then put into a position where he is expected to function as the White man would function. (If the White man stopped buying roses for his woman and started bringing dandelions, what flowers would brothers be expected to bring to the sisters, roses or dandelions?) If the brother copies the White man, he loses (doesn't own a pot to pee in) and if he doesn't copy the White man, he also loses (I'm quitting that cheap bastard, he doesn't really love me). Black women often are confused by their mates who seem hostile and angry with them even when their love is rather obvious. If you do not understand why, reread this section again slowly, and thoroughly. Most Black men have trouble articulating their anger in a thorough, non- argumentative way. Trust me, this is part of the problem in Black male female relationships.

DEFINING MARRIAGEABLE

One of the most irritating concepts to the conscious Black man is the term "marriageable" Black men. The term suggests that a Black man must be "qualified", must be "eligible" "suitable" in order to marry a Black woman. The Black man not only has to pass the test of White people to get hired, he must then pass the test of Black women (and in all likelihood her parents as well) to be considered worthy of having a mate. The term as it is used here is mostly used in conjunction with *men,* suggesting that there are some men who are so bad, lost, poor or hopeless that they need to be seen as virtually non existent. This sounds exactly like the way White people see some Blacks. There are some "niggers" so hopeless that *they* don't exist in the minds of some Whites. When we see Black men (usually they are men) denied legal rights, not counted in the census, not part of the unemployment figures, not eligible for any kind of benefits or welfare, who die homeless as "John Does" and are buried in unmarked graves, these men basically didn't exist in the larger society. Black people, have protested such treatment and perceptions for decades. But then Black women come right behind White folks (their usual position) and insinuate, if not articulate outright, a similar view. If we go back to the infamous page 332 of *Waiting to Exhale* during the hen session where the characters are sounding off about what's wrong with Black men, we get a decent idea of what removes Black men off of the eligibility list: gay, ugly, stupid, imprisoned, unemployed, drug-addicted, short, liars, unreliable, dogs, shallow, wimps, old and set in their ways, etc.

Gay men obviously are not interested in marrying a woman, at least not for the usual reasons that men marry women. Women cannot be expected to want a romantic relationship with a gay man. White folks say gays number ten percent of *their* population which *might* give a rough idea of their percentage in our world. I can understand clearly women's frustration at seeing an appealing brother and then finding out that he is gay or bisexual, with or without the threat of AIDS. As far as men in prison, I'm not sure how Black women interpret this. Many Black prisoners are married already or are (were) with a lady at the time of their incarceration, so they were never in the pool of the available men. Many Black male prisoners are young, sixteen to twenty four and have no reason to think about marriage at those ages anyway. Some prisoners are gay or bisexual, and thus, have already been counted out, unless one wants to count them again so that the situation can seem worse than it is. That way Black men look worse and more sympathy is created for Black women, which is the way the pattern *usually* develops. Needless to say a very large number of drug users are already in jail, so they could be counted twice also.

Are Black women saying, "I would be interested in certain brothers, but I can't get to them because they are in prison", or are they saying "I would never consider marrying a brother if he is an ex-prisoner because being such takes him off my eligibility list"? Is there an assumption that if the White man put you in prison you must have done something wrong and therefore you are too risky to commit to? Are women saying that "ex-inmates" aren't capable of being rehabilitated or that they personally just don't want to take a chance on one themselves? Similar questions can be asked about all the labels that Black women (like Whites) have placed on Black men, from drug addicts to short, shallow, lying dogs (to use their labels and terminology). But all the questions really come back to the same central question. How come we never hear the term "marriageable Black women? ". Are all Blackwomen considered marriageable? Do all Black women deserve to "marry up," and therefore are "entitled" to brothers who have it more together than many of their sorry asses? Doesn't that idea sound exactly like us talking about White folks when we say "you have to be twice as good just to be considered equal (or in this case eligible)? What makes for an ineligible woman besides already being married? What if they are in prison, crack heads, gay, ugly, short, liars, shallow and set in their ways? If you can't be an unmarrriagible single Black woman, what prevents you from being so? And if you can be why don't we ever hear about them; why does it seem that only brothers bear the weight of hearing about one more thing that they are not? Is an unemployed woman poor wife material, in this era of dual career households, as an unemployed brother would be as a husband? If not, why not? I can think of nothing easier to do than to hold someone else to a higher standard than what you can attain or maintain yourself. Black women seem to be very good at this. Many don't have a pot to pee in and yet feel very self righteous in pointing out someone's else's employment status. Don't get me wrong, Black men do talk about women. We mention from time to time whose ugly, skinny, fat, can't cook, sexually inhibited or unsatisfying. And all Black men have experienced Black women's lies but they are seldom *called* lies. They're referred to as exaggerations, understatements, mistatements, over- simplifications, emotional responses, out of context responses, etc. Never lies. Brothers, you see are the only ones in the race actually *capable* of lies, or so we are led to believe. But most brothers do not get a charge out of talking badly about black women. We seldom have a "rooster session" comparable to our sisters' "hen sessions". We might very well get together and talk bad about the White man, because many of us get a charge out of that, but not about our women because we seldom really mistake them for "the enemy". And thus we have no real need to codify, classify, label or categorize them into those that are "qualified" and those that may as well not exist. To have terms like "marriageable" and "unmarriageable" accepted into popular culture, is a way of separating many potentially good brothers from the rest of the Black community. This reaction by brothers to this word might catch some sisters by surprise. But how would you know that we feel this way? Do you expect Oprah to cover it on her show or Sally or Geraldo, Phil or Maurry? Are you kidding? Is Ebony or Essence or Ebony Man likely to discuss the true issues that effect Black men in their relationships? No! To the media, whether you are marriageable or not, most Black men just don't exist. Until you kill. You might not believe this but thousands of brothers have killed just to prove to themselves and to others that they in fact *did* exist. But that's another story.

Getting back to the main story here, a major question has to be asked: Let us say that the basic substance of the Black woman's complaint is true, that a million potential husbands for Black women are not positioned to fulfill that role at the present time (are unmarriageable) because they have one or more significant problems that they have to overcome first. They have to stop stealing or drinking or doing drugs, etc. And they have to start working steady, earn money, support themselves, etc. The question is, do Black women have a responsibility or incentive to work on trying to make this happen or do they simply bitch and complain as if that was a cure for the situation? Do Black women do the right thing by sitting back and waiting for brothers to "get themselves together"? If a brother is strong enough to bring himself back from the brink of disaster during the most challenging period of his life, why in the Hell would he then need a "strong woman for support" when the hardest work was done without her? And if a woman does help a brother with problems, why does she say she "mothered" him instead of just saying she supported him? Why the need to kick a brother psychologically precisely at the time he is down, psychologically and otherwise? Who cares if Black men are lost and washed up, White people, Asians, Hispanics, Indians? Who stands to gain the most for every Black man that regains his balance and his sanity? Black women per chance? Is there a relationship or should there be a relationship between who stands to benefit the most and who should be expected to assume a share of the burden and responsibility? A frightening thing about Black women is how they can deny reality and blame the victim while at the same time claiming to be the ultimate victim. Cases in Point:

a)   Black women see enough of urban school systems to understand that they fail and some know how and why they fail. That is the reality. *But their typical response is to ask,* why don't the Black boys just study and learn? (supposedly like everybody else)?

b)   Black women know that many White police are racist and kill Black men in cold blood. That is the reality. *But their typical response on hearing about a police shooting* is to assume that a brother did something wrong because "the police wouldn't have shot him for no reason at all."

c)   Black Women understand and know about the changing economy, the job cut backs, the exporting of jobs, and the mechanization and computerization of the work place. *But their typical response is to ask:* How come the brothers don't have jobs?

d)   Black women know that prison does not rehabilitate or care about it's prisoners. It does *not* prepare them for life outside. *But their typical response is to ask:* How come brothers always end up back in jail?

e)   Black women know that there are not nearly enough treatment centers for addicts. They *know* that waiting lists are months, even years long. *But their typical response is:* When are you going to stop taking drugs?

After a while some Black men give up trying to explain or communicate with the women in their lives because the same stupid ass question that they ask *before understanding reality* is the same stupid-ass question they ask after they *deny the reality* that has been presented to them. Then they have the nerve to set themselves up as the ultimate victim (for being both Black and female), complain about "society" always blaming the victim (who they think they ultimately represent) while they do a better job than "society" ever could blaming America's ultimate victim, the Black man, for most of their problems! Many people, from Haki, Pearl Cleage (Mad at Miles) and others, say that it is pointless to try to say who White society has hurt the most, the Black man or the Black woman. Ordinarily I would agree. Black men certainly didn't delve into that kind of discussion in the sixties, we were too busy fighting and proving to people who and what we were with our actions. But in the last fifteen years or so we have come under attack by, amongst other people, our own women. So what was pointless before now has a point, mainly to show our sisters the historical blows and deaths Black men have endured to benefit *all of us* (and not just our gender) and to show once again, who the *real* enemy is. Black men are forced to come to our own defense to fight charges that were unexpected from a source that was unexpected, our women. We have to remind that source who has taken the greatest blows, *as measured in deaths*, for the race. If Black women are unwilling to assist the brothers that have problems to get back on track (not suggesting that *all* can be or even want to be saved), then they should shut up and accept the problems that they deserve. Sisters, should accept the fact that many, many brothers did not bring all of their problems on themselves. If the Black man faces disdain from the White, Hispanic and Asian societies, and his own woman talks about him like a dog and he *still* manages to be economically self-sufficient in America, he isn't just marriageable, he is a damn superman.

Pre-Marital Sex - Marital Sex

There are literally thousands of books on the market on the topic of sex. For the most part, Black men and women have neither read nor reflected on sex books written by White folks, and neither have they written very many of their own. Enter any major Black bookstore in the nation and you will find hardly a single substantive volume on sex written by a Black author (Dr. Rosie Mulligan being the great exception.) Thus, one wonders how much mis-information or outdated information Blacks have absorbed on sex. In spite of a three hundred year old reputation of being sexually superior, we seem to suffer just as much, if not more, than all the other races from sexual problems, diseases and myths. It is far beyond the scope of this text to even scratch the surface on any significant sex problem or issue. On the other hand, however, to discuss relationships for over two hundred pages and never mention sex is unrealistic. Therefore, a brief mention must be made to express some Black men's feelings about a couple of sexual matters.

The first question that many men have never had satisfactorily answered is why sex is not considered a fair exchange. Many men growing up in the fifties and sixties thought: a) girls did not like sex: b) girls feared sex; or, c) girls were "giving" you the ultimate gift if they consented to having sex. Old social practices, birth control concerns, religious conservatism, sexism and a number of other factors helped to prop up these ideas. But in the late sixties, seventies and pre-Aids scare eighties, most of these ideas were discarded. Men learned that women liked sex, especially if the right techniques and sensitivity were used to assure that she reached the same climatic heights that men take for granted.   Yet women, inspite of the mutually shared pleasure while participating in "the act", still maintain a certain attitude. The attitude is that they *give* a lot more than the man, or they *deserve* a lot more for simply having made an equal contribution - their body. Yet these same women would very likely complain to their close girlfriends about how horny they were and how they needed some sex if a great deal of time had passed since their last sexual experience. So the question arises, if a woman needs sex from time to time (even if it is less frequently than most males), why is she at the same time assuming that she is *entitled* to something more or extra when it is her need, as well as the man's, being met by the act? I think men in general and Black men specifically are baffled by this. And their confusion seems to be based on the fact that they can't get a truthful answer that is not also contradictory. If a man expects sex without spending any money on the woman, her attitude may very well be "I'm not an easy lay, I'm not a Whore." This surprises some men because they were thinking that emotional feeling and attraction were the key motivating factors pushing people to go to bed. If on the other hand a brother spends money on the lady and expects to have sex, then her attitude is "Look, I'm not a prostitute, I'm not jumping into bed no matter how much money you spend on me." When we finally see the type of brother who is very successful in taking women to bed, we see it's a brother who has a polished act. He buys the roses, opens all the doors, goes through all the *European etiquette*, speaks in soft melodictones, and reveals little of his genuine feelings about living as a Black man in America.   This Don Juan type has sex consistently. I could accept that except for one major contradiction. His sex partners may be the same sisters who consistently say "I can't stand men who are always playing games". Don Juan's whole approach is a game, and women love it enough not only to go to bed with him but tell half her girlfriends about it the next day. And many women will *especialtly* enjoy telling girlfriends *how Don Juan seduced them*. Later on, they will tell Don Juan how they hate men who play games when he begins to reveal his true self to them. Black women I think, have no idea how contradictory and confused they sound. And I think a major reason why brothers do not listen to women more than they do is that they are *scared as hell* that if they did, that they would end up thinking and talking just as confused and contradictory as the women they are trying to follow. And they don't need that, they really don't. Black men are confused about a lot things, a lot of *important* things. And they are denied a lot of things. But sex is not one of the things that they are confused about. They know what they want and when they want it. The last thing they want to add to their list of problems is confusion over and denial of sex, and they know that if they follow most sisters' advice and conversation to the letter, that is exactly where they'll end up. So there's a problem here .

The other point that I think is worth mentioning about sex is the relationship between early sex and sex in later years.   It is absolutely fascinating to listen to talk shows and hear a woman complain about her man's preoccupation with sex during their dating. Because as sure as day follows night this same woman may very well complain later about her (now) husband's extreme lack of interest in sex during their late thirties, forties and beyond.   This difference in sexual interest has been explained in terms of hormones and differences in sexual peaks etc. I'm sure that these ideas are valid, but I'd like to add an idea I'll call "sexual memory". The best way to understand sexual memory is to understand the idea behind riding a bicycle. Once a person learns how to ride a bicycle, they normally don't forget. A person may not ride a bike for ten or fifteen years., but eventually when they do get back on a bike, even if they are out of shape, forty pounds heavier and have other problems, they will eventually be able to pedal down the street in no time. This is because their muscles and nervous system has a "memory". They remember how to respond to actions and motions previously learned years ago. I personally believe that a similar thing, though not to as great a degree, can be said about sex. It is important for a man to have a lot of good sex with his wife in the early years of the relationship. It is important for her to go all out to both enjoy herself and him in the early years, rather than simply service him or wait for her so-called years of sexual maturity. Because if he doesn't have a deeply rich "memory" of both having pleased her and himself, it may cause problems in later years. In the later years, when some women finally allow themselves to really enjoy sex, the man is often sexually bored and unstimulated. If he can not draw mentally on those times when the sex was incredible, both physically and egotistically (in terms of him satisfying the woman), then he has no "memory" to use to make today's sex satisfactory. You can not draw on something that never was, any more than you can withdraw from a bank at which you've made no deposits. So if a woman wants to reach a climax at forty five and fifty, she'd better make sure she regularly does so when she is half that age and not wait for her so called maturity. This is not hardly medical or scientific advice, but if it works for other physical activities, why wouldn't it work for sex also?

As important as it is for the man to have a "sexual memory" for future sexual satisfaction, I would strongly, *very strongly* recommend that women *not* fake orgasms, which according to many studies is a very common practice. Faked orgasms is another in a long series of mixed messages that women give men. Women have no idea how many times they send out these confusing messages. This is not to say that men don't also send out mixed messages, but I think women win this contest hands down. "I like this dress, I don't like this dress; I have a closet full of clothes yet *nothing* to wear, I don't want sex, but I love sex, etc," Most men ignore a great deal of what women say when it is clear that they don't know what the hell they are saying. But when women catch men disregarding their words, they are very quick to charge men with being insensitive. They never focus on their own contradictory messages as the cause of that insensitivity. If it works this way with words, obviously it's even more confusing and disturbing on the higher level of communication, the sexual plane. A faked orgasm tells a man that he has satisfied a woman. For him to hear that he is insensitive to her needs (sexually) in a *later* conversation is very confusing. Because men virtually never fake orgasms, it is hard for them to remember that other people (women) do. And women seldom admit to faking an orgasm to the man that she has faked it to. So a brother has to hear how unsatisfactory he is to a woman he thought he satisfied. The normal male response is to tune the conversation out, because he has no real evidence if what he is hearing at that moment is the truth either. He believes that her actions of ecstasy in the bed are more honest than her rational arguments. And every time she fakes an orgasm she gives him more reason to discount her words, especially since he *wants* to believe that he is pleasing her. In these cases the charge of insensitivity squarely belongs on the shoulders of the *woman*. She is being insensitive to a brothers honest attempt to satisfy her sexually (by doing what ever he knows to do) and she is being being insensitive by her own lying (which is what a faked orgasm is) and her contradictory communications. Don't fake the funk. Be honest until he and/or she gets it right. Otherwise, the frustrations of today due to faking will lead to bigger disasters in the future.

Dating Mothers

Have you ever seen a feature story in a national magazine, Black or White, about the thousands of Black men who adopt Black children every year? Of course not. Perhaps you don't believe it's true. But think about it for a minute. Millions of Black children have mothers but no fathers present in the household. Each year many of these mothers get married or establish long term relationships. Is this possible without the man agreeing, formally or informally, to adopt these children and care for them to some degree? Probably not in most cases, unless those children are nearly grown and about to leave anyway. The truth is that Black men, as in so many situations, are not credited with the massive amount of "step fathering" they do. There are at least three reasons why this should be treated as some kind of a big deal. First, step- fathering is expensive. It's one thing to take a lady out and spend money on her, it's another to take her and her children out for an event that is not only more costly (have you seen children order food when they know mama doesn't have to pay for it?) but often does not lend itself to ending in a romantic interlude! This is real caring and sharing which Black men are not seen as capable of providing. Second, the Black male ego is supposed to prevent Black men from feeling for or supporting "another man's kids" according to our detractors. If a man will not care for his own children, why in hell is it reasonable to expect them to care for another's, the logic goes. Well it might sound logical but grateful mothers all over the country will testify that their experience with some Black men defy logic. The third reason that Black men's support of "step children" should be made known is to counter in some small way all the negative press about the Black man's irresponsibility towards the Black family. As a matter of fact if you think about the few times you actually *do* hear about Black step fathers, it too is almost always in a negative light. First of all, he is more likely referred to as a "live in lover" or "common law husband." What sounds better , those two terms or the concept of an adoptive father? Then the media goes on to say that the brother molested the daughter, killed the baby, beat the baby, etc. It is not the point here to deny that these things happen and unfortunately happen too frequently. But with all the frequency that it does happen, will anyone say that it happens most of the time? Of course not! In the majority of cases, thousands of Black men decide that a part of the reconstruction of their own life requires that they care for children who are not their own. And the cost some men have been willing to pay is in some cases higher than what some women can imagine. Because many of these stepdads have children that they lost custody of in a previous relationship. And some of these biological children grow very angry with their fathers and very jealous that he is showering attention, money and time on children that are not his own, while they go lacking in some or all of those things. How would women handle a situation where their love for someone else's children was causing a serious break between herself and her own children? Could she handle that? Would that draw her closer to her new man or would that be the basis of many an argument? This is what many Black men have to deal with every day all over the country. And sometimes even after two, five or even ten years, the tension, jealousy and anger of his own children, is still there. One answer to the problem is, of course, don't make babies. But an incredible number of young ghetto sisters have this attitude of "I need someone who will love me always and who I can always love," and they are determined to get pregnant. You know and I know that there would be many, many less babies in the Black community if Black women simply didn't want them. That is common sense.

The other answer to some of these issues is of course for the father and step-father to earn more money. Money to provide for *all* the children involved has it's obvious benefits, but also certain drawbacks. It takes time to make money, most people get paid by the hour, directly or indirectly. So even if a Brother was willing and able to work long enough to pay for everything that everybody needed, he would have to deal with *their* complaints that: a) they never see him: b) they don't get to spend much time with him: or, c) he's always asleep. If brothers make a conscious effort *not* to date sisters with children, they will find that they have very severely cut out a large portion of single Black women, women with many excellent qualities, from their pool of potential mates. This would be especially true if the brothers in question were themselves on the lower economic levels, because many of the "educated," career-oriented sisters would not likely find them of much interest. Thus, there is no other option for sexually healthy Black men but to earn *more money*. They either have to make more money to "qualify" for those higher income single women or to pay some of the added expenses (even if it's just baby sitting money) associated with single mothers. There are Black women of course, who are neither financially solid career women nor mothers, and are in the pool of available women. But it's very likely that a higher percentage than normal of these women have characteristics (obesity, mental problems, physical unattractiveness, confirmed virgins, religious extremists, etc.) that a normal sexually active Black male might find unappealing.

Are there any advantages to dating single mothers? Yes, there can be one major advantage in dating such a woman if she has her head screwed on right. Single mothers seem to often develop two different mindsets that are miles apart and can spell heaven or hell for the brothers who deal with them. The key thing is for brothers to first recognize how hard it is to *be* a single mother, especially if there is more than one child. Even with all the agencies and laws set up "to protect the women and children," you can bet that most of these women are still struggling in most aspects of their lives, especially financially. When people, not just women, have a long history of financial pressure, they usually go in one of two directions. Either they become users and manipulate people, agencies, programs and situations and suck as much money and blood as the situation will allow *or* they become very appreciative people who learn that people will usually help you if you just show appreciation for things that come your way.

There are many sisters who are convinced that they will never find a man to trust and love and live with for the rest of their life. But they also understand that men are the key to getting money. So the men that come into this kind of person's life are squeezed like oranges, and when they have no more juice, they are dropped into life's trash pile. This type of woman does not see herself as "blowing" a good thing, because she is already convinced that it will not happen for her. She cannot conceive of herself as having lost something if there is no longer the idea that it is attainable. Her agenda is to merely identify the next man (victim) that is to help her enjoy life's pleasures for as long as that situation lasts. This type of sister sees to it that her predictions about men come true by her attitude and behavior towards them. This type of sister is sometimes killed by an old or current boyfriend, but you will never read her personality profile in the newspaper article. She's assumed to be an innocent victim rather than a vampire that contributed to her own demise.

The other type of single mother is the kind that men dream about. Actually men don't actually dream about single mothers, they dream about women who will appreciate them, even if what they are able to do falls short of televisions' version of White life. These single mothers appreciate favors more *because* they are single mothers. As single mothers they have an understanding of how you make a dollar stretch, how you think of somebody else (in her case her children) first before you think of yourself. Single mothers work harder than most single women, and they understand that the world doesn't owe them or their child a thing if they don't work for it. This type of sister may have had one or more bad relationships but she still holds out hope that a good brother is out there for her even if he isn't the fantasy figure she was raised to look for. When a good brother comes into her life, she doesn't act like he owes her or that she is entitled to use him to catch up on all the things that other women have been getting. On the contrary, she is thankful for the opportunity to do something *for* and to relate to another person in an emotional way. Not surprisingly, this is often the woman who gets a man willing to "leap tall buildings in a single bound." Brothers will, as Dennis Kimbro (author of Think *and Grow Rich - A Black Choice*) said about his wife, crawl through broken glass, simply because the woman is appreciative of what he does or is trying to do. Many of these sisters would not or could not have been so nice and appreciative if they had met this same man in an earlier period of their life. But after dealing with real life issues, taking on the responsibility of caring for another person, and looking for someone to appreciate what that entails, she is now experienced enough to show appreciation towards somone who is trying to do the same for her. The experience of single motherhood then is like a university education for some women in that it teaches them three important lessons: 1) you can do bad by yourself: 2) the world does not owe you anything ; and, 3) when someone does something for you, be thankful. Most brothers would like for women to already know these things simply by growing up, but many brothers take a better-late-than-never attitude and are thankful when they meet this type of woman ,whether she has children or not.

MONEY, STATUS, AND WHITE WOMEN

This writer is in conflict over the topic of Black men and White women and how it should fit, or even *if* it should fit, into this discussion. There are several reasons for this conflict. First, I am strongly against Black men marrying White women. This is an expression of my personal choice and values. So I question my ability to be objective about the matter. Secondly, the topic has so many aspects that it could easily be a separate book by itself.

On the other hand, I questioned how realistic was it to talk about relationships between brothers and sisters and not mention White women? And since this book's focus is on money issues, how could I avoid the problem that some Black women have with financially successful Black men being the main ones to run out and get a White woman? So like it or not, there must be something said about White women and how they impact on our relationships.

There was also a degree of concern I had about *really learning* why brothers go after White women. I felt real comfortable and politically correct in my position against White women. But what if my judgments about them would be affected by my research and new understanding? Would I begin to back up on my own position against them? Could I at least intellectually, start to see the validity of this preference? And if a crack developed in my own views, how far would it go? Would I be converted to the point of saying, "Well, its ok for brothers to be with whoever they love", knowing full well what *that* meant? The bottom line is that the issue of White women has to be somewhat addressed if this book is to meet its mission of expressing how a significant number of Black men feel about various aspects of male female relationships.

In articles about White female-Black male unions, a list of a half dozen or so reasons are usually given as to why such unions develop. One reason the White woman is on the scene is because she believes the notion that, on average, the Black male is sexually superior to the White male. And since she may be one of the many millions of White women who are not sexually fulfilled, this may be a major reason why she positions herself to pursue or be pursued by Black males.

On the other hand, money, status and success are universal attractions to females. Some White women who normally would not give a second thought to a Black male, particularly given their white racist conditioning about Black males, might change their tune when they see one who is successful. Thus, famous and rich athletes, musicians, and entertainers attract White women for all the old "forbidden fruit" reasons, as well as for the financial success and social approval that these select Black males have achieved. But brothers are not available merely for the asking; all have some degree of standards and/or restraint that would keep them from jumping on anything available. The main question might well be, what are the factors which keep a brother in a relationship with a White woman over an extended period of time?

We will omit detailed discussion of the standard reasons commonly found in the magazine articles and books on the subject. These would include some variations of the following:

1. The Black man worships and pursues the White woman because she is the forbidden fruit that he expects or imagines to be the sweetest of all.
2. The Black man pursues the White woman to seek revenge against the White man and desecrate his idol.
3. The Black man wants a trophy of success, and a White woman on your arm is a universally accepted trophy.
4. She's got a Black soul. Some White women have absorbed enough Black culture to enable them to come off as "Black" as many sisters. Tina Marie and a few other White female singers (Lisa Stansfield etc.) might come to mind.
5. Love is Blind: When you fall in love you don't see color and race (yeah, right!)
6. Sisters Did Me Wrong: A brother might be able to chronicle a series of negative experiences with sisters which hurt too much, lasted too long, or proved too costly for him to risk yet another attempt at a relationship with a sister.
7. Sex is Sex: Some brothers simply see all females as sex objects born to be pursued and to give pleasure to males, period. White ones included.

It is not that these reasons are invalid, but simply that they have been discussed in other places, and it serves no purpose to rehash them here. Also, these explanations have no direct relationship to money issues. Thus what we are going to cover here are ideas which do deal with money or shed light on the Black male's emotional perspective.

A. Pursued Instead Of Pursuing; Sacrificing Instead Of Collecting

It will be explained in a later chapter that most brothers who do not live in the Southern part of the US have trouble even getting eye contact or a hello from sisters. There are many reasons or explanations that I'm sure sisters would give to educate us as to why this is the case. And, of course, many sisters would probably just outright lie and say that they always speak to brothers when they are spoken to (Yeah, right!). There are various means that brothers use to adapt to the repeated rejection that a Black male is likely to receive. One method is to make "hitting on" women a game. They take the seriousness out of their approach and their attitude. To keep the seriousness in only makes the rejections hurt more. When made a game, one can at least act like it doesn't make a difference if a sister speaks or not. Socializing is less traumatic. The problem of course with this approach is that the women pick up on the semi-insincerity in the attitude and they don't take brothers seriously. Many feel even more righteous in ignoring Black men who greet them.

Some brothers don't speak to sisters at all unless they receive specific cues from the sister that its ok, or unless he is formally introduced to her. This way both his expectations and disappointments are kept at a minimum. And of course certain brothers are so bitter about repeated rejection, they decide that non speaking sisters will be the butt of some of their raw humorous jokes. You've seen them on the street corner where four or more guys are standing around. When the sister passes they speak. If the sister doesn't respond, she will hear things said about her that usually makes her wish she had.

A White girl who has decided that she wants to "check out" brothers realizes, regardless of how naive she might be, that in the normal course of events, Black men will probably not approach her or speak to her. Thus if she wants a brother she has to let him know in a much more obvious way that she is open to meeting him. Sometimes the only way to do this is to aggressively approach him. Other times if they are in a setting where mixed couples are very common, she may simply give the cues and eye contact that says she is available or interested.

For many Black men this is like ice cold water in a searing hot desert. It is not necessarily the girls whiteness that he is reacting to as much as the idea that somebody has voluntarily made an open move toward *him* for a change. Rather than being ignored for the umpteenth time, he is being recognized by a stranger. A real stranger, a White girl! The curiosity level, the ego and self image are all being stimulated now in this brother because he's asking himself, why me? White women have options, and pretty White women have even more options. Attractive and intelligent White women have many options. And White women who are attractive, intelligent and have money have, to the Black man, unlimited options. Why then would a person with so broad an array of options pick them out as a preferred choice of someone she would like to know. This sparks genuine curiosity.

The Black man's self image is pretty beat up based on how society in general responds to him and how many (maybe even most) Black women respond to him. Many feel like a Reject (with a capital R)! Along comes a person who appears to have a wider array of options to choose from than the Black women he's used to being around, (a white girl) and he discovers that he appeals to her. He is the preferred choice from a larger pool of choices. He is not only being affirmed, he is conquering new territory. Its like pulling up to your high school reunion in a Rolls Royce after having been voted least likely to succeed. His beaten ego now says, I must be of some value because I am valued by a person who I know to be of recognized value to the society at large a White girl. And to top it all off, I didn't have to work for it or place myself in a vulnerable position to get her attention because *she chose me.* Of course these types of relationships are usually of short duration and don't necessarily lead to anything really substantive. But to most brothers that is not the point. The point was that this selection by a White girl was the tonic he needed to understand that he wasn't a reject. And he understands that he's not a reject based not merely on the girls whiteness itself so much as that whiteness is her passport to a variety of choices and of that broad variety he was selected. That's enough proof for him that he must be somebody (even if its only for a short period.)

One of the main reasons that Black women can't understand how White women affirm the Black man's ego is because they usually don't understand (or don't care) how low the Black man's self image often is. Secondly, in her drive to find a "good" Black man, a "marriageable" Black man, she has no idea of her role in bringing his self esteem down to the point that it is. She has stepped on or stepped over many brothers in pursuit of her prince charming. Note this quote by the renown jazz singer Abbey Lincoln taken from an anthology edited by Toni Cade called T*he Black Woman* (Signet, New American Library 1970 N.Y.)

"When a White man "likes colored **girls**," his woman (the White woman) is the last one he wants to know about it. Yet seemingly, when a Negro "likes White **girls**," his woman (the Black woman) is the first he wants to know about it."

This is an interesting statement. I would say this to Ms. Lincoln. The White man is secretive to his woman because he does not want her to know that he believes in the sexual superiority of Black women. At the time this was written (1966) there *was* a definite social stigma against sleeping with Black women. If his attraction to Black women became well known, it would have limited his options and choices when it came time for marriage, something he would not very likely do with a Black woman.

In the case of the Brother, he is parading his White woman around for one of two reasons. Either he thinks she is a trophy and he wants others to see his trophy; *or,* more than likely, he is saying to everyone *"I am not a reject."* "Someone has accepted me who had more options and choices than you. I do not accept the status that you thought I deserved and here is my proof that I am not what you thought I was, a reject." That's what I would tell Ms. Lincoln.

The other side of the coin is even *more impressive* to a "Black reject". When a Black woman "allows" a man to pursue her and finally agrees to be his woman, she expects to collect. She collects status, gifts, trips, favors, money, anything of value. That may well be precisely *why she is* in *the relationship* in the first place. When this is the case, men don't feel they are loved for who they are but for what they have. You have all heard superstars in sports, music or the movies say "Yes I meet a lot of attractive young ladies who appear to like me. But do they like me or my money?" No one, regardless of how much money they have, likes to feel used.

A White girl in an interracial relationship however, is likely *to lose* the most important things in her life; her family and her friends. If you saw the movie *Jungle Fever*, you saw the scene of the White girl being beat to hell by her father and ridiculed by her friends. This is the price that many White girls are willing to pay to stay connected with the Black guy she loves. Many White girls are treated as dead people, written out of wills, and unwelcomed at family gatherings. Many of these White girls have babies by brothers and send baby pictures to the White grandparents. Sometimes these letters are either returned unopened or the pictures are returned in torn pieces. Thus, some Black men feel that their White woman loves them as no Black woman *could* because no Black woman would take such treatment from her family to stay with him.

SUCCESS BREEDS REJECTION?

Why is it that it is the *successful* Black man who often has the White Woman on his arm? The financially successful brother knows down to the core of his bones that Black people put down and doubt their own people when they are trying to succeed in a very competitive, unusual or risky enterprise. But if they succeed and make it, no people on earth will jump on the band wagon quicker. Some Blacks may claim to be a cousin, an old neighbor, an ex-classmate, etc. Why should a successful brother be surprised or impressed when sisters who previously wouldn't give him eye contact, much less the time of day, would be at his door once he's successful. These women have everything to gain and not a damn thing to lose. How is he to measure their sincerity, faithfulness, and other wifely qualities? How do you know she is not just a first class gold digger? You can not measure it by what she is willing to give up to get and keep you.

But with the White woman there is a difference. You learn that this union is causing her pain within her family. She may not be being beaten as in *Jungle Fever*, but perhaps she is being rejected and ostracized by her family, and its driving a stake in her heart. The Black man is certainly not requiring that she go through this. In fact, he is normally angered and saddened by it all. But, when he looks up, the woman is still there. Yes, this White girl may want the same diamonds, furs and exclusive lifestyle that the sisters want, but she is willing to pay a heavier price for them. Similarly, if a Black man is financially successful, he has had to work hard, and has also paid a price and sacrificed for what he's got. Once you have fought for what you have gotten, you respect other people who are willing to fight also. The successful Black man develops feelings for the White woman that bond them together because she is paying a price to have him. This brings on feelings of admiration, respect and pride. And these feelings have a cyclical nature, such that the pride he begins to feel for this White woman, makes the Black man feel prouder of himself based on the fact that someone thinks he is worth giving up so much for.

It is one thing to have a union based on romantic love. That's nice. But romance has a tendency to get beaten down by real world situations and it often dies quickly. But when a relationship possesses not only love but admiration, pride, and respect that is mutual and reinforcing, that relationship is at a higher level than what most of us experience. When *both parties pay heavy dues* and share a sense of struggle to make a relationship work, that makes for a stronger union.

When a brother has this type of relationship with one type of woman (it could also apply to Asian women or others) and he compares it with what he usually experiences from a sister, he sees definite differences. With a sister he sees not only someone who has all to gain and nothing to lose, but someone who would probably have a serious problem sacrificing much of *anything* to get him. In her mind the love game is about gaining , advancing, improving, or prospering, *not* giving, sacrificing and experiencing pain. And what some Black men use to determine who they will commit to is not who *he* loves the most, but who has demonstrated, a willingness to go through the most changes to show their love for *him*. In many cases a White and Black woman can love a brother equally. But because the White woman appears to have more at risk by just being in the relationship, this is interpreted by some brothers as her having done the most for him. Thus, he feels more impressed with the White woman because it fills both his romantic and *ego* needs. Many a sister has been heard to ask "Is he still with that White girl?" Yes, is the answer that frequently comes back. "Damn, I swear I don't know what in the hell he sees in her" is the common reply. And she is absolutely right. She *can't* see what he sees in her as long as she (the Black woman) insists on only seeing our world (the Black world) through her own eyes. If Black women are such good communicators and so sensitive and Black men are such bad communicators and so insensitive, how come Black women are no better at seeing the Black man's perspective than we are at seeing theirs? Sometimes White women make more of an effort to understand the Black man's point of view because *they know* that they don't know much about Black people and thus *have to* make the effort to understand if the relationship is to have any chance. On the other hand, most Black women feel they *already know* Black men and thus clearly make *limited* efforts to try to add new insight to what they *think* they already know about them. And what brothers appreciate much of the time is how much *effort* women put into trying to understand them. Thus a sister can know more about a brother than the White girl but the brother is turned on more by the White girl's effort, interest and sincerity to try to understand him. Got it? Sisters could better compete in some instances with White girls if they just made more of an effort to understand our world the way we see it (Black males) rather than assume that because we're from the same neighborhood we *automatically* see or should see things alike.

In truth, the overwhelming majority of Black male- White female unions don't reach the romantic "us against the world" stage previously mentioned. It appears that in most cases these relationships are the "jungle fever" attacks that Spike Lee illustrated in his movie. Most do not go as far as the father beating the daughter, or the wife putting the husband out of the house. Sex is so absolutely about psychological satisfaction based on intense curiosity that once these curiosities are satisfied, a great deal of the passion is gone. I think that can be said about any relationship, even those within the race.

No Pressure for Commitment

This brings us to the third reason for interracial relationships: *no pressure for commitment.* In many, probably most instances, neither the Black man nor the White woman has any real interest or expectation of marriage in the future of their relationship. They play their relationship a day, a week or a month at a time. Most of them have the intention of returning to their own race when it is time for serious commitments. Thus, the relationship that makes Black women so angry (noncommitment) is a relationship that many White women want, because it *is* a non-committed relationship. Does this make Black men dogs? No, it just means that Black women have to get it through their wigs and weaves that many men have carved out a period of time in their life where they have decided that they want maximum freedom over their decisions regarding their money, time and their women. Period. The fact that this decision is made precisely at the time when his body and his mind are physically and psychologically geared for maximum sexual activity seems to make this decision all the more practical and sensible. But because it is a decision that inconveniences women who are ready to play serious house, men are labeled immature at best, dogs at worse. When should men get married? When the first woman in his life wants him to or when *he* wants to? If the marriage doesn't work out, will a judge accept a "I was pushed or rushed into it" as a defense from the male? I don't think so.

In February of 1993, the poet Nikki Giovanni appeared in a nationally broadcast video conference with several other Black writers. During that program she made a profoundly simple statement which shocked me, in that in all my years of "studying Blackness," I don't ever recall hearing it before. What she basically said was that for all the hundreds of years that White men have been raping or having sex with Black women, we (Black people) never wondered if he was *less* "White" for doing so. The White man, whether slave master, manufacturer, Army leader, entertainer or politician always put forth the White agenda, worked for White power, made White money and developed White culture. And no matter who he slept with, he never missed a beat in carrying out his purposes. The obvious question raised here is whether a Black man is less "Black" if he sleeps White. This controversy goes all the way back to 1884 when Frederick Douglas, our number one Black leader at the time, took a White woman as his second wife. How many Black people even know this today? How many care? How many think Frederick Douglas is less "Black" for doing so? Does what applies to Frederick Douglas also apply to Joe Schmo of the ghetto? If not, why not? If you don't marry a White woman but you marry a non African American woman as was the case with Redd Foxx or Thurgood Marshall whose later wives were Asian, does that wash? If not, why not? The opinions in the Black community are divided but as time goes on Blacks become more tolerant of "multi-cultural" unions.

Symbolism vs Substance

One interesting perspective is the one that compares Black symbolism with Black substance. If Blackness is as it seemed in the 1960's, mostly about symbolism (natural hair, African clothes, African names, the raised Black fist, gun-ownership [supposedly for "Whitey"], the declaration of our women as African Queens) etc., then, yes, being married or connected to a White person sexually kills the whole meaning *of the symbolism*, of Blackness and is therefore a definite No No. The problem with this interpretation, of course, is that it strips Blackness of any true meaning, function, essence or guts. Blackness is seen as a kind of fad, a huge display or show that runs about five years or so (1966-1971) until the long "celebration" is over and things go back to normal.

The other view is that if Blackness is much more than symbolism, if it is about building Black-owned companies for Black jobs that support Black families and financially support Black politicians who put forth a Black agenda, etc., then who a Black person sleeps with makes no difference and is of little importance. Would we love Quincy Jones' incredible musical contribution more if he had a least one Black wife instead of the string of five White ones he has had?

Symbolism versus substance is an approach that we can use in most Black issue discussions. The trouble is that between our peoples hunger for at least "symbols or signs of progress" and the media's daily manipulation of our story, most of us can't tell the difference between the symbolic and the real anyway. And so, many Black people, who doubt our capacity to develop substance (after we define specifically what that is) frantically hold on to the mere symbols of Black progress for fear of losing everything. Each generation seems to hold on to the symbols of Blackness while hoping for and putting the responsibility on the next generation to come up with the *substance* of the Black agenda.

Money's Role

With regard to money and White women, there seems to be several streams of thought. The first is that many White women who are with Black men have already been exposed to money and they consider it over rated. They have seen how the quest for money tears apart marriages, families and communities, and they are not impressed with the idea of the continued competitive quest for money, as a part of their lifestyle. Therefore, when these women meet a brother, money may be one of the furthest things from her mind. She is being introduced to and is impressed with all the things that Black women know all about and take for granted: the way brothers talk, dance, dress, smell, screw, think, play, create etc. How can one expect a sister to be overly impressed with something that she has been around all her life? But on the other hand, how can a person not understand how a man who is used to being every bodies enemy or suspect, is now being appreciated for how he *is* as opposed to how much he's *got*?

The second stream of thought is that there are White women with money who simply look to see how that money can get them what they want. And if what they want is the Black sexual social experience, then so be it. These kinds of White women have no intention of giving up all aspects of the material lifestyle that they lead. They understand, however, that it is unrealistic to expect many Black men to fit in on the basis of their own income, thus, the women use their own money to assist brothers in making the transition. In a sense, the brother is "marrying up" in this situation. Actually marriage is often not the true situation, perhaps shacking "up" is more appropriate. White women understand that many White males are stars in the boardroom and misfits in the bedroom, so they reach a point where satisfying their sexual cravings and curiosities become priorities. Certain brothers are all too ready to accept what they see as the best of all worlds: the American dream (money and the White woman) and acceptance of who they are. Their sense of status, options and self confidence are at levels few Black men ever experience. Can Black women understand this? But only a fraction of Black men " get paid" to be the White woman's lover, especially on a long term basis. It has already been stated that it is the "successful" brothers who seem to have the White girls. But we often don't know who's paying who to do what? Sometimes a brother appears successful when in fact it is his White wife or girlfriend who has paid for everything. Is that ok? If not, why not?

Understanding the Price of Success

Up to this point, the "successful Black man with White woman syndrome", has still not been fully explained. It's been saved for last. It is the most difficult for some to understand, but understanding it is an important part of the healing that must occur if Black male-female relationships are to have a future in our middle and upper middle classes. It might appear elementary or patronizing, but the situation must be explained step by step. Please bear with me.

On page nine of her book *Manhandled* (Winston Derek publisher 1992 Nashville, Tennessee) Victoria King makes the following observation:

> "Sometimes I wished I were a boy so that I could escape
> the fence. As a boy, I would not have to endure the
> agony of having my hair straightened with a hot comb to
> make myself presentable and could help my father cut
> the grass on Saturdays instead of the daily grind of
> sweeping, dusting, and washing dishes.   On the
> occasions when my father would cut grass for white
> people in neighborhoods I had never seen, I would beg

to go. Sometimes daddy would take my brothers, but never me. My "place" was in the house where the world was safe from my inquisitive and prying eyes. Adventures were not for black girls unless they read them in books. And so I retreated to books and worlds in which I was free. I have always suspected that the disparate treatment in childhood is part of the reason girls generally make better students than boys. *Boys are allowed to learn from experience, girls are forced to learn from books.*" (Emphasis mine)

For now, keep the above passage in the back of your mind. We have explained in several places in this book why Black females usually do better and believe more in formalized education than Black males. I believe that because so much credit, trust and emphasis have been given to education and college degrees that many Black women have a very false sense of confidence based on having earned these degrees. It is not that Black women do not get jobs and earn good incomes as a result of their educational credentials, but relatively few seem to reach the higher stages of excellence (and of course that has to be defined) that one might expect. The reasons for this short fall are of course due in part to racism, still healthy and rampant in America, and sexism. But I feel that three other things might account for Black women's failure to push on to the higher levels of achievement. First, there is a relationship between a Black woman's success level and her ability to meet and marry a Black man with whom she feels compatible and vice versa. Thus, many Black women consciously shun achievement at a certain point in order to keep hope alive that a man and family are in her future. This is unfortunate because the Black community truly needs their excellence, power, and their image as role models. I believe the concern of a high achieving Black female finding a mate is real however. Second, I think Black women are more attuned to leading "balanced" lives where a large portion of time is reserved for causes and concerns relating to family, friends, the church, the community, etc. Thus, time that could be committed to the job is siphoned off in other directions. And last, I think some Black women rely too heavily on formal education to "qualify them" for the positions they aspire to. Black women seem to discount the role of experience, the politics of wheeling and dealing, the role of threats, intimidation and blackmail (Oops! I mean whitemail!) to achieve higher success. (One White writer has written an entire book relating to the Sob (Son of a Bitch) factor in achieving success.) Part of this tendency for Black women to do things *by the book* has its basis in the socialization that Ms. King refers to in her book in the quote above. Too few Black women ever learn how real world games are played in the world of power, position, money, status and control. What males learn, even underexposed Black males, is that *it almost never happens the way its written in the book*. We will come back to this point later.

There are three costs that people in general, and the feared Black man in particular, have to pay to be successful. The first cost is the cost you pay to learn your craft well enough to be good at what you do. This might involve learning something out of books such as law, accounting, medicine or some other profession or skill. But in many situations even the skill or expertise is not *academically* grounded, it is based as much on judgment as on skill.

The second cost a successful Black man must pay is the cost it takes to get *recognized* as being good at what you do. As everyone knows, there are plenty of talented people in all areas of life that have not gotten the opportunity to show the decision makers their talents. New "stars" are being "discovered" every day, but many other people are knocking at the same door or trying to find the door to knock on.

The third cost one must pay to be successful is the *getting paid stage*. It seems that every successful person has a story where even after their talent was recognized, they were exploited and asked to work for near nothing as part of a dues paying process. For some the process might be a situation such as when a college athlete brings in millions of dollars to a university, while he receives less than one percent of that. A singer might get paid fifty dollars a night for entertaining hundreds of people in a club. Other stories are similar.

But finally, when the successful person does get paid, they take the biggest step of the success cycle. They *leverage all* their assets - money, media contacts, name recognition, etc. and cease operating as an individual and become a company. They bring in numerous people to take on various roles and functions. For example an athlete not only makes money at his sport, but if he is good enough, he can make two or more times his athletic salary in other areas, from product endorsements to acting in movies.   A carpenter may go from getting paid good wages as a carpenter to having his own construction company, and then to owning some of the buildings his (or her) construction company built.

During this period when that a Black male is going through the steps to be successful, he is not without the sexual and emotional needs that any other individual would have. And as that male is looking for a woman, he uses the familiar standards that most men use to make judgments about women. How does she look? How is she built? What are her likes and dislikes? What most Black men would never think to ask is whether her personality and emotional make-up are compatible with their own desires and *willingness to pay the price required to be successful.* That question, that consideration, is not made because men often see a separation between their work life and their sex life and underestimate a woman's influence to either help or hurt their drive to success. Here, we come to the crucial part of understanding why many successful Black men marry or date White women.

If a brother who is hell bent on a type of notoriety or financial success happens to hook up with an *average* Black woman, she is likely to bring several things with her which could work *against* his success. Specifically these things may be:

1. A fear of Risk:

If you go back to the upbringing and socialization that author Victoria King referred to a few pages back, many of the answers lie there. Women are protected from many real world events as they grow up. They are taught that adventure, risk, taking chances, etc. are *foolish* things to do. They understand and trust things that *go by the book.* And every chance that the average Black woman's opinion is solicited or volunteered, you can bet the rent money that she is going to council brothers *against* taking any risk and *towards playing it safe*, doing things "properly" (and you know what that implies right?) and going by the book. The reality however is a lot different. Achieving success at any significant level, even for Whites let alone Black males, is a risky undertaking. *To give up the willingness to take risks is to get out of the game of trying to be a success.* Period! Also, when Black men are successful in most things, it is often due to their *creativity*, not their political muscle, their contacts, and certainly not their financing. And to be creative, *by definition*, means *not doing things by the book*, not playing along with the status quo! Thus when a brother who is trying to be successful is playing his cards the way his intuition tells him, playing his hunches, and making the moves his gut tells him to make, he is made to think by the average Black woman that he's doing it all wrong. It's often poor advice when he is not encouraged to follow the intuition that has made him successful thus far. The more formal education the Black woman has, usually the more conservative her advice to her man will be and the more self righteous she will be in giving her advice, *precisely* because of her "book learning." The Black man, being told how important education is all his life, is very vulnerable to lose confidence in his judgments, hunches and gut level feelings, and he may then try to compete with White boys in a game following *their* rules (which his Black woman will eagerly give him) rather than come to the table with his own talents and program. John H. Johnson, the founder of Ebony magazine, gave one of the most brilliant responses I have ever heard a successful Black man make about education and success. He was asked one day if he was sorry that he never attended college. He said, "not at all, because if I had gone to college, what I would have learned is that what I've already done would have been impossible to accomplish." Think about that statement. It is extremely on time for the point being made here.

2. The Black Woman's Board of Directors:

If we go back to the book *Waiting To Exhale* by Terry McMillan, one of the strongest points that came out of that book was the Black woman's obsession with blabbing her personal business to her girlfriends and in turn receiving and giving advice to her girlfriends about what *they* should do about *their* personal affairs. I shutter to think that most Black women talk to their girlfriends *that* often, *that* long and with *that* degree of influence as was portrayed in this book. However, on the other hand, I think it would be very *naive to think* that our Black Queens are on the phone, at the hairdresser or in church and *not* putting some of the Black man's business in the street and getting some at random, home spun advice in return. I understand how this society has taken away Black women's confidence and I can see how that confidence can be propped up or restored by her talking with her peers about matters close to them. Men do the same thing to a lesser degree. But it is uncomfortable for a man to be talking to his woman about the conclusions that he has reached regarding his career or business venture, and when asking for her opinion, she offers something that her girlfriend told her at the hairdresser when his wife clumsily half explained what she *thought* his problem or predicament was. Black men don't need their woman's girlfriends to be his board of directors and advisors on how he should run his life. Why is this so important a point? Read on.

3.   Is The Price of Success Too High?

Success from afar looks great. But as you get closer to it, you quickly become more aware of the cost. A point may be reached when you get a view of what success really looks like, feels like, sounds like etc., and you decide that that view is close enough. You conclude that you are not willing to pay the additional cost to get closer to success. I think that the decision to pay or not pay the price for success is a right that every person has. I *do not think* that decision should be made for them by another person.

When a women comes into your life and says she loves you and tells you that she will support you and understands your dreams, some men feel comfortable in telling them about their need to be a success. But too often down the line, when the man is closing in on his goal, the woman screams stop, please stop, the cost of success is too high! Too high for whom? Too high for what?

Because Black people are generally not business people or understand business, we lack the kind of background that really allows us to understand success or know what it takes to have financial success. If you throw in the negative self image most Blacks have of themselves (negative images that they project on to other Blacks as well), add in their fear of risks, and most Black people are just not in tune with success concepts. When you have people that do not understand success, don't expect success, can't handle success, or don't feel *deserving* of success, then almost any price can be seen as too high to pay for success.

So when our Black queen tells her girlfriends what kinds of things her boyfriend/husband is doing to make his dream come true, she receives un-solicited unfiltered opinions from her girlfriends. "Child, if that was my man, there is no way that I'd let him go to that business meeting in London without me!" "Yeah, my man told me he was saving money to start a business too, but I told him I was embarrassed to keep riding in this beat up car, so he ended up getting a new one", "Well, my man told me he was going to resign from his job too, and I told him he was a fool!" And so on it goes.

The overwhelming majority of Black women admire Black men who are successful. They just don't want to be around when that man is paying the dues required to *be* successful. (Remember Savannah in "Exhale,": "Why can't men already *be* what they aspire to.") And most of them don't believe that the man they are with has what it takes to be successful. In their wisdom the women figure why allow him to pay the hard dues for success when he's going to fail anyway, and I'll have to go down with him. Black women listen to their girlfriends who work 9-5 jobs and don't know a damn thing about independence (which is part of most brothers definition of success). And these women often convince one of their girlfriends to persuade her man to stop playing a game that none of them understand. This has been traditionally called the crabs in the barrel mentality and this is one of the primary ways that it comes about. If a Black woman thinks the price of success is too high then she should leave her man if it becomes intolerable. But she should shut her mouth if the brother ends up with a White girl who *can* deal with it.

Sometimes Black women can't deal with success even after it has arrived. What do Muhammad Ali, Sugar Ray Leonard, Joe Frazier, Larry Holmes and George Foreman all have in common? They were all boxers, all very successful World Champions, and multi-millionaires. All of them began boxing *before* they got married. All of their wives *knew they were marrying boxers*. Yet each of these men had to deal with their wives begging them, pleading with them, to quit boxing. Why does a Black man need a person to tell him to quit doing that which has made him (them) a multi-millionaire and world famous in the prime years of his life? Why quit at 30? That's what these Black women wanted, but fortunately all of these brothers continued to follow their dreams.

From ordinary people, working ordinary jobs with ordinary dreams and ordinary education (programming) one can not expect most of these people to be willing to put forth anything but ordinary effort. And that's ok, I have no problem with that. But for that ordinary person to spread their germs of mediocrity and ordinariness to a person that wants to do something really significant in life and is willing to pay the price to do it, that should be grounds for a prison term and a large fine. *What some Black men seem to say about their success and being with White women is that they would probably be with a Black woman if the woman was compatible with their struggle for success.* The White woman has not been around enough Black men to feel that she has "figured them out". Black women have. Thus, at the very point that a Black woman feels confident that she knows what a brother is thinking and why he is thinking it, she may volunteer a discouraging comment. It may be an "innocent" discouraging comment or it may be a critical one that he has to stop and deal with (or ignore). But over time many of these comments add up to be a pain in the ass that seem so unnecessary to have to deal with on the road to success. A White woman, because she's not in a position to second-guess her Black man because she doesn't quite know the Black man's thinking, may not say a word. This silence is golden, and it gives many Black men added confidence, and they push on. I am firmly convinced that many Black women understand this principle already very well. You often hear a sister say a White chick will *let* a brother *get away* with this and *get away* with that, as if the White woman is slacking off her *feminine duty* to be a second guessing royal pain in the you know what. Many sisters understand that their own mouths get them in trouble and get angry at the White girl for being passive and quiet. Some sisters act as if the main goal to be accomplished, by any means necessary, is for somebody to always be a pain to brothers, to ride him into some kind of humble submission, a kind of harmless puppy dog state. Many Black women seem to hate confident (they would say arrogant) proud Black men because they feel the confidence is unearned and undeserved. But it seems that is *precisely* what some White women love about Black men, that some of them are proud and moving forward regardless of the problems that society places in their path.

Are White women socialized different than Black women? Absolutely yes. Probably a lot of them are more sheltered from the real world than sisters are. What kind of sobering reality can you see in the White suburbia of two hundred thousand dollar houses? Sisters understand poverty, dope, fear, death, fire, child abuse, etc. The major question then is what makes for the difference between the White woman's ability to accompany a brother through the gates of success and a sister's apparent inability to do so? I believe the answer is in role models. Historically speaking, Black people have a limited scope of the kinds of really successful people that come from their community . Hard work and a lot of natural talent can make you a professional athlete, a singer, a comedian, whatever. These successes are largely based on individual efforts. But they are not the same as building up ones own enter*prise, where* you need so many other people to do what they are supposed to do for your operation to run properly. It is in these situations that the role of one's woman becomes important. You don't need a woman's help to become an All American or to sign a professional contract. Nor do you need one to become a dancer like Gregory Hines or to write like Alice Walker. Michael Jackson has proven that he can be the best at what he does, and the women in his life until recently were merely props used for an occasional special effect or special event. But when one is trying to establish success; based on creating a company and coordinating a staff, it helps a lot to have a woman by your side and/or to understand the challenges you are trying to meet.

White women have seen their fathers, uncles, grandfathers, cousins, brothers and neighbors build enterprises that define their success. They understand that most of it is not written in a book and that it is about luck, hard work, determination and often going against the flow of public opinion and following gut instinct. White women understand the thin line that separates success from total failure, and therefore appreciates the need to give your all precisely when it looks like disaster is straight ahead. *In other words White women don't seem to fear or anticipate failure the way many Black women do.* Of course being White and seeing White success will likely give her reason to fear failure less than a Black woman. That should be obvious. And what brothers seem to be saying to Black women is that I don't need your negative baggage (and your girlfriends negative baggage) if its going to sink my ship and keep it from coming in. When a man works sixteen straight hours in his enterprise, he doesn't need to hear *even five minutes* of critical commentary that kills the spirit he needs to do the next sixteen hour shift. If it can't be positive support then there needs to be silence, the *right kind* of silence if you know what I mean.

The other thing that the White girl brings with her to the relationship is her knowledge of *how* a woman supports her man in these types of efforts. In the Black community couples work individual *jobs* and mutual support is largely emotional during down times. Black women rarely know *how* to support a Black man in a business enterprise. She may be working her individual job to make sure some money comes in every week. Most Black men couldn't do any better and probably would do worse if the situation were switched around.   Black people, are unaccustomed (and apparently uninterested) in working together in a common enterprise, ever since we left the southern farms two generations or so ago. The White woman knows what role her mother, grandmother and aunt played in helping to make their male partners a success, and many of them seem ready, willing, and able to do likewise for their Black boyfriend or husband. Many brothers have mixed feelings about these relationships but accept all the help that they can get for as long as the relationship lasts. When a Black woman sees a successful brother with a White woman, she often thinks the woman *is the end result of that brothers success*. The brother may see her as *the means*, to get him to the success he is really seeking.

I remember listening to the television program *60 Minutes* about five years ago and they were interviewing a Black superstar I had always admired.! This person said point blank on the show that the reason she married her White mate was for *one reason*: that White mate could help her career. Period! Love apparently wasn't a strong consideration. That show turned me around. That person was Lena Horne. Lena Horne had maybe ten or fifteen million Black men who would have married her for love. Yet when she did marry, it wasn't to a Black and it wasn't for love. Part of me wanted to reach through the screen and smack her. Another part of me was proud as hell to see one honest Black woman let **it** all hang out for all to see and hear. She could have lied and said her love was color blind, blah, blah, blah. But she told the truth. How many other Black "stars" or success motivated Black men would this type of marriage apply to?

It may be too late for many Black men to expect Black women to "fall in line" and support their men with the big egos and the big dreams because today is a new day for all women. Many women refuse to be seen as a mere reflection of her man's success or the strong woman behind the successful man. That type of thinking has gone the way of "Colored" water fountains. Women, especially Black women, with the current lions share of college degrees, want to do their own thing and stand on their own, and any brother who has a problem with that has a problem himself. Black *people* need economic and business advancement, and the last time I checked, Black women were a part of Black people. Today it is no more logical to assume that a Black wife is "supposed" to quit her job to support her husband's enterprise than it is to assume that a brother is "supposed" to quit his to help build hers. The women's movement has made clear such obvious sexist expectations and I personally respect this new position no matter how things *used to be*. If ambitious Black men and women intend on fulfilling most of the ambitions that they have for themselves and still live together in marriage, they are going to just have to figure out how they are going to do it in their own way.

The Sasha Stallone Example

Before I close out this chapter on White women , I must relate a story that really opened my eyes to how a particular White woman reacted to a test of faith in her man. I think 99% of the Black women I know would have reacted very differently to the same situation. The story involves one of Hollywood's biggest stars, Sylvester Stallone. In 1975, Stallone was a starving actor who had stooped so low as to "act" in a porno movie to get money and "experience". He was married to a women named Sasha, his first wife. At twenty-nine years old, he had seen his other actor friends careers take off. He had a child on the way and was living in a ramshackle apartment from which the landlord wanted them evicted. In March of 1975, he went to see Muhammad Ali fight a White boxer named Chuck Wepner who was known to cut and bleed easily. Ali expected to knock him out, but instead Wepner stayed on his feet and lasted the whole fight. Within three months Stallone was able to produce a screen play from this inspiring fight which he called *Rocky*. He took the screenplay all around Hollywood and the idea generated genuine interest. But there was one major problem. Nobody who showed interest in the script wanted Stallone to play Rocky, the star. They wanted to buy the script from Stallone, get a real star to play Rocky, and laugh their way to the bank. Stallone didn't want to sell the script, but he was stone broke and his child was due soon. The producers offered Stallone seventy-five thousand dollars. Stallone was impressed but told them "I have to play this part". The money men raised their offer to one hundred and twenty-five thousand dollars to get Stallone's script and *get him out of the way.* The money men told him that the movie had very little chance of being financed unless it had a big name star to add the sizzle, which made a lot of sense. Stallone said that thinking about that much money gave him a headache but he still insisted on being "the star". The money men then really turned the screw and offered Stallone the incredible sum of three hundred and fifty thousand dollars for something it took him such a short period of time to write after watching the Ali fight. He was blown away by the amount of money, but he still wanted to be the star. So he discussed it with his pregnant wife, Sasha in their run down apartment. She understood why Stallone insisted on being the star. Not only had he put his heart and soul into the script, but he knew that this part was the only shot he would ever get at a truly great, tailor-made, starring role. (Remember, Stallone is already 29, and there are not too many new Hollywood hunks "discovered" in their 30's.) Listen to what went on:

> "What does $350,000 look like?" she asked. Staring at his lap, Sylvester replied, " I don't know." "I don't know either," she said quickly, " so I guess I wouldn't really miss it."
> Sylvester looked up.
> "But if I don't sell it, how do you feel about having to go in the backyard and eat grass?"
> Her reply:
> "I'd sooner move to a trailer in the middle of a swamp than for you to sell Rocky."

Silvester called the producers and as politely as he knew how, told them he wouldn't give them the script "for a million dollars" unless he was the star. (Page 68 Stallone A Hero's Story by Jeff Rovin, Pocket Books N.Y. 1985) Reading this passage really moved me. I was not caught up in the emotionalism or the romance of the book; for but a few minutes I actually understood how some White folks express their determination, guts and faith in themselves very differently than we do. Will we ever get to a point of self confidence like that? I know of no Black woman anywhere in the US who would have supported her broke husband and risk losing a *sure* three hundred and fifty thousand dollars. No need to even mention pregnancy! There are at least a hundred ways to rationalize why it would have made more sense for Stallone to take the money, and all of them would have been valid. But instinct and faith and determination not logic or intelligence, told Sasha that that wasn't the best move to make. In all the reading about real world events that I've done for more than thirty five years, few if any have impressed me more than that brief exchange in the Stallone household in 1975. And whereas all of the Black women that I have known would not have done what Sasha Stallone did, I can also say that I know very, few Black *men* who on principle, would have held out like Stallone did. Ninety-nine percent of the brothers would have taken the money also, which is why Black people need a broader definition of what risk and courage are about. For any woman, to *not take the money* and run when their whole life experience says that they are always to take the money and run, is truly impressive.

As it turned out *Rocky* grossed 56 million dollars from which Stallone received two million. It was nominated for ten Oscars including two for Stallone (best actor, and best screen play). Stallone did not win either award but Rocky did win best picture, best director, and best editing. Since that time, there has been a total of five Rocky films and Stallone has *personally earned* at least a hundred and twenty-five million for himself. This story-book situation doesn't happen to but about one in ten million people. But it perfectly illustrates the idea of a lady in her man's corner when the chips are down and instinct or intuition tells you that the "obvious decision" is not the right one. A cynical person may say that Stallone did not stay with the woman that stood by him in this crisis situation. This is true. But perhaps they, like millions of other marriages, were not destined to be together forever anyway. But the former Mrs. Stallone is not now nor is she ever likely to be poor again. You can believe that!

A MALE SPIN ON THE COMMUNICATION ISSUE

If one were to dig below the surface of the many arguments that Black men and women have and try to discover what the main issues in those arguments consisted of, one of the most repeated words would be *communication*. At least Black women say over and over again during their many wine and cheese socials, in Essence magazine articles, in best selling novels, and during the half-the-night telephone conversations with friends, that they are looking for better communication from men generally, and better communication from *their* man specifically.

Since the progress of the women's movement, the word communication has developed into a buzz word of major proportions in virtually all public debates and especially those involving women's or family issues. And it almost appears that women have seized the power to become the sole authorites to judge or determine what is or is not true communication. As a writer and speaker, I am particularly aware of how women have gained power and forced changes in the last fifteen years or so.

We live in an age that I refer to as the *feminization* of literature. That means that women dominate what is being written, and they dominate the power position of editors in publishing houses. They seem to have the final say in *who* gets published, *what* is expressed and *how* it is expressed. Women dominate as the purchasers of written material, whether it be books or magazines. You don't have to be a genius to see that it's more *profitable* to write what women want to hear (read), because that's where the money is coming from.

In the media that is used to promote books - talk shows, there is an obvious effort to cater to a predominately female audience. The advertising industry has many more ads to sell to the female market than the male market. Thus, the advertising dollars to support female-focused television shows, radio talk shows and women's magazines are much more abundant than what exists for men. Thus it is no accident that the Black woman's perspective is much more prevalent in the media than the Black man's. There is no Black male equivalent to Essence magazine (with its one million copies per month going out to seven million mostly Black female readers). Certainly *Ebony Man* does not represent the common Black man's perspective on life.

It is for all these reasons then, that an effort is being made here to put forth a credible explanation of one Black male's perspective on this topic of communication. There is no claim being made that these views represent the majority viewpoint of Black men. But I believe that it would be beneficial to everyone to have something to add to the tired and repetitious complaints that Black men have had to hear about their shortcomings the last fifteen years or more. I would assume that even women are ready to hear something fresh and different.

Individuality vs Symbolism In Communication

People like to believe that they are individuals, absolutely unique in talent and perspective. To a limited extent we are. But to a greater extent we are the direct results of our environment and our history. This is to say, if each of us had the same genetic makeup as we presently do, but had a different environment and a different history, we would in fact, be very different people than we are now.

When we talk about communication, we cannot pretend that mere individuals talk to each other. I do not believe this is true. Black men carry with them the baggage of being Black men, and they carry it wherever they go. Black women have their baggage also and it affects virtually everything they see and interpret. So when we talk about communication between the Black man and the black woman, we have to first see them *symbolically* before we take into consideration their individuality. Symbolically, a Black man is usually representative of a specific frame of mind, a set of experiences, a history, a value system and a culture, as much as he may represent a specific personality. The same thing can be said of the Black woman. None of us were born or raised in a vacuum. Many influences contribute to who we are.

This being the case, we should be clear about what two mind-sets, what two value and belief systems are vying for influence in the communication process when the Black man and woman talk to each other. And what problems and challenges are going on in this communication process regardless of the specific feelings and personalities of the people involved? In short, what makes for a *built-in* difficulty in communication between Black men and women simply *because* one is a Black man and the other a Black woman?

The Black man who attempts to communicate with the Black woman is basically a rebel. He rebels against authority because that authority is always trying to negate everything of substance that he stands for. That authority is either White or is some person who represents the interests or values of his historical White oppressor. This rebellion may play itself out verbally, physically or through the creation of alternative cultural perspectives in any aspect of culture, religion, art, sport, family life, and so on. Black men have a need to preserve something called a Black or African perspective, however weakly it may be carried through. And while Black men are rebelling, they are also *subject* to the most *intense form of rejection* by the society they are rebelling against. Every conscious Black man hasbeen aware of this rejection by the greater White society.

In addition to the rebel label that Black men wear, they also carry around the baggage of insecurity about their manhood. This manhood insecurity has its foundation going back to the beginning of slavery. Black men have never been allowed to participate within their own community or in the larger society as full-fledged men with all the rights, economic and political privileges and mutual respect that White men have enjoyed. They have had mixed success in maintaining and supporting their families, which again chips away at their masculinity. As a result of this masculine insecurity, Black men *overreact* to minor threats from *non-white* males and blame others for their own frustrations (including Black women) rather than dealing with their real adversary.

Masculine Insecurities

Defining and achieving manhood has always been a problem which has lurked behind the thoughts of Black men (and women). In effect many Black men have accused others of "preventing him" from being a man or "feeling" like a man. We must examine the concept of Black manhood, because it is crucial to understanding what's happening with such issues as communication in Black male/female relationships.

Normally when we read about the Black man being *emasculated*, we usually interpret it in one of several ways:

a) The White man sold off members of the Black family during slavery and therefore prevented the Black man from feeling like a man because he had no means of keeping his family together.

b) The White man did not allow Blacks to be legally married; thus, there was no Black marriage institution legally established which Whites were bound to respect.

c) The White man would visit the slave quarters at night and perform all kinds of both normal and freaky sex acts on the Black woman and keep his own White wife "clean". The Black man could do nothing but stand and watch.

d) When the slave trade came to a halt, the only way to increase the slave population was to have existing slaves to reproduce.

White men bred slaves, which involved forcing any two slaves to mate. In many ways this represented the original pornographic movie, because such breeding was often a spectator event involving Whites standing around watching Blacks in the sex act. Clearly, this was emasculating.

e)   If there was even the suspicion of sexual attraction between a White woman and a Black man (free or slave), or that a rape had been committed against a White woman, the Black man's genitals were often literally cut off. If the victim didn't die, he was certainly physically emasculated.

f)   After slavery and into the twentieth century, when money became even more important as a medium of exchange for a man to provide for his family, the Black man was prevented from earning money by White men.

g)   When the White man did allow "the colored" to earn money, he often selected the Black woman as the wage earner. Thus, the Black man felt emasculated because he became dependent on his woman's earnings. The Black man thus blamed not only the White man but the Black woman for his feelings of inadequacy.

h)   When the Black woman became a mother or attained a degree of financial independence she could threaten to put the Black man out of "his" house and take his children if he got out of line. She could do this with legal and police support. This was again seen as an emasculating situation for the Black man, again caused by both "his" woman and the White man.

Historically, most Black men referred to some combination of the situations listed above when they referred to emasculation. The above situations have a basis in fact, and therefore the feelings of Black men seem legitimate.

Although it is not completely out of order for Black men to feel that in some instances Black women have betrayed them, it is clear that at other times the charges just don't hold up. For example, most Black men have to come to a more mature understanding of those situations when the Black woman was able to work and earn an income and they were not. In the first place, it was not the woman's desire to "take jobs away" from the Black man, there was simply an offer made to her to work and she accepted it. Second, if Black women had not accepted those early menial jobs, many Black families, including the men in them, would not have survived. And last, in most cases, the jobs that were offered to the Black woman (domestics, secretaries, nurses) were so feminine in nature that the Black man would not have accepted them anyway. The idea that Black women worked hand in hand to take away the Black man's manhood doesn't hold up in this historical context. However, it is still important to understand how situations like this made the Black man "feel" much less of a man. The only reason one would not agree with this is if they considered a Black man's feelings as unimportant. Of course that is precisely the message he has been receiving throughout his entire history in America.

Because of the belief, right or wrong, that other people have "taken away" the Black man's masculinity (including his own woman), Black men have often acted desperately "to prove" that their manhood has been "regained". Such actions to prove manhood have varied from very simple acts to the bazaar. In the one hundred and thirty years since "freedom", no clear definitions of manhood have been universally accepted among Black men. Occasionally a famous Black leader like Malcolm X will be projected as a model for Black manhood. But the problem here is that that same leader is often projected as being so special and unique that they are placed beyond the realm to which ordinary men can be expected to reach. It is quite obvious that most men of any group are not leaders but followers, and yet they have to *be* men and get the respect of their fellow men *as* men.

When the other party to a communication process is a Black Woman, you have an entity that is not just different but in some cases the very opposite of the male. She is not the opposite merely because she is of another sex, she is the opposite because her mind-set and values are often the opposite of males. She is *not* a rebel, she usually goes along and accepts things pretty much at face value. Things White and European are often considered correct, sophisticated, tasteful, proper, intelligent, pretty and preferred. She usually does not appreciate or respect the Black mans resentment of and rebelliousness against the status quo of White America. She considers it (and therefore him) childishness or immaturity or, even worse, ignorance. This is all part of the legacy of house slave training referred to in a previous chapter. There is the acceptance by most sisters of material possessions as a valid measure of one's status in life and the quality of life itself. The Black woman in general is not particularly interested in Black or African history or Black political (power) movements that might change Black peoples' perspective or position in the society. She seems much more interested in being accepted by the larger White group, something that interests her Black male mate to a much lesser degree on the whole.

Thus, without even going into the specifics of a particular argument or the differences in personalities, we see here a built-in set of circumstances that will make agreement and compatibility between Black men and women difficult. In any given situation Black women will see things in so- called "practical terms", meaning the *way things are,* ie., the White man is in control, do things *his* way. The Black man in that same situation will demand that his perspective be respected or at least listened to. In many instances the dominating perspective is the White perspective, not necessarily because it is better but simply because White people have more resources (money, media, political and legal clout) to *make* their perspective the reality. And this is what makes the Black man feel weak and powerless in his woman's eyes. It is the fact that his woman does not appreciate the value of his ideas *on the basis of merit* alone. What seems to be respected is *only* the ability to ram your idea down the throats and into the consciousness of the masses. In other words, to program people. Black men do not have the media machinery needed to program people.

Too often Black men can get their women to believe in them only after Black men get a White man to believe in them *first*, because that is who Black women seem to believe in most consistently. We see this happen all the time when a Black man wants to start a business or when Black men get involved in "stardom." A young Black man will say, "I'm going to be a movie star, basketball star, Olympic champion, world champion, a comedian, writer etc. etc." The woman in their lives - mother, sister, girlfriend, wife- doesn't bother to check out the brother's talent and try to access his dream on the basis of his ability, work ethic, and strategy. The women don't bother to ask, "does the man's dream have any merit?" The dreams of the Black male are much too easy to be dismissed as unrealistic or fantasy. But let a White male coach, manager, investor, talent scout, or news paper reporter arrive on the scene, and the Black woman's faith in her "boy" or man rises ten-fold. And its for one reason only: the White man said my guy is good, and he's the one who makes everything happen.

The point here is that Black men and women have difficulty in communication from the jump because they often have opposite points of reference and different aspirations. The woman wants as much of the White world for herself and her children as she can possibly get. Anything that she perceives will help her do that, she's ready for and she will listen. But many Black men, on the other hand, have the perspective that their insight, talent, manhood, creativity and human potential must be recognized, and it is not being recognized if it must always mimic the White man or have his approval. The Black man is trying to create a value system, a philosophy and lifestyle which is the best of his African self and the America in which he presently finds himself. And he can't show this world to anyone because its in his head. He has to create it. The most frustrating and painful thing he has to deal with over and over again is that his own mate a) doesn't know any more of what he's talking about than White people do, and b) questions his ability to improve on anything that the White man has already created.

If this was the only precondition that made for poor communications between Black men and women, things might not be quite so bad. But another precondition, the overreaction to the slighting of manhood, makes the situation much worse. When some Black men feel their manhood is being attacked by their women, they will lash out physically and often severely. They will hit their women usually for one of two reasons. First, they feel that by hitting their women, they are discouraging future disrespectful statements or actions and they are reminding her who "the boss" of the relationship is. But in some cases the men strike out at their women because the woman becomes the White man's representative mouthpiece in his own home. In effect, the ideas accepted and articulated by his woman is almost, word for word, the same kind of criticism that most White men use to criticize Black men. Thus a beating may be viewed like an *exorcism*. The Black man doesn't have the capacity (guts) to take on the devil directly, but he can try to beat out the devil's ideas that have crept into the head of his woman. There is no intent here to endorse such actions, only to try to explain them to people who seem perpetually confused by it all.

Finally, as if these preconditions for poor communications were not bad enough, the whole situation is coated over with a thick covering of *denial*. The women deny that they are imitating White people in any way, deny that they are materialistic, deny that they are ignorant of Black history and its relevance to their life, and will deny anything that upsets their image of themselves as anything other than a good woman looking for a good man. Black men will deny that they have a "manhood hangup," and deny that they are rebellious against the status quo because they don't want to be perceived as militant, angry or uncooperative. The Black man will usually deny that he prefers light skin or White women because there is some guilt associated with that for many men. Both Black men and women deny that they are in anyway programmed or affected by the thousands of messages they get from the media, their coworkers, family, and so on. They would have you believe that all of their decisions and choices are strictly determined on the basis of their deliberate thoughts. What we have here then are two sets of Black people - males and females, who have chosen two different methods to respond to racism and oppression. And because they have had a fundamental disagreement over *how to respond to Whites*, it gets very much in the way of how *they relate and respond to each other.* It is further complicated by the fact that White people respond *to them differently* and therefore reinforces both groups reasoning for responding the way they do. Whites are less threatened by Black women and so treat them "better" than Black men. And because Black women receive better treatment from Whites, they continue to try to convince Black men that Whites are "basically good people."

Disincentives For Black Males To Communicate

I believe that if an idea, a statement or a belief is stated over and over again, year after year, decade after decade, that idea must have some basis in fact. I believe most stereotypes are true to at least some degree or they probably would not have stood the test of time and circumstances. Thus, if it is so widely accepted that the Black man doesn't communicate, or doesn't communicate well, then it might be more beneficial to explain *why* that might be true rather than to deny that is the case simply to put down a stereotypical image. Actually, there are many reasons for the Black man's reluctance to communicate, and it will be no trouble listing a few of them here.

1.   School Habits:
It was stated earlier that the Black man's greatest contribution to America and the world is his creativity. *Original* thoughts, designs, concepts, and so on are usually thought to be the signs of genius. But the public school system has no room for creative thinking in its operation. School is a steady diet of reading, writing and regurgitation. A good student reads what White folks said, accepts and believes what White folks said, memorizes what White folks said, and then spits back out on a test or term paper what White folks have said. This is American education grades 1 through college. Only after your sophomore year in college might a teacher *care what you think* of an idea or subject. But while you are in high school, your responsibility as a student is to memorize and spit out at the appropriate times what you have memorized. What a young Black male child thinks about himself or the world is absolutely of no interest to anybody in the educational system. There are no classes or grades to be earned in something called *Your Philosophy*, only Western or Eastern Philosophy. What the school system seems to be saying is that you are not old enough to have a worthwhile thought yet. Wait until you have read what a thousand other people have thought about things (about 950 of them White men) and then you *might be qualified* to think your own thoughts.

So young Black men tune out of school work because their pride says, "if you have no use for what I think, I have no use for what you are trying to teach me". Proud Black males demand and expect a certain reciprocation even if only ten, twelve or fourteen years old. Black men get little practice in communicating in school because many reject that which is to be communicated. They reject the regurgitation because what is being regurgitated is not "them", it's not *their message* so there is no "communication" as such going on even if they *were* to regurgitate. Black boys tire of the game and do not participate and therefore keep their thoughts to themselves. The other side of this same coin is "inappropriate" classroom participation. A young Black man may try to answer a question but be laughed at because he uses street language, is too blunt, or has an answer that seems perfectly logical to his thinking and experience but is "wrong for the situation". It only takes a few classroom snickers to discourage many people from opening their mouth in the classroom, and thus opportunities to learn to express yourself and communicate are lost.

Why doesn't school effect Black girls he same way? There are many answers to that question, but one is just a repetition of what has been stated previously. Black girls and women do not question the assumed superiority of White people, White textbooks, White teachers or White directives. They are taught to "be nice," "be a lady" and go along with whatever the program is. Black girls do not rebel, and if they do it's seldom on a racial principle. Some young Black girls believe in the White is right ideology almost as much as White people do. Black girls do better in school because they are much more comfortable in school. They are comfortable learning how to "talk proper" and all the other indoctrinating processes that make up "education". Also, as was mentioned earlier, Black girls have Black female teachers as role models with whom they can identify and who help make them feel comfortable. In performing well in their school work, Black girls do pick up greater communication skills, even if much of the rest of what they learn may not be in their best interest.

2.   Home Environment:
Black parents have a tremendous faith in the power of education for their children, and they believe, many times wrongly, that the teachers and school system know what they are doing and have their children's best interest at heart. If there is any problem at school, it is usually assumed to be the child's fault in most cases. When a Black male child comes home, one of the first questions that a parent will ask (especially the mother) is, how are you doing in school? Another way of asking this same question could be, "How well are you

memorizing and spitting back all those things White folks tell you to?" But of course no parent would ever phrase the question in this realistic way. Anyway, when a child is doing well in school they usually get approval to do everything else they want to do. They can visit friends' houses, work after school, go out on weekends, etc., "as long as they keep their grades up". They are ok in their parents' eyes and the relationship tends to be good when the child is doing well in school. When the child is *not* doing well in school, then it tends to hurt the relationship between parents and the child. The child's poor school work is used as the basis for punishment, and *other* avenues of learning and positive experiences are cut off until *they do better in school.* Other ideas the child may have about life are treated as less valid, less important, or less legitimate because poor school work may cause the parent to doubt their child's ability and the parent may begin to perhaps see the child as dumb or a loser in the same way that the school has labeled him. It is a known fact that with all the different nationalities that make up the public school system of the United States, a much higher percentage of Black *male* children are regarded as slow learners, retarded, delinquents, psychotics, autistic, behaviorly-impaired, emotionally-disturbed, etc. than any other sex of any other race. Is this an accident, a coincidence, or an accurate assessment? When the parents accept and go along with these labels that the system has developed for their male children, and when they use school performance as the criteria by which to grant exposure for their children to life's other experiences, they become partners in crime with the school system against their own children. They are telling their boys that their other options to learn and grow in life will be limited until they conform to a "bad system." How do we know the system is bad? Because these *same* parents will tell you, for hours on end, how *bad* their local school systems are. But it doesn't make any difference how bad the system is, the Black male is punished by his own parents for not conforming to this bad system. They act as if their son's cooperation would make this bad system "good." Many a young boy feels so betrayed that his parents would side with the school against him that communication breaks down and the kid may say "hell with my parents and the damn school system" and head straight for the gang that is ready to accept him. In other words, poor communication in school shouldn't be allowed to lead directly to poor communication at home, but it often does. It is not in the scope of this book however to go into how to prevent this from happening.

Another common problem that happens in the home that hurts the ability of young Black men to communicate is the requirement that the young man talk according to the terms dictated to by the parent. For example, a boy might come in and start talking to his parents in street language (but not cursing). Street language is developed by young Black men. When *they* say it, its considered dirty, crude, dumb, unsophiscated, etc. Eventually this "slang" works its way through popular music, television, newscasters, movies and even White politicians may eventually say the word "homeboy" or give a "high five." As usual, when White people do it, its considered acceptable, creative, illustrative, etc. But parents may say to their son, "Look, you either talk to me in English or we have nothing to say. Don't give me any of that jive talk!" A child could comply and talk in standard English or he could be stubborn and say forget it. *Who loses when the child says, "forget it"*? The answer is that they both do.

Finally, there are certain subjects that kids are reluctant to discuss with their parents. Sex, buying a car, learning how to drive, getting an allowance, curfew hours, drinking, birth control, sexual diseases, buying expensive clothes (hundred dollar Air Jordan Nikes), racism, drugs, illiteracy, religious disagreements, etc., are just some of the many topics that teens are reluctant to discuss with parents. And parents are also slow to voluntarily address some of these topics. Many times young girls suffer the same communication blocks with their parents as the young boys. But mothers usually are more present in the home than fathers, and the mother often feels more at ease having a mother-daughter talk than a mother-son talk. Many questions she just doesn't handle well because she has never been a young boy trying to grow into manhood in today's world. But she *can* reflect back to her own childhood when talking to her daughter.

There are often crucial discussions that never take place between young Black males and their fathers or mothers. When these discussions do *not* take, place several things often happen. First, the boy receives misinformation from a peer. Second, he makes a mistake in his decisions or judgements that lands him in jail, injured, into fatherhood or with a sexually transmitted disease. And third, by not having been the recipient of sound and thorough information, he is not in a position to provide sound information when it becomes his responsibility to talk to his kids. Critical communication skills are not learned, and thus can't be internalized and passed on. Daughters may be no more comfortable in talking to *their* sons than their mothers were in talking to her brothers.

3.   **Peer Communication:**
      Before young Black men try to communicate with women, they must first learn to communicate with other young Black men. And what they learn in

these lessons can be summed up very easily: *words don't mean very much.* Among Black males communication is more likely to be transmitted non-verbally through actions and image. There is a *you are what you can do* understanding among Black men. If, for example, you consider yourself an athlete and you want that image, and that respect, then you must produce results which say you are an athlete worthy of respect. All that "talking a good game" subjects you to is ridicule if you are unable to back it up with action. The same can be said about most of the activities that young Black males participate in. Talking, boasting, broadcasting your intentions ahead of time places you in an embarrassing position if you do not deliver on your boasts. So, many young men learn that it is better not to communicate their plans, dreams, intentions, goals, strategies, etc., because if they do not meet their goals, they don't suffer the pain of humiliation and embarrassment because *no one was aware* of what they failed to do. Instead, they are more likely to be given credit for making a good effort at whatever they participated in. Doing a lot of talking can also be seen as a sign of weakness, because "strong men" don't have to talk. As a matter of fact, talking a lot under almost any set of circumstances is seen as a *feminine* characteristic. If you can't perform, talking won't help you win the game, win the fight, pass the test, or get the money. Talking is seen as that which you do when you are powerless to do anything else. Thus, a lot of talk signals powerlessness, which is something that few men want to be perceived as if they can avoid it.

4.   To Avoid Being Exploited, Ignored Or In An Argument:

Black women see Black men's limited use of words as a drawback. But a drawback to whom? As was pointed out in an earlier chapter, Black men begin to feel the rejection and exploitation from other elements of society starting as young as thirteen or fourteen. And what you learn very early is that the more you reveal about yourself the more you put yourself in a position for people to misuse you, frame you, charge or accuse you, or other wise hurt you. When you make known your weaknesses and vulnerabilities, you may seem more sensitive or likeable or honest to some people, but you also reveal to others how they can get the upper hand. One of the reasons why women get frustrated at men not communicating with them is that they are not getting new information on how to better position themselves to get *what they want from the man.* The Black woman pretends that communicating with her more would be better for the *man* in question? But, *it's usually better for her!* The more she knows, the more she has to work with to manipulate her man and circumstances to her advantage. It would be cynical to suggest that this is always the case. But it is very naive to suggest that its rarely the case. Why wouldn't the philosophy of "better safe than sorry" not apply here for most Black men?

I am an avid reader of *Essence Magazine,* even though I do tire of the repetitiousness of the Black female stand on things and the inevitable Black male-bashing that seems to be required to drive home a point. But every once in a while you run into an article that impresses you. Such an article was written by Jill Nelson in the October 1992 issue of *Essence.* Basically Ms. Nelson says that many women try to kid themselves into thinking that they want a man who will communicate, when in fact they are often not ready to even listen to what men have to say

"Frankly, in the past its been easier to blame men for the lack of communication that usually characterizes an unsuccessful relationship than to check out the woman in the mirror. I'm not suggesting that women are responsible for all problems. I'm suggesting that its healthy to own up to where we've messed up and try to change our behavior. We need to take an honest look at what we want from relationships and how much we're willing to do to get it." (Quote from page 85.)

At other times when the men are honest with their feelings (showing their vulnerabilities, fears etc.) women have been known to use their candor against them as I suggested above. Ms Nelson gives a perfect example:

"A few years ago a man I was going with broke down and cried, talking honestly about his fears of being phased out of his job during a corporate reorganization. I was turned off. First I tried to dismiss his feelings by telling him he was "just stressed out". When he persisted, I told him he was "making too big a deal out of it". A few weeks later I broke up with him. I told my girlfriends I "just couldn't deal with a weak man." (Essence P. 85 10/92)

Later Ms. Nelson shares something else worth its weight in gold. (P. 86 Essence)

"I've been known to go off when a man communicates something to me I decided I can't-won't-deal with. This is frequently precipitated by my harassing him to "tell me how you really feel." Not too long ago I asked a male friend to help me decide which of two dresses to wear, even though I had already chosen one. No dummy, he knew he was on dangerous terrain and tried to remain ambiguous, saying he "liked them both." When I insisted he choose, he didn't pick my choice, the red one. Then I had to know why. When he finally told me he thought the red dress made my skin look washed out and was a little tight, I got angry and told him he had no taste. When I was finished raving, he inquired simply, "Why'd you ask my opinion?"

"Is it any wonder that some men are closemouthed, some dishonest and some both when it comes to talking? Why risk being rejected, dismissed or appearing unmanly if it can all be avoided by reverting to macho-type behavior and keeping a stiff upper lip? Or lying?..... I'd conveniently forgotten that communication doesn't mean a man telling me what I want to hear, but what he feels. The hard work is being able to listen to and accept, nonjudgmentally, what he has to say."

Now this writer, who communicates for a living, still labors under the disadvantage of being a Black male communicator. Why do I say that? Because the points Ms. Nelson made above I could have made as easily myself by just pulling out a couple of the episodes I've lived through. But it wouldn't be credible because I would just be seen as another frustrated Black male who is bitching about his girlfriend, wife, or about Black women in general. Right? Ignore it? So I go into my files and pull out an Essence article, written by a distinguished writer, a Black woman "sympathetic to the plight of Black women" and presto, the same points now take on an entirely different meaning and *credibility.*

Black men don't talk because our words don't seem to mean anything to anybody. To the public we are liars and acting suspicious. To our bosses we are probably lying and acting defensive. To our women we are possibly lying and acting arrogant. In response Black men have said, "They may dismiss our poorly articulated words, but we are going to make them deal with our *actions"* Thus, our actions, right or wrong, are our true statements of communication.

One of the things that men and women are supposed to do for each other is help each other fulfill their dreams. In order to do this they have to reveal their dreams to each other . It was previously stated that brothers usually keep their intentions from other brothers for risk of looking like a failure if they don't reach their goal. But when we find a woman who we think we can confide in, we sometimes let it all out. This is a very risky act for a lot of brothers who are counting on their woman's support and confidence to build up their own sometimes shaky confidence. A statement I've recently come across shows what can happen when a brother allows himself to be romantic and revealing, and when he assumes that the women he's dealing with today are the same as the ones he knew when he was growing up. In her best seller, *Waiting To Exhale,* Terry McMillan has one of her characters make a short but very revealing statement. One of her characters is asking GOD to send her a decent man. She wasn't satisfied with what God had previously sent her, so she says:

"Now I'm more specific! Could you make sure he talks about what he feels and not just about what he thinks? Could he have a genuine sense of his purpose in life, a sense of humor, and could he already *be* what he aspired to?" (P. 11 Waiting To Exhale Viking Press 1992 New York)

Lets look at how a Black man might interpret that statement and how the interpretation shows just how far apart Black men and women are.

McMillian's character is asking for a man to reveal his feelings and not just his thoughts. Black men want to feel that in a world where Whites don't like or trust Black men, and Black people don't trust Black men, that there ought to be one person that you can count on to help you become whatever you are trying to become. They want to feel that when those low moments come and confidence, finances, productivity or credibility is running low, that he has at least one other person who believes that he will pull it all together. It's that old-fashioned "behind every good man there is a good woman" concept. The Black man wants to *feel* this. But in truth the Black man doesn't expect this for precisely the reason that McMillian stated. Today's Black woman wants a *finished* product, not *a sensitive developing man*. She wants him to already *be* (McMillian emphasis on the *be*) what-ever he is going to be so she can just consume it, enjoy it, bask in it, reflect her own status and glory in it. She doesn't want to have to do a damn thing but show up when all the work and struggle is finished. She wants no assembly necessary - batteries included. She wants a meal ticket, a status symbol, a good screw, a good father and someone other women envy all rolled into one. She has no concept of being behind a good man, she wants to be the first in line to win him in a lottery once he's "finished". These women offer what to their completed dream boat? Are they themselves (the women) already whatever *they* are going to be? It wouldn't matter in many cases anyway if she was. As soon as some women find a guaranteed quality lifestyle in the form of a man, they are going to get pregnant, quit their job, and live off of him for the rest of their lives, or as long as he puts up with it.

Like Ms. Nelson said in her Essence article, Black women need to "take an honest look at what we want from a relationship and *how much we're willing to do* (emphasis mine) to get it." A six year old can ask the tooth fairy or God to drop something out of the sky. All you need is self- centeredness and greed to pull that off. Indeed, Black women are often protected when men tell them what they think as opposed to what they *feel*. We often have to think about what we say so as to shelter the woman from the rage that some sisters have the incredible ability to effortlessly provoke. Do my *feelings* come through on this?

5. It Failed To Get The Girls:

There are certain points that this book is intent on emphasizing until they are clear. One point is that the relationship problems of Black men and women in their 20's and above have their foundation in attitudes and behaviors that start much earlier, usually around thirteen or fourteen. The second point emphasized is that people are creatures of habit. Once a male or female adopts an attitude or a coping mechanism that helps them through a frustrating experience, it is hard for them to change it unless someone either explains to them *why* they should change or shows them *how*. Usually it takes both and usually it takes a very trusting and understanding person to do both. At thirteen or fourteen, girls *actually teach* boys, by their lack of response to the boys' conversation, that talk doesn't count for very much. It isn't a difficult lesson for boys to learn because they're learning the same thing from boys of their own age in other situations. Girls (and eventually women) are interested in *image*, because the boy's image becomes a part of their own image. To have a boyfriend with a good image makes her look good in the eyes of her girlfriends. How you dress, how you look and carry yourself, how you dance, whether you are respected by the other boys (how you handle yourself physically), if you have any special talents or personality quirks, will say more about your success with girls at that age than your general conversation. Especially since you will be competing with boys who are two to four years older or more. If the women reading this are honest, they know that it is nothing that a fourteen or fifteen year old boy can *say* that could make him competitive (as a boyfriend) with a bigger, older, stronger, more mature boy of sixteen, seventeen or eighteen. Nothing, he loses, end of story, period. Thus image, style, machoism, money, a muscle-bound body, access to a car, jewelry, and a host of other things are the key to crafting the image that will take you places where conversation alone will not.

The problem, from the woman's perspective, is that it never stops. At twenty five or thirty five, the man is still impressing with the car, the clothes, jewelry, money etc. Why? *Because he was never given a signal that the women had stopped playing the game they started twenty years earlier, and because the game still works* for him.

Now the college-educated, corporate Black woman who owns her own condo might be put off by what she considers "childish posturing" by some Black men, but she is in the minority. The brothers are directing themselves to the lowest common denominator. The majority of the women still respond to the very game that they started. Women don't want to know what you really think about anything until they "get serious" about you.

6.   Your Statements Become Public Information

One of the reasons that I think so many African-American women enjoyed reading *Waiting To Exhale* by Terry McMillian was because they appreciated the tight sisterhood that the four main characters enjoyed. The glue that seemed to hold together the sisterhood was the general understanding that you had to spill your guts out to your sisters about what was going on between you and the men in your life. Each woman turned in their reports on a consistent basis regarding what their man said, what he did, how he screwed (if he screwed) and how the women responded to their man's behavior. Each woman needed and depended on the other women's opinions of the dramas in their life, in order to maintain whatever self-confidence they may have had. It was a rather democratic process, where at least three of the four women had to approve the actions that any one sister wanted to take. Thus, a tremendous amount of a man's personal business, whether he was a good or a bad guy, was in the street. And who's to say that each man's personal business will not be spread well beyond these four women?

Thus, a lot of men will not discuss their feelings with a woman because they have no confidence that the discussion will remain the private thing that it is meant to be. It may not be her girlfriend with whom she shares this information, but rather her own mother, an older sister or brother, or a close relative of the very man insisting on the privacy of the conversation. Many men have gotten to the point where they don't even blame *individual* women for these transgressions anymore because they see it as so widespread that they assume that it is something that women can't help from doing. That it's genetic. In other words, to get mad at a sister for putting your business out in the street is to get mad at a sister for having to sit down to pee. It's their way of doing things. Their world begins and ends with their mouth. Are there exceptions to the rule? Of course. Many. But you have no way of knowing without the test of time, because all the blabber- mouths are going to lie and say they never tell anybody anything. Add in the fact that women instinctively cover each others lies and denials, and you've got one hell of a puzzle to unscramble if you have the time and interest to play those kinds of games. So the obvious answer is to keep your mouth closed. She can't tell what you haven't told her. Are you still wondering why Black men don't talk?

A MALE SPIN ON THE CONCEPT OF COMMITMENT

An absolute requirement of any article, book, or talk show on Black male/female relationships is to criticize the Black man for his miserable, wimpish record on making commitments to his natural mate, the Black woman. Here again, because we only have female magazines to consult, with their female editors checking over the manuscripts of the mostly female writers, who have written from a female's perspective, there is not much choice but to believe the worst about the Black man because that is mostly what gets printed. In this chapter we'll look at commitment from another point of view and provide some insight into the Black male's thoughts and feelings about the idea of giving everything to one woman and one relationship "till death do you part". Probably the best way to do this is to review the basic complaints that Black woman have about Black men failing to commit to a long term relationship and then try to address the issues one by one.

Hit and Run:
Probably the biggest complaint is that even at the age of forty and beyond, some Black men still have an approach that many women consider adolescent. It involves sleeping with a woman, not with the idea of "making love to her" but as a means of scoring ego points to measure one's masculinity and desirability. Women see the avoidance of an emotional connection with them after sex as a prime example of the uncommitted, uninvolved, utilitarian nature that men put on relationships, and that it demeans and shames the women participating in the act.

Limited Emotional Capability:
There are brothers who are not the hit-and-run type but who are faulted because of the poor *quality* of their emotional involvement. Some men seemingly do not have the capacity to feel deeply about females or at least not deeply enough about the one they happen to be with at that moment. Other brothers who clearly have the capacity to "fall in love" disappoint their mate by ending the relationship because he fears, is confused by, or feels trapped by the *depth* of his emotional feelings. In any case, the females are left feeling frustrated, with a sense of disappointment and dishonor when their affections have not been reciprocated. The men usually leave under real or imagined problematic circumstances and the women feel betrayed and angry.

The Cheating Husband:

Many, many Black men will go through all the necessary steps and ceremonies to legalize and maintain a permanent connection with his "main" squeeze. However, they either had no intention or not enough discipline to break away from their many "minor" squeezes as well. Thus, many Black women over the last decade or so have discovered that their husbands were involved in a social and or sexual way with another woman. This unauthorized union is proof of a lack of fidelity and commitment to the marriage.

The Unsupportive Father:

Perhaps the worse of the entire lot is the father who ignores, doesn't support and doesn't even inquire about his children. Most people of both sexes and all races have a low tolerance for men in this category. A husband and a wife will always be two separate people but children are a part of them both, physically, legally and otherwise. The very height of uncommittedness is a father (or mother) not taking care of or at least relating to his offspring.

If the above will adequately serve as the basic categories of uncommitted men, we must next look at what it is that people are committing to. A lot of time could be spent discussing the rather vague concept of a *relationship,* but since *marriage* is the desired relationship for most, it makes more sense to focus on that.

Defining The Commitment Called Marriage:

I don't remember the first wedding I attended in our family, but we had many because I had a lot of aunts and uncles who married. I was no more than about fourteen years old when I noticed that there were definite differences in how men reacted to the idea of marriage as compared to the women. The men seemed to be rather cool and reserved to the idea of marriage. The men always had this attitude of, "I think I'm doing the right thing but its hard to be *absolutely positive.*" The women on the other hand were so excited that it was clearly seen as the biggest thing in their life. When a woman in our family became engaged, the excitement would spread to many other female members of the family, and they would start to talk about details like gowns, shoes, food, and so forth months ahead of time. Throughout my life the signals and messages I have received about marriage have not changed very much. Women still get a lot more excited than men, and one woman's preparations for marriage are enough to excite a dozen more of her female friends. Most men still wonder if they are making the right move, or making it at the right time. Immediately prior to my own marriages, I had questions about whether I was doing something that I might later regret. I went ahead anyway because I knew

I would regret not marrying them even more. But none of this is the feeling of absolute ecstasy you believe you are suppose to feel when getting married. And I felt guilty because I didn't have that feeling. Both times. But in my informal discussions over the years with brothers, I've never yet met one brother who was ecstatic over his marriage. Happy, pleased, confident, a feeling of being lucky, yes. But ecstasy, no.

What is it then about this thing called marriage that almost everybody wants to do sooner or later, but which causes such different responses in men and women? Unless we get some clarity on that point, we are not on firm ground in talking about commitment.

Frankly, I think that most men would say that there is much more in marriage for the women than it is for the men. Marriage was designed to protect the interests of women and children and such protection limits the options and freedoms that men had before marriage.

Marriage is a set of responsibilities for both husband and wife, but Black men would say that the pressure is greater on them. What are the pressures on Black men in marriage and what is it about marriage that would make even "nice guys" (if you sisters still believe there is such a thing) have reservations about entering into such an agreement? How can we better understand lack of commitment by getting a better idea of what commitment is and what it costs? When a thinking man looks at marriage, he looks at three things. He looks at himself first, because that's who he has lived with all his life and will continue to live with until the day he dies. He looks at marriage, the institution, and at the lady he is thinking of marrying. And then he thinks about outcomes, benefits, costs and rewards in the marriage and attempts to tally it all up to see if the bottom line adds up the way he thinks it should.

Personal Considerations and Sacrifices
Based on the areas we have covered in the life of young Black men, there is not much in the general society to encourage these young men to achieve status, security and economic satisfaction. That is the way it is and always has been. Young Black men have no rational reason to believe that life is going to treat them well. Even if he graduated from high school, has average intelligence, is not involved in dope or gangs, goes to church, has never been arrested, has two parents and is not ugly, life still has a whole lot of whipping reserved for the average Black man. If a young Black man is working, he probably is not making enough to satisfy his own modest needs of a home, car, clothes, food and a minimum number of adult toys and trophies. Savings are probably non-existent. So the first consideration a brother usually makes in the consideration of marriage (otherwise known as full commitment) is a financial

one. If I am not making enough money to adequately support myself, how can I possibly take on the responsibility of another person? And if I am making enough only to live the way I want to live, am I willing to go backwards financially for the pleasure of being with this young lady forever?

Another major factor is whether the bride already has children, as millions seem to today. A male must look at his current economic status and future prospects more critically when children are already present. Because of their role as providers, men have to (or at least *should think*) about their new responsibilities. They cannot afford the luxury of simply getting wrapped up in the emotionalism of marriage as women seen to do. Men also look at their sex lives and ask themselves questions. In addition to having my financial situation disrupted and having the pressure of having to find a way to make more money (work longer hours) just to live at the same level that I'm already living, am I also willing to give up the idea of ever having sex under *any* circumstances with another woman for the rest of my days on this earth? That may be twenty, thirty, forty or fifty years into the future! If women don't think that is an incredibly hard idea for a man to think about, then they do not have the foggiest notion of the male psycho-sexual make up and thus are *not in a position* to critically comment on a male's sexual commitment. When a man cannot *promise* this particular part of the marriage vow, there is basically only one word to describe him-*honest*. He *honestly* can not say to himself, to the bride or to any God he might worship that he will *never* under *any* circumstances sleep with another woman. But this honesty kicks Black men in the butt because this is not the answer Black women, the religion of Christianity and the laws of at least forty nine states (I don't know about Utah but we're not likely to be living there anyway) in the U.S. want to hear.

The problem, in part has to do with human nature. There is human nature, male nature, female nature and a whole range of other natures that we call gays, lesbians, and bisexuals. And there are differences. For a woman to really understand how hard it is for some men to promise fidelity, imagine a man coming up to you and saying I will marry you if you promise not to menstruate every month. I think most women, after registering complete shock, would then proceed to talk about how "natural" the menstrual cycle was and how hormones and body chemistry determines the various changes that women go through. And while they are giving the male this lecture they would *act like* men have no natural hormones or body chemistry determining *their* moods, desires, and actions. I believe part of the reason that men "stray" is hormonal and psychological.

The third decision a male might ponder in considering marriage could be broadly called his freedom. In addition to all the other things that must be sacrificed or rethought, a man has to ask himself would he be in charge of his free time to do as he chooses or would the duties of marriage prevent him from visiting friends, doing old activities in sports or hobbies, etc.. What about personal development activities like going to school, studying computers, or involvement in painting, music, karate, and so on. In marriage, especially in one with kids and one that is under-financed, *is there such a thing as free time (freedom)?* These are the types of questions and conclusions that many men might reach when contemplating the full commitment of marriage.

Let's assume that despite the life-changing and challenging situation marriage might mean for a man, that he is ready for marriage. Then what? Well, the man next would look at his mate, his bride. He would likely say to himself, "This is what I'm getting in return for the decision to restructure my life". But men realize that if they marry, they marry not only the girl, *they marry marriage.* And there is a big, big difference between marrying the women and marrying the *institution* of marriage.

Marriage is more complicated today because for every question that had only two or three answers twenty years ago, there are now more than half a dozen answers to that same question today. And of course there are new questions which did not even come into anyone's mind twenty or more years ago, such as whether his wife will carry his name. What this means is that there are more opportunities for there to be disagreements in marriage than ever before. It's like walking into a restaurant and ordering meals. If there are only two main meals to select from, it is likely that the husband and wife will have the same meal. But if that restaurant offers forty different meals, and people have stopped thinking that its necessary for the man and woman to eat the same meal, then its almost guaranteed that the couple will have very different ideas of what makes the perfect dinner. In marriage we now have a menu of many choices; and rather than the husband and wife agreeing on things together, most want as often as possible to select the choice that best meets *their personal needs.* So with more choices and options (more freedom of choice) come also more misunderstandings, disagreements, arguments, "fights", yelling, screaming, cursing, vindictiveness etc. And the male is normally paying, *spending his money* to be a participant in these disagreements no matter whose "fault" it may be.

But the increased options in life and marriage also reveal something else in relationships. Not only do the increased decisions make it easier to have arguments (for example whether your Sunday dinner should be really cooked in the stove for two hours or simply nuked in the microwave) but it makes it easier for husbands and wives to "judge" each other and keep score about the various decisions they've made over the last year or more. In other words, in the past, when the gender roles were so well defined that you didn't have to really *think* about what to do as a husband or wife, it was harder to *be* a *bad* husband or wife if you simply followed the traditional script. But today, as you have to *think, choose, weigh, and calculate* your decisions as a husband, or a wife, and as you have to accept responsibility for how those decisions affect everyone else, it then becomes much easier to be considered a dumb-ass husband or stupid-ass wife. And of course holding one of these prized titles is not good for insuring the longevity of the union.

The other things that come with marriage are increased fears and concerns. Life will take on a more serious tone which some people like to call "growing up" or "maturity." In addition to worrying about there being enough money to support a family, there may be the fear of not having a job at all. There is no need here to discuss Black male unemployment, because every reader knows the story. And as many Fortune 500 companies like Sears, IBM, and Boeing lay off thousands of white collar, college grad, experienced worker types, there is no way in hell that a Black man, even with all the right credentials, can be sure that he is safe in any company. Hell, the Army is even laying off people, if you can believe that.

There is the fear that you might not be able to keep your pledge of fidelity, and there is the curiosity of whether your wife is keeping hers. If you have children from a previous relationship, there is the fear that marriage will effect your relationship with them - financially, emotionally and in your ability to spend quality time with them. With a jealous, insensitive wife, this can be especially difficult. Most women get to take their children wherever they go and stay angry at the father of their children over such a long period of time that some (many) lose the ability to even believe that a man can agonize over being separated from his children. Savannah in *Waiting To Exhale* shows such insensitivity to an old boyfriend, Kenneth. (p.391)

"........ and a month or two later, you'll call me up all pitiful
and probably say something like, even though you love me to
death, you can't leave your wife right now because you'd feel
too guilty about leaving your kid, or it's too much money
involved, or whatever other excuses you motherfuckers always
manage to come up with."

A major fear that many men have if they have gotten past the point of wondering if they can *support* a family is wondering if they can support a family to the level of material comfort that the wife wants and or expects. There are many men who would be really appreciated by some women but who are openly ridiculed by their own wives because the man can not provide bigger, better, or more of what they are already providing for her.

It is the nature of American society to give women the license to feel this way because of the long history of hypergamy in the U.S. (as well as in many other places, I presume). Hypergamy means "to marry upward" (Haki, page 86) and women are expected in traditional ways of thinking to move a step up in social class when they marry. In the context of today's reality, this concept is not dead but it is dying.

Today, if you listen to the conversations and expectations of some Black women, they feel perfectly justified having their cake and eating it too. Using an old traditional way of thinking, they want to "marry up." They want the husband to have more age and experience, more education, more money and status, more social connections and an overall higher profile than herself. Then she wants to be able to quickly change up, and put on her feminist hat, and expect to be treated *equally* with her husband. And she can express these views with a straight face. She sees no inconsistency between liking a man *because* he has more of everything, yet demanding that that same man treat her (who may not have a pot to pee in) as an equal! An equal in what?

It is not my purpose to try to chronicle all the fears and concerns that some Black men have about marriage. I wish to list only a few representative ones so that females will see that these concerns are real. Fortunately (or unfortunately depending on your frame of mind) for Black women, Black men *do not think these things through thoroughly*. If all Black men did so, a very significant number would *not* marry and even *fewer* Black women would be married today than actually are. Most Black men do what women do which is to respond emotionally rather than logically, something people like Terry McMillian would like us men to do more of.

But the state of being married does not correct mistakes in judgment that people make in the marriage, nor does it protect you from the weaknesses that you knew you had prior to the marriage. Thus, those who ignored their promiscuous ways, their spend thrift ways, their erratic work habits, their traditional rather than modern or liberated values, will have all these problems crop up in the marriage, resulting in either two miserable married people or a destroyed marriage. Thus, Black men are often confused by charges of their lack of commitment, because Black women act as if *any* marriage can work. That two people can come together who do not have harmonious or compatible personalities and yet make it simply because they go through a ceremony and are proclaimed married is a ridiculous assumption.

How many problem marriages or destroyed marriages do Black women have to see to learn that that is simply not the way it is? So if a brother says no, I do not want to marry you (either because I am not the one for you or you are not the one for me) rather than be angry at non-commitment from the brother, she should be somewhat grateful (though she still may be disappointed) that she did not get faked off into a situation that would have only back fired anyway, and would have left at least two more people's lives disrupted. But Black women don't look at it that way. They look at the decision not to marry as a sign of weakness. They assume that they can intimidate, brow beat or embarrass a brother into marrying them and still believe the relationship can last "till death do us part". That makes no sense at all. What kind of a self-image does a woman have if she thinks she has to embarrass a brother into marrying her? Does she think he loves her? Does she really think they would have a good and lasting sex life? Does she think he will remain monogamous? Does she even care? Does being married mean that much to these women?

Black women are smart, and those who aren't are greedy; so either way you look at it both kinds of Black women know how to go after what they want. And, yes, they do want to be married because that is the broad umbrella under which all the goodies fall.

Why is Being Married so Important to Black Women?

In all honesty, I cannot say that Black women want to marry for reasons any different from other women. Whatever the self serving goals listed here, I cannot say that it is any worse (and perhaps may not even be as bad) as the motives of other women.

1) Status: Among the sisterhood there is a definite status for simply *being* married. Perhaps it is assumed that you "married up" and therefore are a real Mrs. Somebody now. Maybe it's assumed that you will soon have children, or you're wearing an expensive diamond ring. Maybe it's the romantic idea that somebody would want you forever. Obviously it could be all of these things and more. Clearly, however, there is much more envy and status that women show toward married women than what single men show toward married men.

2) Children: The character Robin in *Waiting To Exhale* would be an absolutely frightening kind of woman for me to be around and fortunately I've been spared the agony. Here is a woman who selects her men in part based on the beauty of the babies she thinks will be produced by the man's genes. What a way to pick a lifetime mate. I had heard the same statement about fifteen years ago and assumed that a person who would do something like that was rare. But after coming across Robin, I've found that women in the ghetto say such things all the time. So much for crediting myself for being tuned into "The Hood."

The stigma of single motherhood is not what it use to be in society in general or in the Black community specifically. Still, if given a choice, women would certainly prefer to have children with a father, not only for financial reasons but also for moral, religious, and social reasons. Based on the court system in most states, a woman just about has a lock on keeping her children if the marriage should go sour. Therefore, you could call this an "in-the-bag benefit" of marriage: Women get to keep the kids.

3) Better Income and Lifestyle: In doing the research for this book, the single most frustrating area was trying to document the differences in income between Black men and women. One reason it was so difficult was because Black women writers had a different perspective and set of statistics to prove whatever point they wanted to make. For example, to prove that the Black woman was still at the bottom of the income totem pole, Black female writers showed statistics which said she made less than White and Black men. But to show Black women brought just as much to the marriage table as the men and therefore weren't "being taken care of," other Black female writers would show that Black women had more college degrees, more white collar positions, longer periods of consistent employment and just about equal amounts of pay. This argument was to bolster Black female egos and images and take away any credit that the Black man may have earned in being proclaimed the chief provider, a recognized manhood role. Finally, in the statistics that show what happens when a marriage ends, the figures are trotted out to show that the man does much better after the divorce and the woman does much worse. These statistics are designed to create sympathy again for Black women and give judges and lawyers the moral authority to ask for the sky and at least get the moon from the Black man in terms of alimony and child support, the residence and other assets obtained during the course of the marriage.

Marriage *is* an income for some Black women. A gold digger is simply one who has higher goals and is more obvious in her intent than the average Black woman. But I want to repeat what was said earlier, namely that there is no proof that Black women are more or less mercenary than other women. In fact she's probably *less* of a gold digger since Black men have less gold to be dug. There are three lines of thought that Black women use to justify their entitlement to financially benefit in the marriage game. The first line of reasoning is from the poor girl who comes from the projects, never had a father, etc. Her thinking is, "I deserve a man to provide me with the things that I never got from the father that was never there". So the husband has to do double duty. He has to be both father and husband to his bride and hope that he doesn't fail by managing to play only one role well. When a Black woman is both consciously and subconsciously trying to make up for past deprivation in this way, (particularly when she is beginning with nothing), it's not difficult to see how her demands and expectations can grow quickly and completely out of line with reality. Often this same female says to all who want to hear "My kids are not going to live like I did; they shouldn't have to. They are going to get everything they deserve and everything I didn't get." Please pity the poor man who marries this type of woman because she will develop an all-consuming urge to spend, to have and to consume, all in an effort to fill an emotional hole that material things are not designed to fill.

The second line of thought comes from a woman who is the product of a solid middle class family and who thinks that her husband should provide for her the way her father provided for her mother. However, the catch is that her mother didn't work outside the home because that was the thinking of that day (and of her father). So whereas this college-educated woman and her husband could be doing very well working together, and may in fact *be* doing well, he still doesn't measure up because according to the wife's standards, he should be able to provide the lifestyle *by himself.* She wants the luxury of quitting work and raising one or more children without a drop in the lifestyle. She's not dumb. She passed math and, she can add *and subtract;* but that's not the point. She wants what she wants and doesn't see why her husband shouldn't be able to do it if her "daddy" did it! Pity the brother who marries this type of woman also.

Finally we have the social striver who comes from a family of social strivers. Daddy is a judge, surgeon, high political office holder, a successful business owner, etc. This woman will likely marry a doctor, lawyer, dentist, engineer or businessman. He will already be very comfortable, content and stable. But it will not be enough for her. This woman will push him to want more, be more, have more, and control more. The husband will feel that nothing is enough for her. He will soon see that he must be a super achiever just to be acceptable.

Women use their fathers to be the financial baseline that their husbands must meet just to get a passing grade. Unsuspecting husbands labor for years not realizing that they have this shadow, this ghost, following them wherever they go. It is "daddy" and all that he either did or didn't do. And you, the male, have to make up for it or surpass "daddy" whatever the case may be. The idea that you are the captain in your house is an idea that's present only in your own head. Daddy's shadow is calling the shots. Is there something wrong with a woman wanting to improve her lifestyle or at least match what she's use to? No, it isn't. But when it's hidden and denied and then revealed and used later to manipulate the husband, it sure as hell puts a damper on the idea of romance, commitment and "till death do us part".

By far the worse part of marriage for most Black men is the legal divorce. You stand before a White judge (and usually they are consulting with White lawyers) who says "you will pay X amount of dollars to your ex-wife and we are going to take it directly out of your pay anyway if you do not comply". There are few things more humiliating that a Black man can experience. If all prospective Black grooms spent a day in divorce court and saw how little power he had to direct the rest of his life after he tried to live the married life, a significant percentage would cancel marriage so fast it would give you whiplash. Black women ought to be on their knees nightly praying not for a man, but for the Black man to never come to understand what he's getting himself into legally when he says "I do." The White boy is fighting back in his own marriages with prenuptial agreements. As Black men make more money they may use the same tool in order to prevent being taken to the divorce cleaners. White judges don't give a damn about Black women or their children. But White judges love to strip Black men of whatever they have, every chance they get, even if its not coming to them personally. After working through this abbreviated version of a Black males interpretation of marriage, it will hopefully be easier for the Black woman to appreciate why the men are resistant to this comprehensive commitment. If it is still not any clearer, the subject will come up at a later point in this volume.

Let us review and explain in greater detail the four or five character types of non committal Black men that were identified at the beginning of this chapter. The hit and run brother is usually a young brother who is trying to do several things at once. He is trying to experience as often as possible, the incredible pleasure of sex which may be a relatively new phenomena for him. He is also biochemically driven to do this; thus a part of his motivation is not totally in his complete control. He is also trying to establish a sense of manhood in three areas and sex is allowing him to address all three areas simultaneously. Sexual conquests provide manhood points (and status) among his peers, and it gives *him* self-confidence and reaffirmation. Sex also establishes among his circle of young women that he at least satisfies one manhood criteria: the brother is a "performing" male. The question, though, is at what age does this behavior seem or become immature. I don't think many people today *expect* a man between twenty-one to twenty-five to marry, do you? But what about a twenty-nine year old? What about a once- divorced thirty-two year old or a twice-divorced forty-four year old? And does what they are doing with the major portion of their time and talent (their occupation) carry any weight in judging them to be mature or immature? Does playing the field as a Black male constitute a crime simply because there are women out there who want to be married and men who don't? I challenge anyone to come up with a one size fits all answer to these questions. However Napoleon Hill, author of *Think and Grow Rich*, has some interesting comments to make on this subject and we will look at them in another section of this book.

The brothers of limited emotional capacity are again not of a single type. Some people have real psychological problems in relating emotionally to others. I don't think it is a cop-out to say that a significant number of young Black men have this problem. There is a natural law that says "for every action there is an equal and opposite reaction." I have no doubt that for all the rejection, scorn, abuse and ridicule that has been dumped on Black males, that a lot of disturbed personalities have been formed as a result. Instead of sitting back and getting angry for not getting what they want (marriage), I would like to see more Black women help brothers get professional help, on the basis of the *friendship*, that they are assumed to share. If a sister helps a brother find his better self through professional help, she may or may not inspire a commitment that would become her dream come true. But even if that deep romantic commitment doesn't come, men would learn that having a female as a friend has its value. Just as men have to learn how to help Black women without the carrot of sex as an incentive, Black women have to learn how to help Black men without the carrot of lifetime commitment as the incentive. And with this kind of openness, both may get what they are looking for.

The cheating husband is probably more the rule than the exception today, if by cheating you mean a brother who has ever had sex outside his marriage. There are many ways to explore this idea, but for our purpose the focus will be the issue of realism. What highlights the misunderstandings between men and women seems to be the fact that they disagree on what is *real*. The problem is more than one gender not understanding what the other gender is saying but rather what the opposite sex perceives as a realistic expectation. For example, a woman of relatively modest means can talk about her wedding costing thirty thousand dollars and see that as real and say it with a straight face. But most men looking at that kind of money for a mere ceremony that lasts one day, with few material assets left behind, see that idea as something from the Fantasyland studio in Disneyland, *regardless* of who's paying the tab. That much money for such an event seems completely unreal to him. On the other hand, a woman will see the extreme celebration and expense dedicated to the Super Bowl and all the holiday atmosphere trappings associated with that event, and think that is unreal. Or young women can see the fact that one young man will kill another one for his sneakers, gold chain, coat or for *nothing* and feel quite unconcerned seems absolutely unreal to her.

With respect to married men not ever having sex outside of marriage, the question that many, perhaps most men would ask is "how real of an expectation is that"? Even if it was something that men *wanted* to comply with, like avoiding a pot belly, their hair turning gray, being without a job, or some other lofty idea; how realistic is the expectation? Certainly if we look at African traditions going back thousands of years we do not see this promise there. Perhaps this is one reason why most Black women are not that fond of exploring African traditions, because it can be used to rationalize longstanding "sexist practices and beliefs". In any event, what *binds* the African-American man to this promise that he can't seem to keep? It is the religious dogma of Christianity which he had little choice but to accept from his original slave master and the converted slaves and the culture which they developed? He is also bound by the laws of the United States, which he had no hand in establishing. Thus Black men break a promise that they only *circumstantially* agreed to and not something that they freely initiated or acted on voluntarily. This might sound like so much bull to people who have completely bought into and swallowed hook line, and sinker the religious, moral and legal underpinnings to White American society. But to others it is but another example of how the Black man pays a price for not being in a position to clearly *define himself*, what *he* believes in and thus define what he promises to do or not do. So much of what the Black man fails to achieve are parts of "package deals" that he *had to* buy into simply by just being here in America. Package deals which he did not assemble, nor were assembled with him in mind.

Marriage vows aside, I would like to think that individual couples of Black men and women can decide among themselves what they will and will not tolerate from each other. It is preposterous to think that Black men can change the religious and legal underpinnings of this country and shape them according to their will or their historical traditions. But I sure as hell hope that doesn't mean that Black men and women can't agree on a one to one basis with each other about what they need to make each other happy and enable their marriage to survive. In fact, many people have been writing out their own marriage vows for the past twenty-five years now, so this idea is not new.

It might be interesting to point out here what often happens to a brother who does comply with the strict fidelity requirements of a christian marriage. What often happens is that, after a few years, he loses his interest and capacity to adequately perform sexually altogether. The same women who worried their heads off about the promiscuous boyfriend or the unfaithful husband now complain that *they* can not get enough sex to satisfy their modest sexual requests. Whole areas in mental and physical medicine have developed to address the problems of these non functional but faithful husbands. Before closing the door on any compromise in your standard wedding vows, you may want to make some adjustments in light of this possible sexual consequence.

The brother who doesn't commit to support his children has the least amount of sympathy and understanding from this writer. Whether a brother can comply with regular on time child-support payments to the mother of his children is obviously tied to whether American society will enable him to receive regular on time payments for the work he has done or is willing to do. But not even this question should get in the way of a Black man supporting his offspring. With billions and billions of dollars passing hands every hour of every day, the Black man's will and intelligence should make a way, a legal way, for him to capture enough of those dollars so that his children have a place to stay, food to eat and clothes to wear. Any other answer substantially different than that might reduce the man we think we are talking about to a "boy". And of course as a "boy" he would be disqualified from general consideration of what is being talked about here.

It is sincerely hoped that the information provided here will give some added insight to the inability of the average Black man to see the joy and excitement in marriage in the same way that women do. There is little basis for it, because it's an uneven deal. Women, no matter how gainfully employed, see a boost in their lifestyle as a result of marriage. Most would probably not consider marriage *without* seeing such a boost. Brothers, on the other hand, see a dramatic increase in a range of responsibilities, not the least of which is financial. By marrying, a brother is paired with another human being that is normally more materialistic and more status conscious, which signals a likely rise in financial expectations. Many men could very well see more work hours and added pressure coming into their life for no other purpose than to meet their bride's new demands or expectations.

It is absolutely understandable why a woman would want a financial partner to come into her life. By simply sustaining her affection for him and sharing her body with him, she gets him to work his entire lifetime to supply her with the things she wants. Men would also like to have such a financial partner designed to meet those specific needs as well, but such is very rarely the case. It is also understandable how the Black woman could feel much more secure as a human being after getting involved in even the most nonsensical marriage, as she has the added leverage of the White legal system to force certain minimum payments to her at the marriage's end. All of us should be so lucky as to have some "guaranteed money" on the side coming to us for years in the future. In that sense, marriage can be the single best financial instrument for the woman. She can't lose. She gets it if the marriage works. She gets it if the marriage doesn't work. But as men we are asking the women to understand our lack of shared enthusiasm. We see our money, our time, our sense of fun fading into the sunset. Even if marriage is something that we do see ourselves eventually submitting to, is it too much to ask that it be on *our timetable* rather than yours?

THE BLACK MAN'S BURDEN - DON'T BELIEVE THE HYPE

In the 1960's the term *Black Man's Burden* was used to refer to the extra pressure and problems Black people faced as a result of racism. It was acceptable in those days to use Black *man* to refer collectively to both Black men and women - i.e. the race.

Today there is still a *Black Man's Burden*. But more and more in today's society, Black Man's Burden means just that, The Black *Man's* Burden.

The Black man in particular is being made to feel that he is the cause of *everybody's problems* - White males, White females, Black females, the Koreans, the Japanese, the Jews etc.

One of the things that the Black man is supposed to have destroyed is the Black family.

But Don't Believe The Hype

The chart below gives some reasons for the break up of the Black family that the media and quite a few Black women forget to mention. It is not the intention of this chart to deny the fact that hundreds of thousands of Black men shirk their responsibility as fathers, providers, protectors and leaders in the Black family. It is, however, an attempt to show that in many tens of thousands of cases, either

a) the man acts out of desperation (placed on him by the larger society) to do what he feels might be in the best interest of his family

b) the man has a legitimate reason for not maintaining the relationship,

c) the female is the primary person ending the relationship or

d) the female is actively participating in activities that would make the formation of a new family unit very difficult.

e) A Black man is not even involved in the situation or is not aware that he is involved.

As long as White America and Black women feel justified in always blaming Black men for all that ails Black and White America, do not expect much cooperation in problem solving from Black men. No one, including Black men, want to be the perpetual scape goats and whipping boys for all the ills of America. Everyone must stop believing the hype and Black women should stop helping to create it.

THIS IS WHAT YOU SEE	THIS IS THE MEDIA HYPE	THE REAL DEAL IN THIS SITUATION
Single Black woman with a child and no mate	Irresponsible Black man walks away from his family	The woman plotted to capture the man by purposely getting pregnant. Lied about birth control. When man learns of the plot, he refuses to marry such a conniving woman
SAME AS ABOVE	SAME AS ABOVE	Man and wife have a peaceful separation. Both parents apply for child custody. Court automatically awards children to mother.
SAME AS ABOVE	SAME AS ABOVE	Woman fears never being asked to marry. Biological clock is ticking and she wants to experience pregnancy and motherhood. Gets pregnant by unsuspecting man who may never learn he is a father.

THIS IS WHAT YOU SEE	THIS IS THE MEDIA HYPE	THE REAL DEAL IN THIS SITUATION
SAME AS ABOVE	SAME AS ABOVE	Woman gets pregnant by unsuspecting male. This woman is additionally motivated because she thinks this particular man would make some "pretty babies" (light skin, straight hair, Anglo features etc.)
SAME AS ABOVE	Poor Black women can't find a marriageable Black man.	Divorced Black woman is not interested in getting married again
Single Black woman with a child and no mate. Receives welfare, housing, and food stamps.	Irresponsible Black man walks away from his family	Male mate could not find a job. Becomes aware that the family can get more financial support if he leaves. Painfully, he leaves.

THIS IS WHAT YOU SEE	THIS IS THE MEDIA HYPE	THE REAL DEAL IN THIS SITUATION
Single Black woman with a child and no mate. Receives welfare.	Irresponsible Black man commits crime and goes to prison.	Male could not find a job. Love for family and pride prevented him from leaving. Decided to risk his life on a one-shot deal to rob White America of some of its money. He got caught.
Single Black woman with a child and no mate. Modest Lifestyle	Pimp Black man introduces Black woman to prostitution and drugs.	Female with no job skill tires of welfare life. On her own turns to prostitution and drugs to fight poverty and depression. Does not know who the father is.
Grandmother, adult woman and children. No mate	Irresponsible Black man leaves family.	Black man willingly accepts mother-in-law into his home. She causes problems. Wife constantly sides with her mother, not her husband. He leaves.

THIS IS WHAT YOU SEE	THIS IS THE MEDIA HYPE	THE REAL DEAL IN THIS SITUATION
Single Black woman with a child and no mate.	SAME AS ABOVE	Black man leaves "good job" to start his own business. She can't endure the hard, lean years of the business start-up. She leaves and takes children.
Successful Black woman with children and no mate	SAME AS ABOVE	Successful husband is transferred out of state. Successful wife refuses to leave her job. Keeps children.
Black woman with a child and no mate	Irresponsible Black Man leaves family	Black man never in the picture. The woman's parents have died. She takes care of younger siblings.
SAME AS ABOVE	SAME AS ABOVE	Black man dies a typical, early death - heart attack, cancer, stroke, diabetes, car accident.

THIS IS WHAT YOU SEE	THIS IS THE MEDIA HYPE	THE REAL DEAL IN THIS SITUATION
SAME AS ABOVE	SAME AS ABOVE	Black man injured in accident at work, home or in car. Becomes wheelchair-bound. Cannot perform sexually. She leaves with child.
SAME AS ABOVE	SAME AS ABOVE	She becomes born-again Christian. Once satisfactory husband suddenly is seen as the devil himself. She leaves and takes child.
SAME AS ABOVE	SAME AS ABOVE	Black man is in the service fighting some other people to send a few dollars home to his family.
SAME AS ABOVE	SAME AS ABOVE	Innocent Black man killed in everyday urban violence: robbery, drug shoot-out, police brutality, etc.
SAME AS ABOVE		

THIS IS WHAT YOU SEE	THIS IS THE MEDIA HYPE	THE REAL DEAL IN THIS SITUATION
SAME AS ABOVE	SAME AS ABOVE	Innocent Black man jailed in everyday miscarriage of justice.
Single Black woman with a child and no mate. No father interaction.	Irresponsible Black man walks away from his family	Woman left father and took child. Dislikes mate so much that she prevents him from seeing child as often as possible.
Single Black woman with a child and no mate.	SAME AS ABOVE	In her desire to be wined and dined as often as possible, woman dates 2-3 men at once. Gets pregnant. Honestly doesn't know who the father is.

THIS IS WHAT YOU SEE	THIS IS THE MEDIA HYPE	THE REAL DEAL IN THIS SITUATION
Black woman with a child and no mate. No assets, public housing	SAME AS ABOVE	All money entrusted with wife during marriage spent obsessively on hair care, jewelry cosmetics, and clothes. Brother leaves home but sends child support. Support money, in too many cases, still pays for hair car, jewelry, cosmetics, and clothes.
Black woman with a child and no mate.	SAME AS ABOVE	Black man tries to live a "normal" life, but finally comes to terms with his homosexuality. Woman leaves him.
SAME AS ABOVE	SAME AS ABOVE	Woman comes to terms with her homosexuality; she leaves man, taking the child.

THIS IS WHAT YOU SEE	THIS IS THE MEDIA HYPE	THE REAL DEAL IN THIS SITUATION
SAME AS ABOVE	SAME AS ABOVE	Black men loses his high-salaried job. Her meal ticket now gone, she leaves and takes child.
Single successful Black woman, no children. Highly immersed in White culture and values. Sometimes a White girl trapped in Black skin.	Irresponsible Black man doesn't have his thing together like sisters do. Not marriage material.	Woman insists on "marrying up." Man must do more than just match her success, he must surpass it. White man trapped in Black skin highly preferred.
Successful Black woman with a child and no mate	Irresponsible Black man leaves family	Black man was never in the picture. "Successful" woman married White. He left/she left.

AND COMING SOONER THAN YOU THINK

THIS IS WHAT YOU SEE	THIS IS THE MEDIA HYPE	THE REAL DEAL IN THIS SITUATION
Successful Black woman with a child. No mate	SAME AS ABOVE	Black man never Physically present. Black woman choses Artificial Insemination to impregnate self.

George Subira

I find it is extremely difficult to talk to Black people about business and be very informative and very emotionally moving at the same time. Every speaker I know either does one or the other, not both. I honestly believe that I am the best in giving the kind of answers and perspectives that grass roots' folks need to understand in order to start a small business. Of course, there are many people who know a lot more about all aspects of business than I do. But I try harder than anyone I know to get into the heads of average Black folks and see things from their perspective, a Black perspective. Very few of your business heavy-weights do this. I think I'm much easier for the Black masses to understand and I take a lot of pride in that.

John Raye on the other hand, won't give you the details about business that I will but he will move you, stir you up, and cause you to take some action towards moving to independence. I don't know of anyone in the country that does what he can do. Imagine a Baptist minister at a revival meeting preaching about business instead of religion; that's John Raye. He is the total package with the powerful voice, the belief, and faith in Black people and in his commitment to the cause of Black economic empowerment. He is good, *real* good.

If a church, college, or community group ever got both of us together in a full day business seminar, I guarantee you it would be the most motivating business program that their participants ever attended. But, of course, the struggle is to get our people interested in business in the first place.

John Raye is available through Dudley Cosmetology University, Greensboro, NC (910) 996-2030.

Other Books Available from VSBE Include

BLACK FOLKS' GUIDE TO MAKING BIG MONEY IN AMERICA

After 14 years and better than 75,000 copies sold, **Black FOLKS' GUIDE TO MAKING BIG MONEY IN AMERICA** continues to find its way to self reliant Black Americans.

BLACK FOLKS' GUIDE TO MAKING BIG MONEY IN AMERICA was written to answer many of our most pressing financial questions. Topics include job searching skills, credit counseling, home buying techniques, bargain shopping, time management, saving plans, income tax strategies and much, much, more. There is a review of the 24 principles that virtually all wealthy Americans use to develop and maintain their wealth. There is a chapter discussing the 13 roadblocks that keep Black Folks in continued poverty.

This publication deals with the special financial problems of the single Black female parent. It discusses the relationship of Black Folks to land (real estate) and business.

The most important and innovative aspect of this work is that it includes a STEP- BY-STEP PLAN OF ACTION designed to instruct the serious African American how to increase their wealth and improve their lifestyle.

BLACK FOLKS' GUIDE TO BUSINESS SUCCESS

Black Folks' Guide to Business Success tells the reader what practices to use and which practices to avoid in establishing a stable enterprise. The information is presented in a clear and understandable style that makes for easy and enjoyable reading.

Other topics covered in this book include:
- Specific business ideas for the Black community - What, Why and How?
- A discussion of Black People's attitudes towards money. Do they help or hinder the quest for the dollar?
- A discussion of Black business attitudes. Do Blacks go into business to make money?
- The true cost of establishing a successful business. Besides money and time, what are other costs?
- The Black Brain Drain and the Corporate Junkie. Who are they? Do they help or hinder Black business development?
- Extensive listing of organizations, networks and business resources.

GETTING BLACK FOLKS TO SELL

Getting Black Folks to Sell is a volume which hammers home one dominant idea. That idea is that the single most important factor in determining the success of a Black business (or any business for that matter) will be that business owner's ability to sell.

In the last twenty years there been thousands of business conferences and workshops held all over the nation. These conferences have informed the attendees on forms of business ownership, accounting practices, tax payments and general management principles. What is virtually never discussed in any degree of depth however, is the art of selling. This is quite ironic when one considers that it is the activity of selling that puts money into the cash register. This volume will answer the following questions:

- How have recent changes in the American Labor system put more pressure on Black Americans to sell?
- What other benefits does the Black community gain by having a skilled sales force?
- Why have Black Americans shied away from sales in the past?
- How does one prepare to be successful in sales?
- What are the extra challenges that Black salespersons have to be prepared for to be successful in sales?
- How do you set goals in sales and improve your performance and income?

$14.00   Retail
$ 8.40   Wholesale

1ST TIME ON AUDIO TAPE --THE MIS EDUCATION OF THE NEGRO   By Dr. Carter G. Woodson

All 16 Chapters - slightly edited for today's readers are included in this 6 cassette 5 1/2 hour presentation. This is an all time classical work in Black History. Reading Done by George Subira.
* Includes attractive vinyl case
* Enjoy this important book over and over again.
* Play it for your children, churches, classrooms, and organizations.
* Excellent as a gift for all occasions.
* Use it as a fundraiser and spread the word.

$30.00 Retail
$18.00 Wholesale

I'll tell you why George Fraser's book is so important for the really success minded African American. Most books on success try to convince the reader that you can become an individual success by mastering certain techniques or ways of thinking. But that is only half true. Everyone needs a number of different people to help them along the road to success. People assume that they will eventually run into these people but they have no plan on how to make *sure* that they meet them.

George's book shows you how and where to meet them. Everyone understands that *who you know* is just as important as *what you know*. George's book explains how to meet the people you need to know to achieve the success that you are seeking. That is what makes it a very different kind of success book.

THE ECONOMIC EMANCIPATION OF AFRICAN-AMERICANS

"Let the Church say, Amen"

BY RICHARD E. BARBER, SR.

YES! Please send ____ copy(ies) of THE ECONOMIC EMANCIPATION OF AFRICAN-AMERICANS @ $7.95 per copy plus $2.00 postage and handing to the following address:

NAME_____

ADDRESS _____

CITY _____

STATE _____ZIP_____

method of payment

CHECK____ MONEY ORDER____ VISA____ MASTERCARD____

_____   _____
CREDIT CARD NUMBER   EXPIRATION DATE

    The overwhelming majority of Black people are not going to start a business and I accept that. But that should not mean that they are then free of any responsibility of helping to develop the Black economy. One thing people might feel comfortable in participating in is the Penny Lovers Program developed by brother Richard Barber. It is a hell of a concept because it can work and is working.

    It is all based around the penny. Black people have many, many thousands of dollars laying around their house as pennies. These pennies are in drawers, jars, cups, boxes, bottles, on dressers, and floors everywhere. Barbers program consists of using all these pennies for economic projects. And all the people who would donate the pennies wouldn't miss them because they aren't using the money now anyway.

    Barber is the brother who formed the first Black bank in Pittsburgh, PA twenty years ago, so he has always been serious about Black economics. I'm going to do what I can to promote him and his book because he has definitely got a place from which all of us can start.

MONEY ISSUES IN MARRIAGE

The preceding pages, as well as what follows, contain numerous perspectives which tend to cast serious doubt on whether the Black man and the Black woman are even suppose to be together as partners and family. That was not my intent. My intent is only to show real gender differences in outlook, experiences and values. Realistic people understand that good relationships require work and understanding, and we shouldn't necessarily expect good relationships to happen *automatically*. The more we recognize those differences and understand that they vary greatly from person to person and from situation to situation, the more we should be able to succeed in our relationships.

Black men and women do in fact get together and marry or have long term relationships. Most Black men and women would fit into this category. This section will examine certain economic ideas and realities that many Black men see in this thing called marriage. Unfortunately most Black people do not see enough of the economic realities of marriage, and that is a problem. It is my belief that the economic ignorance of the Black community has a major negative effect on us as a people generally and on our relationships specifically.

The Motivation to Marry

While Black men have been targets of criticism for not wanting to commit in a relationship, few people have ever questioned the motivation of women in *wanting* such a commitment. Some women simply want to marry a better lifestyle. They are tired of being poor, and see a man as the surest way out of that situation. Some women simply want a child and would rather do it within the structure of a marriage. In this situation, many woman seem to be minimally fazed when the marriage doesn't work out; and perhaps that might be because the marriage was originally just a means to get what she really wanted (a baby) and was not intended to be an end in itself. The desire to get away from their parental domination encourages some women to want to marry, while for others the motivation is the fear that they probably won't attract anyone better than who they have currently. I have heard that some mothers even tell their daughters that, for the sake of security in a marriage, they should marry someone who *loves them more* than their own love for the husband. I'm sure some women find themselves in this situation, and they respond accordingly. Other women marry only because the husband-to-be is considered by everyone else to be quite a catch. Thus, for the sake of status, a woman might move forward with marriage.

Why is it important to question the motives of women wanting to marry? Well, for several reasons. In the first place there is an assumption that just the act of getting married is a good thing in itself, and this assumption is historical. But that assumption was more valid it seems when most couples stayed together for life, when they worked together rather than in competition with each other, and when it was clear that children would enjoy the daily nurturing care of the mother and the exemplary work effort of "the man of the house". When marriage was viewed as something permanent and strong without "victims", it was seen as something that strengthened the whole family and community. Thus, marriage was viewed in a more positive light. Surely, therefore, anyone who was pushing for something so completely positive had to be viewed as a positive person themselves, and the person who was holding things up (the male) was seen as a drag, not only for the woman involved but for their community as well.

Today none of those old assumptions about marriage hold true anymore. It is not necessarily seen as permanent; the couple is not necessarily part of a specific community; the children do not get adequate care very often; and when the marriage ends (or even while it is intact) people claim to be *victims* of the marriage. In no way should marriage today be assumed to be the all-positive experience it was seen as in the past. Yet, in most cases it is still seen that way even when all the realities about marriage are clear for all to see. And because the image of marriage has barely changed, the image of the person most wanting to marry (usually the woman) has maintained the position of being the most positive person, while the reluctant male is still viewed negatively. This is true even when a woman's motivation to marry is completely selfish and self-serving. This reluctance by the male, rather than being seen as a negative, should be seen as a sign of mature contemplation and caution. There are many more things to consider in marriage these days than in generations past. It should not take a rocket scientist to figure out that if the institution of marriage is crumbling, that it's probably due to the actions of the married people. And there would be good reason to suspect problems will develop in a marriage if either of the parties went into the marriage with the wrong assumptions and the wrong motivations. Thus, while a woman is almost always perceived as the positive person who is trying to make this marriage happen, she is often the very person that insures its eventual destruction because of her faulty motivations, assumptions and reasoning. And who might be the only one aware of this situation? You guessed it, the contemplating groom, who often marries because of the sheer weight of peer pressure, which is another poor motivation to marry. So what we have here is another situation where the image of the woman is more positive than it often deserves to be, and the image of the less enthusiastic male is worse than it should be.

Another value judgment that people make regarding the personalities of the woman and man considering marriage involves maturity level. We know, for example, that throughout history the Black man has always been referred to as "boy" by disrespecting White folks who precisely intended to convey the idea of disrespect with that word. The Black man has understandably developed a sensitivity to the suggestion that he is not an adult or not fully grown. When a man wavers on his decision to marry, there is a tendency for people to say that he is immature or not ready to grow up, which is equivalent to calling him a "boy". On the other hand, the person who wants *somebody else* to take care of them for life, the woman, is considered in this situation the *mature* one. In any *other* normal situation we would call someone who needed to be taken care of immature or a boy, girl, etc. Can you see the contradiction in interpretation here and how it just so happens to go against the man? Warren Farrell makes the point from a slightly different angle in his book (pg.154 *Why Men Are The Way They Are*)

> "I have discussed how a single woman who supports herself is called a career woman, while a single man who supports himself is called a playboy. He may pay for her play as well as his own- but he hasn't "grown up" until he pays for her life. Ironically, a woman who commits and becomes financially *dependent* is considered more mature than a man who does not commit but is financially *independent*. When we pressure a man to commit by implying he has not grown up, we become like the coach who calls a man "sissy" to egg him on to perform. Maybe commitment is just the modern word for pressuring men to perform."

There is almost no way for a person to really understand the word commitment without understanding the idea that it involves a *taking away* of your options, and a reduction in your freedom. And every Black man in America almost has it as a part of his genetic makeup to stop and give deep thought to *anything* which threatens the very thing he has fought so long to achieve and has yet to obtain, this thing called freedom. The Black man is well aware that his labor has been key to other people experiencing more freedom and wealth than he. He is not all that impressed that he is being asked to be a part of a similar relationship again, even if the person asking, his future wife, does have all that he desires in a woman. It is one of the most illusive of things, this thing called freedom, that the Black man rightfully ponders when he's asked to make the move to marry. We have called into question the motivation of why some women want to marry, but we should get a glimpse of what some brothers think about that issue as well. It is interesting that while we constantly hear about role models for young boys or young girls to follow, we seldom hear about "role model couples". Just as many young people in the ghetto have been surrounded by *individuals* who ruined their lives by the bad decisions that they made, so the same can be said about many marriages that young people have been exposed to. As a matter of fact, young people have even seen the marriages of many of their role models come apart. This would include many athletes and entertainers; they seem to divorce constantly. If they are realistic and judge by what they see and hear, young people have no real reason to assume that marriage is either permanent or positive. How could anybody Black possibly disagree with that? Even if you were fortunate enough to have been born into an intact, even happy family, you still couldn't help but notice so many other families disintegrating. In his book *The Black Woman In America,* Dr. Robert Staples cites a study that was done by Elliot Liebrow in the sociological classic *Tally's Corner* (pg.106).

> "Elliot Liebrow also noted a pervasive disenchantment with marriage among a group of lower-class Black men. Marriage was seen as a *series of problems*: public and private fights between spouses; how to feed, clothe, and house a wife; anxiety about being able to ward off attacks on the health and safety of their children. These men could not recollect a single marriage in their community that they recognized as a "good marriage."

For many men, it is one thing to have a "series of problems" in one's own life; but to actually *pay* to have these series of problems as one does in a marriage is ridiculous. And to have to *pay* to get away from the problems (as in a divorce) is even worse.

If all this is so, why do men marry? Apparently it's because of intense love; love that could very well be deeper than that of his bride. Why do I say this? Because look what men have to *give up* to get married. Men have a deep appreciation for their freedom prior to marriage. These freedoms are numerous, but let's focus on only two: a) the freedom to go to bed with whoever you want, as much as you want, whenever you want, without guilt. That is a fantastic amount of freedom that men take for granted when they are single and only truly appreciate after a few years of marriage. The second great freedom is the freedom from the pressure of having to earn great sums of money for yourself and to meet the needs of one, two or more additional people. Freedom from the pressure of having to do that *every week* of every year is one helluva relief.

Although many men are not emotionally or experientially aware of the degree to which these two freedoms are sacrificed at the time of marriage (because they can't be experienced until *after* marriage), its pretty safe to say that all men think about them very deeply. When men hesitate to marry, it is seldom because they don't love the would-be-bride. It is because they question their own ability to *happily give up their freedoms, forever*. So when a man is motivated to marry, it is usually because of intense love. It usually isn't due to sex because often that's already been experienced countless times with the would be bride. It usually isn't money, because the average Black woman still makes less than the average Black man, and the increased expenses brought on by marriage usually eat up the wife's additional income anyway. And men seldom marry for status. It's ego-boosting to have an attractive wife, but you can't do much with that in the real world. There are millions of attractive women, so how much status could one nice looking woman have if she doesn't have other status bearing qualities to go along with the good looks.

Men marry for love because that's usually all the average brother can marry for, since money, status, security and sex are not significant factors. To be aware of the loss of freedom and still marry - it's got to be love! Now how long the love lasts is another question. But we should not read the often terrible circumstances under which *some* relationships end in such a way that we fail to credit Black men with loving, giving up freedom for love, and marrying for love.

On this same point Dr. Farrell makes an interesting observation as to how this applies to women. On page 182 he says:

"How can a man distinguish devotion out of fear from devotion out of love? If a woman can support herself financially and is not attached to the idea of marriage, it is a good bet she is devoted out of love. A man cannot tell whether a woman is in love with him or his security blanket until she is financially and psychologically independent enough to leave. Until a woman has learned how to leave even she cannot be sure she has learned to love."

THE WASTEFULNESS OF EXPENSIVE WEDDINGS

I live about twelve miles from the Taj Mahal Casino Hotel in Atlantic City. Less than twenty four hours ago, Randall Cunningham, the Black quarterback for the Philadelphia Eagles football team, got married in a ceremony that cost $800,000. For a person to pay $800,000 in expenses, they must earn more than a million dollars before taxes. This ceremony included five (yes, I said five) wedding rings. The gowns, cakes, dinners, decorations, etc. were all designed to demonstrate that Black people could waste money just as fast as their oppressors. The most current issue of Ebony magazine has Eddie Murphy and his new bride on the cover. His wedding is suppose to have cost a million dollars. Last year, the Whitney Houston-Bobby Brown wedding was the spectacle that captured people's interest. Is this what our ancestors died for? Did Dr. King and Malcolm take bullets to the head so that our Black monied class can casually blow millions of dollars in a day while the masses of Blacks wallow in poverty? I don't have any personal gripes against these wealthy celebrities; but I think expensive weddings send a bad message to Black people. It says if you have the money, this is how you should spend it. Even worse, to those Blacks who lack the money, (which is most of them) it encourages them to *wish* that they could be just as wasteful. It says the amount of money spent represents how much I love you. The Black and White media, by giving so much coverage to these events, is essentially saying that of all the many important things going on in the lives of thirty million African-Americans, we should stop everything and focus on this ceremony. An expensive wedding sends all the wrong messages to a people that need all the right messages. We hear stories of wealthy Black people dying broke because of poor money management decisions and spending priorities and yet we celebrate the very wasteful events (like expensive weddings) that perpetuate these tragedies. Who would have thought that Sammy Davis Jr. and Alex Haley would both have to have their personal possessions auctioned off after their deaths to pay off debts? And who in their right mind thinks that the amount of money spent on a wedding has anything at all to do with how happy or long lasting the marriage is likely to be? As a matter of fact, and practicality, it may do the exact opposite. How can a couple expect to start off on "the right foot" when they strap themselves with the ball and chain of wedding debt. The likelihood of them arguing over the expense or the wisdom of such a wedding is very real as that debt lingers on. How many other things will they not be able to do or purchase because of that one day of pomp and ceremony? If the economic strain of the wedding day lingers on, both parties may begin to remember their wedding day with more negative than positive feelings.

THE BLIND LEADING THE BLIND

Let us pretend that every single problem or misunderstanding that has been presented thus far was a non-factor in your current relationship. Going even further, let us pretend that your current romance comes right out of an old fashioned Hollywood movie, and is characterized by fidelity, communication, mutual respect, sensitivity and all the things that only seem to happen in books and movies. Would your marriage be in any kind of danger anyway? The answer is *absolutely yes*. And the reason it would be in danger is that the overwhelming majority of Black Americans are financially ignorant. Black people are only taught the basics of making a living. The emphasis is usually on getting "an education" (actually getting a degree), searching for job opportunities, resume writing, interviewing skills, and so on. Eventually, up to ninety percent of Black people do find some form of work that allows them to start piecing together some form of livelihood and lifestyle. But their financial education usually doesn't go any further than that, and there are many things other than how to get a job that one must know to avoid financial disaster. What are some of these other things one should know about? A normal list would include how to manage money, how to spend it, save it, invest it, negotiate with it, and even how, in some cases, to give it away for tax purposes. Another area of information would be understanding the world of credit, the very thing that America runs on *more than* money itself. Learning how to buy a house is not part of most Black people's education, which may account for: a) why most Black people do not own their own homes; b) why most Blacks over-pay for the houses they do own; and, c) why many Blacks unnecessarily lose value in their homes over the years. Much more goes into having a financial education, but it wouldn't matter to most Blacks because they get virtually none of it in the normal course of their lives.

Marriage, for all the emotion that the word brings forth, is as much a long-term, legal, financial partnership as it is anything else. Many Black couples, in the course of this supposedly lifetime relationship, will have more than a million dollars go through their hands. Some will have much more. In addition, there will be other assets such as inheritances, homes, insurance policies, pensions, etc. Thus, with so many assets and so much money passing through the hands of a couple over a forty year period, there are plenty of situations where arguments and bad feelings over money can arise. When both parties are ignorant about money, are unaware of how ignorant they are, and have no plan to become *informed* about financial matters, it is certain that they will struggle over money often. It is a classic case of the blind trying to lead the blind.

Financially ignorant couples would not be so bad if they were few and there were well known means of bringing them financially "up to speed". But if a Black couple lives in the Black community, the chances are great that they live in *a community of ignorance* where the lack of information about economic realities is equally experienced across the board by virtually everyone. Thus, it is that much more difficult for people to be aware of what's missing from their consciousness when it also doesn't exist in the consciousness of the people that they interact with daily. I am not putting Black people down as being *incapable* of understanding money management. It's just that the *proper information* about money management has no systematic way of entering their lives. The information is not part of their high school or college education, is not part of the Black media (except Black Enterprise), is not offered in our churches or social organizations, and is generally not discussed intelligently at the family dinner table. Most Black people think they have struck a gold mine when they merely find out about the services of their job- related credit union.

So the answer to the original question is yes, one's marriage can be as romantic as Romeo and Juliet and still become a disaster by people making financial mistakes in their efforts to provide for themselves and their family. Actually the reality is a bit more complicated (and worse) than Black people simply not having the proper information to make good decisions about money. Because in addition to not having the right information, we as a people have very negative attitudes about money and business, and these attitudes have become a part of our cultural tradition. Because of these attitudes, the proper information about money and business would have a difficult time being absorbed and acted on even if it was made available. All habits in mature people are hard to change.

About fifteen years ago, I wrote a book about these problems. That book, *Black Folks Guide to Making Big Money In America*, has been called the first Black-self help book, and I am happy to say that at this point it is still selling well. Also during that period I published two other books dealing with Black people's attitudes about money. They are *Black Folks Guide To Business Success* and *Getting Black Folks To Sell.* Thus, if the reader wants to get a more detailed explanation to support the unflattering statements that are being made here about Black people, these books should be purchased, because it is not possible to cover those subjects here.

The new freedoms that women exercise today make financial ignorance even more likely to cause problems in a marriage. In generations past when the man was the accepted "leader" in the marriage, the woman generally followed the husband, right or wrong. Any suggestions or advice the wife gave to the husband was usually done in a relatively subservient manner. Thus, it was quite possible for the family as a unit to *not* make maximum financial progress if the husband made bad money decisions, but the marriage *itself* could have maintained stability because of the secondary role women played as financial-decision makers and their commitment to stay with the husband.

Today, women are not expected to be passive followers of husbands and feel comfortable in questioning and challenging anything. Many more options are available to both Black males and females. And there are many less completely right answers to questions because the many options provide a variety of "correct" answers depending on a person's goal and perspective. Thus, it is much easier today for men and women to *both* be right, in what they are saying and yet still argue because the answers are based on their different perspectives.

Money especially lends itself to these kinds of arguments because everybody *thinks* they already know clearly what to do with money. But conditions in the Black community regarding economic development, show that few actually know how to manage their resources properly. Does that mean that we should go back to the days when women kept their mouth shut and family "harmony" was preserved? Absolutely not! Does this mean that every financial decision should be put to a vote? Who breaks the frequent one to one ties? Does this mean that, the woman should spend "her" money the way she wants and the man spends "his" money the way he wants so that there's true equality in the house? I can tell you that it's extremely difficult to buy a house that way, or deal with emergencies or long-term planning, but it may work for some. The reality is that nothing should excuse our people from investing the time it takes to study and learn personal financial management. Nor is it good if only one person is doing the studying and making all the financial decisions, even if they are correct ones. Why? Because people die and many people, especially older women, have been financially wiped out because they made a number of bad decisions when the husband (and financial decision maker) died suddenly. Some wives don't even know what or where all the assets are (as Terry's friend Bernadine found out). When both people are reading from the same financial management book, they're more likely to be on the same page when making financial decisions. And because today's marriages have a higher probability of failing, it's much better to have two informed people trying to start their lives over rather than two financially ignorant ones. On the other hand, if the husband and wife team become skilled making a quality lifestyle through intelligent spending and planning, poverty, a major cause of divorce, will have been eliminated. Basically it's an all win can't lose situation. But someone has to educate Black people and show Black people how to do it. And that is what's missing in our community: economic leadership. We have plenty of institutions and organizations in our community that are always *asking* for money but not a one that tells us how to get it and manage it.

Black people have a history of mass action when the challenge facing them was clearly recognized. In the nineteen twenties and thirties when there

were good wage jobs in the North and the Klu Klux Klan in the South, Black
people came North in the hundreds of thousands. It was called "the great
migration". When it was thought that integration (or at least the removal of
segregation) was the way to go, Black people developed a legal and activist
plan of action to make that a reality. Many tens of thousands participated in
that effort. And when all Black leaders seemed to say that Black elected
officials would improve our lives, millions of Black people voted to put
thousands of Black people in office. We have always tried to do what seemed
at the time to be the right thing. Today it is very obvious that we need a
financial education, whether we intend on getting married or not. Today we
hear about banks going under, credit crunches, the deficit, mortgage interest
rates, CD's, stocks and bonds, mutual funds, Dow Jones average, and so on.
But unlike other times in our history when we acted in mass in response to a
problem or new opportunity, today we just seem to do nothing, hear nothing
and understand nothing. Many people think that the issues don't effect them,
until they get turned down for a mortgage or a credit card, or get laid off from
their job. Then they are ready to holler racism, when in fact they don't have the
slightest idea what the hell's going on. If women seek equality, then they are
going to have to spend time understanding what these mostly traditional male
areas of finance are all about. White folks have always told Blacks that "with
freedom comes responsibility". I think men could say the same to women. A
part of women's freedom will come from successfully understanding and
dealing with the financial system. In our current financial crisis, Black leaders
and Black people in general seem unaware that our financial ignorance is at
crisis proportions. Our inaction in addressing that ignorance is a major part of
the crisis. And because there doesn't appear to be a person, organization or
institution that is ready to teach Blacks about finance, this situation makes for
yet another and more depressing part of the total financial mess. Meanwhile,
we talk about how much money flows through the Black community, how we
should support Black businesses and each other, and how we should boycott
company A, B, and C. We talk until we're tired, and because we are tired we
fool ourselves into thinking that we actually did something.

One report that should have jolted Black people into action was the
national study done to compare the wealth (net worth) between Black and
White families .

In that report of 1984, by Dr. William Bradford from the University of
Maryland, entitled *Wealth, Assets and Income of Black Households*, much
needed new information came to light. The gist of that information is as
follows:

1. The median net worth (half of the people owning more and half own less
   - the middle point) of the Black American Family was only about

$4,200.

2. About 29%, almost one third of Black families, either had a net worth of zero or less than zero.

3. The Black middle class with family incomes of $24,000 - $48,000 make up about a quarter of all Black families (26.7%). This group had a net worth of only $17,600. The White family with a similar income had a total net worth of $54,600, more than three times as much.

4. Upper income Black families earning over $50,000 per year make up only 12.6% of Black families as of 1980. But their net worth was still only half of that of Whites.

What these figures show is basically what most observers of the Black community already knew: that Black people do not invest their money but instead spend it on consumed items. This is not to say that the various forms of racism are not responsible for these gaps in wealth, but certainly they can't be blamed for it all.

It is my opinion that shortly after these figures were released, leaders in the Black community should have made sure that the average African American saw them, understood what they meant, and came up with an economic education program that would help turn the situation around. That is not at all what happened. Instead every major Black leader used these figures in their speeches as proof that racism was alive in America because the Black man wasn't getting his fair share. Tell me, what is new or revealing about that? Black leaders are not to merely announce the obvious, they are to form plans, strategies, programs, and educational tools so that we can progress. By doing nothing, Black leaders leave everyone on their own acting as individuals, still trapped in financial ignorance. Failure to act makes the average Black family likely to be worth only $4,000 after years of work, with a one in three chance of being worth nothing. White people have been saying Black people aren't worth anything for centuries. It would be ironic if they could come up with the figures to prove their point.

Why don't Blacks, either as individuals or family units, do a better job of managing their money? Why wouldn't they use the services of a financial planner if it's that obvious that our spending is out of hand and our assets are so few? Several reasons come to mind.

a) There is a false sense of security among many Blacks that they have arrived. They have a comfortable job in a White Corporation, and they own a nice car, wear nice clothes and live in a nicely furnished apartment in the integrated side of town. This person or family has achieved, in their mind, the total success package that Black people were told to dream about during their youth. They already *are* successful in their minds, so why would they need a financial planner or a money management course? They make the fatal assumptions that: 1.) the job will last forever, and 2.) no major event is ever going to come along (divorce, death, disability, a fire, car accident, etc.) that will dramatically alter their lives.

     b) Money management is believed to be necessary only when a person makes a lot of money, say, over a hundred thousand dollars a year or more. Having a financial plan on a salary of thirty to fifty thousand a year is considered unnecessary. Because the majority of Black families make a lot less than fifty thousand a year, many Black people think this way, therefore they don't bother with planning.

     c)   There is a healthy suspicion by many that financial planners want to sell you something other than their planning services. They usually try to sell extra insurance, stocks, bonds, etc. Many people find these sales pitches intimidating and back off. Others find the planners hourly fees of up to fifty dollars an hour too expensive.

     d)   People do mostly what their peers do, and because so few Blacks use the services of a financial planner, it doesn't catch on and grow. Most Blacks whose friends are doing well financially are doing so because of a raise in salary or success in their business, not because of great moves in financial planning. Planning is not seen as significantly instrumental in lifestyle improvement in any significant way.

     e)   Black people certainly can't count on Black leaders to shed light on the need for better money management. In thirty years of listening to Black leaders, and in all the books that I've read about them, the only economic advice I've ever heard dealt with boycotting certain companies because of unfair racial practices. If Black leaders never address money management in their presentations, how are Black people ever to be made aware of their options. To be honest, most Black leaders don't know anymore about wealth accumulation or money management than the people they profess to lead. The Black community has no conception of economic leaders like they do religious, political or educational leaders. We have a profound case of the Blind leading the Blind leading the Blind. We have an entire community of Blind people from top to the bottom, with nothing on the horizon to suggest that there is going to be a mass awakening in the foreseeable future.

MARRIAGE, SUCCESS AND INFIDELITY

     The news that Magic Johnson tested HIV positive in 1991 sent shock waves throughout the nation, and caused millions of people to rethink their sexual behavior. It was important for many people who followed or cared about the situation to find out exactly *how* Magic became infected. He couldn't possibly be a drug user who shared needles, so that meant that he was gay, right? Wrong! Magic came forward and admitted that he had had unprotected sex with literally hundreds and hundreds of women during his NBA career and that this was how he obtained the infection. This story was a hot news item for months and raised questions about Magic's sexual behavior and other sex-related issues. I would like to use this unfortunate event to highlight a dilemma that some Black men experience after they marry and become successful.

Most men of all races will never have the opportunity to go to bed with the number of women that Magic Johnson, Wilt Chamberlain, Warren Beatty, Prince and other stars have reportedly gone to bed with. The reason is very simple. Most men are not as rich, mobile, famous and nice looking as these men are. But let us imagine for a minute what it might be like to be a professional basketball player who travels to thirty cities in the course of three months. Let us assume that although our model is not a star, he is nice looking, muscular, and earns a half a million dollars a year (ten thousand dollars a week). Assume that this athlete is married and has two children. When he arrives at any city, groupies (women who perform sex for stars that they adore) are already in the hotel waiting for the team to arrive. These groupies are not ugly women. On the contrary, they are very attractive and well built. They can be found lounging at bar, the restaurant, the pool, —everywhere, and they make their sexual interest known to the athletes that they seek. These athletes see similarly attractive women at their pre-game practices, during and after the game, and back at the hotel. Assume that the athlete in question has been approached, directly or indirectly by fifty seven different women during this two-day stay, but he manages to say no to all of them. Does he receive any benefit, praise, reward or special mention for turning down these young ladies? No. Does he deserve any? Most people would say no, especially women, which is probably true. But it is human nature, not male nature or female nature, to want some form of credit, encouragement, or reinforcement when you successfully *discipline* yourself to do the right thing. Men often want sex with attractive women (and if you are a Black man with a head case, with White women). The fact that men say no when their body says yes is a noteworthy achievement. Assume that this particular athlete rejects the offers of fifty women in the next town and the next town after that. But in town number four he says yes to an extremely attractive woman who also happened to be his two hundred and twenty seventh temptation in the past few weeks. Being human (and horny by now), he goes to bed with her. Now project this situation over a five year period. How will this athlete be portrayed by Black women? Is either of the following an accurate portrayal of his character:

a)   He is very disciplined and generally faithful to his wife. It takes more than two hundred temptations by some of the most attractive women in the country before he succumbs to his male nature.

b)   He is a dog. He cheated on his wife dozens of times in the last five years. The fact that he responded less than one half of a percent of the time is no excuse and unimportant. He should be *perfect* if he really loved his wife.

People recognize the power of environment in influencing behavior. You *can't* ask a man to be successful and not put himself in an environment which helps develop and support that success. And if he enters a success oriented environment, he is going to attract women, because women love *successful* men as much as men love *sexy* women. There are women who hang around lawyers, doctors, actors and other professionals and they in a sense are just as much groupies as those who follow rock stars and athletes.

The message here is the following: First, women who want a successful husband must accept the fact that other women will also find him attractive, and will let him know it. Second, even if that husband has all the right intentions of remaining faithful, he is subject to a great deal of pressure. The more women approach him, the more likely he will eventually submit to sexual urges. Third, corporate America has its groupies like the world of sports and music. Some women consider finding a successful husband "on their level" at work just as important, if not more important, than their own professional career. Therefore, before a wife takes the usual self- righteous position she is bound to take if she discovers that her successful husband has had an affair, she needs to consider the human dimensions and inclinations at work. Probably, if a man can force himself to resist every single sexual invitation, he might also develop problems in sexual performance at home as well. Women are certainly as quick to leave home because of the latter problem as they are for the former. Essentially the Black man is being asked to be perfect. Anything short of perfection is a legitimate excuse to give him Hell!

Finally, it is very easy to criticize someone for being unfaithful when the accuser has not been tested themselves. Unless a person is tested in life, they don't know how they are going to respond to a challenging situation. Men are only dawgs if we presume that the morality of women is higher. Yet, almost all the research on women since the start of the women's movement show that given "equal opportunity" in new situations, they act remarkably like men (which is to say like dawgs) much of the time.

BLACK MEN ASK WHAT DO THEY REALLY CONTROL?

A Black middle class couple decide that the time has come to make the move from apartment living to having their own home. Both of them have been looking at houses seriously for a year. The apartment's den is littered with the monthly real estate booklets that showcase the areas newest houses for sale. Money has been put aside for more than three years. This couple (let's call them Jerry and Janice Johnson) is serious. After many discussions on the costs of owning a home, the features they want it to have, and their preferred neighborhoods, the Johnsons begin their regular weekend visits to the homes for sale. After a run of thirteen weekends, the Johnsons have taken a liking to nine of the more than sixty houses they have inspected. Actually that's not quite true. Jerry likes nine of the houses. Janice only seems enthusiastic about three and only one of those three is in the nine that Jerry liked. Two of the houses that Janice likes, Jerry doesn't particularly care for. Its not that Jerry doesn't like the houses per se, but the neighborhood seemed a little too White for him. Yes, it had a "good school system", but the school was damn near all White. Based on the mortgage company's evaluation of Jerry and Janice, they are qualified to purchase every house that they have seen except one of the ones that Janice liked. Who do you think is going to have the ultimate say on which house is to be purchased? Ask any practicing real estate sales person and they will tell you *the woman* is much more successful in persuading the husband to buy the house *she* wants than the other way around. Under ideal circumstances both husband and wife will like their new home equally. But the woman bases her enthusiasm on things that don't really mean that much to many husbands. The woman is interested in the size and modernness of the kitchen and bathrooms. The number of bathrooms is important, as is closet space, the fireplace, central vacuuming etc. So the reality is that the single biggest financial obligation that men commit themselves to, the house, is very often *not* something that they have the ultimate say in selecting. Why do men do it? Basically because they want their woman to be happy. It doesn't make sense to commit to a smaller mortgage (the man's choice of a home is almost always cheaper) if the wife is going to be disappointed or dissatisfied. Why spend money to get dissatisfaction? Many times this process is the first lesson that Black men experience in learning that they *are not* really "in charge" of the relationship as they had been raised to believe. After the house is purchased, and if money is not a limiting factor, most Black men will find that every appliance and every piece of furniture is selected and specifically arranged basically because "that's what she wanted." For all the times that we've heard the expression "a home is a man's castle", it's pure bull. Most men are "given permission" to control only three places in the house: the attic, the basement and the garage. And many houses don't even have one or two of these spaces. This arrangement, whether men talk about it or not, effects how men look at their job and their life. When they get stressed out from the job, White folks and so on, and ask themselves "what the hell am I working for?" It bothers them that they are working for a package of expenses that they feel they have little control over.

Most men like to see their wife and children happy. But often that is not what they hear. What men often hear is what the family *doesn't have* and *what it wants*. Thus, how is a man suppose to respond to the institution of marriage when his voice is so often overruled on the expenses that he inevitably has to pay for anyway, and then the person who actually made those purchase decisions still isn't satisfied and wants more?

The male looks for a way to put himself in a position where his ideas and opinions count. Since it is often not at work or in his own home, he may begin to think about starting his own business. A business is often not just a means to make money, it is a means for the business owner to make a statement about who they are or who they want to become. A business is a means for a person to express his creativity and explore his ideas and hunches. For many men, if his home can't be his castle, maybe his place of business will be.

What would happen if someone convinced you to join an organization that everyone said was great, but when you joined you found out that your opinion didn't count for anything? What if every time there was a show of hands on an issue, your side lost most of the time? What if the organization asked you to pay substantial dues, but you didn't like how your dues were being spent? If most people were part of an organization like this they would quit, right? Many men feel that marriage is just such an institution.

As if it wasn't bad enough to have such little say about the design and decor of the house, some men find that they also have little authority in how their children are raised as well. Because many women are able to "marry up", they often carry with them what might be called a "ghetto complex". This ghetto complex is an extreme version of "I'm going to provide for my child the things that I didn't have when I was growing up." Of course this is generally a good attitude to have, but like anything else it can be carried to an extreme. As mothers many Black women decide to compensate for their past poverty by dressing their children as if they were auditioning for Parisian designers. And in many cases there is not a lot that the husband can say about it. How many outfits does a small boy or girl need? How many shoes? Should they be asked to wear hand-me-downs? Should kids respond to every fad and fashion? Should the young boys get all of those designs cut into their hair, and how many times should a ten year old girl go to the beauty parlor? Should every major holiday demand a new outfit? Should church be used as an excuse to buy clothes? Should young boys pay a hundred dollars to "be like Mike?" Should young kids be pushed into the modeling business? And when the hell is enough?

Many Black men find that they are ignored when they offer their advice about children's clothes. And what makes it even more difficult for practical Black men is that the general marketplace in the Black community caters to Black people's near *obsession* with looking good. Clothing stores (especially for women) and shoe stores (especially for women) dominate *all* Black shopping areas. Thus even if a sister wanted to maintain some sense of financial sanity, many stores are there to tempt her to go overboard. And whereas these women may not ask the husband to spend all *his* money on the clothes, they will spend all of *their* money on clothes, and then tell the husband that they don't have the money to pay household bills.   Thus, in effect, the husband does pay for all the unnecessary clothes.

As if this ghetto complex alone is not enough to push women to extravagant spending, there is another factor pushing this wild spending competition among women. Women like to show off their children to other women much in the same way men like to show off their cars to other men. But a car is a material thing, whereas children are human and should be treated as such. The idea that a woman is a *better* mother because she makes her children look nicer than another woman's children is a misplacing of values and priorities to say the least. Black people's obsession with *consuming* things as opposed to *developing* things starts here in this I-can- look- better- than- you contest. The value of a mother should be in her ability to implant the proper values in her children, not instill in the next generation her own twisted values. Some of the most vicious people I know always looked good on the outside. I can say the same about some of the dumbest people I know. Many men stand by and have to allow this madness to go on. The alternative is to engage in repeated arguments over the issue, usually with only limited or no results. This might seem like a minor issue, but it is very symptomatic of the problems in our community in many ways.

1)   It is a problem in that it perpetuates the poor self image Black people have of themselves and their possibilities. It tells Black people that if you don't like who you are, rather than develop your mind and "become somebody", dress the body, look good and people will like you anyway, even if you still have a poor image on the inside.

2)   It is a problem in that a tremendous amount of Black capital that

could be used to start a business, pay for dental care, pay for insurance policies and investment is burned up in clothes. Foreign clothing manufacturers love our stupidity because they make a fortune from it.

3)   It is a problem because so little of this spending is directed back to Black clothing stores, because of our obsession for buying name brand labels and patronizing the most exclusive White department and clothing stores. And when a Black person finally does buy a piece of clothing from another Black person, it turns out to be only a Martin or Malcolm T-shirt. And instead of paying the ten dollar asking price, they want the brother to accept five or eight dollars.

Men often see that they really don't have much say in their family life or the house they pay for. It is as if his only purpose is to provide the money so that everyone does whatever they feel like doing. So much has been said about the absence of the Black male role model in the home. The truth is that many family members don't want to follow the male role model, but would rather follow the ignorant masses instead. Sometimes the male can only get attention and respect when he acts nasty or threatening or violent, and then of course, he's not looked at as a role model anymore. So he walks away from the total package, the woman, the kids, the house, the bills, everything! Society will say he is another irresponsible Black man. The wife will often pretend that she doesn't know *what* the problem was. Many brothers don't willingly walk away, they are pushed away, or ignored, and drift away.

Using Children To Get Money

Many men complain that their ex-wives and girlfriends use the couple's children to extort money from them. Many people know men who are unable to see their children because of the man's inability to pay the amount of money that the wife, her lawyer, and the court system consider fair. I will not expound on this issue, because it has been sufficiently covered in the media. But what is necessary to recognize is that this strategy follows a pattern that often begins at the very pregnancy of a girlfriend. She might start asking for money to pay for one thing (prenatal care, for example) and then obtain that care free of charge and use the money for something else. Once the baby is born, the pattern continues. Ask for money for one thing, exaggerate the cost, collect the money, buy the thing at a lesser cost (or don't buy it at all), and spend the change on something that the mother wanted all the time. We are not talking about junkies or alcoholics here, but women who have just rationalized that their motherhood entitles them to all that they can get. Men often receive many mixed messages during this time. The baby is the greatest thing in a woman's life, yet the man, who is fifty percent responsible for this great thing, is now somehow viewed as a villain of some sort. Some women become angry at men and see them as villains because it's so much *easier* to be a "father" than a mother. A father can share in all the same benefits of parenthood as the mother but doesn't have to go through the many physical, hormonal, psychological "costs" that mothers have to experience. Mothers sometimes resent the fact that men "get off so easy". This resentment causes him to be seen sometime as the bad guy. And in being viewed as the villain, he must therefore *pay* for how his woman perceives him. Usually these women never admit that they use their children to get money, because that sounds foul even to themselves. Thus they continuously deny their behavior even as they continue to do it. The law and public opinion almost always finds a way to place blame on the Black man. His reputation for non support is legendary. Even in situations where men pay what is asked of them, if the woman says it hasn't been paid, the public assumption is that the women are probably correct. Whoever heard of a woman lying?

The Finale of Marriage

It has been said that people are aware when the end of their life is near. Of course, this could not possibly be true most of the time, because so many people die in strange and unexpected ways that puzzle even the living who are left to investigate the causes of death. But doctors and hospital personnel insist that people "decide to die" in many cases. We know that both Dr. Martin Luther King and Malcolm X sensed their own deaths very shortly before they occurred.

Let us pretend that all Black men who had married and had done all the right things could see their death three to six months down the road. What could they say about their lives in many cases. Most Black men could honestly say that everybody got paid except them. The work effort of most committed married Black men materially benefits someone other than themselves. Generally speaking, most people probably feel this way at one time or another. But evidence points to Black men as the ultimate "slave ". When the African American male gets hired, it is usually by a White-owned company. To make a profit, that company, must make more money off the worker than what the worker costs to keep employed. When the worker is paid, all taxes and pension payments are taken out before he gets his "real" pay. When he goes shopping to purchase the goods and services for himself and his family, he spends 94% of his after tax money with White American businesses or those owned by other nationalities. The money spent with these companies has little or no chance of coming back to him or his community in ways that would benefit him or his community.

Within the home, it is fair to say that the real majority of the purchase decisions made with the male's money, whether the wife is earning income or not, is dictated by the wife and children. The only real purchase decisions that the Black male makes are those that are for his personal use. Many times these purchases are very limited because they are not considered part of "the necessities." Furthermore many of these personal items are not for his personal *pleasure* but are things required for him to *merely maintain* his function as the family provider.

When some men spend money for recreation, personal pleasure, or to relieve stress, they often feel a sense of guilt or shame. They may conceal their spending "vices" out of fear that they may be seen as a typical Black man who blows time and money. Spending money on an athletic event or on other forms of "good times" results in many brothers having to hear their wives complain that "you could have taken all that money and ...." (done something *she* felt was more practical). Are there *any* luxuries or activities that Black men can indulge in that are not considered either sinful, wasteful, dangerous or dumb? Yes, its when those activities are done with the family. The Black man, (and other men in general) is *supposed* to make enough money so that his entire family can enjoy a trip, activity or good time without his worrying about the expense. But many Black men do not make enough money to do this. Therefore, because he can not afford to please everyone in the family, he is considered selfish or wasteful if he, as the chief provider in the family, treats *himself* on rare occasions.

If we fast forward to the age of sixty two, the average Black man sees his death six months down the road. He has worked hard for more than forty years. He has pleased his boss; he has mostly pleased his wife; he has pleased his children; he has pleased White America for being a loyal consumer; and he has pleased the government for paying more than his fair share of taxes (for years the family claimed minimum deductions). And although our male workhorse is happy that he has pleased so many people, a part of him feels shortchanged. "What did I do for me?", he asks himself. Where did I go *for me*, what did I buy *for me?* How much of my life was for me? After all this work in behalf of other people, I now face death years before my wife. And I'll die years before collecting any of the thousands of dollars of social security that I've paid for decades. I will die before collecting any of the pension funds I worked so hard to provide for myself. I will die before I can treat myself to anything from the few dollars I put away in the bank. I will die before I can cash in on any of the assets I've finally paid off such as the house. And I will certainly not collect any of the insurance money whose premiums I've faithfully paid for more than a generation. When I die *it will be just a bigger version of my life, everybody will get paid but me* , and everybody will live even longer to enjoy it. And even at my funeral, people will feel more sorry for the people still alive and collecting the fruits of *my* effort than they will for me who never got the chance to eat much of the fruit I produced."

Does the above analysis mean that Black men should avoid marriage because its going to leave him miserable and feeling ripped off? No, not by a long shot. But it does mean that Black men must make conscious decisions to enjoy the statistically shortened life that has been forecast for them. This may mean doing things the wife feels is wasteful. And to that wife I would say this: Since a great part of a man's happiness must be obtained by his making other people happy, because so little of what he does goes to himself, could you, the wife, allow *yourself* to be happy by seeing your husband make himself happy on his own terms? And since it is universally acknowledged that this Black man will die before you and that you will get the remaining fruits of his labor, isn't that even more reason for him to be allowed *to live while he is alive*?

Many Black men do not wait for their wives to give them permission to live life on their own terms; they take it. And this taking back of one's life is often the root cause of many financial problems in marriages. If Black people made enough money to purchase "the necessities" and experienced a sense of being free and in control of their lives, many of these financial arguments and problems wouldn't exist. Or if Black people weren't the suicidal consumers that they were, having to always have the latest styles, brands and colors, they wouldn't experience some of these problems. But that is generally not the case. And one more time I will make the case of Black men needing to go into business.

The way to attack this problem of Black men not really being in control of their life is for them to tackle the challenge of running their own business. Working in your own business should make at least part of the work effort enjoyable. Also through business, a man can treat himself to trips, meals, entertainment, and recreation in the course of carrying out that business. And if you make it big in business (bigger than you would have been if you had stayed on the job), there's even the chance that you will live longer to spend the money and enjoy the freedom that you earned. But then that brings us back to Black America's ultimate challenge, which is to convince our people to go into business. Right now, most Black men *seem to prefer* working for Whites and working themselves to an early death.

CLASH OF CAREERS; MONEY, POWER AND SEX

In many people's eyes the essence of the money problems between Black men and women is centered on two major developments of the last twenty or so years. The first is the idea that women should be treated equally in all ways, as men are treated. The second development is that besides all the rights, privileges and respect that are due women, they also deserve to obtain equal pay for the work that they do comparable to men in the same position, company, level of responsibility, seniority, etc. These two ideas are not yet fully realized in any place in America, especially for Black women. But every year sees progress being made on many fronts. In the mid-nineteen-nineties, Black women have economic clout and spending power like never before. Because of their increasing dollars, the rapid closing of the numerical gap between Black male and female professionals as well as the females numerical superiority, Black females and males find themselves debating each other. Who should control what in our families, neighborhoods and in our national agendas? Opinions are expressed at cocktail parties and other meeting places and each side vies for support. There is the "Black women are taking over everything and emasculating us men" point of view. You have the "I'm liberated, may the best person win" point of view. You have the "it's the Black woman's turn to step forward" point of view. And you have many combinations of these with exceptions, deletions and addendum, with various degrees of support for each. In the nineteen sixties we used to call this "the woman question," and to some extent people still refer to it that way. In the last twenty years, many books have been written dealing with women's career issues, but like most books, they have been geared toward White women. Some Black women, in spite of their Blackness, have "gobbled up" these books and swallowed them hook, line and sinker. This tendency of some Black women to identify closely with White women has been repeatedly mentioned in this book. There are some sisters who read women's literature and understand that there *is* a relationship between the women's movement and themselves, but they are very clear that they, as Black women, have to establish their own agenda. And there are also Black women who reject the women's movement almost entirely for no other reason than the fact that it is a White female- inspired, controlled and dominated movement which they have no interest in being a part of. And then there is a large segment of Black women who are basically apathetic and ignorant of many women's issues, and who simply hear only bits and pieces on the eleven o'clock news.

I cannot cover all bases, books, opinions and perspectives of the woman's movement in this chapter. My intention here is to make some observations and comments about what some Black women seem to want, what they seem to be saying (and doing) and what some Black men think of these things both positively and negatively. The main reference used as the framework for this discussion is a book which was written by a very well known Black writer but which never became a big seller in the Black community. The writer was sister Bebe Moore Campbell, and the book is entitled *Successful Women, Angry Men*. Other books were consulted, some of which won't be quoted, but this book for me captures much of the essence of today's issues. Of course, Warren Farrells book, *Why Men Are They Way They Are* previously quoted, was also very useful.

Why Are We Even Able to Discuss this?

Before we discuss the specific rights and entitlements that women in general (and Black women in particular) think they are due , we must properly set the stage by giving the necessary background information.

Prior to 1970, the role of all women had not changed very much in the many decades of this century. Even the many employment advances that women won during World War II , when millions of men were in the military, were reversed as soon as these men returned home. For twenty years after World War II, women in general were viewed as homemakers , mothers , wives and reflections of and support for their husbands. Women were generally not seen as independent careerists, nor did a large percentage of them seem to want to be that. Those women who did remain single and pursued careers were often derogatorily referred to as "old maids". In any event, they didn't appear to be looked up to or envied by the majority of other women who seemed to prefer a "happy family life."

In the case of Black women, this was generally not the situation . Black women worked inside the home, outside the home *and* raised families. Their income was needed to help provide an adequate family income. But Black women also worked because it was their tradition to work, both in Africa and certainly during enslavement. And maybe because of this long history of working, Black women had more understanding not only of the difference between a White job and a Black job, but a male job and a female job.

With such clear lines of tradition established over many years about who was expected to do what and when, how is it that all hell broke loose in recent years about women's rights? And from the Black males perspective, how did Black women figure to be entitled to so much? A perspective is offered here to not only explain how Black female advancement came to be, but to also give credit where it is due. The Black man is not only responsible for his own movement up the social, political and economic ladders in this country, but he has also handed ladders to every other group that has wanted to climb also. Unfortunately he hasn't gotten the hype that he deserves for doing so.

Hype is massive continuous and sometimes sickening publicity. But hype works. People, at least for a while, recognize an event or person far out of proportion to its real life significance because of hype. Black men receive, the wrong kind of hype. The reputation of Black men as mindless dope dealers, rapists and useless father figures is legendary and is caused by three parts hype for every one part of reality. Black men need a very healthy dose of the right kind of hype. Whereas Black people have been complaining for years about correcting interpretations of early African- American and African history, we fail to see that even the Black movement within the last 30 years has been grossly distorted. It was the *Black male* who started the engines of the Black movement and kept them running throughout the sixties.   Eventually everyone with a social grievance jumped on the coattails of the movement to reach their own particular destination. Every feminist, gay person, Hispanic, Asian, or handicapped person who challenged the status quo to recognize their legal rights should themselves remember that Black men were at the very core of the struggle for those rights. When these oppressed groups take to the streets or challenge courts, most of them do so with the mistaken notion that their struggle began only after their group had a rise in consciousness and began to fight back.

The reality of course is very different. Other than the Native American, Black men have the country's most consistent record of challenging the special privileges and powers of American White men. That fight reached a peak in the twenty year period between 1950 and 1970. During that time, two different but related movements were taking place.   The first was the Civil Rights Movement, which had as its main goal the revamping of the state and federal laws in this country such that Black people and any other people could be legally entitled to all the rights that were provided to White males. The second movement, which was very much a part of the first, was the Black Power movement. The Black Power movement had as its major goal the redefining of the American Negro into the American Black man with strong linkages with his African roots. It also called for Black Americans to seek power and not just the rights given them by Whites passing laws in their behalf.

The leading civil rights organizations such as the NAACP, CORE, SCLC and the Urban League were led by Black men. Black women were highly visible and active in marches, sit in demonstrations, voter registration drives, and the many administrative office functions. But when there was a *body count* of who had been shot, hung, or otherwise killed, it was almost always the Black male. A notable exception was the death of four little girls in a Birmingham, Alabama church that had been destroyed with a bomb.

In the Black Power movement you had groups like the Black Panther Party, the Nation of Islam, SNCC, US, and other groups who were much more about intimidating the White power structure to respond to Black demands or face violent confrontations with Black men ready to burn, kill and destroy. These groups were led by Black men with many loyal female supporters. As these groups did in fact challenge the system, the body count was made up of Black males.

When the rebellion in the cities took place in the 60's and 70's, it was virtually all Black males that lit the fires that caused the nation and the world to take notice that: a) something was very wrong in America, and b) something had to be done about it. When the body count was made at the end of the rebellions, it was mostly made up of Black males, hundreds of them. The Black women that were killed were mostly casualties of accidents or cross fire. Whatever few Whites or police that were killed (a very important part of the message being sent out to the country) were killed by Black males.

White people perhaps had hoped that while the uneducated and un-employed Blacks could be expected to rebel in the streets, that there was hope of compromise with the Black elite college students. Such was not the case. Black student unions sprang up on college campuses all over the country, from the smallest schools to the Ivy League universities. In almost every instance, they were led by Black males who were ready to take over a university building or take on the campus police. Even on college campuses there were casualties, such as the deaths of Black men at Jackson State U. in Mississippi and in Orangeburg, South Carolina.

The point here is that whereas Black women made invaluable, consistent and sacrificial contributions to the movements at that time, and had such outstanding heroines as Rosa Parks, Fannie Lou Hamer, Angela Davis and many others, Black men paid the ultimate price for everybody's freedom. We did not see Black women hanging from trees or shot through the head. Black women did not have their body parts exploded into pieces like Ralph Featherstone of SNCC nor were they found in swamps like Emmett Till, and the three civil rights workers in Philadelphia, Mississippi.

Black women fought in the movement, but Black men died. There is a distinct difference between fighting and dying. And death and the threat of death were a necessary part of the plan of action that would cause enough drama, enough sympathy and enough guilt to make old, pale White men "voluntarily" change their own legal system in such a way that, at least on paper, basic human rights would be granted to all, regardless of race, color, creed, etc. If the hype machinery would have been working in the interest of Black men, nobody would ever forget that. But it was not in operation, so many people, even (or especially) Black female writers, forget who laid the foundation for other people's struggles. The reason this issue about conflict between Black men and women in the home and workplace is taking place is because of the many advances that women have made in both areas. And many of those advances were and are traceable to both the Black movement and the feminist movement. But feminism used the legal foundations brought on by civil rights organizations and, indeed, in some instances used the advice and help of some civil rights leaders to form their movement. And the fact that the women's movement gathered its greatest thrust of momentum in the years of 1969-1970, the very height of the civil rights/ Black power era, is also no accident or coincidence. Thus, Black men's blood can be seen as being as much a part of any women's equality discussion or activity as any contribution that any White feminist has ever made.

Ms. Moore Campbell recognizes this genesis of the women's movement in recalling her own period of raised consciousness. (page 36)

"The texture of her words took me back to the space inside myself where I could feel the sixties and seventies, the memories of that era's activism and *my own* tentative stumbling toward a new kind of womanhood. I could hear Hendrix and Baez, smell burning incense and the biting odor of grass wading through campus dorms. I could see brass medallions, fashioned in the symbol of peace, and furiously colored dashikis, mile-high afros, wildly waving fists. And I saw women with soft, unfettered breasts underneath tie-dyed cotton shirts, talking quietly in support groups, mouthing the strange sounding new title of Ms., screaming and yelling and raising their fists."

Certainly the references to "dashikis, mile-high afros and wildly waving fists" had much more to do with the Black movement than the women's movement. But as the two movements were going on at the same time, it is quite easy to see how aware Black women would see them as inter-related.

Unfortunately, the Black women of today in their thirties (and younger) who have not taken the time to study their history either as a Black person *or* as a woman, are not aware of these important details. Thus, when they discuss the issues of money and competition with Black men in the work place, they usually make all the incorrect assumptions, which dramatically showcases their ignorance. These women assume a) we (women) are here in corporate America because of our education and qualifications, b) we are here because White people are generally fair and just want to see results regardless of race, and c) Black men are *not* here because they are militant or lazy and use racism as their excuse. These women are wrong on all three counts. Black women hold many of the positions they do today because Black men put themselves on the line to be lynched, fire bombed or shot so that all people, especially their own women and children, could live lives as normal respected human beings. But the rhetoric coming from Black women spokespersons has been so negative and angry in the last fifteen years that many people might find the truth hard to believe in today's social environment. So if it is now clear why and how it came to be that we can even discuss the questions and issues concerning gender equality in the workplace, we can now proceed with the understanding of who is largely responsible for these progressive social developments, whether he's given the hype for it or not.

Changing History Is a Bitch

As much as I hate racism and it's ugly legacy, sexism's history appears to be more challenging. Sexism's history is certainly a hell of a lot longer than racism, seemingly going back to the beginning of time. Incredibly it falls on my generation of men to try to change the entire course of human history, and try to do so immediately! With no guidelines, warnings, forecasts or real sense of direction, men are suppose to move with all deliberate speed to change the nature of gender interaction as we have known it from the beginning of time to 1970. And while much progress towards that end has been made in the last twenty-five years, it so happens that, simultaneously, the family unit in the Black community is at rock bottom. Is this a coincidence or is there a direct relationship between the pluses of one movement leading to the downfall of a basic social institution? That question lurks in the back of the minds of many men and of women who are still trying to digest this thing called feminism.

Black women had a long history of "doing it all" long before the women's movement. Their tradition of raising a family (and large families at that), working outside of the home, and keeping the house clean and in order is legendary. The Black woman's role as unofficial leader of the family has also been documented in countless books and articles. So what are the issues today for Black women with respect to career, compensation and control. The primary issue appears to be how to strike a balance among all the new options that some "educated" Black females now enjoy. Another related issue seems to be whether this balance should be struck in favor of those things which are more likely to make for domestic tranquility with a male mate or in favor of more "freedom" for the woman.

One thing that is really clear is that it is not easy to change traditions that are not only extremely old but also have a fair amount of reasoning behind them.   In the reasonable expectation of men and women to reproduce themselves, it seems logical that the one who actually gives birth to a new being would also be the best qualified to care for the child, especially given women's superior biological feeding equipment. But humans are millions of years from their original existence, and they insist that changes are in order. How to change and how much change appear to be the major questions that need to be answered.

As previously stated some Black men, are used to seeing their women having an easier time finding a job and than themselves. Many men seem to overlook the fact that these women were (and are) grossly underpaid for the work they perform, but then Black people have a long history of being underpaid, so maybe it doesn't seem to be a big deal. What the women's movement has done to the psyche of a significant number of Black men is to aggravate a situation that was already bad to begin with. And the purpose here is articulate what those feelings of aggravation are.

A good beginning might be to spell out what it is that some Black men think Black women are saying, and what they appear to want.

1) Black women appear to not want the White man's particular antagonisms (and fears of) Black men to hurt their own options for employment. This is particularly due to the belief that the women will eventually have to shoulder the responsibility of caring for children by men who for various reasons will no longer be present. Thus, they welcome all new options that come with being a "twofer" (a Black and a woman).

2) Black women do not agree that masculinity alone and a tradition of being the provider should automatically dictate that a man's salary should be superior to the women's particularly when she has more qualifications to offer to the marketplace in terms of skills, education, experience, "chemistry" and etc.

3) Black women do not know why in a society that constantly emphasizes to "be all you can be", she should suffer for trying to do exactly that. Black women suffer by either angering the man that they are with or intimidating and "scaring off" the men that they could potentially develop a relationship with, simply by maximizing their potentials.

4) Black women feel that because men are always complaining about how women always spend the men's money, men should now appreciate that women can earn their own money and therefore provide men with more financial options and freedom.

5) Black women want to be stroked. If they are doing a hell of a job as a super woman, competing successfully with White men at work and fulfilling her wifely and motherly duties at home, why don't husbands and other people stand up and say "Hallelujah, more power to you"? Why, instead, do women feel like they're walking on egg shells?

6) And finally for those Black women dedicated to the Black community, there is another important question: Does a community with so many negatives going against it have the luxury of turning down contributions from Black people who also happen to be female?

These questions and subsequent answers are put forth in an effort to demonstrate, particularly to the female readers, that an honest attempt is being made to address some of the concerns of those Black females working in competitive job situations.

Quantifying Before Qualifying

Before discussing Black couples struggling with money, careers, power and decision making, it makes sense to determine approximately how many people are likely to even be engaged in this argument. Some people say that too often the Black middle class perspective is portrayed as the ultimate reality in our community when usually it is not a truly representative picture of our people. Victoria King, in her book, *Manhandled,* says on page 13:

" ... and frequently the black communities insistent focus on the well-to-do black woman of corporate America when discussing the problems of the black family is ludicrous. Considering that only 11% of blacks have college degrees, and that an even smaller number of these graduates are able to penetrate the invisible corporate barriers and glass ceilings, these well-heeled sisters probably represent less than 2 to 3 percent of Black American women . And yet when focussing on the problems in the black community and the so-called emasculation of the black male by the competitive black female, we choose to focus on the overachieving superstar sisters to escape the harsh reality of the abhorrent condition of life for many of the other 98 percent of Black women in America."

In *Children of the Dream* by Audrey Edwards and Dr. Craig Polite, a slightly different set of statistics are quoted. On page 159 they say:

Moreover, the number of black women now working in white-collar administrative support services such as clerical work virtually doubled during the period, going from 634,000 in 1970 to

1,201,000 in 1980.   And at the upper class professional end, in
1970 only 56,000 of the 3,309,000 black women in the American
work force held executive, administrative or managerial positions.
By 1980, 219,000 out of 4,659,000 black women held such posts.

In the nearly fifteen years since those 1980 statistics, Black women have
made many economic gains and received tens of thousands of baccalaureate and
professional degrees.   Yet, it's probably safe to say that no more than ten
percent of Black American women are in professionally competitive positions
with all the accompanying pressures, status, pay and responsibility . However,
it should be clear that as leaders and role models, these women do establish the
guidelines and procedures for less professional women to follow. As role
models their impact is greater than simply their numbers. Only 300 Black men
play in the NBA, but they influence millions.

Beginning at the Beginning

Without any available evidence to the contrary, we can only assume that
Black couples of the baby boom generation (those people born between 1946
and 1964) married for the same reasons that Black people have always married
Namely, that there were physical, intellectual and emotional attractions which
encouraged them to formalize the relationship into the long- term deal we call
marriage. But these people came of age when the various social movements
were creating opportunities that, though demanded, were unable to be fully
understood and appreciated at the time. Thus, Black men and women got
together with the idea of supporting each other, but with no real ideas what they
were agreeing to support, *how far* they would go to support, or *how long* they
were committed to support the wishes of the other spouse.

As opportunities for females developed into one of the largest areas of
employment in the last twenty years, Black women focused more intently on
their careers. The idea of being both Black and female made some employers
more likely to give Black women unprecedented opportunities. The reaction
from Black men was mixed, with some being totally supportive, while others
were discouraging. What happened then and what's happening now around
these new roles is the issue.

Anger and blame are two of the easiest and most effective emotions to
project on others. Naturally people will do the easiest things first; and recipients
of anger and blame normally react immediately. Thus, because it is both easy
and effective in creating a reaction, people are quick to get angry and place
blame. But in no way are these the wisest actions in a complicated situation.
It is merely the easy way out. Black women by way of their books, articles,

workshops, groups, etc, have made it a mission during last fifteen years to let Black men know how angry they are with them, and how they blame Black men for not responding to their problems and new opportunities in the ways that the women had wanted and expected. This is an unfortunate situation but it is also ironic because Black women had less to do with the new opportunities that they enjoy today than anybody else. She of all people should have been the most prepared to sympathetically discuss and   cooperate rather than get angry and blame Black men.. Why do I say that? Let's look at the facts. On the one hand Black men loss more blood, died in greater numbers, took more risks, spent more time in jail, waged more legal battles, killed more people and, destroyed more property than Black women ever thought about to get Black peoples' demands at the top of this nations social agenda. White women, on the other hand, launched an all out assault against sexism and the White male establishment to demand that women be put at the top of the White males' agenda. In this war, Black women, for various reasons, played no or an almost insignificant role. Thus while winning new opportunities as both Black and a female, Black women in fact played secondary roles in the Black movement against Whites, and a nearly invisible role in the feminist struggle against the White male status quo. Therefore, how in the hell does the Black woman justify being angry at anybody, given that she is getting most of her mileage from the work of other people. The last thing that powerful White men would have paid any attention to in terms of threatening his world would have been angry Black women. Black women aren't seen and never have been seen as a threat. But White men changed conditions because they have always feared Black men, and they had to make peace with their own mates (White women). This is why Black women have the new opportunities that they have today, and for no other reason.

If Black men had come forward, say, by the early 1980's to express this side of the story, perhaps Black women would not have become so self-righteous in their criticisms and attitudes towards Black men. But because male bashing was becoming the industry that it is, with all the "I-was-abused" talk shows to sell the Hype, Black women obviously felt comfortable adding their two cents. One purpose of this book is to correct certain perceptions that have been allowed to stand as truth for much too long, Unfortunately, books like Haki's *Black Men: Obsolete, Single, Dangerous* don't help the situation at all.

If we as Black men, love Black women, love unity, love to see ourselves and our community develop and grow, we must look past the anger and the blame that is hurled our way no matter how unfair we may think it is. And we must present a perspective that addresses the legitimate issues that Black women have raised.

Dual Career Couples vs. Working Couples

One approach to exploring the conflict that affects the families of working couples is to distinguish between dual- career couples and working couples. A person who views their work as a career has usually attended college or engaged in specific training programs. Thus, people see law, music, art, medicine, and engineering, and so on as careers and pursue work in these "fields" as part of a career track. Also there are career ladders within particular industries where a person may perform a series of different jobs but which all relate to, say, the television, construction or the computer industry, etc. Society tends give more value to the people who pursue careers rather than those who simply work jobs. A career person is more likely to be seen as a professional or expert, and will normally be paid accordingly. If a person is not in a career but they work, we usually call that person a job holder. They are usually not emotionally or intellectually connected to their job and would quit in a minute if a better job came along. It is therefore assumed that the stress is greater for a couple engaged in career jobs than a couple where one or both partners simply work jobs in which they have little emotional investment . But problems can be just as intense for both.. Often the female wants her job to be seen as a career, not necessarily because it is, but because she wants her work and money earning efforts to be taken as seriously as the "career" of her husband. Most people normally give more respect to careers than jobs; and for someone to try to put jobs and careers on the same level can be judged by some as merely a ploy for attention and respect. Each family of course establishes it's own view about vocational respect. Perhaps this only perpetuates class bias in a capitalistic society. But let's be serious, it takes more effort to work in the hospital's operating room than it takes to cover the lamp department at K-Mart.

Let us assume that our hypothetical, troubled Black couple is a dual-career couple. One is an accountant, engineer or chemist while the other is a radio personality, college professor or corporate executive. It doesn't matter who is which because each assumes that their talent and income is comparable to the rest. Under these circumstances, what are the potential problems? How do women and men look at those problems? One potential problem concerns time and functions. Dedicated professionals put in hours that are longer than the 9 to 5 norm, especially if they are maneuvering for a promotion . The first question is whether the husband expects his professional wife to function in the same way as the traditional wife of the past with a spotless house, completed laundry, home- cooked meals and a normal sexual appetite. Are the expectations realistic considering the circumstances? Personally, I don't think so. But many brothers say that they have no problem with their wives being a professional as long as she does not neglect her wifely and motherly duties. Some women accept this arrangement because they sincerely want to excel in both areas of life; thus we have the " superwoman syndrome" of the nonstop wife working at home as hard as she does at work. Other people think that a maid or housekeeper should be employed to lighten the wife 's load. Some men accept this as a workable solution and some don't. Those that don't might reject the idea because a housekeeper is too expensive and would cut into the financial difference that the wife's professional salary is supposed to make. Mathematically some men say, one could make almost as much financial progress with the wife staying home and not working at all as one would when you factor in the cost of going to work, the cost of child care, and the cost of a housekeeper. Men would tend to look at matters in dollars and cents because that is their main role: the provider. As much as he would like to consider other points of view, his first concern is to question a person or situation that undermines his effort to provide a decent income for the family. If a situation threatens the family income, he would want to see how the situation can be addressed so that he doesn't feel pressed to work harder or longer than he already does. On the other hand, some brothers would reject the housekeeper solution because they feel that making a happy, clean, comfortable home is (or should be) the woman's way of expressing her appreciation for her man. She should want to preserve "his castle". Modern- day women contend that vacuuming the rugs has nothing at all to do with their love for their man and he should be smart enough to see that. In this situation we obviously have a potential problem and my suggestion would be for the brother to retreat from his demands. Feminist women some how see this situation as an expression of a man's *resentment* of his wife's success and a feeling of being threatened by it. I fail to see how that conclusion can be reached. Baby- boomers were programmed to believe that their lives would be the best in American history if they got their college degrees, did the right things, and kept their noses clean. Many brothers assume that if this is so, they ought to at least be able to receive the same type of treatment that their uneducated mothers gave their uneducated fathers who made only one fifth the income that they now make. A brother's expectations may be a little naive but only those women who are determined to see Black men in their worst light will conclude that there is malice in the hearts of all brothers who don't automatically approve of their wife's agenda. There are, of course exceptions. Another extreme case is the woman who routinely works at night and who is not only not home to fix dinner but comes in exhausted late in the evening. Her concern when she arrives home is to cool

out, rest and not try to "make up" for her absence on the home front. Under
these circumstances, some men feel they have a case for proclaiming neglect.
Yet some women, rather than admitting that they are out of balance in their
priorities, poke their lips out and feel that "my man can't handle a successful
woman". The reality is that we call females who are married *wives*. The word
wife has a definition like every other word that comes out of our mouth. And
the wife has duties or responsibilities just as the husband. And although we are
living in a time when that definition is being revised, questioned, and tested, the
word should still in fact stand for *something*. Otherwise, why in hell get
married and become a wife in the first place?

Some women think they need "support" during their long work days
away from their husbands. Although each case will be different there should be
some kind of definition or understanding about the arrangement. Is the man to
understand that, "she will be coming home late untilI she completes her degree,
finishes her project, finishes the training session, gets her promotion or gets
past her probation period"? Or is it a matter of "This is the way it's going to
be for as long as she works, period? " If the average woman thinks the average
brother is to accept the latter at face value without raising an eyebrow, then she
should question whether he really needs her at all under the circumstances.
Once you have a pattern of working couples who take their jobs seriously (even
if they aren't both professionals,) several other problems are likely to develop.
One might be the too- tired- for- sex-problem. This needs no explanation.
When something as important in a relationship as sex declines as a priority for
one person (often the newly liberated working woman) and it becomes a source
of frustration for the other (the male), you have a problem situation. Oddly
enough, you will still have some women who, with a straight face, will say that
the man's anger is because of his inability to handle her success. And I guess
the fact that he can't get a good meal or some good sex has nothing at all to do
with it?

It perhaps should be mentioned here that the feminist movement has
been compared to the Black movement in countless ways. One of the things that
Black men would often do during that period was to pass off every conceivable
problem the Black community faced to racism. If it rained and it was
supposed to be sunny, some brother some where would have you believe that
the White man's racism caused the weather to change. And many times the
people listening would let it go, not call the brother on it, leaving him to
believe that he had actually passed on a piece of wisdom rather than a crock of
crap. So too is the case with some liberated women who have a knack for
blaming all unsatisfactory and/or uncooperative responses from Black men on
their egos, their machismo, their feeling threatened, or their need for control.

Its a cop out for women who just want and expect to get their way all the time.

With prolonged sexual dissatisfaction comes the inevitable affair by some Black men. Whereas wives of a generation ago thought they had a leg to stand on in insisting on fidelity because she was nearly always ready, willing and able, today's liberated woman thinks she can stand on that same leg even though she is not as accommodating. In material that I studied in preparation for this chapter, some women actually said that their mates desire to have extra-marital sex was based on "his need to dominate submissive women". Again, her unavailability for sex, she would like you to believe, has no bearing on the matter. Other women, more honest with themselves, admit that they can't seem to say no to heavy job assignments because as a Black and a woman they are under that much more pressure to *prove* that they are qualified and not just another affirmative action hire. Black people, especially Black women, have a history of getting all wrapped up in White folks agendas and claiming them as their own. If it happened on the plantation, the site of her own enslavement, it can certainly happen more subtly in a corporation. Black women do come home tired and do need to recuperate not only from work and pressure but also from the office politics, the gossip and whatever racism they experienced that day. But she should also assume the responsibility for determining when she intends to extract herself from some of her job pressure so that she may still function as a wife. After all, most women still call the wedding "the most important day in my life". If its so important to get married and become a wife, why isn't it important to *act* like one *afterwards?* Having an affair may relieve a degree of frustration in some men, but there are certain problems that affairs cannot satisfy. For example, while the wife maybe too busy or too tired to perform duties for her husband, she is often ready to go overboard for her boss who more often than not is a White male. So what we have here is a replay of the plantation. The "master" needs her from sun up to sundown. When ever he calls, she will—must go. One hundred and thirty years after freedom, she is not yet free enough to tell him to kiss her ass. How is a brother supposed to feel in the 1990's when White men indirectly still rule his house? Of course his wife will say "Come on, don't make this a racial thing." But Black women always say that. Black women see the *good* in White men *first* until the men prove themselves to be racist. Often these same women will see the *bad* in brothers *first* before (if he gets a chance) he proves himself a good guy. Strange, huh?

One of the disturbing and frustrating things to some men when they have certain discussions with women, including their wives and girlfriends, is the tendency of women to at first deny a specific truism and then, after the fact, come back and admit to its accuracy . This is certainly the case in discussions on women in the workplace. Black men have been in most work places longer than Black women because of sexism in hiring. And in those places where Black men worked that employed at least some women, the brothers know what happens to women, how it happens, and why it happens. They have witnessed sexual harassment, and they have seen females seduce men for promotions, as well as other unfair tactics. They know what goes on at the workplace, including the so-called sophisticated employers like universities, hospitals and law firms, etc. When they marry and realize their wife is going into those same work places, there is a protective urge on the part of some men because they are concerned that their wives will fall prey to the same exploitive situations that they have witnessed. I would consider this reaction to be a form of caring, concern, even love.

Unfortunately, some women consider it be men's insecurity or paranoia. But if one man found a particular woman attractive, appealing and intelligent enough to marry her, isn't it possible that at least one other man might find her appealing also? And if this other man and your wife spent nearly as much or even more hours around each other as the husband did, might not there be the eventual opportunity for a mutual attraction to develop and grow? If this is true, then why do women pretend that it is an impossibility? Why do they think that men's concerns about their attractive wife working around men is so unwarranted? Why must an expression of sincere feelings be misinterpreted as misplaced male ego tripping?

Women of course, pretend that even the idea of sleeping with another man is beyond their comprehension. They are much too moral, in control, focused, careful, loyal, faithful and businesslike to slip into a compromising position like that. That's what they would have you believe. Two women interviewed in Ms. Moore Campbell's book, *Successful Women, Angry Men* (page 112-113) make their point.

> "Often, men experience an almost paranoid perception that a wife's co workers and work friends are aiding and abetting her insubordination to her husband. Some say they feel competition coming from their husbands towards their office mates. Lena, a 43-year-old executive in a public-relations firm was counseled by her husband when her career and marriage began. Subsequently he dropped out of public relations to go into real estate. Lena proceeded to ascend to startling professional heights. A superstar in her business, she says her fantastic success has been misinterpreted by her husband. "He's become hideously jealous of all the associations with

men I've had in my job. He began to see me as someone he couldn't control anymore. I was going away everyday, out of his clutches. He projected all his self-doubts onto me. For some reason he had this image of me as a very, very loose woman doing all kinds of things. His jealousy drove me bananas. Another woman says the following: "George used to always say to me, 'Why do you have to go to meetings with so many men,? Donna said with a long heavy sigh. "I'd explain to him that I just happened to work in a male- dominated field, but I always got the feeling he suspected I was up to something."

In another part of her book, Ms. Campbell says the following:

"Working women often have more opportunity to meet men than do women who stay at home, and their schedules give them more latitude to make time *for affairs* (emphasis mine, page 151)

Ms. Campbell's representations here confirm the mixed message mumbo jumbo that men can't stand to deal with. On the one hand, something is wrong with men if we dare suspect that our wives might fall prey to an office romance. We are sick, mistrusting, insecure, and so on. Yet, Ms. Campbell tells us that if she did want to do it, the working woman is certainly in a better position to pull it off than the old-fashioned stay- at-home wife. She's got more men to select from and more time. So what does all this mean to the man? It means that the women are talking out of both sides of their mouths and still doing a good job of making you think that you are the one who is crazy.

At this point, a fair question that a woman might ask is why would a man suspect that his wife might establish an office romance? Would it be because all men are dogs and a dog at work would attract his wife, or is it because all women are loose and can't say no? The answer is neither. The truth is that men and women have spent much of their lives finding out what the other sex wants or likes, and once they learn what these things are, they use them from *time to time*. We've often heard both men and women say "I wonder if my stuff is still good". "Stuff" can mean anything from a flirty smile, a powerful line, to a stiff penis and anything in between. Thus sex is often more about a competitive person testing their own appeal then truly caring for another person. Men have heard women talk about 50/50 marriages, equality, partnership, equal sharing of duties and responsibility, equal pay for equal work, equal this and equal that. It sounds good, it's even believable sometimes, but its basically untrue. Because women will continue to be turned on to power and money just as men will always be turned on by a cute face, D-cups and a tight butt.   And when you are turned on by a person more powerful and wealthier than you, then by definition you are not dealing with an equal, but a superior.   And women have been trained to date up, marry up, etc.   Therefore, when a woman marries a man who is her equal, she has essentially *settled* for someone other than her dream man, no matter how "nice" her husband may be. Men believe that it is human *nature*, not male or female nature, to move toward your old fantasies and dreams even if you've just about given up on them.   So if a married woman can manage to get just a little taste of the powerful, rich type of man she has always dreamed about, *especially if he's hitting on her,* (it relieves the guilt), she just might do it at least once to check it out.   This sexual freedom appears to be an unspoken part of the feminist movement and distinguishes working women from the domesticated one.   And one of the pat lines that feminists always use (and its usually true too) is "men have been doing this for years".   So in many women's eyes, two wrongs, in this case, make a right.

In *Successful Women, Angry Men*, Ms. Campbell uses the whole book to document women's frustrations at being the first generation of female competitors to White male power and the costs it extracts from them personally and in their marriage in particular.   As a feminist, one would expect that Ms. Moore Campbell would lay more than a fair share of the blame on the uncooperative men that are part of this new experiment.   However, I am very glad that she had the courage and honesty to give enough of the other side of the story to help me make my case as well.   Let us look closely at the following statements, and then discuss the accuracy of men's suspicions and the source of their frustrations.

> "Women, of course, have affairs too and many of them suffer from the same feelings of neglect and abandonment as their husbands.   Others seek lovers in retaliation for their husband's dalliance.   Most, however, look to extramarital affairs to provide them with a love relationship in which they don't have to be adversarial.   Often their burnout has put them in touch with their own human and sexual needs, feelings that had been suppressed. When female self-esteem is *low,* many look to bolster their self-confidence with the attention of another man.   Women say they have affairs with the kind of high powered, self-assured men they wish their husbands were.   Others just want to spend time with someone who will be nice to them.   They want attention, excitement, and the intimacy lacking in their marriages.   "When I did have an affair," said a woman from Alabama, whose salary and position far exceeded her husband's, "it was with a person

whose position was more prestigious than my husband's. He was good to me. We could talk about a variety of subjects without his becoming intimidated because I knew something he didn't. It was nice to have someone on my level. And, of course, we didn't have any real problem, so the sex was great."
(pages 159-160)

If we study these revealing statements, we see not only much of what is wrong with today's two-career (or even working couple) marriages, but how men are deceived as well.

A)   The first sentence says the reason for women having affairs is the "same feelings of neglect and abandonment as their husbands." This is a flat out lie. A husband's role is to provide for his family. By leaving the house he is not abandoning anyone, he is doing his job by working a job. The change in the nature of the institution of marriage is the woman going away all day to work and then coming home many nights late because of business meetings, deadlines, and "networking".

It is the *duties of the house* that used to be done by what we called the wife that have been abandoned. And if they have not been taken care of by hired help, then we can only assume that the wife has abandoned these duties. How can a wife have the "same feelings of neglect and abandonment" if the husband has fulfilled his main obligation while she has neglected one of hers?

When the wife comes home from her exhausting day filled with racism, pressure,, deadlines, etc and declines sexual relations, it is understandable. But does the *reason for the decline* in relations change the fact that the male has been turned down? And if he has been turned down, is he not in fact being neglected and abandoned so to speak? And if there *is* sex, is it not because *she* is *not* tired and therefore its being engaged in when she wants it? So if *she* is getting sex when she wants it, how in the hell could someone say she has suffered abandonment and neglect?   Comprende?

B)   "others seek lovers in retaliation for their husband's dalliance (affairs)". If in this case, two wrongs make a right, then *women* lose their right to pretend that they have higher morals than men do which they frequently pre-tend.   And if *they don't make sure* that their husband finds out about their affair, then they are not having an affair in retaliation to their husband. Why do I say that? Because what hurt the wife was the emotional pain she suffered after she *found out* about the affair, not the affair itself. She could act in retaliation only after finding out the infidelity. If she has an affair and makes sure that her husband *doesn't know* about it, then she is sparing him the very pain that she experienced when she found out. In which case she is not retaliating at all. If she is not retaliating, then what is she doing? She is simply using her husband's act as an excuse to do something that she wanted to do all the time, which is to screw another man; not hurt her husband. This makes her intentions much more like her husband's original intent. It shows actually how much they are alike, at least in terms of sex drive and deceit.

    c) "Most, however, look to extramarital affairs to provide them with a love relationship in which they don't have to be adversarial." The entire nature of the feminist movement is adversarial. Feminists believe, teach and act according to a set of ideas that say "men have been against us, we are now launching a counter-attack against them to claim rights that we assume to be ours". In the "marriage of equals" it is the woman who takes the initiative to assert and proclaim her rights and demands, with many men being given more than a hint of a take it or leave it ultimatum. Ms. Moore Campbell's work is laced with many references to women working in the corporate world and having to "beat" men at their own game, being uncharacteristically aggressive, presenting an authoritative voice or demeanor, and so on. Look at this quote by Campbell herself on page 85:

> "They haven't learned to limit the energy they give to their jobs and outside interests so they have something left for their personal lives. In many cases they have sacrificed their personal lives to the goal of independence and self-fulfillment They emulate the same men they declare are their oppressors: those who work late, compete hard, and give only 2 percent of themselves to their families."

    Given these realities, how in the hell could the husband in her life be accused as being the *source* of the adversarial relationship, when every aspect of the new woman constitutes a battle. A battle for respect, a fight for money, for excellence and professional advancement, all of which comes at the expense of family life. On the other hand, if the husband said, "Look, honey, cool out, come home, take care of the house and kids, and I'll take care of everything else", he'd be accused of being a backward- thinking sexist. So the Black man not only can't win no matter which way he turns, he also has to swallow lame B.S. excuses that the wife actually believes explains her behavior. Wow!

    D) "Often their burnout has put them in touch with their own human and sexual needs, feelings that had been suppressed. When female self-esteem is low, many look to bolster their self-confidence with the attention of another man." If you have been following the line of reasoning up to this point, you ought to very easily see the ridiculousness of this statement. First of all a woman can only burn out in the business world because her *man* gives her absolute free reign to do as she wishes and to maximumily expend her energies. That is what burn out is. If he insisted on her coming home, fixing dinner, etc, she wouldn't get the chance to burn out. Burning out is proof that the man allowed the woman maximum latitude to do what she wanted to do and the condition of being burnt out is the condition that she drove *herself* to, *not* the husband. You can not feel sorry for a woman who against the desire of her mate drove herself to a condition that she now finds unpleasant. Besides, she isn't the only one paying the cost. While she is burning herself out, he is eating microwave dinners every night, taking care of the kids, not having sex with his exhausted wife and not getting the attention and affection one expects in a marriage. So when the point of burnout comes and she decides to get back in touch with her needs for sex and human kindness, does she go back to the man that has been understanding and trying hard to be the modern man (even if he has been complaining the whole time)? No, she seeks another man to have her revived sex urges satisfied and her self-confidence bolstered. The husband loses coming and going. What is the husband supposed to do? If he splits, you know he'll be accused of being unable to handle a successful wife—the standard party line. If the man gets out and gets himself a girlfriend so that he can "bolster his self esteem and confidence", would the wife or women in general go for it? You can answer that.

E) "Women say they have affairs with the kind of high-powered, self assured men they wish their husbands were... "When I did have an affair, it was with a person whose position was more prestigious than my husband's. He was good to me. We could talk about a variety of subjects without his becoming intimidated because I knew something that he didn't. It was nice to have somebody on my level".

Of all the statements made in Ms. Moore Campbell's book, none were more revealing, confirming or important than the above. First the statement confirms the great fear of many men. That being that when the wife is in the working world, she will eventually become attracted to and go to bed with a man she considers *more of a man* because he has more power and presumably more money than her husband. Yet, when men express this fear openly, they are considered insecure or unstable. Many of these same women will look you straight in your face and say things like, "I just don't see money as being that important", "men with power are on ego trips, I'm not attracted to that type", and so on. They will always deny what you, the man, knows they would prefer if they had their choice. "Honey, I like you just the way you are", is possibly the biggest lie that ever came out of a female's mouth. How many women have dreamed about a man "on their level"? Keep in mind women's twisted idea of " on their level". To a woman in middle management, making sixty thousand a year, a man on *her level* is not a man in middle management also making sixty thousand a year. To a woman, a man on *her level* is an *upper* level manager making one hundred thousand dollars a year. According to women's logic, that is the type of man a woman at her level "deserves". Understand? So as women complain about having to be *twice as good* on the job just to be accepted, many husbands, even of so- called liberated wives, must make *twice as much money* as the wife to really be accepted by her. To help prevent her from being tempted to sleep with men "whose salary and position for exceeded her husband's".

Many times women will say that what they really want is not really sex but "someone to talk to and listen to me". Sex is given by the woman as payment for a listening ear. These women exaggerate very often the receptiveness of their listener/lover while doing the same in the opposite direction for their "pig headed" husband. Warren Farrell makes a good point on page 143 of his book *Why Men Are The Way They Are*. He says that comparing qualities of a husband and another person is a false comparison, like that made between apples and oranges. Listening is easy when the person we're listening to is not complaining about us; when we don't have to live with the outcome; when we don't have to negotiate the everyday terms of life; when we don't have an emotional and financial history and an emotional and financial future. In contrast, when all these circumstances are combined, our listening skills are tested.

Of course the brilliant working woman with the MBA and high paying executive position might not be smart enough to realize this. She *is* smart enough to blame the husband for not fulfilling a role that he cannot possibly fulfill, which is that of an *unaffected,* objective listener.

The intent of this chapter is not to lower the boom and crush the ideas and goals of working women. It is to say that we are all walking on new ground here, and anyone of either sex who thinks they've got it all figured out is an arrogant fool. As a Black male however, it becomes extremely annoying to hear women in general and Black women in particular express such baseless self righteous attitudes about the " correctness" of their views, when half the time their arguments eventually crumble like a house of cards upon more serious examination. Our annoyance increases when Black women explain their frustrations, and use the limitations of the Black male as the universal answer or excuse for the failings that Black women experience. Black men are no more responsible for all of Black women's problems than White people are responsible for all of Black peoples problem's. The purpose of this chapter was to dissect some of the complaints of working Black women, and show that in many cases their arguments had no logic with reference to blaming Black husbands. And as Ms. Moore Campbell has suggested in her work, given the opportunity, women behave just like men in many similar situations. So whose right and whose wrong?

Attitudes

People have many dimensions that define who they are. But when we distinguish one person from another, we usually refer to their *personality* as representing who they are. Personality can include a number of things: intelligence, sense of humor, smile, moods, attitudes, etc. When we marry someone we understand that many things about them will change in the years ahead. Physically we know they will age. But as long as the personality of our mate remains pretty much the same, we still consider ourselves married to the same person no matter how much they change physically. Even when a person becomes permanently injured, disfigured or disabled, we still view that person as more or less the same after we adjust to the new restrictions.

But when the personality of a person changes, when what makes them laugh, cry, talk, make love, joke and play change, we then begin to see them as a different person. In trying to adjust our personality to respond to a new personality, we are not always successful. In such cases, people often decide to go their separate ways.

When men and women talk about each others attitudes, it is a conversation to be taken seriously. A person's attitude has a great impact on their personality, and their personality, as we said, is who they are. When men and women say they are having trouble getting along, what is usually involved is their attitudes towards each other or things in general. Thus, in discussing the impact of money in Black relationships, we must look at how having or not having money affects the attitudes of the parties involved. In the April 1993 issue of *Essence Magazine* the lead article concerned itself with Black women's negative attitudes. I must say that it continues to frustrate me personally as a writer when I see good pieces written and know that the Black community's reaction to the article is going to be good or bad not based on the accuracy of *what's* being said but on *who* is writing it. If this same article had been written by a man (rather than a female using a *false* name,) the magazine may not have chosen to print it. Or *Essence* may have been printed it and thousands of negative letters would have come pouring in. In any event the article describes three basic negative female attitudes. After some discussion about how these attitudes may have developed, some words of advice are offered regarding "making peace." I think its fair to say that the people with whom these sisters with an attitude have to make peace with are Black men. The article represented a public recognition of an attitude/personality conflict between a significant number of Black females and certain types of Black men. These attitudes of Black women are consistent and prevalent enough that recognizable names are assigned to them and their probable causes are explained. All of this is being recognized as fact by Essence Magazine, the bible for many Black women.

It bears asking, then, that if some Black women already have attitude problems (which is not to say that Black men don't have their own fair share of attitude problems) how does the corporate or professional career track affect those attitudes which may already be difficult? Do brothers who decide to marry these type of career-minded sisters catch more hell or does it even out in the mix? This is a serious question because currently, Black women are convinced that "most Black men can't deal with a successful Black woman." And some Black men, Haki being one, agree. But perhaps what some Black men can't deal with is the bitchy attitude that was always a part of some sisters *before* they became successful. And perhaps financial success has given some
  women the security to act more like a bitch as often as they wish. These are just a few of the many questions that Black men have that are never raised, written about or addressed in any public forum or publication. Are they valid questions? Many men think so.

Let's assume the impossible. Let us assume that no Black woman in America who is pushing hard for career and professional success possess a single prediagnosed attitude problem. Given this, we must ask the question: Does the mere striving and struggle to reach and maintain career success cause certain new personality traits (attitudes) to develop that might also cause an otherwise supportive brother to head South? Attitudes are formed by conditions and experiences. Do certain job conditions and experiences posses enough power and influence to change a woman from the personality someone married yesterday to somebody that today is only vaguely recognizable? . And is a husband obliged to remain married to this new person when he only made his promise of "till death do us part" to the someone who's obviously now missing? Brothers need to ask themselves these questions and then some.

Our main guide through this maze of confusion, Ms. Bebe Moore Campbell, has the following quotes in her book *Successful Women,Angry Men*.

"Cheryl said that her husband accused her of not being a good wife because of her businesslike attitude. "Sometimes if I came home, keyed up from work, and I told him to do something, he'd say, 'You better turn off that work stuff. I'm not someone you're supervising." The analyst admitted that sometimes she was overbearing." It's true. There have been times that I've had trouble shifting gears and I'd treat him like someone I was managing." (pages 106-107)

"Husbands shout that they get their wives' leftover time, leftover enthusiasm, and leftover attention. The job, they assert, comes first with these women who have become so businesslike they've lost their warmth and femininity. They would rather work than be mothers or lovers." (Page 101)

"Some women who have accomplished their professional and economic goals may unwittingly bring their job personalities into their homes. The increased self-confidence that succeeding at a job engenders is expected in men in this society, not in women. Many husbands find it uncomfortable to live with a woman who appears to be their intellectual or financial equal." (Page 60)

" What has happened in the more than twenty years since the Civil Rights Act is that in order to succeed, many women, already convinced they must deliberately masculinize their dress, speech, method of working, and how they express leadership and emotions, have also adopted the male value system that consciously and unconsciously denigrates female cultural expression in the workplace. Research reveals that the young women who are ascending in fields that were traditionally male exhibit more of the characteristics associated with male leadership than do men.   A "macho female" has emerged, a suited and tied individual who succeeds in her job by making her male co-workers and superiors feel culturally comfortable with her even though she may feel very uncomfortable herself. "(Page 189)

There are many other passages in this work which express the main two thoughts which are: a) the work place is affecting women's attitudes and b) their husbands are not happy with this new personality. This phenomenon is a cross- cultural and cross- racial problem. White women as well as Blacks are being sucked into a masculinization process that is quite evident. Usually Black woman excuse many of the changes they go through by saying "Well this is what they (White folks)are doing now" and brothers are just suppose to accept it and shut up. And we must never forget that in her long history of trying to be acceptable to White folks, a certain type of Black women will do just about anything . Hell, some have tried so hard to change their racial identity that the only thing left is her sexual identity. An astute person understands that once inside the "corporate culture," the environment changes you in ways that one cannot be aware of on a conscious level most of the time. And it is especially difficult when the precise attitude that turns your husband off is the exact same attitude which wins you the respect of your peers and gets you the favorable nod of a job well done by your supervisor. For a Black woman starting at the bottom of America's totem pole, that's heavy stuff. Some men understand that. But, sisters, can you also understand that in the general scope of things, the Black man's day is probably even more stressful than yours? Why do I say that? Because in addition to having to prove that he is as good, as qualified, and as smart at the workplace like you do, he may also have to prove to someone each day, in some degrading manner, that he is *not* a thief, drug addict, or a criminal- and that is added pressure that Black women don't have. When the Black man comes home he wants to feel safe, and comfortable and that he can relax. Most Black men are not on ego trips that require a wife to serve as maid, waitress and sex slave. *They just want peace.* Which is why the very last thing a Black man needs is a woman who enters the house that he is largely responsible for paying for, sounding and acting like the White boss he just left. That's not what or who he married. Neither is this type of woman what he considers to be a good role model for his children. He would like for his daughter to at least be exposed to a femine mother in her early years so that she'll know what that's like, even if she too opts to be a masculinized female success story when *she* "grows up". The one point I'd like to challenge in Ms. Moore Campbell's work is her reference, on more than one occasion, that aggressiveness and intellect are one and the same. True there are men who do want to feel that they are smarter than their wives because it makes them more secure in their leadership role. (They can justify telling them what to do.)But there are also guys who have no problem with a woman knowing more than them, but who still dislike being bossed. Intellect and aggressiveness are not the same. Many of us have been fortunate enough to have heard brilliant teachers, ministers, writers, doctors, or even comedians, and they weren't necessarily aggressive at all. Perhaps Ms. Moore Campbell connects aggressiveness and intellect as one in order to make aggressive behavior more acceptable to men. The truth is Black men don't respond well, to aggressive, pushy, or bossy behavior from other men either, or even police. So most brothers don't even think about accepting it from a woman, and especially his own woman. Thus, Black men and Black women are going to have to learn how to be bicultural. European-American male culture might be required to make it in the world of work. But everybody should agree that when your feet hit the door, male and female African-American culture is spoken and practiced here.

I Can Do Good By Myself.

There's an expression that African-American women often use that drives me up the wall, across the ceiling and down the other side. The expression is "I can do bad by myself." I'm told men also use the phrase but I've never heard them. I associate this expression with Black women. What the expression says to me is "Brother your only true value to me, the purpose of your existence as far as I am concerned, is to help me do better because I can do bad by myself." I might be overly sensitive, but I can tell you that my respect level for a sister immediately falls whenever I hear use the phrase. I feel a bit hypocritical because these sisters are merely telling the truth and I am always preaching about the truth. The statistics clearly say that Black women indeed are doing bad by themselves. Actually Black women with children (which means they aren't by themselves) are doing pretty bad. That discussion has been beat to death, so we won't cover it here.

What we will examine are the consequences that await a brother who happens to hook up with a woman, who can do good by herself, but their marriage fails. Are the results any different than with a woman who can do bad by herself?

Many feminists say that the idea of a woman having her own money, maybe even in some instances more money than the husband, is a terrifying idea to a lot of men. You will get no argument from me on that point. Money has always been used by people in all sorts of relationships to control, influence, demand, force, and manipulate behavior that agrees with the person who controls the purse strings. Men have certainly done that to women in marriage. One of the benefits, the perceived advances of a dual career marriage, is that women don't have to play by the same old rules. Their professional incomes dictate that there is a new game in town, and men have to deal with that or else.

This chapter has looked at various changes that men and women have gone through to reach this goal of equality. Obviously I have sought to highlight the Black male perspective, the one you almost never hear about. In this last segment, we need to look at what happens when the marriage doesn't work out in a marriage of equals. If a woman who believes strongly in feminist ideas decides to marry, she is not likely to select just any type of brother as a mate. She is most likely to pick a brother that she feels has more than average respect for women, admits to sexism, at least mouths the principles of gender equality, and supports her, as well as he's able to at the time, in her quest for career success. But let's be realistic, couples not only do not have a crystal ball to look into the future, they don't even have a road map which shows how to get from where they are to where *they think* they want to go. People in this position we call trail blazers. Trail blazers are not necessarily smarter or more capable than ordinary people. They just have a vision in mind that makes the old trail the wrong road for where they want to go.

Thus, any brother who would to marry a woman who embraced these new ideas would deserve to be looked at favorably just for being willing to try a new direction to help Black women be more of what they want to be. I believe this is a fair assumption. Now because the feminist road is not charted and laid out, because feminism is not a *major* cause within the Black community, and because the general society is still sexist and fighting change at every turn, the brothers in this position do not *really know* what they are up against. They will have their ideological principles tested not only by the general society, but also by the very woman that they entered into this experiment with. What kinds of things can happen if things don't work out well?

A dual- career Black couple is likely to have very high debt, because Black people are still the ultimate consumers. A big mortgage, two expensive car notes for late model (expensive) cars, and maybe also a boat, camper, van or truck note as well. A wide variety of credit cards, bank credit lines, and expenses for in home offices may also to be assumed as part of this lifestyle package. Like most high consumption couples, there will be the trap of overestimating just how much you can afford to comfortably pay for. And in spite of the hundred thousand plus dollars a year in income, it will be a struggle every month to make sure each and every bill gets paid.

Meanwhile, the complaints and problems and clashes that were described previously are spiraling upwards. The biggest single problem in the brother's mind is that, after having made what he knows to be great strides in doing" women's work," having accepted the fact that his sex life is never going to be what it was, and having scaled back his own career goals to make room for his wife's plans, he still feels pushed to do more, more and more. On the one hand it is ridiculous to congratulate a man for fixing his own food or watching his own children, even if it is something that his father and brothers have never done. But on the other hand people need to feel appreciated and supported when they are performing tasks and duties which for them are a challenge because it goes against the grain of their training, their original expectations and their psychological self image. If a brother spends an hour cleaning the house, he doesn't need to hear how badly he did it if the intent is to make him feel comfortable in doing it on a regular basis. But this is what some men experience. A woman is programmed to push men. If he'll take me to a six dollar movie, maybe I can get him to take me to a twenty dollar play the next time. If he'll buy me a ten dollar meal at this restaurant, maybe we can go to the more exclusive one downtown next time. Following that line of thinking, some women might feel, " If I come home from work at eight o clock this week, maybe it will be OK if I'm out till ten next week". The brothers who are trying to adjust to the liberated woman do not have a cheering section on the side line edging them on. As a matter of fact, some of his best friends and relatives might suggest that his marriage has turned him into a wimp. Thus, if the woman for whom he is extending himself is not supporting his efforts, then he's in a no win situation. Most people quit no win situations. So let us assume that the marriage ends and has left its ugly mark. What position is the brother in?

Trailblazing brothers are likely to be put into a position of assuming a high degree of debt. The court system in the U.S. have not changed from their original mission of trying to preserve the lifestyle of women and children. Thus, the debt that was incurred in the marriage by two high income earners, now must be assumed by each spouse separately. And more times that not, the man is assigned the task of paying for stuff which he never wanted in the first place. On top of this debt, there will be requests for steep child support payments because of the lifestyle the couple lived collectively. If the wife and kids are awarded the house, the brother will have to pay a heavy payment for an asset that he no longer enjoys. The worse case situation occurs when the payments are not made, the bank forecloses on the house and the equity on the property is lost for both spouses.

When a brother emerges from his failed efforts at a challenging marriage, based on feminist ideas, he is almost a misfit. He's too use to a woman pulling her own weight to tolerate any sister who wants a free ride. But his experience with an independent woman was not positive enough to risk trying it a second time. How is he suppose to respond to Black women's continued complaints about Black men when he's so aware that his efforts at change satisfied nobody. (To better understand this situation see *It Pays To Be A Trifling Husband.*)

In the end, in situations where a brother marries a woman who can "take care of herself," the divorce laws sometimes do not allow them to do exactly that and he is often in the same or worse position than if he had married a poor woman. Of course, if his independent-minded woman offers a fair settlement proposal that they can agree to, then the end results might not be so bad. But women are notorious for seeing dollar signs at divorce time, and suddenly women who normally have something to say about every topic in the world all of a sudden need an attorney to state their "substantial interests and claims." The lawyer is now the only person the husband has to talk to and the lawyer is looking for as much blood as he can get.

It was made clear at the start of this commentary that only a small percentage of Black couples ever get into these kinds of financial and professional conflicts simply because relatively few Black people are powerful professionals to begin with. What are some of the other attitudes and situations that create difficulties for Black couples attempting to live a financially harmonious life together. One difficulty relates to ideas presented at the beginning of this book. When a young female adopts the mentality of measuring her self worth not on the basis of what she can do for herself but on what she can get men to do *for her*, her life is headed downhill. Because once that becomes the game that she decides to play, then it is into this game she will invest most of her thinking, creativity and action. Quite often sex and - motherhood follows shortly thereafter. At that point she allows her lifestyle, benefits, opportunities and future to be largely dictated by what her boyfriend (and eventually the husband') does for her while forgetting that she has ability that she can use for herself and family as well. If the boyfriend walks, she then places herself at the mercy of the state welfare system or relies on parents, grandparents etc. A significant number of such females eventually wake up to their potential and get their acts together. Unfortunately most do not.

In the book *The Black Male in America* by Doris Y. Wilkinson and Donald Taylor (Nelson-Hall Chicago 1977). There is a chapter entitled *The Myth of the Impotent Black Male* by author Robert Staples. On page 136 There is the following:

> "Economically destitute Black families may be forced into a welfare system where it makes "sense" in terms of daily economic security for Black men to leave their families. An example is this Black woman who refused to permit her husband back into the family after he got a job. She said:"

> "Not me! With him away I've got security. I know when my welfare check is coming and I know I can take him to court if he doesn't pay me child support. But as soon as he comes back in, then I don't know if he's going to keep his job or if he's going to start acting up and staying up drinking and spending his pay away from home. This way I might be poor, but at least I know how much I got."

Black women, like all people, look for the "best deal they can cut". Some look for a man to take care of them. Some, like the one quoted above, would prefer to have both the state and the man make contributions for her security. And then many women take a lot of pride in putting themselves in a position where "I don't need no damn man to take care of me." These independent sisters are interesting to study for their contradictory behavior. On the one hand a lot of lip service is given about marriage being a *sharing relationship*. Of course! If I'm a traditional woman and all I've got is fifty cents, and I see a man who has a thousand dollars, of course I'm going to talk about sharing because that means I am due to receive four hundred ninety nine dollars and seventy five cents (half of $1,000.50). All I have to do is convince him that having sex with me is worth that much (but don't call me no whore). Yet the sister who *actually has money to share* is in many instances the last ones to get married and share what they do have with their mate. Such Black women normally explain their situation as: a) because "they can't find a man on their level" (which I say is still a man that makes more money), or b) can't find a man that is not threatened by an independent woman. Some of that may very well be true. But look what Warren Farrell says in his book on page 171:

"Item: The largest study of singles in the eighties found that women earning high incomes are almost twice as likely to *want to remain uncommitted* as are women earning low incomes. (emphasis mine)

Item: The authors of American Couples found that lesbians were more likely than other women to claim that income and status were irrelevant. However, the authors found, to their surprise, that the high-income and high-status partner in lesbian relationship was almost always the one to leave. Taken together, what the items reveal is that the more income a woman makes, the less willing she is to commit. Which makes her just like a man - and therefore helps us understand why men (who earn more) commit more cautiously".

These two studies just prove what is common sense: its just human nature not to give away (excuse me, I mean "share")your money and assets. This is especially true when you have to work as hard for them as Black people do. What irritates men is that for many years we have said if women were in our position, they would think like we think and do like we do. Women have, on the other hand, always pretended that just being born female carried with it some moral superiority that enabled them to automatically do the right thing. Men believe that money and the things you have to do to get it obscures the behavior differences between the sexes.

Interestingly enough some women accept obscuring the gender roles and behaviors and will do a "man's job for a man's pay." Thus, we see female police and firemen, airline pilots and astronauts, etc. Victoria King on page 49 and 50 of her book, makes the following observations during her twelve years as one of the first Black female union electricians working on commercial construction sites in New York City.

"In the midst of all this poverty and despair, I happened to stop an elevator one day to transport a ladder and a bundle of pipe when I over heard one Black pregnant teen whisper to another, "You couldn't pay me enough to do that kind of work." At the time, 1986, I was making about $1500 a week and seldom had less than $300 in my wallet, while they were at the hospital in search of free medical services. Although I was dressed in jeans and work boots, I lived in a beautiful three bedroom apartment on the upper westside of Manhattan and my son and I had just returned from our annual two week Christmas vacation, this time in the Virgin Islands. In spite of the fact that I worked hard for a living, I had doors opened to me of which these girls could only dream. Two years later I could afford to quit the electrical trade to attend law school.

The irony was heartbreaking. I wanted to grab them and shake them and shout, "Wake up! No one is going to save you from this hell hole!" Here were two young Black teenage females, both pregnant, one with a baby in her arm; neither wearing a wedding ring. All that they were trained to see when looking at a woman in other than a traditional or subordinate position was that it was not cute. Working hard or sweating for a living was a crime against femininity. They were trapped as surely as if someone were holding a gun on them, but by their own thinking."

Black people, males and females, are very confused about money, and that confusion makes for the mishandling of just about all other things *related* to money including marriage. Some believe that we should attack all the problems of crime, housing, racism, drugs etc. separately. I, for years have advocated the idea that if we as a people make a concerted effort to understand money *first*, many other problems will be much easier to understand and probably easier to solve.

WHEN MEN MAKE LESS THAN WOMEN

Once upon a time there were two middle aged white lawyers living in the deep South. The male "head" of the family had a good job but it paid only thirty five thousand dollars a year, and it had been at that level for years. This man's wife was a feminist and her legal education led her to a job that paid one hundred and thirty thousand dollars a year. How on earth could that man have possibly felt that he was truly the head of the household if his outspoken feminist wife made almost a hundred thousand dollars a year more in income? Because governor Bill Clinton had his eyes on a much bigger dream, a dream in which money is not even the issue. Today as President of the U.S., his salary is a quarter million a year. The benefits that come with the job make the salary almost unimportant. His wife, Hillary, has no salary that most people are aware of, but then at this stage of her life she doesn't need one either. Is this an unusual turn of events? Of course it is. But some of the principles still hold true even if you aren't White, a Rhodes Scholar and a lawyer. There are many, different situations where Black women make more money than their husbands or boyfriends. And there are just as many reactions that men can have when placed in this situation. In other words, one can easily write an entire book (and I'm surprised no one has by now) on this topic alone. Since so much is made of the Black woman's "progress" and the Black mans "decline" in education, and status, and income, the issue bears at least some discussion.

Why Is It a Major Issue?

If you were from another planet and came to America, you would hear a contradictory conversation going on that would confuse you. On the one hand you would hear about the issue of gender equality and women rights and equal pay for equal work, etc. But on the other hand there would be an underlying assumption that, when all is said and done, women should "marry up" and that men should not. Men should not place themselves in a position where their wife earns a substantially greater income than they do. The obvious question is: Why not? What is the big deal if the woman makes more or not? What precisely is wrong with that situation, particularly when so many married, employed women have unemployed husbands with no income at all?

African American marriages have lasted under the most trying of circumstances, and the community of Africans in America is always looking to advance itself.

The first reality that has to be faced in this struggle for advancement is that there is no security or guarantees for Black Americans. We do not control the economy of our own community; we are only twelve percent of the national population; and, we take in at best only eight percent of its total income. Most Black people overwhelmingly work for White people and for companies where their jobs can be taken away at the stroke of a pen. So, one of the biggest mistakes that any Black person can make, male or female, is to get caught up into thinking that they are employed in some lofty fixed position that is destined to last forever. We all know people who use to be doing well who are not doing well now. There are tens of thousands of skilled, educated, experienced White men trying very hard to make it after losing comfortable positions in the top corporations in America. These men are offered as proof that security as we use to understand the word is basically a thing of the past. Despite that grim reality, there are still people, including some Black women, who appear to have relatively secure jobs that will assure them that their material needs will be met for the foreseeable future. And the question remains as to why it may not be a good thing for the well positioned Black woman to commit to a brother who is much less able to supply the material aspects of life?

The Manhood Issues:

a)   In the United States there is a direct relationship between the money that you make and the respect you receive, at least in non racial situations. There is a relationship between your income and what you are and are not able to do in life for yourself or for other people. There is a relationship between your money and how the society makes you feel about yourself. There are a broad range of other factors and relationships that money helps to shape, if not outright determine. And despite the millions of printed words that says that *should not* be the case, a reality check says that is the way it is. Thus money affects what you can and can not do. It defines your power to move, change, control and protect. Black men, like most men, see money as a very important part of their ability to carry out their agenda and act as men. Money is part of a man's means to manipulate the world. Without money, the Black man sometimes has to act somewhat child-like and wait for someone else more powerful, more respected, more entitled and more in control to manipulate the world for him, and hopefully in his best interests.

The Black man's experience has been that he cannot count on other people, particularly White people, to spend money in Black people's interests, quite the contrary in fact. Thus in America if Black people are to see their agenda carried out and their goals fulfilled, it is even more crucial for them to have money because of the historical pattern of White monied interests specifically using their money and power to keep Black people and the Black man in particular in a subservient position. But Black men have another reason to associate money with manhood. Black men have a history of being denied the normal and natural ways to express their manhood in ways that have nothing at all to do with money. This tragic history has made him very sensitive to the subject of manhood and has in fact caused him to have a manhood deficit. Such a deficit is as natural as if you denied a car gasoline. Without gasoline a car can not move, which is the very thing a car is intended to do. The Black man throughout American history has repeatedly decided not to exercise his manhood in the way that man has done historically, which is to confront and kill his enemy in war. To me, slavery was a war situation. Because of the decision not to express manhood in this way, the Black man had to find other means of expressing the manhood he eventually felt entitled to express. Thus, in a kind of "if-you can't-beat-them-join-them" philosophy, the Black man, right or wrong, finds that he is currently engaged in the *money is your manhood* philosophy that is so much a part of the White world of which he is now a part. In summary, money is a part of the definition of manhood generally, and a part of Black manhood especially. One of the most fundamental means of measuring his progress in winning his fight for money and manhood is whether he is winning this struggle within the smallest group of which he is a part, his own household. Failure to win within his own home is what destroys for many Black men the idea that they can or should continue to compete in the real world. Some Black men stop struggling to be men and simply submit to who ever wishes to make them submit, wife included.

    b)   Of the various groupings of people that make up America, Black women rank near the bottom in economic accomplishment. Thus, it is natural that they look to Black men to improve their economic status, particularly in light of their legendary consumer buying patterns. Black women, though beneficiaries of the feminist movement, never bought into feminist philosophy or activity for as long or as deeply as their "White sisters". Given the prospect of living alone and raising children by themselves, they insist on equal pay for equal work. But having generally been denied the opportunity to live the traditional American wife lifestyle of staying home and being cared for by a working husband, I think the majority would opt for such a lifestyle if it was offered to them. *Black men making more money than women helps both sexes see themselves as they would prefer to be seen rather than how they have been seen traditionally.* I think Black women are tired of seeing the images and references to "the powerful Black matriarch" being father and mother to the children, the leader and "backbone" of the family (suggesting that the Black male *had no* backbone), and unable to attract a good man for a long term (or permanent) relationship. I think many are tired of that. To some the idea of being a $70,000 educated executive woman married to an uneducated $35,000 fireman is just a 21st century update of a nineteenth century image. For many Black women there are things more reinforcing to their self image than the size of their personal pay check. Success at "marrying up" is one of those things. For the Black man to be the breadwinner in the family not only elevates the man but also puts her in alignment with virtually all other human societies in the history of the world. Few societies in history have sent women out as hunters and gatherers to bring home the bacon while the domesticated male stayed home to watch the children. The man as breadwinner also kills the persistent images of the lazy Black man, the homeless Black man, the useless or burdensome Black man, and the criminally inclined Black man.

c)   Both young Black boys and girls would likely benefit from experiencing more of the traditional family arrangements in their life than what many see today. Based on what they see it would be hard for me to believe that many young boys don't think that men are *suppose* to walk away from their wives and children. They probably feel that, at the very worse its an acceptable thing to do. To see men shouldering the brunt of the responsibility for raising the family would probably be the single greatest lesson a young boy could learn. It would also put him in alignment with the rest of the world and show that there is something else besides money and material things that defines manhood. Boys are subject to many negative temptations every day. By having a strong father, the boy can see that those temptations don't need to be tested. But the father will need more than his fist, his religion or his mouth to demonstrate his strength. When the son can see his father's ability to earn money, he will learn that it can be obtained without falling for the various illegal temptations.

Young girls need to believe that there is hope for Black boys and men. They see Black men die and drop out of society. They hear all the statistics that forecast their loneliness. But I don't think Black women get a thrill at seeing their men defeated. No matter how much or how bad Black women talk about Black men, I believe they would very much love to look up to them. Many say that no one should have to look up to anyone else. But my instinct and gut tells me that girls will always envy another girl who has a father to look up to. Money should not be the defining factor but only naivete assumes it's not part of the package.

What Do Black Men Fear?

Many of the things that Black men fear in relationships where the woman is the superior earner has already been covered in another chapter.

1) Black men fear that the effort required to earn the income that the woman earns will not allow her enough time and energy to "perform" as a wife, lover and mother. In that sense, men see themselves as married, but without a true wife.

2) Black men fear that, despite the best intentions in the world, the wife would eventually find another man "on her level" who she just uncontrollably would fall in love with because of a new feeling of exhilaration that his money and position would give to her.

3) The Black man fears the "double whammy" of such a marriage. Whammy number one is the emasculation that a man might feel because he's made "to feel like a woman" in asking for money, "borrowing" money, being introduced as the "husband of," etc. Whammy number two is when he is asked to do women's work, work which he might not have a problem with if he was secure in his position as "head of household". But when a man finds himself cleaning the house, cooking meals, changing diapers, washing clothes and generally keeping house while the main provider is still out making the money, it distorts his sense masculinity. Also there is no time limit as to how long he is to endure the situation. It could last for as long as they are together. The marriage could mark the very time where he feels his identity became somewhat questionable. Most men cannot be paid enough to be made to feel like a woman.

4) Black men fear the attitudes that come with a woman of greater income. She may be very feminine most of the time, but on those occasions where there is a slip into bossy or demanding postures, there could be danger. Some men would seek to take action to "remind the lady who the boss really is". That action could very well be physical and will no doubt be ugly in any event. It is also unfair to many women who may feel pressured to be unduly submissive.

5) Black men fear that at the workplace their wife's supervisor will be in a much more influential position of controlling her time, actions, tastes and preferences than the husband.

6) Some Black men fear that a Europeanization (under the guise of "sophistication") of their wife will take place. As she becomes more visible to and socializes with White folks and picks up "corporate culture," she will cease to be the sister the brother fell in love with initially. She may start to come off like a White girl from time to time. This is especially likely to happen if her busy schedule prevents her from keeping in touch with her family roots. In striving to advance, she will do what it takes "to fit in," which is another way to say assimilate. Some sisters won't or can't turn it off at the front door, and problems begin.

7)   Black men fear that most of the extra money will not be spent on family needs but on the excessive material things that Black people usually buy to prove that they have money (jewelry, furs, designer clothes, etc). Arguments may result from statements like "At least I'm spending <u>my own</u> money."

8)   Black men fear that there own work will have little recognition or value in his wife's eyes because it doesn't have the status or/money that her's does. This is a major concern to many men in this position.

9)   Black men fear that they will not mix well with the wife's educated, "cultured" friends and her community of peers that he is likely to have to socialize with from time to time. He is as afraid of embarrassing his wife as he is of his own insecurity.   He is especially uncomfortable in "playing the role" at formal affairs.

In the discussions that have been a part of the changes in gender roles, one issue has been lost, or so it seems. And that issue is the fact the historically men and women derived some genuine joy in fulfilling their "traditional" roles. Men loved to see their wives and children get excited over gifts and surprises that they were able to provide with their hard earned money. Women, though experiencing the pain of child birth liked the idea of being a mother. They liked to bring a smile to the faces of their family members when they tasted a meal that they spent hours preparing. However old fashion some of the tasks that men and women were asked to perform, no one out grows the joy of giving and being appreciated. Note the quote from Ms. Moore Campbell's book (pages -185-186)

"Three years later, Ms. Fast Foods stood in front of a stove stirring at least four different pots, while the man in my life, my future husband, reclined on his sofa. What was amazing wasn't that I was cooking for a man again, but that I no longer resisted the act as a betrayal of feminist principles. It felt natural cooking for a man. The scene was blissfully domestic and I was happier than I'd been in a long, long time. Trying to please the man I cared for was satisfying. Maybe part of my pleasure was knowing that this particular man would set the table, clear it, and wash the dishes. Maybe not. More than his doing his share, what was personally fulfilling to me was the relish with which he ate the meal I'd prepared. To be honest, I enjoyed being the cause of his satisfaction every bit as much as I liked researching magazine articles and seeing my name in print. That admission, as unremarkable as it seems today, coming after several years of denial and suppression, made me feel as though I'd rediscovered some missing part of myself."

Black men fear marrying women of stature, money and deadlines because the simple pleasures described so well by Ms. Moore Campbell above seem to be beyond their ability to provide and appreciate. *People* make a home, not the furniture or the appliances. If there is not an atmosphere of mutual service, then most would agree that a critical part of the sense of home is missing. A lady who has become accustomed to room service in hotels might have lost her ability to distinguish the difference.

Responding To a Growing Pattern

Successful Black women want and deserve husbands and a happy home life. But there is no law, regulation or requirement that the men in these womens lives must earn more income than they do. But even if there were, sheer numbers and conditions may eventually make that idea much more difficult, if not impossible, to implement. There are many more women getting a formal education in undergraduate and graduate schools than Black men. Job markets continue to give more opportunities and higher salaries to those with the degrees than those without. Black women outnumber Black men. Black women are more likely to marry within their race than are Black men. Black women seem to have less homosexuals among them than Black men. White women will continue to push for the rights of women and become more "multicultural" in their orientation and thereby open up doors that Black women can use (Who would have guessed that the next Black Senator would have been female? Don't think that the "year of the Woman" election emphasis didn't have something to do with it). Whether Black men are ready or not, like it or not, or can deal with it or not is not a factor now. Black women are going to increasingly become the Black man's equal, or superior, in the money game. Since that is the coming reality, a major question is: How should men and women deal with that reality? It would be a mistake, I think, if either sex adapted the "it shouldn't make any difference" stand in light of all that has been presented here thus far. On the other hand, I think it's overly fatalistic to sentence all the "successful" sisters to a lonely spinster lifestyle or to have them seek White men or "others" as mates. Some general advice and direction is offered here to prevent obvious disasters and to help promising relationships to succeed.

a) Longer Dating Period

The old saying that "time will tell" probably holds a lot of relevance here. When men and women are first attracted to each other, they often cannot put their finger on precisely all the factors that form the basis of the attraction. Over a period of time, communication with the mate and oneself provides more clarity as to what is happening or working in the relationship. It would therefore make sense to prolong the dating and feeling-out process before any serious commitments are made. Of course, in many situations it is years into a marriage before the woman surpasses the husband in money, status, and ambition levels, and this situation constitutes an entirely different set of circumstances which may prove easier to deal with.

b) Honest Communication

Time in a relationship in itself doesn't mean anything if the communication in a relationship is poor and honest feelings are not expressed. But it is particularly important that communication be honest in situations where both parties realize that they are in an unusual or atypical relationship. In a situation where a woman's income is significantly greater than the males, both parties should be clear what constitutes the attraction. Why do they think a relationship would last? Why does the women want this particular man? Is it that he supplies the best sex she's ever had? If so, how long can a relationship last that is based mostly on sex? Is her biological clock ticking, and she's determined to have children, and he's the best man available at the time when her clock is making the most noise? Is she marrying for professional reasons, because having a husband will make her look more normal in the professional world and enable her to advance? Is she marrying because he's very attractive and is simply another trophy that balances well with her professional trophies? Whatever the real motivation for marriage, a brother should be very clear what it is, because it may contain hints as to the probability of the relationship lasting. Men in this position should be clear and confident in what they are bringing to the table and believe that those talents and qualities are respected by the woman. Otherwise the woman could easily walk, as men have done for hundreds of years, because her money provides a degree of independence and alternatives that most women never have. Obviously the woman should be on guard as well. There are many brothers who would very much like to find a woman who would take care of them. They will tell you they love you or anything else you want to hear for an opportunity to be kept. A prenuptial agreement ought to be seriously considered if the personal wealth is that great.

c) Personal Motivation

Very few Black people are born into wealth or born into a situation where a good paying job is virtually handed to them. Most of us who have anything, obtained it because we earned it. Two key parts of that capacity to earn are our "smarts" and our work ethic. If a person is smart and works hard and follows other "success principles", there is a decent chance that even as a Black person they may do ok in life. So if we find a woman who has done well and a brother who has not done as well, we might ask ourselves might it be due to the fact that they have different "makeups". Is the woman a real studious type who reads, studies and analyses while the brother gets his cues from the cosmos and astrology? Does she routinely work in some capacity for ten or more hours a day while the brother soaks up the best from all the movie channels? If this is the pattern that we see here, love might not be enough to keep this relationship together. High achieving people tend to lose respect for people who do not have ambition and drive at levels near their own. Successful people are that way because they *think* their way through the problems they encounter and to the opportunities that come their way. They get very upset when their achievements are seen as only luck. It is one thing for a man's under-achievement to be traced to bad luck or societies prejudices. Its another if its largely due to him being on cruise control. Two people going at two different speeds are bound to develop a large distance between them even if they are going to the same place and traveling the same road to get there. These habits should serve as a guide in reading the direction that the relationship might be heading.

Playing Catchup

In some relationships where the woman makes more money than the man, the man has no problem with it because he understands that she is simply earning what she deserves based on the decisions she has made and the work she has accomplished. He also recognizes that he has a similar potential but has not reached similar heights because of his poor decisions, which is a pattern that he specifically intends to change. In many of these types of relationships the woman has no desire to always be the bigger wage earner, but she is in the relationship because the man has promised (and she believes) that he is going to "go back to school" and get his life together. He is pledging to "catch up" to her so that they will be on a more even level.

Often a productive woman can inspire a man to reorganize and reprioritize his life to become more productive career-wise. But there are other issues that must be faced. Many Black men have permanent scars on their record which will prevent them from gaining access to the types of jobs that many sisters have. In addition to the half million Black men currently in prison, there are at least twice the number who have been in jail or prison for crimes the corporate employer will certainly view as serious. Will a college degree itself change that? Not in the hard job market we are in today. Many Black men have had their bouts with drugs. Will a plum job be lost because of that history? Its quite likely. Many Black men have military records where they may have less than honorable discharges. Will that have any weight? In many instances very much so. Some Black men complete college but their academic performance is so poor that it does not open the doors that it was suppose to open. What I'm pointing out here is the same theme that has been pointed out earlier in this book. The natural tendency of the Black man is to rebel against the status quo in any and all ways, and it comes back to haunt him when he pretends later that he can be a part of a system that was never intended for him. Politics plays a part in all decisions. When a Black woman gets hired, how she comes off in the interview, how she dresses and carries herself (is she Afrocentric or Eurocentric in appearance and mannerisms?) is as much a part of the decision process as her college degree, because she will represent the company during all types of business dealings, every day. If she poses no threat and is anxious to be a "team player", her application may sail through. It is very naive for the Black woman to assume that Black men can "catch up" merely by doing the same things that she did because *he* will not be looked at like *she* was looked at. Brothers need more *proof* that they are not guilty of all the things that America assumes we are guilty of. Thus sometimes we need more experience, more education, and *definitely* more references. White corporate America wants to know "can you supply us with the names of other White folks you've worked for before we allow you in here? " Many Black men cannot provide all that is needed to "catch up" to their woman. And because women do not understand or believe that White decision makers respond differently to Black men than they do Black women, many of them blame the man for not trying hard enough when their plans don't come to pass. Some of these Black women get to know some of these White male decision makers quite well. Sometimes these White males get to know these sisters so well that they begin to see them as women first and Black second, especially if they are attractive and Eurocentric in behavior (A new sister on a popular national morning news show not only knows how to talk like a White girl, as they all seem to do, but she has mastered how to shake her hair back from her forehead just like the White girls.) Some of these White men may develop a sexual attraction and grant special favors to these sisters for that reason. It is likely that some sisters may misread this "niceness" and see it as a true personality trait of her fair-minded boss. She begins to think he's really a good guy. When her six foot three, two hundred and thirty pound, dark skin boyfriend comes in for the interview, does she really think he's going to be perceived in reviewed the same way?

I think it's fair to say that when many women, Black or White, see a Black man, they often find the size, power, attitude and posture very appealing. They often see strength and security in some types of Black men. When this same Black man goes for an interview with a White male, those very same factors go against him because the White man feels intimidated by that strength (see Andrew Hacker's comments in the Essence article, White Men on *Black Power,* page 68, November, 1992). A small nerdy-looking, passive, accounting type of Black man has a better chance of receiving White folk's approval in many instances than other types of Black males. Women, because they appreciate other qualities, don't pick up on this distinction unless it is specifically explained to them, and even then they sometimes don't accept it. The only type of White man that doesn't mind dealing with macho type brothers are White policemen. And even they need to have the greater numbers, the guns, the batons, and etc. on their side. Witness the Rodney King beating. The police saw it as a competitive sport where they had to win. But only certain types of White men like these types of jobs. Most White men want anything *but* that type of job.

Sometimes men and women get to a point in the "catch-up mode of thinking" where they see that they have reached a philosophical impasse. They differ not on the idea that having a lot of money is a good thing, but on how many changes one should go through to get it. Women see the changes as merely so much work and effort. Men may see it not as a matter of effort but as a matter of compromising the nature of their personality eight hours a day, every day. There is a major, major difference between compromising on work and effort and compromising yourself. Black men have always been told to be like someone else rather than themselves. Black women compromise much more easily, partially because they have been imitating Miss Ann all along anyway. For some sister the idea of being at a place (her job)where she can actually *get paid* to play a role that she's wanted to play anyway (a White woman) actually makes work a *fun place* to be. It's a combination fashion show, rumor and gossip mill, educational center and a place to meet successful men all rolled in one. Black men on the other hand have seldom wanted to be White men, we just wanted what they had (power) or wanted to be left alone. Even if a brother actually decides "to do whatever it takes" to try to fit in and make it in the corporate world, there will eventually be a defining moment when a significant statement, policy, directive, argument, incident or other takes place. And he will all of a sudden ask himself , "what in the hell am I doing here? I hate this job, my boss and what I've become." That point has been both the end and the beginning of many life changes and relationships in the Black community.

On the other hand, life is competitive, and it is almost always in the heat of competition that people perform their best. Some men look very eagerly to the task of proving to people (prove to their father, mother, wife and children) that they are somebody special. A million athletes will tell you that they are successful today because of the motivation they drew on in trying to prove to somebody that they could play the game and compete. I would imagine that success in the work place is very much the same thing. So playing catch up is a very viable plan of action for some brothers.

Other Options

Ideally when two people marry it should be a case of two already happy people coming together because they believe they will be even happier together than apart. And a persons financial, educational, and occupational profiles are important aspects of a person experiencing that happiness. Thus, part of what couples should look for are two people already happy with themselves, trying to see if the union has a chance to be a happy one. Money can sometimes be very much secondary to happiness. Bobby Brown will probably never make the money that his wife, Whitney Houston, makes, especially if she also develops a film career. But Brown appears happy with his career even though he is in the same field as his wife. If you listen to those members of the public who do not think their marriage will last, they are not suggesting that money will be the issue but that Mr. Brown will eventually make Mrs. Brown unhappy enough to split.

As Black women become more wealthy, they should help finance the ongoing development of the Black community. This can be done in many ways such that talented or determined people do not miss the opportunity to move forward. A woman of means could support the ambitions of those brothers who clearly do not fit nor are not interested in the corporate world. Some of these developments might include the following:

1. Political Aspirations

Mention was made at the very beginning of this chapter of President Bill Clinton's past as a lowly paid politician in Arkansas. We may never know the true nature and history of the relationship between Bill and Hillary Clinton but we can assume that she had a great impact on his political aspirations. If a Black man can see his future as a city councilman or other elected office, a financially secure wife could help him get there if she wanted to. And the benefits would no doubt come back to her in more ways than one.

2. Artistic Talents

Have you ever heard the expression "Backed by the Mafia?" What about "Backed by the Jews" or "owned by the Koreans, Japanese or Cubans?" How often do you ever hear "Backed by Black people?" Almost never right? Well, everything has a beginning and that beginning always starts with the first person. The entire world knows that the Black community is a gold mine of artistic talent, from singing to needlework, from painting to writing. But artists need to have the freedom to create and the means to eat at the same time. If they have to work to eat, they can't give much time to their craft. If they pursue their craft, they become "starving artists". A woman may invest in her mate and enable him to become what he can become in his creative field. If not, we in the Black community can expect that other people will continue to see our people as fair game to make a quick dollar. They will continue to front us money, we do all the work, and they, being the financier, walk away with most of the profit. The music business is but one case in point.

3. Community Service
Many of our best and brightest have a vision of serving the Black community as their ultimate goal. In the sixties and seventies, this was accepted as both noble and necessary. By the eighties, the mentality of the "me generation" had taken over and anybody that wasn't chasing a dollar was considered a fool in a lot of communities, including some Black ones. Everyone wanted an MBA, CPA or law degree as a license to charge top dollar. But we have still cranked out people who perform social service. Of course most of those people do not earn very much. To many who value community service and empowerment, these people are important. Some men will always see themselves "working in the hood." Might a marriage between this type of man and a higher earning corporate woman work? Perhaps, but only if she could clearly a) still relate to the Black community, and b) see value in something other than dollars. For some Black women in corporate America that's asking a hell of a lot.

4. Religious Aspirations
Some men feel that they are "called to preach" in the later years of their life. Sometimes this requires a return to school and the purchase of a building for worship. A financially secure wife can be a big asset in this instance. Need I explain how our people have been helped by religious leaders who weren't just out looking to make money? Malcolm and Martin come to mind.

Undefined Options

When a Black man has been led to believe that there are things he is not qualified to do, and there are things he has failed at doing, and things he is not interested in doing, he can become discouraged. There are many fields that Black men don't even know about. It doesn't take a lot of imagination to

conclude that there are a lot of men who honestly don't know *what* to do with
their time and talents. Especially when they are told that what they are
currently doing is wrong or illegal or not good enough. We know that school
systems misdiagnose and misguide Black students, especially males, yet we still
wonder why they don't have their act together. We know that the home life was
rough, the role models were absent, and the gangs and dope dealers were just
around the corner, but we still get angry at why this guy doesn't have his life
together. And we know that prisons don't rehabilitate, nor does the Army
provide much training that relates to the real world, but we think this guy is
weak or sick or dumb *or something* because he's grown up and still doesn't
have his life together. Sometimes all that a man needs is really the same thing
he needed as a child. Namely, someone who will spend quality time with him,
believe in him, and orient him to the world beyond the street. He may not have
had a single person like that in his life. Either the person with the time was too
dumb or those who did know what was happening lived far away or didn't have
the time. The school system didn't have the belief. And the social agencies
were so busy telling him to say NO to this, that and the other that they never got
around to telling him what to say yes to. The community told him to say yes to
the very school that had lost faith in and misdirected him. So there are many
brothers who need some serious and sincere counseling on a personal level.
The problem however is that the busy successful woman is possibly least likely
to compassionately advise a brother, because she too is wondering why he
doesn't have his thing together. She may be in a great position to advise him,
given her exposure to the world and her knowledge of him. But she doesn't feel
like "mothering a man". She would begin to loose respect for him if she felt
she was mothering him. Isn't it odd how we don't think twice about a woman
marrying a "father figure" who is fifteen or more years older but we look down
on a brother who asks for advice and accuse him of wanting to be mothered.
That's why so many brothers have adopted a very simple way of running their
lives. They simply take the shit they want and if they get killed, so what?
Imagine the degree of rejection one must experience to get to that point.

   We have heard so much about and give so much blame to the absentee
father, might we give sisters more permission to mother? Black women like to
have the image of nurturers. And they always talk about "nurturing a
relationship". But the only other person in their relationship besides
themselves is their man, and every time its time for him to get "nurtured" its
called mothering and is discouraged. So apparently the only thing women want
nurtured in a relationship is themselves.

The Business Alternative

As a person who has spent the last fifteen years preaching the gospel of Black Business, I could easily write on and on about this topic. Other books have been written to cover the topic of business more thoroughly than what can be done here. However there are several points I'd like to make that fit well into this discussion.

In the first book that I wrote on Black self help,-*Black Folks Guide To Making Big Money In America*, I made a statement that turned out to be the most quoted line from the book. The statement was, "White folks go into business to make money, Black folks go into business to be the boss". My point in that statement and in the discussion that followed was that it was important that Black people go into business for the *right reasons*. It is not enough to merely go into business for any kind of reason. Why? Because your motivation for going into business will largely determine how you run your business, and how you run your business will determine if you are successful in your business. The point being made in that discussion was that too often Black people get fed up with all the injustices of their job and tire of always having a White boss. So out of *frustration*, rather than as a direct result of planning, they quit their jobs in order to place themselves in the position of being their own boss. As a "boss man" they can develop attitudes which turn customers off and thereby kill their business before it has a chance to even begin. Its quite interesting that seven years later, Ms. Moore Campbell would refer in her book to a similar practice that men of all races use out of a similar frustration with their wives professional and financial success. In her book she explains the business efforts of some men as a means that they employ to regain the status as "the boss" in their home.

> "Others, whose wives earn significantly more money, quit their jobs and strike out on their own, posturing as entrepreneurs who can earn more than their successful wives. These businesses usually appear suddenly and seem poorly planned to the wives. They are always "his" business although a great deal of the time the men will demand that their wives help them and invest the family money much of which the wife has earned. For many husbands, these enterprises represent the means by which they can rescue their manhood. Wives say the businesses take on a fantasy quality, the men will make a million dollars, regain the control of their wives and thus their masculinity. Unfortunately, what often results is an even greater loss of ego. When these businesses do not get off the

ground, wives are forced to become the sole supporters of their
family, giving men even less control and rankling women."
(Page 144)

Ms. Moore Campbell's statement above not only points out the needs,
frustrations and dangers for individual Black men and their families, but
demonstrates a major problem for the Black community as well.

The Black community needs a massive increase in the number of Black-
owned businesses, period! There is no one who is calling themselves a Black
leader of any kind who does not agree with that idea. But the reality is that all
businesses are risky to some degree or another. There is the risk of leaving the
work you were doing before the business venture and the risk of losing money,
time, effort, reputation, credit, and etc. Many things are put at risk in a
business enterprise including your relationship with those people closest to you.
Black businesses are much more risky than a mainstream business for a number
of reasons. And as if that wasn't enough, under-financed, poorly-planned
Black businesses are virtually guaranteed to fail. Thus the thing that the Black
community most desperately needs is the very thing that is most risky to do.
But that's not all; there is another problem that is important to consider. The
very thing that it takes to start a business, the assumption of a lot of debt and
risk, is the very last and worst thing that most Black women, (and women in
general) want to do. It is perceived as a loss of security. Women love, and
need security. Most women marry in part because of the greatly increased
feelings of security (financial, physical, emotional and other) that are felt
simply by being married. Today it is not popular for women to admit this. But
these recent feminist years were preceded by thousands of years when that was
most certainly the case.

For the Black man who simply wants to do the right thing, a real puzzle is
waiting for him. Does he start a business with all its risks because it is
something he wants to do and something the community needs, or does he not
start a business because his wife doesn't want to assume the risk and he wants
peace in his household? Its a hell of a situation not only for the particular man
in question but for the Black community at large.

Despite how strongly I personally believe in the importance of Black
business, I cannot dismiss Black women's concerns as being without substance
or merit. They are looking at things that many men do not look at. They could
easily say that saving for a home or the kids education, the paying off of twenty
percent interest credit cards or just having a nest egg for the inevitable lay off
or firing makes more financial sense than taking a chance on a business. And
a business in the Black community fails much more than half the time. Those
are some serious considerations. On the other hand the Black man can ask,

"when do we get out of slavery"? There was some security in staying on the plantation after the Civil War too, but people who asked for freedom had to experience the good and the bad (risk) of freedom sooner or later. When does the Black men do his own thing? Its been more than a hundred and thirty years since emancipation and more than ninety percent of us still work for the White man. Will we get to do it before Jesus returns or before the end of the world? This is a serious debate that is currently going on in thousands of Black families. And while we are debating, there are people from all parts of the world very thankful that we have allowed them the opportunity to set up their businesses in our community while we engage in our "heavy" debates. And if after another twenty years or so the Black man and his wife finally decide that its time to go into business, I hope they will be prepared to relocate to the desert and serve the Indians and rattle snakes. Because the Black community that they knew will be so full of Koreans, Japanese, East Indians, Arabs, Cubans, and so on that there will be no more room for other businesses, Black or otherwise. Most Blacks have absolutely no idea the position our community is in, and I'm afraid many would not even care if they did!

IT PAYS TO BE A TRIFLING HUSBAND

As a person originally trained in history, I've been aware for a long time that although history rarely repeats itself as many say, there are definitely patterns to the events that we observe. There are patterns in music, in sports, in the stock market and in marriages. One of the reasons that wee see patterns and what often appears as history repeating itself is that we are actually observing
human behavior. Human beings have not changed a whole lot in the last few thousand years. The same things that made them feel hungry, angry, lazy, happy, sick, excited, or any of the other human emotions five thousand years ago are pretty much the same things that cause them to feel all those emotions today. Thus, human behavior is rather *predictable*. If this is pretty clear then the idea that people can be conditioned or programmed shouldn't be to hard to understand either. When a person learns to associate hard work with good results, over eating with being fat, or weight lifting with bulging muscles, even people who aren't very bright eventually catch on.

This very brief chapter seeks to make one point concerning marriage, divorce and being a husband and a father. It is intended to show how some Black men actually learn by association, programming and laws *how not to do the right thing*. It is not to justify Black men shirking their duties as men, providers and fathers. But it is an attempt, like so much of this book, to explain how Black men learn to see and react to certain situations. It is directed, like much of this book, at people (usually sisters) who are constantly saying, "I just don't understand why brothers say this, do that or think this way". I am trying to bring greater clarity to the dialogue that is sporadically going on between Black men and women.

Good Guy - Bad Guy?

Imagine if you will two Black families that are almost identical to each other. Both husbands make thirty five thousand dollars a year and both wives make twenty five thousand a year. Both couples married eight years ago. Both have two children, and both are in the final stages of a divorce. Couple number one leaves the court room with the husband legally bound to pay his wife three hundred dollars a month in child support. Couple number two leaves a different court room with the husband having to pay his ex-wife five hundred dollars a month in support plus make a three thousand dollar a year contribution to his two children's education. In effect husband number two has to pay more than twice as much money to his ex-wife as husband number one. How is this possible, you might ask? The incomes and circumstances are similar, but why are the outcomes so different? Its a good question. Let's look at the specifics.

Husband number one is a truck driver with a high school education. Although the image of a truck driver suggests that of a person with low job skills, the fact is that a continuously employed driver makes a pretty decent salary. Husband number one was a typical Black consumer that spent his money on anything that made him look and feel good. He indulged in every fad that came along in an effort to be stylish and current. His closet was full of clothes; he had plenty of jewelry; two expensive watches; and of course a flashy car which he traded about every three years. Because he spent a lot of time on the road, he felt guilty about all the time he was away from home. So almost every month he took his wife and kids out to someplace nice. But just as often, he also made time for himself with the fellas. There were plenty of weekends when he drank, gambled, went to the track, etc. Husband number one didn't have any savings to speak of, and the couple lived in a decent apartment in the better part of the Black community. The kids were doing ok in the local public school. Husband number one was not a bad guy at all; he was what most people would call an average brother. And what the court has asked him to pay in child support is about what the average brother is asked to pay.

Husband number two is not average in many ways due to his level of ambition. He really seems like he wants to go places. He is a self-employed carpenter, also with a high school education. His business experiences good times and bad times thus his income is not as steady as a salaried employee. As a matter of fact, the tensions in the household during these down periods seemed to contribute to the causes of his divorce. Husband number two knew all along about the cycles of his business, which is why he has invested in rental properties to cover his slow periods. He owns four rental units in which he has invested a great deal of time and money in fixing up. They are located in the inner city, and in spite of careful renting procedures, he always draws tenants with problems that keep them from consistently paying their rent. People often skip out without paying. Husband number two is often in court trying to get someone evicted. In any event, the average profit is seldom more than three hundred dollars a month, which works out to be exactly what he tries to give to his church every month. Husband number two was reared in a religious family that believed in tithing, and he has tried to maintain that habit despite having taken on many other responsibilities as an adult. Thus, in a way, husband number two takes all the results of his efforts and fights with tenants and hands them directly to his minister. He doesn't see much more than a few dimes.

Five years ago husband number two found a nice house for his family; and because he was so good with his hands, he was able to restore the house which had been badly damaged by a fire. There is no way that this man would have qualified for a mortgage big enough to pay for this house in its repaired condition. Fortunately, he worked out a deal directly with the original owner, and both of them came away satisfied.

Husband number two has always bought the idea of the importance of education. At the urging of his wife, he committed very early to sending his children to the best schools that he could afford. Since the first grade, his two children have been attending a private school that not only has a good record scholastically but is very safe and has policies that reduce the peer pressures that make school a fashion show. But it costs two thousand dollars a year per child and husband number two can only afford it by cutting out all the fat from his personal needs. Thus, husband number two has no jewelry (except his wedding ring), has a poor out of date wardrobe, and his only transportation is a Van with almost a hundred thousand miles on it. Husband number two would never go out to drink and gamble and most of his socializing is with the people at the job sites. Husband number two is one of these hardworking, hustling, church going men that seem like a throwback to our grandparent's day. But for whatever reasons this man's marriage is over.

What is important here is to show how each husband is treated by the legal system, because marriage, for all its romantic emphasis, is a legal contract like any other. According to the original laws of divorce, it was the intention of the system to protect women and children from experiencing a great reduction in lifestyle in the event that the main provider should take a hike. Alimony (money to be paid to the wife) in addition to child support was usually required of men so that the family could continue to live the "lifestyle to which they had grown accustomed". In more recent years the courts have routinely disallowed alimony on the assumption that women can work to take care of themselves. They have not discontinued, however, the requirement that men make a consistent financial contribution to their children's upbringing. Men in general and Black men in particular are legendary in their reputations for not paying such support. Many reasons have been cited for this, with irresponsibility being accurately placed at the top of the list. But what will be shown here is that part of men's refusal to meet court stipulated support payments are in some instances due to the unfair judgements made at the time the payments amounts were first determined.

When husband number one went to court, what the judge saw was your typical Black couple. They owned flashy clothes and cars but basically didn't have a pot to pee in. There were no assets to divide because there were no assets obtained in the course of the eight year marriage. Nothing divided by two equals two nothings. Couple number one kept their own clothes, cars and jewelry and went their separate ways. The husband is ordered to pay what most women would consider minimum support, and everybody crosses their fingers and hopes he pays *that* on a regular basis.

But couple number two is a different case entirely. The wife in this instance is no more vindictive or troublesome than wife number one. But she is wise enough to understand that because there *are assets,* maybe she had better hire a "good" (White) lawyer, which wife number one did not bother to do. It is important here to understand the lawyers perspective. The lawyer for the wife is an independent businessman who practices law for a living. For him to make a good living as a lawyer he has to have a reputation as an attorney that can win more than what his client expects, from the settlement. A lawyer, then, *is not* concerned with "fairness" in most instances, because what is *fair* is not viewed as a "win" for him or his client. A *win* for the attorney is getting the court to require what seems *more than fair* for the woman involved. If what is won is *more than fair for the woman*, it automatically means that its *unfair for the man*. If you have a situation where the two opposing attorney's are evenly matched, the court is more likely to lean in the direction of the woman simply because divorce laws were originally set up to protect women.

With couple number two the court sees that there is property involved beyond personal items, so there must be a property settlement. In many, perhaps most cases the resident house is given to the wife and children. If it is determined that this arrangement still leaves the man with more property (in this case, four houses to one) then is it fair to assume that there will likely be a forced sale to further compensate the wife. Husband number two, being a religious man, is not antagonistic and basically just wants the relationship to end as peacefully as possible so that it will not strain his relationship with his children. His wife's lawyer *loves* that since it will make his "win" that much easier. Husband number two's lawyer tries to advise his client to challenge certain demands but is told by the husband to "be cooperative." When the process is all over, the wife has the "good house" and money from the sale of one of the rental houses, healthy child support payments and three fourths of the private school bill paid for every year. She has child custody and the furnishings in the house. Husband number two is left with three houses located in the ghetto. He would prefer not to live in any of them.

Let us look more closely at this situation and answer some questions. The lifestyle of the family of husband number two was definitely better than the lifestyle of couple number one in terms of substance and security. This was possible only because husband number two sacrificed all manner of personal toys and fun for himself and invested his earnings in his church and his family. This is what most people would call praiseworthy behavior. And its reasonable to assume that this praiseworthy behavior did in fact get at least some praise as long as the marriage was intact. But as soon as the marriage hit the skids, the same behavior that caused husband number two to be praised is now used against him to force him *to continue* giving beyond the call of reasonable expectation. There is no law that says that children who begin private school must complete private school. But because the couple started the children in private school the court (and the wife's lawyer) decided that this four thousand dollar a year expense should continue even though the conditions which made it possible (the husbands sacrifice) are being changed. The house the husband acquired through shrewd negotiation and repaired during endless days and nights of painstaking effort was not given away voluntarily by him to his wife but basically was taken from him by the court. Without going on and on, the question is: What *benefits come to husband number* two for being a better husband, father, and provider than husband number one? I don't see any. As a matter of fact, I see that the more that a man provides for his family, the more will be taken away from him when he leaves, and the more he will be asked to pay in child support. In other words it costs you as a man, to be a good provider. In marriage the financial reality of the man and woman are very different. For the man the reality is: I will only get what I work my ass off for and even then I might not get all that I'm due. For a married women the legal reality is often: I am entitled to continue to receive whatever I am accustomed to receiving even if the conditions that made it possible have changed. Men therefore are made to see that it is foolish to give to your family. Because when you give, you are simply putting yourself in a position where you are going to be expected and forced to give more if the relationship doesn't work out. And the last person to be thought about is the person who made most things happen, the husband. Do the judges and lawyers care about the past sacrifices that husband number two made to make his family comfortable and secure? HELL NO! Does the wife care about her husband's past sacrifices? Sometimes. A couple years after the divorce is over, she realizes how hard it is making it solely on her own efforts. She thinks about it and appreciates his sacrifices then, but not when she's on the prowl looking to get all she can get during the divorce. Even if she does think about what her man was able to accomplish with limited resources and hard work, she may never tell him and he would have no way of knowing that it even crossed her mind. Will the children know what their father did for them? Probably not. In most instances children are too young to realize what happened and why, and when they do have questions, it is usually the mother who gets to answer them. Even if she is nice enough not to bad mouth the man, he still doesn't usually come out as a hero. What about the church that husband number two has been giving three hundred dollars a month to? Do they understand? Usually not. Most divorces are made to look like its the man's fault. People will normally gossip about him and say things like "you never know what goes on behind closed doors". It is very difficult being a good, strong Black man in America because no one expects you to be. You have to constantly prove yourself. And after you have, people place their burdens, responsibilities, expectations and problems on your shoulders. After a certain point they either convince you that the problem you took on is now really *your* problem, or, you solve the problem and receive no thanks in return. Once you show you have a strong back, people will load things on it until it breaks. When it breaks, they just look for another strong back. Does it pay to have a strong back?

Let's go back and look at husband number one and compare his new situation with husband number two. Both men are now in the pool of "available" Black men. Which one is mostly likely to be successful with the single women? Will it be husband number one with the flashy clothes, jewelry and nice car or the carpenter with a horrible wardrobe, an old beat up van and a house in the less desirable part of town? Which man is likely to have the most money in his pocket to take a new young lady out: the one who pays three hundred dollars in child support or the one who pays about seven hundred? So good men really pay *twice* for being good men. They pay the ex-wife for having provided her a certain quality lifestyle, and then they pay again by having to live a limited new lifestyle because of limited resources.

Women's usual response is to say, "Yeah, but he left her "strapped" with children, which limits her new life style." Yeah, right, but let him go to court and try to "unstrap" her from the children, and she'll fight him tooth and nail. Without those children "strapping her," she'll lose a lot of money every month. If husband number two managed to find a girlfriend, would she likely appreciate the fact that he took care of his *past* family? Yes. But her main concern would be *what he could do for her,* the new woman in his life. The more he tells her about his past sacrifices, the more the new woman may use this information to see if he's as willing to do those same things for her. It's a way of her measuring his feelings for her. Instead of feeling a degree of sympathy and compassion for the brother, she just may expect the brother to make all the same mistakes again but in *her* behalf. If on the other hand, she determines that the brother is now more cautious (which is only reasonable considering his experience) then she might very well split and accuse him of "carrying around too much baggage". In reality she's saying, "This well is too dry; somebody got there before me; I've got to keep looking."

The issue is character. When does it help the Black man to be a good guy (as most people define good)? Of all the millions of "good slaves" that have lived in America, how come we can't name a single one whose name lived on in history simply because he was a good man? We read instead about men who escaped slavery or who fought against slavery. To some, being a good husband, where you take on all the things that anybody throws at you, is another form of slavery. And if you seek to escape that form of slavery, you will pay for it no matter how good a slave *you were*. And if you were a good slave for a *long time*, and left your wife after, say, twenty five years then you will really pay. The longer you provide for a woman, the more angry society and the legal system gets at the man for having the audacity, the nerve, to want to leave. Thus, Black men learn that even if they succeed in a society that discourages their success and they share that success with a wife, that shared success should not be *great* success. Because he will pay dearly for his sharing if the marriage fails, regardless of whose "fault" it is.

Near the beginning of this book we made the point that at fifteen or sixteen years old young boys do not win girls by being "good". That grades, church membership, boy scout membership, having an honest (but low paying) job, helping around the house, and so on had nothing at all to do with your desirability to a female in your own age group. In the examples in this section we have shown how twenty years later being the good guy still shortchanges Black men. This is not a call for Black men to further rebel against society or to abandon the institution of the family. Rather it is just to point out how careful Black men must be in making decisions regarding their future and in examining the rules they are told to live by.

ARE Drug Dealers Monogamous?

In the above comparison of divorcing couples the central point was that Black men often have a
hard time understanding how they benefit in the long run in being a good guy. Neither of the men profiled were really "trifling" as most of us would define the word. Neither man would be seen as a problem for the Black community. But let's look at a Black male who *would* be considered a problem for the Black community - a drug dealer.

I try very hard not to let my hatred of drugs and the misery they cause the Black community from getting in the way of trying to get into the head of drug dealers. I can't see anybody solving the drug problem without spending substantial time trying to see the world as drug dealers see it. If you want to take a dealer from his viewpoint to yours, you are going to have to recognize his viewpoint. And in writing the piece above about good husband, average-poor husband, I asked myself about what benefits await those brothers who are beyond poor husbands. These brothers often are the so called "dogs" that some women think all Black men are. And I asked myself if these men were monogamous? Do they only deal with one woman at a time? And of course the answer the overwhelming majority of the time is that they are not. If that is true, if each drug dealer has two, three or more women, then that says a lot about the make up of the character of the Black woman. If a sister knowingly dates, has babies by, spends the money of and or uses the drugs of a dope dealer, then how is she any different than the dope dealer himself? How is her character better? And if we use the term "drug culture," aren't we including women and what they do for and with drug dealers as part of that culture? And if every dope dealer has more than one woman (I doubt seriously if they share any women for any length of time), then wouldn't that mean that more Black women were in the drug culture than Black men?

The point here is not to accuse Black women of being the cause of the drug problem but to show over and over again how what we are told by society and the media is so untrue. We believe that people are rewarded for good behavior - not necessarily true. We believe the bad people are punished. Again not necessarily true. We believe that we know who the good guys and the bad guys, are. Again not true. Everyone in American Society is asking why the Black man is the way he is. Why does he commit so many crimes, why does he abandon his family, why does he sell drugs, why this and why that? It is not enough to say he's oppressed or that he's unemployed or that he's rebelling against a system that never has accepted him as a man. All that is true but it is not enough of the truth. A bigger, clearer part of the truth is that there is *little reinforcement* for Black men *to be a good guy*. And there is a substantial amount of positive reinforcement for Black men *to be a bad guy*. The issue isn't if Black men *know* right from wrong, its which one *pays* the most, which one can help him survive.

Black men's values and behavior is not shaped only by economic pressure, racism and White folks. The reactions of the women in the men's lives greatly effect them as well. If many men act a certain way or believe a certain principle, there is a reasonable chance that the actions and responses of women (*not* what they say) has given them reason to act or believe as they do. If men have killed each other over women, its obvious that they will likely do about anything else to win them, please them and keep them. And contrary to what teachers and preachers, parents and police might think it is not at all obvious how a man is suppose to treat a woman or wife if he values his own interest. What we have tried to show in this chapter is the following:

a.   That a hard working, sacrificing "good guy" can get screwed by the system with the active participation of the women that he has worked long and hard to support. And after he is separated from that woman, his continued goodness (fulfilling his financial responsibilities) can and will handicap him in developing another meaningful relationship.

b.   That an average man with typical Black American consumer behavior can be spared the hassle of unjustified responsibilities and pressure just because he never willingly assumed them in the marriage in the first place. And by not assuming heavy responsibility during marriage, a man is in a much better position to resume a normal social life should that marriage come apart. And since most marriages today eventually break up, is that not then the best strategy to take?

c.   That a drug dealing thug raining misery down on the Black community can still attract more women to him than the "good guy". And even as the women learn of a drug dealers income source and his other women, many are more likely to stick with the drug dealer (and his money) than they are to stick with the struggling good guys.

This backward set of results described here are not the way they are because *Black men* made them that way. They are backward because of the backward way that Black women respond to the situations that the three types of men are in. And unfortunately a major, major factor is determining what men will do in most situations is very simple to understand; namely, *what will attract the women*? Period.

So if you see brothers smile, and make jokes when sisters ask "where are the good Black men"? You should understand now.

BLACKS MALES AND HIGHER EDUCATION

Hardly a month (or is it more like a week) goes by without the average African American hearing the statement, "there are more Black men in jail than there are in college." Like many similar statements, people sometimes act as if the more times they say it, the more likely some sudden change is going to come about. Actually it works the other way around; the more times people say something, the more likely people will feel that its just one more unalterable reality that they have to accept, and they'll usually do nothing to try to change the situation.

Any honest discussion about the future of Black male female relationships would require addressing the situation of Black men and college, because of the current perceptions by Black women and social observers. The perception is that the most upwardly mobile, middle class future leaders of Black America, who also happen to be female, have before them a discouraging set of prospects. One prospect is that they will have difficulty in finding a similarly educated and professionally positioned Black male to marry when they graduate. Another is that if they fail to find such a man, they will have to marry someone outside of their race, or they will have to marry a non-professional Black male. And if they decide not to compromise their "standards," they may not marry at all. Finally, even if Black female college grads are lucky enough to find a compatable mate, if that marriage doesn't work out, she will be thrown into the pot with her unlucky sisters anyway at a time when its even more difficult to find a mate.

The other aspect of this human resource tragedy is the tremendous loss of human potential for the development of the Black community. The potential doctors, lawyers, professionals and businessmen that the community needs will not come into existence because of the Black man's absence on campus.

While nothing discussed here is likely to change these real dilemmas, it still might be helpful or enlightening to go over why this situation exists. Perhaps those in a position to change the conditions can get a clue as to how to do just that.

I am surprised frankly that either White or Black America would be surprised that there are more Black males in jail than in college. College caters to a small sector of the general population. It focuses primarily on people who are recent high school graduates between the ages of 18 and 22. Within this limited age group they focus on people who have at least three years of specific college prep courses and who have gotten high grades in those courses. But even if you fall within, the very limited number of people bound by these criteria, it's of little meaning if you do not have the twenty to eighty thousand dollars it may take to finance a four year education. Of course, the hundreds of community colleges allow a wider spectrum of people to attend college.But eventually the financial realities of the 4-year college will kick in for all people wanting to legitimately call themselves college grads.

Prison, on the other, hand starts targeting males as early as fifteen years old. More and more youth offenders are being "tried as adults", especially in gang and drug-related crimes. The age range goes from the early teens to beyond fifty. Thus, the chances of having a larger number of people would logically follow if one institution focuses on a four year age span while the other looks at a time frame ten times wider. Not only is the age range wider for prison but within that range they care nothing about the offenders brains, grades or financial background. These are objective criteria which common sense would show would make for easier entry to prison.

In addition to the objective facts noted above, it is in the subjective decisions made about Black men that make for their high incarceration rate. The American justice system has as part of its entire history a pattern of not only imprisoning Black men for crimes that they did not commit but also sentencing them for longer periods of time, than people (including Black women) who have done similar crimes. This is basically because the typical White male has seen the Black man as someone to be confined, controlled, observed and excluded. This is not to say that the Black male is not guilty of many crimes. But to see his crimes without looking at the history of crimes perpetuated against him and the conditions he is expected to survive in, is to ignore the complete story. The Black male is put in a position where crime appears to be the only way out of poverty. And in the trial phase of his judgement, he is without the financial resources to pay for the proper legal representation. Thus he does hard and long time in prison.

Having said that, we will look at the educational perspective of the non-criminal Black male as they are still in the majority inspite of what the media seems to suggest. One way to look at the Black males perspective on education is to compare the approach of a high school athletic coach to the approach of a high school academic teacher in terms of how they relate to Black males and the results that each achieves.

A coach (track, football, basketball, etc.) makes it their business to identify talent or potential. He doesn't wait for the student to perform at a high level of excellence, he looks to see if the potential for high performance is there. He does this even if the student is unaware of their own potential or shows merely marginal interest. A teacher on the other hand will wait to see if a student does well in Math or History or English before they take notice and recognize the student's potential. If the student fails in a subject but has the potential to do well, most teachers have no intention of exploring that possibility. This is not the case all the time, but because Black male students are often assumed to be academically weak, it is the case much too often.

In order to do well in almost anything a person must have some natural ability, a level of competence with fundamental techniques (supported by coaching and/or instruction) and the   motivation   to work hard and consistently at the task at hand. We have already seen how a coach is normally better at recognizing potential or ability. In the teaching of techniques phase, a coach will drill his athlete over and over again for hours a day until they have mastered a specific move or reaction. A teacher on the other hand will not insure that a student has mastered something as fundamental as reading at grade level or writing in clear and complete sentences. Instead, teachers will pass a student on from grade to grade and even graduate him without even so much as an elementary mastery of reading and writing. Would a coach send a player in the game who didn't know the plays?

Coaches have highly respected reputations for being able to motivate their athletes to run till they drop from exhaustion. Teachers on the other hand are usually very poor motivators and do not even see it as part of their job. The best positive motivation teachers can come up with is "if you work hard, you'll get a good grade." Their specialty, however, is in threats, "if you don't do your work, you'll flunk, get kicked out of class, suspended" etc. Coaches care about each athlete doing well and feeling apart of a winning team. Teachers stress individual accomplishment and gloat over the A students while accepting at face value the idea that "there will always be those that fail" (read Black Males)

By the time a Black male's experience with a coach and a teacher is over, his regard for them are miles apart. A coach has worked the student to nearly exhaustion, cursed him, maybe embarrassed him in front of his peers and perhaps in the extreme even punched, slapped or kicked him. Yet the bond that exists between athlete and coach rivals that of father and son, and often exceeds it. The bond between many teachers and students is virtually non-existent. The teacher never expected much from the Black male and never found a reason to motivate him. The student never felt confident in the class, and was never made to feel that he even belonged in the class. Both student and teacher quickly forget that each other ever existed.

The coach has often taught the student lessons in discipline, work ethics, teamwork and general principles of living that may never again be matched in that young persons life. The teacher on the other hand may stick in that student's mind as just another adult authority figure who doubted that students ability and potential.

It was discussed in an earlier chapter of this volume when and how young Black boys get turned off from school and how school and society in general gets turned off to them. This has been another example of the same principle. And just as male- female relationship problems start in the early teen years, so it appears that academic problems begin then also. Black males do not stop being college candidates at seventeen. They usually stop at fourteen, if not before. Certainly a good two years before college, it seems rather obvious who is and who is not headed for college. Thus, my continued surprise at why people seem to be puzzled at the Black male shortage there. The Black male shortage in college, if projected and based on what's happening to Black males in the lower levels of school, is as predictable as reading the gasoline gauge in your car.

The great irony of the situation described above is that in many instances the athletic coach, who supposedly couldn't care less about his athletes mental development, is more responsible for numbers of Black males getting into college than many of the so-called academic teachers. Teachers are often the people who really couldn't care less about the males development.

If you the think that colleges are down in Black male enrollment now, try to imagine what it would be like if all Black athletes were to disappear tomorrow. How many thousands more Black males would be gone? Who do you think you have to thank for those males: caring academic teachers or caring (but also ambitious and manipulative) coaches?

Justifiable Faith?

If we accept the fact that both athletes of college scholarship caliber and criminals of prison caliber represent the extremes of the Black male youth spectrum, a fair question might be what is a realistic expectation for the average Black male student in high school?

I believe that a great deal of faith and confidence would be necessary for the average Black male to believe he they could survive four years of college. He would need:

    a.   Faith that he could do college level work even though it would be a great deal harder than what he did in high school. As an average student, only doing average work in high school, is that faith justified?

    b.   Faith that he and his family could afford the cost of college or qualify for college loans and grants. Is that faith justified?

    c.   Faith that he would have a clear direction as to what he wanted to do with his life (what to major in) once he got to college.

d.   Faith that there would be informed and caring people around him to help him if he stumbled and fell along the way while in college. Is that faith justified?

f.   Faith that his world view and values would some-how fit in and be at least marginally acknowledged at the majority of colleges (White) in this country. Is that faith justified?

g.   And faith that after the entire struggle to graduate was over, that he would leave college with marketable skills and the high probability of finding immediate and rewarding work. Is that faith justified?

All Black youth have reason to doubt their ability to survive in college, especially on White campuses. But I don't think its unreal to say that Black males have more reason to doubt their chances. Normally, their grades, standard test scores and communication skills are lower than the average Black females. Because of a long history of "compromising", "adjusting," and "fitting in"(that has already been discussed repeatedly), Black girls will seek to blend in with the greater White student body (and be more accepted by that same student body) than the Black male.

Its been more than twenty five years since the big explosion of Black students on White colleges. We are no longer a campus experiment. What do the results say? The results say that not only do most college teachers not care if students learn, the teachers don't even appear in the classroom to teach the classes. In most large universities the classes are taught by graduate students with minimal teaching experience themselves. They talk to classes of two, three hundred or more students at a time. A student could not show up for the whole semester and nobody would know it or care.

The results, also say that whereas, even the prices of houses and cars have come down in the past few years, the cost of college tuition, like the cost of health care, has greatly out run normal inflation and is more ridiculously priced now than ever before. This is especially true when you are paying for highly paid professors who don't even show up to teach.

The results, also say that because so many people have college degrees now, its value as an aide in employment has been greatly reduced, because so many people show up for a job, with the same credentials. The results say that because urban public schools are getting worse, they are less able to prepare college-ready students. Thus, students either don't get admitted as often, spend an extra year in remedial courses to prepare for the other four years, or are forced to drop out due to an inability to survive academically.

Students find that the overwhelming majority of the information they are forced to learn in college does not relate to either of the two worlds of which these students are seeking to be a part. It doesn't relate to the Black world to which they will likely return after they graduate. Nor does it relate to the practical world of work which they hope to enter after graduation. Thus, this place called college which some people see nearly as sacred as church, is a virtual sea of pointless, directionless, impractical "information" which students are paying dearly for in time, faith and money. But the single most devastating reality is that more and more Black people personally know of friends, relatives and neighbors who are either unemployed college graduates or under employed college grads. And in the face of corporate down sizing, White males with years of experience in positions that Black graduates are striving for, are being let go. Furthermore job prospects for non-technical specialists do not look very promising for years to come. Is the faith in college justified?

Money On Campus

Even though the male and female may be equally "broke" on the campus scene, the Black male, because he is a male, will be expected to provide the transportation and the bulk of the expense money needed for the broad range of coed campus life activities. Failure to be able to do so will likely place him in a losing situation in the campus social scene. There are many who would argue that " he should not be thinking about women, he should be concentrating on his studies." To ask a healthy male at the height of his sexual hormonal activity period to refrain from sex and interaction for a few months, or even a year, is not out of the question. But to expect him to sustain that discipline for four long years is completely unrealistic. The chances are most women will pick boyfriends on the same basis as they did at fourteen years old. Namely who can confer on them some type of "status" and "show them a good time"(read dollars). A negative social and financial reality that Black people have placed around their own necks has to do with the continued emphasis on status symbols. With high school students wearing expensive gold chains, gold earrings, designer clothes and hundred dollar basketball shoes, it stands to reason that Black youth on college campuses would carry this madness with them to these schools as well. Thus, the cost to "look good" in detailed cars, jewelry, clothing and personal care (finger nails, toe nails, hair care, etc)has risen higher than the normal educational costs. Even concert ticket costs and meals can set a student back an easy hundred dollars in a single night. Weekly "spending money" for some students has to be measured in hundreds of dollars per week.

Many Black males have looked at the total picture of college life (usually after a year or two) and from their perspective determined that its not worth the effort, cost and restrictions. And as much of an advocate of college as you the reader might be, can you not see any reasoning to any of the Black males' analysis? They are asking; Why pay up to $40,000 or more (and go into serious debt) to pay for an education where, through inferior teaching, I am taught information that relates to neither me and my lifestyle nor the places where I intend to work? And while the hype behind college is that it qualifies you for better employment, why pay forty thousand dollars for the status of being a college educated unemployed or underemployed person?

Sisters On Campus

A fair question might be why do Black females go through this experience? If the facts are that plain to see and Black women are as intelligent (if not more intelligent) than Black men, then why do they continue the sham of college if that's what it often is?

This author has given the answers in many ways already through out this book, so it may sound rather repetitious here. Black American women probably care about the "cultural" values of college more than Black men. The courses in European philosophy, psychology,"art appreciation," and the "great" European literary figures, etc. probably genuinely fascinate them. Black women probably believe that they are actually getting educated, rather than being indoctrinated, in many of these courses. In other words, they are more attracted to and appreciative of the content of the many liberal arts courses than the males are.

Second, Black women probably do better scholastically than Black men. If they bring more academic skills and a deeper base of" knowledge" to the campus in the first place, and they find the courses more interesting as well, it stands to reason why they would get better grades. Doing well (or at least ok) in school would obviously be a big factor in sticking with it. If one is doing poorly and flunks out, the decision not to return to school is made for them.

Third, Black women have strong motivation for staying in college because that is the best place, in their mind, to find "a good man." If one wants a college educated man, what better place to find one than at the college? At twenty or so years old, college educated young men are seldom thinking of marriage. Many men don't care if their eventual wives are college educated or not. So college is not necessarily the same hunting ground for a mate for brother's as it is for sisters. Of course many sisters would boo and hiss this writer and deny that part of college's value is that it is a good place to look for a good man. But these same sisters will be complaining about their difficulty in finding a man "on their level" in a few years if they don't find a college grad.

You can bet on it.

Fourth, Black women probably buy into the status value of having a college degree more than Black men do. I don't think they can be faulted for that too harshly. If you are a Black woman and for hundreds of years you've been told that all you were good for was to spread your legs, suckle babies, cook food and scrub floors, I can see how they would want to demonstrate that they also had a brain, particularly if they were motivated by "proving things to White Folks".

Finally I think Black women stick with college because of the different realities that Black men and women experience in the broader world. It's seems Black female grads have an easier time getting jobs than Black male grads. As racism dies a slow death, White people continue to have the option to pick and choose *which* Blacks they will deal with until that final day (if it ever comes?) when they will deal with us all equally. Until that time, they will almost always choose light ones over dark ones, articulate ones over mumbling ones, and females over males. If you happen to be light, articulate, and female, you're usually home free. White employers pick their preferred employees the same way cab drivers pick their preferred customers. And big, dark, African looking (ie. mean looking) men will be the last selected every time. Bet on it. Degree or no degree.

If Black men are having a harder time leaving high school with the necessary skills to enter college, what can improve their chances for success? If Black men are not impressed with the courses, status and "worldliness" of college, what do they need to motivate them to go to college? And if college is not the answer for many of them, what is the answer? These are legitimate questions and people of both sexes and various political persuasions are looking for answers. There is the assumption that Black women, Black families and the Black community will not be right until "the brothers get their thing together." And a big part of that getting things together has always been "education" which has always been a code name for college.

The Prison Model of Education

I think a key to how the Black man operates with regard to education is to see what happens to him when he is imprisoned. There are many stories about how Black men have learned to read in prison and then begin to read almost obsessively. Malcolm X is one person who comes to mind. Reading, more than any other skill, has to be the focus of the Black mans education, even if other so-called important subjects are left for later. But its not enough for brothers to simply learn to read. Black men must develop the *habit* of reading.

This is what's done in prison. Once Black men get into the habit of reading, they are then in a position to keep up with what others have said and are saying about Black people's conditions and the means of improving those conditions. It only stands to reason that if anyone is to truly gain an appreciation for knowledge, it would seem easiest to direct them to the subject matter that is of most interest to them. And it is not all that out of line for people to be interested in their own history and culture first before looking into other fields seen as more remote. Thus in prison Black males usually go thru a long period of reading about themselves (Black History) before broadening their prospective into other areas. The history foundation gives them a framework from which to interpret the other information that they absorb. This seems basic and common sense to many average people, prisoners or not.

Unfortunately this common sense strategy can still run counter to White folks efforts to restrict and control the Black mind. A case in point is that of former World Heavyweight Champion Mike Tyson. Tyson is a high school drop out with a history of poor scholastic performance. In prison he started reading like a madman; biographies, the Koran, Black history, etc. The legal system is set up in such a way that it supposedly promotes education, as long as of course, the system gets to *define* what constitutes education for the Black man (what else is new?). Tyson studied for his General Education Diploma (G.E.D.). If he successfully passed his exam he would have gotten three months knocked off his prison sentence. He took the test, but failed the math portion, thereby flunking the test. He had to say so long to the three months early release from prison. Later on, newspapers all over the nation printed the questions that stumped Tyson. The broad base of opinion seemed to say that these were tricky questions and that many high school grads, even some college grads, would have been stopped in their tracks also. The point here is that the Black man, if he is a true man, should not submit to another man's definition of what constitutes knowledge or enlightenment any more than he should yield to the opinion of others about who he should worship or marry. In order for Black men to be motivated to go to college, they may have to feel that they have a say over some of what they are learning and have that body of knowledge legitimized as valid. In the past the Black man has legitimized over time his ideas about music, dance, painting, poetry, religion, medicine, etc. We as Black men have not changed our position and apparently White folks haven't either.

Part of the problem with Black men and formal education could be addressed with good counseling. But what is good counseling? The many White and Black counselors, accept at face value all the hype and assumed benefits of higher education, regardless of statistics that say otherwise. They have less objectivity than what Black men need. They are ready to tell Black men what to do rather than help them go about making decisions based on their own criteria. In order to be a good counselor, a person has to see how a Black man wants to position himself as a total human being, not simply how to do well as a student. A person is a student for just a few years, they must live as total human beings for the rest of their lives. Because many Black men desire autonomy as much as possible, and because many counselors have difficulty understanding that concept or taking it seriously (especially when they themselves are not independent or autonomous), relationships between Black men and counselor types often don't work out. But theoretically a good counselor could be a very big help to Black men. But a *good* counselor could only earn the respect of that title over a period of time like a coach earns his respect of coach and father figure over time. A strong Black man will seldom do something simply because he's told to. Children usually do that. A man will do as is suggested to him only after he's convinced that the person advising him knows him(or his situation) well enough to have his best interest at heart. Thus one of the major problems with education in reference to the Black man is that people are unwilling to give him their time. Either they are too important or too busy, to give of their time to justifiably suspicious and doubting Black men. Black men have a right to be suspicious of virtually everything coming from the dominant culture. Time and only time in most cases is the only element which can melt away distrust and allow Black men to feel comfortable being counseled. But that's not how educators, administrators, and counselors see it. They look at the need to give Black men extra time as spoon feeding them, coddling them, pampering them, spoiling them or, as Black women are fond of saying, "mothering them." It seems that whenever Black men ask for time and attention, they are ridiculed as something akin to weak. How many stupid acts of violence by Black men were intended to merely be statements that they weren't weak? How many were statements that they were looking for some quality time, attention and advice. Black men will not give you any of their time or attention if you are too busy or important to give them yours.

I don't see a big increase in Black men going to college any time soon. I would like to say that as more Black men obtain positions of authority in colleges, the more chances exist that current systems can be adapted to fit some African American males. But that will not be the case and proves the futility of having faith in "so called education." If Black male educators were truly educated to think critically and analytically, they could see and understand what is being presented here and develop innovative educational programs that would appeal to other Black males. Black male educators who perhaps at one time thought about righting a system that has always wronged Black men, now find that they are often at the helm of such a system. But precisely because they have been educated and embraced by that same system, they too develope blinders and cannot see anything other than "going by the book." A book they, as Black men, had no part in writing, and they, as ambitious (looking to move up) Black administrators, have no interest in changing. Many Black educators have no idea that they personally represent and personify the futility, inadequacy, and contradictory nature of the very educational system that they champion. While many Black male educators tell students about analyzing a problem and solving it with skills learned in college, the educators do not use their brian power to address the problem of the Black male shortage on campuses. They use their brain power to advance themselves within the system they are in. And that advancement has often more to do with doing things the way they were always done (not rocking any boats) than coming up with creative solutions to old problems. In this way many Black male educators are a contradiction to everything they talk about. They are proof that power, guts and racial consciousness, not merely superior brain power, really determine the efforts to push for change not only in educational institutions, but in public institutions in general.

Compromising Wimps?

While the general society moans the shortage of Black men in college, and all means of finding an adequate explanation are explored, sometimes the obvious is overlooked. Could it be that many thousands of Black males do not like the final product that they see emerging from college? A college is an institution and as such has the power to recast or remold individuals who very eagerly go there "to be educated." Many people, especially those from "culturally deprived environments", come to college full of trust. They willingly submit to the power of the faculty and adminstrators. They believe that all the relevant and practical principles for prospering in tomorrow's society will be shared with them in an honest and candid way. They believe that the education will serve their best interests, not just societies. But maybe thousands of young Black males, on seeing some of these graduates, decide very early that they don't like what they see coming back from college. What they see, from their perspective sometimes, is that an easily identifiable Black man from the hood entered college and emerged four or five years later as a compromising, Eurocentric wimp. This seems to be especially true when they return from the "most prestigious" colleges, the ones that the Black community are the most excited about them attending. How and why does this scenario get played out?

Often in colleges, brothers meet soul-less nerds with prep school backgrounds from isolated corners of America. The White student campus culture, in many ways a primer for the White corporate culture to follow, renders obsolete much of the "street smarts" that brothers bring to the campus. Over time (4-5 years), these brothers may be tempted to see their neighborhoods (and thus its people) as the same decadent, hopeless hell holes that many of their classmates do. The tendency to adopt White slang, dress styles, hair cuts and codes of behavior becomes more of a possibility with every additional semester spent on campus. And whereas these superficial changes could be seen as temporary phases that most college students pass through, they sometimes represent yet another means that Black people use to demonstrate their well known tendencies of self hate on one hand and the striving for White acceptance on the other. After four or more years, this "educated" brother from the neighborhood sometimes emerges as a young man with an identity problem. He clearly feels uncomfortable in many ways in his old neighborhood (if he even goes back there), yet is just as sure that he will not be as accepted in the real White world as he seemed to be at times in the cocoon of college. And it seems that the more prestigious the school, the more technical his education, the more expensive the school (thus less Blacks), the more suburban the campus, the more likely our neighborhood brother may turn out to be a Wannabe White boy or at least a lost or confused Black man. I feel very sure that each reader knows exactly what I am talking about and may in fact know one or more brothers that fit this set of circumstances. Young Black men of fourteen or so also know neighbors, friends and maybe even brothers who fit this general description and are turned off by it. Instead of longing for college, they learn to fear it. Look what it did to my cousin, uncle or friend, they say. "He's not the same person anymore, but it doesn't matter because we don't see him much anymore anyway. College did this to him." This is what many young Black men are thinking.

And they are also asking about the upside. For the price of a sold out soul, what is the trade-off? He gets the opportunity to work downtown in the big office building in a sea of White folks, doing what he's told and complaining everyday about it. He says his salary isn't right, his boss isn't right, his job description isn't right, and he's not treated right. Why would a person spend fifty thousand dollars and thousands of hours of effort to place themselves in a position where they are unhappy? Is this not a reasonable question for a fifteen or sixteen year old mind to ask? If college's value is clear, then how come the college grads that many Black males know do not seem to be that much happier or doing that much better than the non- college grads who they also know? That too is not an unreasonable question for a young mind to ask.

Young Black males hear how hard college is, how expensive it is, how much sacrifice you must endure, how much time it takes and how much debt you will be in when it's over. It should not be one bit of a surprise why intelligent young Black males would question why the experience was worth it. When you realize that a large portion of those men who do complete college complain about how hard it is for them to find a job after they have completed this whole process, the questioning of college's value becomes even more understandable. On the other hand, if many of those graduates do get jobs and live a materially comfortable lifestyle, some socially or racially conscious youngsters might still question college's value. Many young Black men conclude that if the main function of college is merely financial stability, they would rather take their chances and survive on their wits than to go through the college experience. As hard as it may be to believe, some of these young brothers like themselves the way they are. They have a sense of hope and confidence, which may be shattered by real world conditions later on, but it has gotten them to where they are now. Those persons who excessively push the college route to success should think about one thing. It is very contradictory and confusing for a young Black male to be preached to about pride, self-love, self-esteem, self-confidence and resistance to peer pressure and then be cast into a situation (White college) where he is a minority and it is continually implied by that environment that his "success" will be determined by how well he mirrors the majority! That is a sure prescription for four years of confusion.

Young Black females, thrust into identical situations, may not think twice about not going to college. If you have to ask why that is the case, then you have totally missed the point of this book and you should close it and pass it on to someone who might understand it better. As more Black women enter college, the size of the sisterhood on campus grows, making it that much easier for the ones that come later to feel a sense of community on these White islands.

Intervention Strategies

The idea of cultural shock and identity crisis for Black college students on White campuses is decades old. Thousands of people have wrestled with this problem for years. At least four means can be used to prevent the alienation from happening to Black youth. The simplest means is to send Black students to Black colleges. In this way emotional and intellectual energy need not be needlessly expended trying to fit into a strange environment. Focus can be directed to the classroom work and typically lifelong friendships develop in the process.

The second safeguard would be to attend those White colleges located in the real world. Sending a Black student to Temple University in North Philadelphia, Rutgers University in Camden or Newark, New Jersey or a Columbia University in Harlem is not likely to leave them snowed under in Whiteness. If anything, many Whites take on a temporary veneer of hip hop culture before they hippty hop back to the White world they're preparing themselves for.

A third strategy is for the student to recieve good counseling. If mothers fathers, sisters and brothers and other advisors can explain to the student how to get only what is necessary from their college experience and not get swept up into the garbage, the student may not become a lost soul. Obviously a lot will depend on how anchored he is in his culture, neighborhood and values before he leaves for school.

The last means that can be used to steer young people clear of some of the confusion in college is to make sure the student gets exposed to African American Studies Classes, cultural centers and Black Student Organizations. These entities are over twenty five years old in many colleges and are a virtual university within a university.At worst these programs reinforce the value of Black people and their achievements in an environment where they might almost forget Black people exist. At best these programs expose students to some of the most brilliant Black thinkers in the country and can help students interpret the meaning and function of the courses that they are taking in their overall program. The problem here however is that these Black programs seem to always be under attack from both Blacks and Whites. Whites attack with the purse strings. By withdrawing funds, courses, faculty, outside lectures and films, musical and cultural events all suffer. It is a constant roller coaster situation on most campuses.

Black students threaten these courses by not taking them for some of these usual reasons (excuses):

a) these classes will not help me get a job.
b) these classes might label me as a militant and hurt my chances of getting a job or getting accepted into graduate school.
c) I don't need these classes because I already know I'm Black.
d) I won't take these courses because its not factual information-its just propaganda.
e) My study program is too packed with "solid" courses and strongly recommended electives. I don't have "room" to add any to my load.

Many young pre-college Black males do not know that these safety valves exist that can keep them from being snowed under at college. Some brothers deliberately "mess up" in high school so that they don't have to worry about being forced to go to college. We all realize that most young Black males have more capability than what their school records indicate. We must understand that if a teenager is smart enough to enter college, he may also be smart enough to sense the alienation on some campuses, and also, resent college's restrictions and conformities. In that case we shouldn't be at all surprised if some pass on going to college during theirs teenage years.

The Black Athlete

A major purpose of this volume is to continually make the point that Black males feel the need to have their own values and ideas affirmed and respected. White colleges may very well not be the place where that would happen. But when would young Black men attend White colleges enthusiastically? Answer: When they are star scholarship athletes going to college on their own terms. Whereas Black women outnumber Black men on most college campuses, there are a number of campuses (like the University of Montana or Wyoming for instance) where nearly all the Black students are the Black male athletes. These brothers are on these campuses because every school expense is being covered by the school. Lucrative campus jobs await them and provide generous pocket money. Rather than chase the females, the females chase them; not just the college's females but the whole town's! In these schools, athletes have personal tutors paid to guide them over the academic terrain. Coaches are training them for a possible professional career. Daily stress and pain is worked out in private whirlpools or with private massage therapists. And the Black male is made in other ways to feel much more like a king than a slave. Rather than imitating the White folks on campus, they are imitating him. They pay money to wear tee shirts with the athlete's number or face plastered on it. Under such circumstances the Black male will come to the White campus because he is in a more controlling situation. If things do not go his way, he's free to leave, and another college will gladly make him more comfortable than his previous college.

Many Black females come to despise some of these brothers and see them as spoiled, pampered, egotistical brats. Who is to say this negative feeling is not pure jealousy over how the brothers have positioned themselves to be catered to rather than humbly seeking to fit in as so many sisters try to do. Many Black women resent the fact that whereas they have played the college game "above board and by the book," many Black male athletes consistently get "taken care of" and all the while ignoring the rule book. Some of these "sisters" wait impatiently to see brothers get tripped up in the seemingly endless number of favors and privileges granted them. But all of this is further proof of what has been stated all along. Black men's success often has nothing at all to do with going by the rule book (the White man's success either, for that matter). Black men have been writing their own book of rules as they went along and few people, including many Black women, seem to either understand or accept that.

Does the Black female perspective have any validity at all? The answer is both yes and no. Yes, some of these Black male athletes may indeed be egotistical bastards. But it was this same ego that pushed this young man to work hard, have faith in himself, and become a top athlete. His ego is what brought this young man to the point where he felt "entitled" to a fifty thousand dollar college education without pulling a dime out of his own pocket. That he got what he thought he was entitled to by the time he was eighteen years old, bolsters and reinforces his ego even more. Should Black women be proud of this success, jealous of this success, imitate this success themselves or not pay it any attention at all? Black men have noticed that the negative attitude of Black female students towards Black male athletes is more directly connected to whether that athlete seems to exclusively date White girls than any other single factor. (Thus a second cause of jealousy and resentment).

Eventually most Black athlete's egos will come crashing down, and they will have to play by the same rule book as every one else. The overwhelming majority will never get a professional contact much less one for multi-millions. So what? At least they would have experienced at some time in their life, living on their terms, where they went first class, where people treated them with respect even if they were still presumed to be inferior. Most Black people never experience that feeling. Black people will always be given the opportunity to be a slave to societies rules, White folks requirements, and the media's stereotypical images. Rest assured that a job market hostile to self-assured, independent-thinking Black men will always be there. But some athletes will use that same ego drive to do well in other aspects of life. Once you have done one thing well, it's a lot easier to believe that you can do something else well also. And even if most Black Athletes don't do too well in another field, so what? Most people of any race don't do real well in what-ever it is that they do. The Black athlete would still be ahead of the game. And for those who say many Black male athletes don't belong in college anyway because they don't have the smarts, I again say so what? Would these men and our community and society in general have been better served if they had been left on the street corner drinking a forty ounce and intimidating people? As the old expression says, "better a has-been than a never-was."

Prison's "Appeal"

Not only may there be more Black men in prison than in college because of demographics, societal pressures, money shortages and just the plain lack of appeal of college to some Black men, but something else has to be considered. As strange as it might sound, there is a warped sense of appeal of prison to some Black males. Some mention the security of prison: 3 meals a day, a place to lay down, your own space, hot showers, and the knowledge that in most cases you have less of a chance of getting shot or beat up in prison than on the outside. Others say that prison allows them to beat their addictions and become a more disciplined person. Self-education in the form of a reading regimen is the single most important thing to other inmates. Still others note that many fellow prisoners are family, friends and neighbors who they re-establish connections with. In other words, to some Black men prison is more of a place they can conceptualize as a type of home away from home, than college where there is sometimes not a single person, place or thing that is familiar. That might seem sad, or incredible, but it is true. And prison personnel, as restrictive and macho as they are, have a code of behavior very recognizable to the prisoners. The guards in some cases are much like the prisoners. Prison personnel to an extent have to tolerate and affirm Black male culture inside the prison because so many Black males make up the prison population. To some Black men the psychological transformation that one has to make as a Black male is less traumatic in prison than it would be on a White college campus. They would be less stressed in prison than in college. Before one reads that as an incredible testimony to the backwardness of the Black male, think about this. On May 10, 1994, Nelson Mandela, the highest example of Black manhood, was sworn in as President of South Africa. Many, many more dignitaries and world leaders were present at his inauguration than were present at the funeral of a U.S.President (Richard Nixon) a couple of weeks before. Yet with all the pomp and ceremony, a special VIP seat was reserved for Mister James Gregory. James Gregory was the chief White jailer during the twenty seven years that Mr. Mandela spent in prison.   President Mandela said:

> "I spent so many years in prison," Mandelea told a lunch of dignitaries after his inauguration. "You will be surprised to know the friendships, the strong friendships, which were built between black prisoners and White warders. It was difficult for the policy-makers to persecute us as they wanted because we became friends with our warders."

Now if a Nelson Mandela, a man of high political, cultural, and racial awareness, can make a statement like that, then it's conceivable how your local drug dealer might feel the same way about his environment at your nearest state prison.

All the explanations of racism, the in-appropriateness of college for large numbers of Black men, the "benefits" and evils of the justice system, and so on, does not in any way change the fact that African American men must find ways to be highly productive in this country. They must do this not because it will please White folks or Black women, but because *it is a requirement if they want to refer to themselves as men.* And also because they are the potential leaders of their families and communities. But we live in a soceity that says that only through education (i.e. college) can a person develop the ability to become productive. That is a myth and always has been a myth. What this soceity respects are people who are good at anything that is valued. If people are skilled at something that is valued, let a lot of people know about it and serve these people at a fair price, they will be looked at as a success in this country. There are many ways to learn to be very good at something without going to college. The most popular word used to describe the activity that I'm talking about is the word *business.* Business is the Black males greatest challenge and opportunity.

If you were to look at the social structure of White America and other ethnic groups within America, you would find a consistent working unity between the business and professional people of that group. Within the Jewish, Italian, Korean or Chinese communities, you would see many organizations with the title Business and Professional Association. What this suggests is that there is a cooperative working relationship between the business people and professionals. It is not necessarily assumed that the business people in this group have the same educational credentials as the professionals. It is only assumed that they meet a certain level of success as business people. They are respected due to their level of service to the city and the reputation they have earned in delivering their goods and services. These types of reputations far exceed whatever college degrees they may have earned. This is the answer to the Black mans dilemma. He must not be measured by another persons criteria necessarily, but eventually he must be measured by something. Business is that something.

Unfortunately as you might guess, the Black community is not set up like most other communities. For the most part we have no functioning business and professional groups to speak of. Our professionals are segregated into their respective groups - The Black MBA's, Black Social Workers, "Urban" Bankers, Black Accountants, etc. These groups come together both regionally and nationally on an annual basis. They produce a lot of good work that affects not only themselves and the Black community but also national policies within the larger White professional associations and the government. But these groups rarely come together with the Black Business Community to form any business and professional associations. I doubt the professionals are to blame for this. My guess is that in far too many cases the term "Black Business Community" is an overly optimistic one. Many Black business owners are not at all united with any other Black business owner. In city after city one finds hundreds of Black enterprises that may come together only superficially; for example they may all be listed in a "Black Pages" type of business directory. But the assumption that they have formed a "community" among themselves is an illusion. At least the Black professionals are organized.

The work of the Black man is staring him right in the face. He need not go to college. All he has to do is work fourteen, sixteen, eighteen hours a day, everyday, until he has built a business that he's proud of, serves his people, and allows him to pay his bills. Then he must look hard to identify other businesses like his own (and those of Black women as well) and work to bring them together so that they can work towards solving problems that affect them all. These businesses, though in competition with each other in some instances, must still see themselves as part of a single family, "a community." Then this community of business people must reach out and make overtures or proposals to the already organized (some might say clannish or snobbish) Black professional groups and establish a relationship there. Finally when the Business and Professional group does come together, they must then take on challenges which reflect their collective intellectual, financial and political power. If all they end up doing is sponsoring banquets to hand out scholarships, sip scotch and engage in small talk, it would appear to me to be a great disappointment. What you the reader must understand is that no people in America (including most Black people) *expect* this degree of organizing among Black People to happen. And no people in America (including most Black people unfortunately) really *care* if it happens or not. Thus few people will be *disappointed* if it never happens. But that has absolutely nothing to do with whether it *should* happen!! For the Black man to simply go to college, get a degree and become just another sometime job holder in the system is actually a cop-out compared to the work that he should be doing.

BROTHER HAKI-HOW DID WE GET SO FAR APART?

In doing the research for this book, I read materials of all kinds to make sure that this book would not be just a collection of my personal opinions. I wanted to examine the conclusions of others who were looking at some of the same issues. At the top of my list was a book entitled *Black Men-Obsolete, Single, Dangerous.* by Haki Madhubuti. The sub-title of the book was *The African American Family in Transition.* I had tremendous respect for the work by Haki Madhubuti, going back to the mid -1960's when I first became aware of him during my Black nationalist days with Maulana Karenga in Los Angeles. I had met or seen many famous Black militants in those days and Haki, then known as Don L. Lee, was the easiest for me to personally identify with. This was somewhat odd because I had no significant interest in poetry, no matter how Black it was, and Haki was known at that time primarily as a poet. But there are some people that you like regardless of differences, and Haki was one such brother. We did not actually meet in those days, he was just one of many that I noted and admired from afar. In the more than twenty five years since those days, a lot of the "famous" Blacks I had met have changed their priorities, values and commitments toward the Black community. Not Haki. Haki is still going strong and is on the case more than ever before. His publishing company, Third World Press out of Chicago, is an established institution in the Black community and does more to produce the truth about the Black American experience than any other entity in America. My respect for the man has grown substantially and without question he is one of my role models in my own work. No one has made more effort to make crystal clear, in plain words, the nature of the many challenges that face us as African people living in America, than Haki Madhabuti

Now having said all that, I need not remind you that we are all capable of having serious disagreements with people we love, respect and admire including parents, siblings, children or mates and that is exactly how I felt after I read brother Haki's best selling book. I had serious problems with how he views some of the issues that are being discussed here. On page twenty five of his book he has given me a tacit OK to constructively criticize him as I do not consider him a Black leader with an unsecured ego.

The Black man has been bombarded with unbelievable criticism about how screwed up he is; how he does so many things wrong and so few things right. I think the phrase is "male-bashing" or, in this case, Black male-bashing. It has been going on at least the last fifteen years. If male-bashing was an effective technique for "straightening out" the Black man, and for making him understand and commit to a better path in life, then maybe the male-bashing strategy could be justified. But male- bashing has just made the Black man a convenient scapegoat for the shortcomings of the rest of American society, and male-bashing has disillusioned the brothers to the point where many of them have said to hell with everybody.

In Haki's book we do not get a sympathetic understanding of the Black man's plight. Instead we get an attitude that assumes that every wrong ever assigned to brothers is true and correct as charged. I found this attitude shocking and disappointing. The Black man does not need yet another male-basher who is saying many of the same things, with the same intensity, and from the same perspective as countess others have said already. What the Black man needs is someone to get inside his head and explain to the rest of the Black male-bashing world how and why he thinks the way he does. The Black men needs a spokesman for his social circumstances, not for the purpose of gaining sympathy, but for the purpose of reinterpreting the reality that so many people assume they already understand.

Haki's book is written in a tone that assumes the opposite of what I have found to be true. His men are weak and totally irresponsible. His women are super-heroes doing the man's job as well as her own, and doing them both well. His tone differs little from, say, a Black feminist booklet like *Mad at Miles* by Pearl Cleage. While there is nothing wrong with supporting many Black feminist views, a brother of Haki's knowledge and experience should have added the Black male perspective in his commentary. Instead we get comments like these:

1) Often Black women understand Black men at a greater level than the men understand themselves. Many African American women realize that if Black men are going to rise to meet the real needs of the Black world, they have to stop "mothering" them and really work for partnerships in struggle and life. Black men as a collective body have not been able to get our act together, and it is not accurate or in our best interest to blame Black women for our current condition. In this war situation that we are in, our women can not effectively deal with White men; they need us-that's our job. (Page 89 Black Men Obsolete, Single, Dangerous \Third World Press 1990 Chicago, IL)

First of all most Black women of today do not see a "Black World". They see White America. The only Black things most of them care about are a Black man and their children. They care little or nothing about building "Black institutions" for a "Black world." Most Black women see the world from a White perspective and today there is less guilt attached to being a *true*

American and desiring the American dreams than ever before. This is where most of the sisters that I know are coming from. Second, I am not and never have been aware of any great amount of "mothering" that Black women are giving Black men. This term is often used to diminish the Black man's ego whenever he appeals for for a degree of empathy during an especially trying moment (of which we have many). Black women routinely knock us for being super macho and hiding our feelings, and but then also criticize us as weak when we reveal our hurt and pain. But this current criticism is coming from a brother, Haki, not a woman. Third, his view that "Black men as a collective body have not been able to get our act together, and it is not accurate or in our best interest to blame Black women for our current condition," is a phrase that is way out of line if you understand where Black people are and how we got there.

I thought that the civil rights and Black nationalist movements were the specific acts of a collective body of Black men (and women), and that both led to the increased opportunity of all Americans, including Jews, women, Hispanics, and Asians to get better justice in this country. Black men, and virtually no one else, gave their lives for these rights.

In the seventies Black men amassed their political power and gained political offices in cities and states all over the U.S.. Wasn't that some form of getting our act together as a collective body? In the eighties Black men acted to increase multifold the number and kinds of businesses that served our community in our effort to control the economy of our people. I believe that speaks to some form of collective action. Haki implies in his statement that there is some noticeable tendency for Black men to blame sisters for our problems. I am not aware of any significant, organized efforts by Black men to blame Black women for our current condition. What I *am* aware of is a mountain of literature from a certain group of Black females who are now household names who have implied that Black men *are* to blame for *their* (Black Women) current condition. Our protests against their right to say that were few and weak. So I really don't know what brother Haki is talking about.

Finally our women *do not by any means* consider themselves in a "war situation" with White men. In fact many get upset at Black men and tell us we are "living in the 60's" when we suggest that we are in a war situation. And as has been pointed out throughout this book, Black women *can* effectively deal with White men, enough to get jobs, housing, and assistance from them when Black men cannot. As a matter of fact most Black women would think that the idea that they can't deal effectively with White men, and that it was our job to do it for them, was an extremely backward and chauvinistic statement. And I would have to agree.

Starting on page 110 , Haki gives some suggestions intended to undo the negative programming that is a part of the slave legacy that plagues us today. Under number 9 of the suggestions he has the following:

9) "Become responsible men and stand up. Stop crying on wives/lovers breasts about how the "man" treats you on the job, in the streets, at school and elsewhere. It is not that we need to present a false picture of our lives, but sisters are under enough weight themselves and do not need their man's *false* tears. That is how our women lose respect for us. They are actually waiting on us to do something about the "man" if we are going to continue to call ourselves men. If Black women can't occasionally lean on the shoulders of African American men, who can they lean on? We are incomplete without each other.

I don't know how you feel about the above passage but it I find it disturbing. First of all, here again is the notion that Black men are weak because we are "crying" on our wives/lovers breasts. I have to ask several questions. Do Black men catch *more hell* from White folks or not? Are we suppose to pretend that we can take it in at all times under all conditions and not wince? If *we are* allowed a little humanity to occasionally express frustration, anger, or fear, who should we express it to? To a sympathetic White policeman? An animal in the zoo? Or to our *soul mate*. I don't feel that it's shameful to show a mixture of feelings to your mate. Isn't that precisely what Black women have been asking for; that the Black man express his feelings and not just his thoughts (Terry McMillans favorite line)? Isn't that what they have been calling "communication? " Black women have a problem with the idea that men believe that men shouldn't cry and that they should be men. Haki, without any empirical evidence whatever seems to believe that we cry too much. It's interesting how one of Black America's biggest male supporters of feminism can still find interesting ways to disagree with them.

Moving on: "Sisters are under enough weight themselves and do not need their men's false tears". What in the hell does that mean? It is not clear what weight Haki is referring to here. Considering that sisters have better responses from private sector employers and much more financial aide from public assistance providers, she certainly has more help carrying her weight than Black men do. If she is single as so many women seem to be, where are all these men crying false tears coming from? This statement is troublesome not only because it goes out of the way to attack Black men but because it does so with a non sensical logic.

The least accurate statement in Haki's entire book is the idea that *Black women lose respect for us (Black men) because they are waiting for us to do something about the man.* Nothing, could be further from the truth. If anything, Black woman lose respect for Black men because many of us *refuse* to play the White man's game, the game that most of our women have decided to play. Black women want Black men to go to college, graduate (become "sophisticated") put on a suit and tie, shine our shoes, go down town and find the best job we can find working with as many "influential" Whites as possible. Then they want us to go house-shopping in the suburbs every Sunday until we find a decent, safe and affordable house so they can get the hell out of their horrible (Black) neighborhood. That is what most Black women want. They are by no means waiting for us to do anything about the man except be more like him. Why some may lose respect for Black men is because we don't have an *alternative* to their plan. We reject their integrationist plan but have no nationalist plan we are actively pursuing. But please, brother Haki, don't try to convince your thousands of readers that today's Black women are ready for some kind of action against "the man". That's Bullshit! If sisters in the sixties didn't support the idea of brothers taking action against "the man" back then, you can hardly expect them to support that now. Today's Black women would marry many, many more White men, if the White men would accept them as wives and not just as exotic sexual experiences. That's what a lot of today's sisters want to do about "the man".

Even on a point that brother Haki and I agree on, we see the situation very differently. On page 104 he says: "Another important point is that young women should be left for young men. Young Black men have enough to deal with without worrying about losing their mates to older, more "experienced," financially secure Black men. It is extremely difficult and nearly impossible for a young, inexperienced (sexually and otherwise), poor Black man to compete with a more "worldly" older brother who has resources."

There are several questions that Haki's statement raises that leave the issue very unclear. At what age should the older Black man leave the young girls alone? How much of an age gap between male and female constitutes the prohibitive barrier? But an even more important question is: How do the relations between less experienced girls and older more experienced boys get started and when do they get started? If, as I have claimed, it starts at about fourteen years old, then there will be little success in trying to prevent a seventeen year old boy from dating a fourteen or fifteen year old girl. And if the pattern does start at that young an age, then at what point do you try to break the pattern if indeed one could actually do so?

Second Haki suggests that it is the men who are pursuing the women which is only half true. Once a young women knows who she wants and determines that he is a status symbol, she will make her intentions so clear that she will appear to be doing the pursuing herself. Long before women "marry up," they seek to "date up". As a matter of fact without "dating up" you cannot get to "*marry* up."

From the male's point of view, I'm sure most would prefer to date women their own age but these women are the very ones who often don't speak or ever make eye contact, and see you as "no better than themselves". When a sexually active man receives constant rejection, it's only natural for him to pursue a female who responds and makes him feel like he is somebody worthy of respect and attention. Women are attracted by the age-maturity gap. Evidently It's as much a turn on as the extra money that the women assume these older brothers have. You can't stop a female from looking for a (sugar) "daddy." If that's what she's looking for (and many of them *are* looking for him) then that's who she will eventually find.

It is not my intent to do a full critique of brother Haki's book, nor to take potshots at isolated phrases which one could say "were taken out of context." But it is important to show how even the strong and knowledgeable among us (like Haki) can take to heart and internalize the steady flow of criticisms directed at Black men and how we then begin to sound much like our oppressors. For centuries many believed we were hopeless simply because we were Black. Now many of us believe that we are just as hopeless because we are male. Haki's book is full of headings and statements like:

1. Black males in a beggar mentality
2. Black men avoiding social responsibility
3. Black men ... immersed in self pity
4. The impotence of the Black male population has forced Black women to be strong........
5. High level of non-involvement of Black men in the family structure...and so on

Each statement could be rationalized and made to appear accurate within a certain context. But for any normal Black male to read this 250 page book and see literally scores of such references like those above, he could only reach one conclusion: that what Black women said a long time ago must be true, namely: "A Nigga man ain't shit!" It's one thing for a woman to scream that out of the frustration of her personal experiences. Its another thing for a brother who knows better to try to document and legitimize such remarks.

On page one hundred and sixty nine there is a section entitled "Five Most Often Used Excuses Black Men Give Black Women." This section was part and parcel of Haki's failure to see the world through eyes of Black males; he instead came off like a diehard Black feminist fanatic.

These excuses are Haki's idea of why Black men fail to commit to Black women.

> "The essence of this short essay is to call Black men on the games that most of us have been taught to play. Pulling the covers off of this "meanspirited" and often unknown habit of lying and running from relationship to relationship only shows how Black men and women are shadows of each other."

As I see it, after much consultation with African American men and women, these are the five excuses Black men use most often to avoid commitment and responsibility:

1)   You don't understand me! Anytime a Black woman arrives at the crucial point of truly understanding the brother she is with, he says she doesn't understand him. Somebody is wrong; generally, it is the brother. Most Black men fear analysis of their actions from anybody, especially the sisters with whom they are living or relating. This denial of reality is not uncommon among Blackmen...
Until Black men can honestly face themselves and communicate with themselves they will not be able to relate meaningfully to Black women. Understanding one's self starts with an admission of not understanding.

2)   yes you are right, but ... ! Few Black men are willing to admit to errors or mistakes. Even though the sister may have read the brother to the bone, he cannot allow her the last word. This inability to be honest and accept responsibility when one is clearly at fault is a problem among many Black men... Facing reality is difficult enough, but lying to one's self about reality can be tragic. Listening to one's partner, rather than challenging her ever utterance, is maturity.

3)   You are too good for me! This excuse is probably the closest to the truth........................ By downplaying and questioning his own qualities, he is attempting to put the woman on the defense and solicit sorrow and understanding. If the sister has been around the block, she will see through this immediately. She will understand that this man is not willing to make a long-term commitment and is not strong or honest enough to face the woman with the truth. Many Black men avoid the truth like it is a drug that will keep their penis soft...

4)   I need my space! Generally, this comes from brothers who couldn't define space if their lives depended on it. Often, they don't have a pot to pee in, but they are ready to call it quits and run. There may be another sister or the current relationship has moved to the point where a "higher" commitment needs

to be made, articulated and practiced. These space-based brothers are generally men who have children and who have not developed/matured to the point of being fathers...

5) I don't have any money and I don't have the time! The man is on my back. This is the brother who is working on a job that demands a lot of time. Generally, his mate knows little about his finances, and he is always crying "broke". When the relationship started, nothing was too good or cost too much. However, as the months and years rolled by, the lack of communication around resources, enlargement of responsibility and probably undisciplined spending have led to financial problems. Rather than sit down like a mature adult and come up with a plan to save and pay bills, he just cries "poverty." The time question is very important. Most Black men do not have enough money. However, they do have time. If one's time (quality time) is not given to the relationship, where is it going? " (Pages 170-171)

My perspectives on Black men not committing to marriage or even marriage-like (living together) relationships have been related in an earlier chapter. In looking at Haki's "five excuses," I will try not to repeat much of that commentary.

In the first place, if Black men have been taught to play games, who taught us? Our mothers, our absentee fathers, older brothers? No. Most Black men respond directly to how women respond to us. It is the male's role to pursue the female. *All of us* receive rejection many more times than we receive acceptance and most of us never quite get use to the rejection. Any games that we have "been taught" to play with sisters have almost always been taught to us *by* sisters. Haki does not even *suggest* that sisters play games with the brothers. Does that compare favorably with your experience? Have you been spared all the games that sisters play in life?

Excuse

1) **You don't understand me!** If Black women say that Black men don't communicate and if *sisters say that they* don't understand men or Black men, I take them at their word. If a Terry McMillan says (in a book that hundreds of thousands of Black woman identify with) to the Black man, "Tell me how you feel and not just what you think," I take her at her word. *How* can Haki say that Black women understand us better than we do ourselves? Now I will admit that there is such little positive information available about the Black man, written from a Black male's perspective, that the average Black man may not understand himself nearly as well as he should. But just because

the Black man doesn't know himself as well as *he* should hardly suggests that the Black woman knows him better. That's bullshit!

2) Yes you are right but ....

This "excuse" is more bogus bull on the same basic issue: The idea that Black women have this uncanny ability to always be right and the brothers are equally consistent in being wrong. Such a sweeping generalization by Haki with no examples as to what precisely he is talking about is grounds for dismissing it entirely.

3) You are too good for me!

The first and last sentence of this quote seems to demonstrate mean spiritedness by Haki toward Black men. I don't understand it. If you were asked to guess who wrote such words, you would probably assume they came from an angry, man-hating Black feminist, not Haki Madhubuti.

As mentioned earlier a woman generally is almost always looking to "marry up." She is looking for men with more of everything that she doesn't have. She doesn't always succeed but she tries. So why would a brother who probably has more going for him tell a sister that she is too good for him? Women often have their hand out either literally or figuratively speaking. They want or expect something from males and what they want to give men in return (if anything) is not at all likely to be of equal value. So why would this type of female be too good for brothers?   Even if you disagree with every criticism that I've made so far regarding this book, I'm positive you will agree that the statement regarding "a soft penis" is completely uncalled for.

4) I need my space!

Haki continues his generalizing and doesn't explain exactly what he's talking about. But it doesn't matter. Because you only have to study one sentence to see how wrong his logic is: "Often, they don't have a pot to pee in, but they are ready to call it quits and run."

Now answer this question.

> Lets say you have a son who is twenty six years old. For reasons either legitimate or bogus "he doesn't have a pot to pee in". However he is in love and the girl he loves wants him to marry her.

How would you advise your son

a) Go on ahead and marry her son, love alone will take care of everything or

b) Look son if you are that serious about this lady you better backup and get to working. Before you decide to get married you are going to have to have a whole lot more than just a pot to pee in!

Haki's statement here suggests that the only thing that a Black man should consider before making the full commitment is whether the woman wants you to. I must really be getting old. I remember the days when the brothers proposed to the sisters but I guess now its the other way around and you are a no good son of a bitch if you turn them down - for whatever reason.

5) I don't have any money and I don't have the time!

First Haki says this brother's job requires " a lot of time". A couple of sentences later he says most brothers have time. Obviously this isn't one of *those* brothers because Haki himself says that this particular brother's job *requires* a lot of time. When a person bashes Black males just for the sake of bashing them, contradictions like this come up, where after a while they don't even care if they make sense or not as long as they bash brothers. I really don't know if:

a)   Haki has been hanging around some very different kind of brothers and it has confused him,

or.

b)   If he was trying to write a best seller by catering to the frustrations of a few hundred thousand book-buying Black women. (That sounds completely out of character for him) or

c)   If the anti-Black male literature by Black women has been so pervasive and effective that he has accepted it and is now turning on himself and taking a lot of us who trust his words with him.

My last statement on Haki's book is a criticism that Haki only symbolically represents. I'm sure if I picked up a book by any of our real heavy afrocentric thinkers such as Dr. Leonard Jefferies, Dr. Molefi Asante, Dr. Maulana Karenga, or Dr. John H. Clarke I would find much of the same views. This represents an important contradiction that must be noted by the serious thinker/activist. Listed below are four quotes from Haki's book. Note this quote from Page 88.

However women must understand that the positive masculine releases that White men have are not functioning within the Black community for Black men. White men in this world build cities, run countries, develop businesses, start political parties, maintain armies, develop technology, run universities, go to the moon and live in and on the ocean. Most Black men generally watch White men do these things, play a supporting role, or clean up after them.

This quote is from Page 20

> The Black rich and the White rich are different and respond
> differently to their respective communities. The two groups also
> view their responsibilities to their people differently. The White
> rich start foundations, build art centers, finance new wings for
> museums and libraries, endow university chairs and create scholar-
> ships for the less fortunate of their people and others. The White
> rich finance all types of summer camps, help keep White businesses
> viable, start independent think tanks, support their writers, artists
> and musicians and buy sports franchises.

This last quote is from pages 76 and 77

> "It is said that when a people has more religious leaders than
> business and military men in a world ruled by business and military
> men, that people is in serious trouble."

> Also on page 207 Haki lists poverty as the number two thing that Black
> people battle daily in America.

These four quotes demonstrate that brother Haki is very much aware of the role
of business and money in a people's development and prosperity. He
understands that money to build those institutions, finance those chairs and
scholarships., start those think tanks and build cities is very, very necessary.
Yet like virtually all afrocentric Black scholars, he lists hardly a single reference
to books dealing with Black business, income improvement, or how to escape
from poverty, among his list of over 300 books by White and Black writers.
The books listed cover a broad range of issues, broader even than most reading
lists suggested by Black scholars. And if you were to actually read these books,
recommended by one of Black America's most consistent and committed
thinkers, you will undoubtedly be an expert on all matters of African and
African American history, racism and the role of Black women in our history.
You would also become familiar with our best poets and novelists who focus
on Black life. And if you read all the White authors you would learn about the
conspiracies that White folk have in place to rule the world and so on.
        But after spending 5-10 years reading all these books, you still wouldn't
know anything about how *to make the money to* build the Black institutions
that Haki knows is necessary for the Black community. Only one book, *Real
Estate is the Gold in Your Future* by Dempsey Travis might help you learn
how to buy and own the roof over your head. Only one book out of more than
three Hundred is about giving you information that you can act on and by

taking such action, improve your ability to control your life. Why is that the case? Why is that the case not only here but in all of the reading materials that deep, scholarly afrocentric scholars recommend?

The answer is complex. First there is the reality that the economic system of Capitalism fueled the slave trade, the destruction of the Native American people, the exploitation of millions of White and Black workers in America's factories, and so on. Thus it would appear contradictory for Black scholars to advocate that Black people master and use very system that led to their enslavement. On the other hand there have been no significant efforts to come up with any alternative to the economic system that Black scholars insist has been so bad for us. Our Black thinkers therefore chose to sit on the fence with respect to economic matters. They neither talk to our people about how to survive within a capitalist system, nor what to do to over turn it, change it, etc. *Meanwhile we all are participating in the capitalist system anyway.* We work for a capitalist company, we shop in capitalist stores and we pay our mortgage and car notes to the capitalist banks that financed the capitalist built houses we live in and cars we drive. And at the same time we are playing the game, we are *playing it poorly.* We are playing it poorly because no one is teaching us how to play for their respective reasons. White instructors are not teaching us to play because Whites want to remain the chief capitalist and stifle unnecessary competition. Black scholars like Haki will not teach you (or recommend reading material that will teach you) because:

A) You need to spend all your time reading about what Blackness is

and

B) You don't need to understand how to master capitalism because that is the evil system that gave you all the problems you currently have.

Meanwhile the word has gone out, or appears to have gone out, to people all over the world that any people, speaking in any tongue, of any skin color, believing in any or no God, can come to any Black community, anywhere in America because the people there are just too dumb, lazy and or fearful to open a business in their own community.

The first sentence from the quote from page 88 is Bullshit. "However Black women must understand that the positive masculine releases that White men have are not functioning within the Black community for Black men."

Of course it's not functioning in the Black community , because the brothers are too busy studying about how much gold Mansa Musa took across the Sahara desert in the fourteenth century on his Hajji between the Mali empire and Mecca. That kind of reading might make you feel good as a proud Black African man, but that won't not help to put baby formula in his baby's bottle. And while Black men are reading about bygone days of glory in West African Empires, the Korean is buying the building down the street for little of nothing at the city tax auction sale. And in two weeks when the brother finishes reading about West African empires and he happens to find a few dollars in his pocket, he will pay top dollar for some baby formula from the new Korean merchant who just miraculously opened a store down the street from his house. This is the vicious cycle that Black people are going though and there is no reason to expect any change as long as people like Haki, who run *multi million dollar enterprises* fail to turn Black people on to the information where they can learn to do the same. Almost all of your afrocentric scholars live well above the economic levels of the Black people they preach to. A college professorship here, one or two books there, several $2,000.00 speaking engagements each month, and you are looking at a hundred grand a year, easy. Some can make more then fifty thousand dollars in February (Black History month) alone. *I have absolutely no problem with any of that*. I do have a problem with Black scholars saying that they are about helping to advance Black people and when their loyal readers and listeners await what steps they should take, information on economic improvement is always left out. All the African History books in the world are not going to get you the down payment you need for a house with the two bathrooms that you need for your growing family.

The idea of commitment which Haki believes Black men evade is at least as much an economic issue as it is an emotional one! The sisters say no romance without finance. A brother's economic level helps him decide if he is ready for marriage. All statistics show that when Black men loose jobs it leads to families breaking up and women collecting welfare. One of the best things that an afrocentric scholar can do to encourage commitment and family unity is to tell all the brothers and sisters how you make money. We can not depend on the White man *giving* the Black man the number or the kind of jobs needed to raise a family in urban America. If a Black scholar who cares so much about Black people cannot supply this information, then who is to do it? The gurus on the late night T.V. with the how-to-get-rich-quick informericals? If Black scholars do not show Black people how to economically survive, then we need to shut up about the selling of drugs, the car-jackings, and the burglaries in our communities, because no human being is going to just sit by and watch themselves become homeless and starve to death. Not in the richest country in the history of the world. That would be insane.

Having said all of this , I still respect and admire brother Haki for his past, present and future contributions to the African American struggle. Don't laugh, I'm serious. Perhaps he will produce other material which will clarify or negate some of the information that he has put forth in this book. As much as I respect him, I think its dangerous when we allow our leaders to say any and everything and never challenge or question any of it. I think even Haki believes that. I hope you feel that way too.

COMMITTING TO TERRY'S GIRLFRIENDS

When a company, organization, institution or person in the public eye, is accused of crimes, unethical behavior or dishonest acts, they have the option of either refuting the accusations and proving their innocence or simply not addressing the issues at all. If they choose to ignore the accusations and let the controversy ride out its time in the public's consciousness, that company, organization or person stands the risk of being assumed guilty of all the charges and rumors that have been brought against it.

When we look at the reputation of the Black man in the 1970's, 1980's and 1990's, we see a group against whom all kinds of shameful charges have been brought. Partly because so very few Black men have stepped forward in these last twenty years and given an adequate defense, explanation or refutation of all these charges, it has been assumed by Whites, Blacks, Hispanics and Asians alike that the American Black man must be guilty of everything that has been charged against him. When you get that kind of a negative reputation, a reputation that becomes more believable not only because of your non-existent defense, but also because of the media's bombardment of new negative images on a daily basis, certain perspectives and questions stop even being considered for thought.

For example a major issue in just about every article published on Black male/female relationships has been "where are the good, decent Black men to be the good, decent husbands for the large number of single and deserving Black women out here?" When the question is routinely put this way, and with such feeling, concern and conviction, the idea of reversing it ("Where are the good, decent Black women to be wives of the deserving Black men ") is *never* entertained. The question of the availability of good women for Black men is assumed to be a non-issue, due to the alleged or supposed large number of Black women ("quality" women at that) available for single Black men. Well, this writer and a fair amount of other Black men are not at all convinced that the second question doesn't need to be asked.

What constitutes a good Black woman, and whose standards does she meet besides her own? Are the expectations of a good Black woman so unrealistic that they detract from her desirability? These questions and others will be examined as we look at Terry's famous girlfriends and check out their qualifications as "good Black women". Terry, of course, is Terry McMillan, the red-hot author of *Waiting to Exhale,* (Viking Press N.Y. 1992), a truly phenomenal bestselling book in the Black community (1992 - 1994).

I can think of five major reasons why Terry McMillan's book has been a blockbuster best seller. First, hundreds of thousands of Black women are able to identify with the difficulties that her four Black female characters have in finding, keeping and being happy with Black men. Second, most Black women can identify with the characters and can see in them a bit of themselves. Third, the book contains enough semi-pornographic sex to arouse the average adult. Fourth, Ms. McMillan herself criss-crossed the nation to at least twenty major cities promoting her book. Television appearances on Oprah, Arsenio Hall and other national shows is the fifth major reason for her book's popularity. It only seems right then to study the characters with which today's Black women identify in order to get a decent reading on the state of Black male/female relations, at least from the female point of view.

Terry's girlfriends are Savannah Jackson, Bernadine Harris, Robin Stokes and Gloria Matthews, and all live in the city of Phoenix, Arizona in our day and time. We will look at these women from at least one Black male's perspective to see if Black men are infact irresponsibly avoiding commitments to these Black women who are presumed to be so good for the Black man.

Savannah Jackson

Ms. Jackson is a thirty-six year old Black female who moves to Phoenix from Denver, in part because she has given up on Denver's weather and crop of Black men. She takes a salary cut from $50,000 to 38,000 a year in order to make the move. She arrives in town and immediately hooks up with the three other women who then become a rather unusual quartet.

In this book, Savannah is depicted as probably the "best catch" of the group of four women. Not only does she earn a nice income (by Black women's standards), she is also well-traveled, fitness conscious, attractive, confident and carries less personal baggage from previous relationships that would turn brothers off. But there is still a great deal to dislike (or at least get turned off by) about Miss Jackson. First of all, she cusses like a sailor. I don't think its too prudish to expect a woman to avoid routine use of the F-word in her everyday informal conversations. In my life, I always have related a woman's cursing to her being angry. At forty plus years, its difficult to change my attitude. If in conversations I have to wonder everytime I hear her talk whether she's angry or pissed off , then being around her will be a nerve racking experience that's adds stress that I don't need. This is assuming, of course, that I'm sensitive to and care about her feelings. If I don't care to associate her words with her feelings and I treat her conversation like I do the brothers', then that's another story. But why would I want a sister who sounds just like one of the brothers? Why desensitize me to her words? If she's flat-chested already, she needs to add to her femininity, not take away from it. Plus she smokes too! Was she ever in the military? Ms. Jackson says that she's lived with three different men for a total of nine years, but wouldn't do it again. She says she's glad she didn't marry them because all three were mistakes. She would only live with another man if they were married because "people aren't so quick to call it quits when they are married." This is a classic misconception that many women (not just Black women) have. They think there is something magic about marriage that can make a bad thing good. Nothing could be more untrue, and many married people will tell you that. The goal is for people to find happiness within themselves first and then with another person. Unfortunately, it takes a long time to determine if that's what you really have when you only think you have it. It's as easy to make a mistake with yourself as it is with the other person. Nobody *tries* to make a mistake in marriage, because too much is at stake. Sounds to me like Savannah just wants to trap a man. If that's the way its supposed to really be, let's make divorce illegal and impossible.

It was Savannah who prayed to God to send her a man *that was already what he was aspiring to be* and I've previously stated my feelings on that. This woman doesn't want to help nurture a relationship, she wants a finished product. In one part of the book she brags about her self-sufficiency yet in another she says that the income of a potential mate is not unimportant. Sounds like your normal talking out of both sides of your mouth sister to me. On page eleven she makes clear her dislike of Black men who are arrogant or cocky, yet she wants *to be* treated like she has a "tiara" on her head. I had to look this word up, and it turns out that a tiara is a crown's crown. A triple crown. The Pope's crown. Thus it's acceptable for her to be treated like a queen's queen so long as her mate, despite his own accomplishments, is not arrogant or cocky. Is this a contradiction or what? sure it went right by her.

Now on page 12 Ms. Jackson blasts Black men for being among other things selfish, manipulative and overly concerned with how much sex they can get. Yet on page 117 in her escapade with Lionel, she is thinking strictly about herself.

> "Part of my fantasy was to get *myself* a little piece out here on the road ... even though Lionel had gotten on my nerves ... I can block his bullshit out of my mind, *because I've done it before*, (my emphasis). I should go ahead and get me some. If I'm *lucky* (my emphasis), I may never see this man again after tomorrow."

Is Ms. Jackson's selfish manipulativeness any different, more excusable, or less devilish than what she accuses men of? Is she as bad as men, or as free as men, or as human as men? I'd like to ask her that. On page 201, Savannah can't understand for the life of her why Robin has such a hang up about going out to a restaurant by herself to eat. "Women who think like that really piss me off", she says of Robin. But on page 206 we read:

> "We spent hours on the phone, talking about everything except how we felt about each other. By the time I realized I was in love with him, I was too scared to tell him. I knew what he thought about me, but I didn't know how he felt. I'd never been in *this* position before. I didn't know if he was going out with other women at the same time or if I was considered recreation, a past time, some temporary form of entertainment. I got tired of guessing. And I didn't feel comfortable questioning him about it. So one day I wrote him a letter and told him I didn't want to go out with him anymore. He couldn't understand why. I lied and said I had met somebody else. I haven't heard a word from him until now."

Now how difficult is it to ask somebody who you love and spend hours on the phone with how they feel about you? Is it more or less difficult than say eating in a restaurant by yourself? Just like Savannah instructed Robin to open her mouth and "eat the goddamn food", I could instruct her to open her mouth and ask Kenneth "how do you feel about me?" I don't see a lot of difference here. She works in media, she's on television, she's a communicator, or so she wants people to think. What kind of interviewer - communicator can she possibly be if she can't ask a man who supposedly means a lot to her how he feels? No, that's too easy. She has to get creative and cowardly. She writes a letter, lies in the letter in saying she found someone else and says she doesn't want to see him again. What was that supposed to be, a test? Was he supposed to break down her door and beg her to come back? I thought the 1990's women said *No meant no*. Or does he know that no meant try again? And if she wasn't playing a game with him, why would she act surprised that she hadn't heard from him since? Why couldn't she interpret that as his respecting the fact that she wanted somebody else in her life rather than him and he was to swallow hard and move on. Is the Black man to be credited with respecting people's feelings in relationships when he acts like Kenneth does, or must there always be a negative attached to his actions? In this case she probably was thinking he must not have loved her much, he never tried to call back and patch things up. Bullshit! Don't sisters know that we not only get tired of playing games, but we get tired of being damned if we play the game and damned if we don't. This woman is not nearly as grown up and mature as she thinks she is. When she finally joins up with Kenneth again on page 257, she makes it clear her feminine ego got in the way of what could have been her best relationship.

"... I've never had to *ask* a *man how* he feels about me. Its usually obvious."

Instead of her admitting to herself that she blew it (and lied on top of that), she accuses Kenneth of being not "exactly the most communicative man in the world". Right! And I guess her own inability to ask Kenneth a straight question and her decision to lie to him were the works of a great communicator, professional that she is. Please, she needs to be spanked like the wishy-washy spoiled brat she's acting like.

On page 347 near the end of the book, we see that it is very similar to page 12. In both situations, as well as throughout this book, she's on a mission to try to get to know Black men. In Phoenix all she's met are "nothing but a few no-name creeps." Now do you think that feeling toward Black men is eventually communicated to the outside world through body language, facial expressions and speech? Of course it is. Might that have something to do with why Ms. Professional is still without a man? You answer that!

Why can't a guy just be okay? Why does he have to be either Mr. Wonderful or a No Name Creep? What kind of man was she looking for any-way? Charles Barkley? He's already married. Before Phoenix Ms Jackson had three years of "dates from hell" in Denver. And of course there were the nine years with three men who were mistakes. If Savannah were a man, wouldn't Black women be the first to say that *something's got to be wrong with him*?

Well what happens when the "him" is a "her"? Are women equal opportunity social critics or is it just their habit of making Black men the all-purpose villain.

By the time I had digested the Savannah Jackson-Charles Turner affair, it was very clear to me that Savannah doesn't deserve a good, strong man. Not at all. Let me explain. All of us have had periods in our lives where we have had some good luck and some bad luck. Only the most naive depend entirely on good luck to guide them through life forever. The rest of us depend on work, effort, intelligence, determination and the pursuit of our goals.

A Black man in America gets whatever he gets through work and determination. No tooth fairy or angel gives us a damn thing. And rejection? Nobody knows rejection like the Black man. We are the only group that everybody fears and rejects. Even dark-skinned male babies are the single most difficult babies to be adopted in this country. We are assumed to be either dumb or evil from birth. Don't tell the Black man about rejection, having to work hard or not having things go his way.

A loving, compatible mate is a very valuable thing to have. A good mate is so valuable that a person should do whatever they can within the law to get one, if they can. People work hard for jobs, college degrees, promotions, home ownership, and other things. A good mate is more important than all of these, so there is no question that you should work hard to get what you want in a mate. Most men have to pursue the woman they want. They have to sell themselves, spend money, give up time, play roles and games and do what it takes to win A woman's interest, respect, affection and so on. And you tend to respect people who follow the same principles and play by the same rules that you play by. You tend to *disrespect* people who expect something for nothing or who expect luck, God or their horoscope configuration to do all their work for them.

Now there is no reasonable and immediate explanation for why Charles Turner "dissed" Savannah, as he apparently did. But how much did Savannah *do* to get what she thought was so important to her. Not a damn thing, really. One phone call to an answering machine. Hell, you'd do that to get the exterminator. If she really wanted the man or at least wanted an explanation, she should have put her ass on a plane to San Francisco, walked into his office, and said "Hey, we have to talk." Would that have solved things? Who knows. Turner could have encountered a serious problem and decided to go undercover from everybody, not just Savannah. But women are notoriously slow in accepting the blame for the dumb stuff that they do or fail to do. On page 382 it sounds like she's taking the weight, but she's not. There is nothing wrong with opening up your heart to a man or woman. Hell, its a requirement to establish the kind of relationship most people want. Where Savannah messed up was not following through with *action* and *effort* to get what she wanted. No, this woman is like too many others; she expects everything to fall into place, one-two-three, in a nice neat package; and if it doesn't, then its not meant to be. Bull! If things don't work out immediately, you work around, over, under, or on top of the problem to get what you want, until you either win or decide it's not worth it. What you lose in time, money and disappointment, you gain in character, emotional strength, knowledge and preparedness for the next go round. That's not a man thing, a Black thing or a White thing, that is the way of the world. When more Black women learn this lesson, they will have better relationships and feel better about themselves. A little pride is cool, but Black people have had to swallow their pride a lot of times to get what they wanted if they thought it was important. A lot of the pride that many of today's Black women carry on their backside is false pride. Savannah is one example of this; thus many of the women who identified with her may have a lot of false pride also. The other reason that Savannah turns me off is because she disses Kenneth, the brother who pursues her, because he can't *guarantee* her wants. Savannah, like so many Black women, wants and expects a guarantee. They want it all guaranteed in a contract -baby, house, happiness, fidelity, freedom, equality, money, career, friends, travel, love, etc., into infinity. Period! This world offers no such guarantees. If they could pull themselves away from Danielle Steele, Cosmo magazine and Harlequin romance novels and study a little Black history, maybe it eventually will dawn on them. Savannah is *not* qualified to be put on the list of good Black woman looking for a good Black man.

Robin Stokes

Robin is the ultimate dingbat of this group. She has an obsession with a no-good brother, Russell, who sets records in proving how many ways he can misuse women in general and Robin in particular. Robin would never have this circle of friends if she were a man. Because men lose respect for other men who are just weak and dumb and do the same stupid stuff over and over again. But women like Robin can have this group of Middle class women friends because women excuse and tolerate stupidity and disrespect when it's one of their own, another Black woman. They simply can't tolerate those same actions and attitudes in a man. Why not? use men are supposed to be strong. Its okay if a woman is weak. Robin would have to be a crack addict if she were a man because crack would justify her stupidity and other crack addicts would accept her as a member. There is an acknowledgement of weakness and problems among addicts. Men turn to drugs because it helps them feel strong and they know they are expected to be strong. But women can be weak and be perfectly accepted as a member of a strong female group. Is it a credit to Black sisterhood that Black women tolerate weak, dumb women that can be accepted and protected within its ranks? Or do Black women simply have a double standard of judging behavior where certain weaknesses are accepted among females but are not tolerated in males, even though males have more pressure placed on them by the greater society and would be more likely to cave in to those same weaknesses?

In any event, Robin wants a man (basically Russell), two babies, and the status of housewife as long as she's not treated like one (I'm not sure I know what that means). She doesn't want to have to worry about money for things like phone bills and rent increases. She really wants a house, wants to take weekend trips and do charity work. Just your basic Black woman's wish list. Nothing too heavy here. But instead of just playing it straight and honest, some mystical power told her that the way to her goals was best reached by playing games with a sincere man who likes her named Michael.

"I just heard the doorbell. Before I answered it, I checked to
make sure the flowers I bought myself with the card signed by
a man I made up were prominently displayed. I want Michael
to think he's got some competition." (P. 52 Waiting to Exhale)

Why in the world Black women do things like this, I'll never know. Do
they have some secret scientifically based study that proves these tricks actually
help them in getting what they want? All it seems to do is add to the general
climate of deceit, one upmanship and competition that doesn't do anything
positive for the relationship. But even this could be tolerated if they would just
except the consequences. Its when they talk about wanting an *honest* man
when they are the ones who start dumb games like this that you feel like
stuffing newspapers in their mouths.

Its not enough that Robin has screwed and been screwed by a generous
number of the Black men in town. She has to come up with her own ranking
scale on how good or bad they were, and then she broadcasts the news to all of
her girlfriends.

Robin does not get turned on sexually by Michael and thinks he's funny-
looking and rebels at the idea of bearing his children. Being the honest, sincere
woman that she is, she accepts all the gifts, money and goodies that he showers
on her and then pronounces him a sucker and a chump. At the same time that
she's trying to get rid of him, she swears that she is going to repay the loan he
made to her to pay a tax bill.

Michael, like most Black men who know what they want, is not taking
the hints that Robin is dissatisfied in the relationship. He's willing to *hang in
there,* which, though an admirable quality in other aspects of life, gets you
designated as a sucker in the eyes of many Black women. Michael finally
backs away after pledging love for Robin, and agrees to chill. For Robin,
Russell is still the man and she checks him out again. Russell's claim to fame
is that he screws and dresses well, is fine, and is assumed to be a person who
can father pretty babies. The same criteria of male excellence that you would
expect to hear from an eighteen-year-old junior high school drop out from the
projects in the Big city, you are hearing instead from this thirty-six-year-old
woman who does multi-million dollar deals at work every day.

In classic form and fashion, Robin shows incredible jealousy when
Michael has the nerve to show up at a public affair with another woman on his
arm shortly after his break up with Robin. Gloria reminded her that she had no
reason to be jealous because she was the one who pushed for the break up. The
other two women vaguely agree with her. It might have been the only part of
the entire book where at least three of the four women agreed to a basic
principle of human fairness. But I wasn't impressed.

There's not much to say about Robin other than "she's got to have it". After she includes some new brother in her stable of studs she gets pregnant by Russell who she then cancels out completely. Now you don't have to be a rocket scientist to conclude that Russell was bad news for any sister. But women have a way of discounting any sense of legitimacy from a person who is generally looked at as a bad character. In other words, once Black women give you their stamp of disapproval, then *nothing* you say is to have *any* weight, forever. Russell asked Robin a legitimate question on page 406. He asked how he could be sure that the baby was his. No woman wants to hear that question because the question suggests that the woman was loose and slept around with several people. But in this case Robin *was* loose and *did* sleep around with several people and did not use condoms all the time. Robin got mad at the question and her friend Bernadine backed her up.

Why oh why don't women own up to their own mess? While Russell did use Robin, Robin used Russell too. She had made up her mind that she wanted a baby by a certain age and Russell's value to her was based in part on her idea that he would "sire" a pretty baby. Once she became pregnant, she did a typical woman thing. The baby they conceived together was all of a sudden *hers* and hers alone. She wasn't even going to tell him about it until "its too late to do anything except to have it". So who is using who? The reader is lulled into thinking that Robin is 100% Miss Good Girl and that Russell should be taken out and hung. No! Robin got exactly what she wanted, not just a baby, but a "pretty" baby by Russell, a married man, and not Michael, a man who loved and wanted to marry her. After Russell gave her exactly what she wanted, the greatest gift of all, Robin then feels justified in calling no good Russell a bastard, a M F, and anything else she can think of. She got what she wanted, and plotted to get it all along. Anybody that doesn't see that and doesn't call *that* using, is one sorry son of a you know what. Robin is the ultimate user, and is completely disqualified from consideration by "good Black men."

Gloria Matthews

Gloria is about the only woman in the book who occasionally behaved like she had some principles or morals. Her Catholic upbringing forced her to have a son that she originally had no intention of having. As a single parent, she did a good job of not only raising her son, but of being a mom to many neighborhood kids. She was a hard worker who seldom left her business and was an all-around good person.

Her biggest problem was her weight. Viewed as being some seventy or more pounds overweight,,she was still considered pretty by her friends. Her more pounds overweight,,she was still considered pretty by her friends. Her weight, religion and responsibilities to her son and business made her "socially crippled and emotionally bankrupt for years." She forgot about men. But her son was leaving home for college, and she had to think about the type of life she would live in his absence. Would it include men? Gloria slowly developed a relationship with a new neighbor about twelve years her senior, a widower from the South. A handyman type, he came over occasionally and they shared simple pleasures as he repaired various mechanical things around the house. It was the purest aboveboard relationship in the entire book. That is not to say that Gloria was ever satisfied or had overcome the wall that she had built between herself and males in general. She wasn't rushing sex and sex certainly wasn't rushing to her.

But as nice as Gloria was, she wasn't above doing what many women do; which is to talk about things she really knew nothing about and putting men into one broad category. On page 180, Gloria is home from a short night out with the girls, which once again proved of limited value for her. There were no dances and no new introductions. "What's the use," she ponders? Then, on her sofa, she begins to question why Black women have to suffer so. She asks in part:

> "Why are we all ᴖut here by ourselves? Are we just going to
> have to learn how to live the rest of our lives and make do with
> inferiors like Russell and John and maybe even the Michaels of
> the world? "

Now let's examine this statement in some detail so that maybe some real meaning will emerge from this asinine remark by Gloria.

First of all, there are reasons why men don't talk as much as women do. And there are reasons why performance, actions, and accomplishments make up a large part of the male communication process. You see, males realized a long time ago that anybody can talk, but not everybody is *qualified* to talk. So men adopted the principle that you have to *earn* the right to say certain things, give certain instructions and give pieces of advice. Just because you had a mouth and knew the English language didn't necessarily give you the right to expect everyone to listen, to believe or obey you when you opened your mouth. Thus if you are on the bench as a reserve in a team sport, you don't have a right to call the winning play for the team. That is the coach's right, the captain's right, or the star player's right. Due to their accomplishments and assumed knowledge, they can speak that others might listen and obey. On the battle field, the general, not the private, calls the battle plan. At work, it's the boss or the foreman or the manager that talks about what will or will not be, not the new employee.

But among women, it seems nobody is anymore qualified to speak than anybody else, or each woman is as equally *unqualified* to speak as the next woman. Among women, anybody that has a mouth can just open it and say whatever they feel like, whether they have any knowledge, experience or understanding of what they are talking about, or not.

Now, getting back to Gloria and her reflection, here we have this obese woman, seventy to a hundred pounds overweight, embarrassing even her son by her appearance. Her first question is "Why are we all out here by ourselves? " Well for starters, in her specific case, there's at least seventy pounds of fat that nobody wants anything to do with. Most people do not connect excessive weight with sexual attractiveness. This holds true for both men and women, but especially for men. Right or wrong, good or bad, that has been the way it has been for at least the last 100 years . The second reason why Gloria might be alone is that she has taken herself out of the social scene and directed her energy to her church, son, business and community work. If you take yourself out of the game, you can't win the game. That shouldn't be difficult to understand. She also had built a wall between herself and men in general and considered them less important than her girlfriends. Thus, unless you expect a man to drop down your chimney like Santa Claus, you are not likely to have a man in your life. Now these may not be the same reasons why Robin, Savannah or Bernadine are alone, but they clearly describe Gloria's situation. Besides, a lot of times her girlfriends are not alone.

The second part of her statement asks if she and her friends have to "make do with inferiors like Russell, John and maybe even the Michaels of the world". In this instance Gloria symbolizes the woman who just opens her mouth and says anything without thinking. She *is NOT QUALIFIED TO TALK ABOUT INFERIORS*. Based on a quality of feminine appeal, physical beauty, she is clearly at the end of the line. From a man's point of view of communication, she has not accomplished enough to earn the right to judge people as inferiors. She is a heart attack waiting to happen (and, in fact, did happen) yet *she* calls others "inferior? " At least their supposed inferiority didn't lead to a near death as hers almost did. And who said she and her friends were "promised" better? Black America and White America are at war and have been for over four hundred years, but few sisters seem to want to acknowledge it. The greatest casualties of this war are Black men, in case you haven't noticed. We lose our lives, our liberty (jail) and our sanity (drugs). The greatest beneficiaries of this war is the Black woman (in terms of new opportunities offered to them). Sorry we can't clone ourselves and be with you right now, but we are a little crazy, detained or dead right now! Check on us later to see if we have survived! Black men are in a war but I don't think many

Black women will realize it until there are only a handful of Black men to chose from. When this happens, many will cross racial lines and marry the enemy anyway, and *still* won't have a clue as to what the hell is going on. More than likely they will blame the Black man for his own extinction.

The third thing that Gloria did was to put Russell, John and Michael all in the same bag of inferiority. How in the hell it that justified? Russell represents lust and non-accountability. Michael is about love and accountability. Russell takes and Michael gives. The only thing that links Russell and Michael is that they both slept with Robin. Why is Michael an inferior? Because Robin didn't like the way he made love and she let everybody know it? That doesn't make sense. And John is inferior? Why, because he hurt Bernadine by not letting her start her business, or because he left her for a White girl? If I could get a *quarter* for every Black woman that would be willing to live with a guy in style for eleven years and then break up with him and get nine hundred and sixty four thousand dollars, I would have *more than* nine hundred sixty four thousand dollars myself and John would become the most popular inferior man in Black American history.

As nice as Gloria seemed to be, she was as potentially problematic as the rest of them. Still, by stretching ones imagination, even with the weight, Gloria may be qualified to be on some peoples list of "good Black woman looking for a good Black man."

Bernadine Harris

If Gloria represent the most principled character in the book, and the one most easily sympathized with, Bernadine was the opposite. Bernadine was close to the total package of Black female attitudes and reactions that are a major stumbling block in the further development of the Black community today.

In the beginning, Bernadine did all the right things in her marriage and her husband's business to make both the business and the marriage a success. She expended a great deal of time and effort, she wore multiple hats to make the business survive and grow and to make the marriage do likewise.

John, her husband, was not sitting on his butt doing nothing. He was building his company, which in the United States of America, is one of the hardest things for a Black man to do, especially in a White male industry stronghold like computers and high tech. Ms. McMillan does not give John Harris much credit for his accomplishments because then the reader might not hate him and may begin to see his side of the story. That would defeat the purpose of books like this.

As it turns out, Bernadine is not happy with the rich lifestyle that her husband seems to require. But it is not clear exactly *when* she started to become unhappy. We do not know at what point she really said to herself, "this is not taking me where I want to go." We find out that Bernadine "has no courage" in so far as telling her husband what she did and did not want to do and why. Being the aggressive type, and insensitive, he pushed onward and assumed that she would both see and appreciate the big picture when they "arrived." In this sense she was the opposite of Savannah, who wanted her man *to be* what he was aspiring to be; Bernadine was helping her man get there.

It is clear that Bernadine was too compromising of her goals and needs, and went overboard in conforming with her husband's wishes. But it is too simplistic to blame John for being a domineering family leader. Many women of all races want a take-charge husband exactly like John. Black men have been consistently ridiculed for not being capable of producing enough aggressive men like John Harris. There are no correct or obvious formulas or role models for modern, aggressive Black men to follow, so they go for what they know, and a lot of their mistakes are only clear in hindsight and then only in certain people's eyes. Bernadine's sense of frustration didn't really come out until years after the marriage.

So what we have here is something of a tie. There is either double blame or no blame at all. John was pursuing the American dream that he thought was important, and Bernadine could not figure out and express where she was coming from. The question is, was the root cause of her failure to talk to John her genuine fear of making it on her own? I think so.

When you examine Bernadine's story, a couple of contradictions hit you in the face. In the first place, on page twenty-four, the writer McMillan says:

"They had both known for over a year that *everything* (emphasis mine) between them was wrong. There weren't any more excuses, apologies or explanations for his not coming home. Intimacy was out of the question. Neither desired the other."

On page twenty-eight, McMillan clearly suggests that Bernadine is not surprised at this separation in her life when Bernadine says to herself:

"Take it easy, Bernadine, *You knew this was coming* (emphasis mine) so let's not get theatrical." A couple of sentences later the narrative says, "Bernadine wanted to tell him that he could take his little Barbie doll and leave now." Then on page thirty-two, it says in reference to very poor sexual relations between Bernadine and John, "Of course by then you knew something was terribly wrong, but you didn't know how to fix it *and didn't want to* (emphasis mine)."

Yet on page thirty-five the author wants us to believe that the separation is a big shock to Bernadine. "I hadn't planned for this, she thought. Never even

anticipated what I'd do if my marriage didn't last. It was *supposed* to last."
(emphasis McMillan)

There are several points to be noted here:

     1.   Bernadine, for all her intelligence and education, was clearly playing games with herself. She, like many women, did not want to assume the responsibility of making herself content, but rather wanted the man in her life to do that for her. When the men are successful in making themselves happy, they are made to feel guilty because they usually do not at that same time make their wives just *as* happy, which, after all, they are supposed to *understand is part of their job*. The woman's job, to her warped way of thinking is to simply sit and wait to be pleased by her man and hope he does all the right things. In this situation, John was doing his thing and discouraging Bernadine from doing hers, which was not good at all. But Bernadine did not stand up for what she believed in. The more meek and weak her own character became the more of a villain John became. We don't know what John would have done if Bernadine had ever put her foot down. Maybe she could have had her way. Maybe they could have reached a compromise, or would have divorced, and freed themselves earlier. Bernadine always had the power to shape her destiny in her own hands. She wasn't retarded. But she could have been like a lot of women: scared to put up, so instead she shut up.

     2.   As the above quotes show, Bernadine knew very well that her marriage was in trouble. But she failed to act on these problems just like she failed to act on her own personal goals. She neither relieved herself nor got off the pot. She knew something was wrong, "but didn't know how to fix it and didn't want to." Obviously she had lost value for her husband and marriage and didn't want to improve it. Yet she didn't take the action to go on her own either. In this situation, a person of inaction, will always find themselves the subject to somebody *else's* action who is not afraid to act. Thus Bernadine was subject to John's decisions and her own indecision.

     3.   There are many negative consequences of *not knowing Black history and not understanding Black people*. One of the biggest mistakes made by ignorant Blacks is that they assume that the typical White American success story is *supposed* to be their own story. And it is very hard for them to see otherwise.

     When Bernadine thought the marriage was *supposed* to last, where did she get that idea from? Did she get it by understanding what usually happens to Black people in America? Not hardly, because that's not the reality. Did she get it from Cosmopolitan magazine and Danielle Steele novels? Perhaps. Did she get that idea from her own determination to work and do whatever was necessary to make her marriage work? Of course not, because she knew things were wrong and "didn't know how to fix it and didn't want to." Bernadine obviously lived in a fantasy and didn't want to deal responsibly with reality. Because so many of the readers of this book were Black women, and because so many of them think as irresponsibly as Bernadine, I'm sure she was a favorite character. But this is the type of sister that routinely drives brothers crazy because they refuse to carry their own weight, yet get mad when you get tired of carrying them too. It all goes back to the fundamental assumption held by many women that they are entitled to guarantees and promises carved in stone. Life was never that way even in Africa. A Black man certainly *can not* insure much of anything in White America. Sooner or later Black women will understand the connection between political and economic power for Black people and their own domestic wishes and tranquility. Guaranteed Marital Bliss? A pipe dream if there ever was one!

On page thirty-five we see what Bernadine was fearful of all the time, why she didn't make a move, and why she's really angry at John Harris:

"You son of a bitch she said, and jumped up from the toilet to look at herself again. Who's gonna want me? How am I supposed to start over, when in fact I'm not starting over? This is the middle of my damn life! And I've got two kids!"

A lot is revealed in this passionate outburst. Obviously the major point is that Bernadine doesn't really think that they should stay together for the sake of improving a dead marriage. But she also wants to be spared the challenge of finding a new man, something she has serious doubts she can do. But even more surprising was that her immediate concern would be for a new man instead of the new freedom she would enjoy to live and do whatever she wanted. If John had been such a tyrant all these years, wouldn't she likely have given more thought to what it would be like to be free? If she wanted her catering business so badly, wouldn't she think that now would be the time to make that dream come true? If she so hated the house among the White folks, wouldn't she have though about all the new places where she was free to go, including back to Philadelphia if she wanted to? But no, that was not the case. This woman is a carbon copy of the kind of woman I have been referring to since the beginning of this book. This is the kind of woman who has lost the ability to appreciate herself as an independent, functioning, important, worthy human being capable of standing alone. She can only see her worth and status as a reflection of the man she is with. Which is why she is immediately thinking about the *next* man even before she is even close to divorcing her current one! She is thinking about her next man because she is *trying to picture her next identity,* and she needs to see the next man in her own mind in order to see who *she'll be.* That is very sad, but a lot of sisters, a lot of women period, are captives of this mind-set. When you build a life based on role-playing rather than your own substance, life could easily end up like this. By far the saddest comment was her last; "And I've got two kids!" Now this statement does not mean I've got two kids, how am I going to take care of them? It means, I've got two kids, how am I possibly going to find a good man who will accept the burden of two kids? She is saying that her kids are *in the way,* excess baggage that she has to lug around while she searches for her next man. That is the saddest part of this sister's outburst. Instead of thinking about how the divorce would effect her children, she was worrying about how her children would affect her ability to get beyond her divorce. If that is not self-centered, then I don't know what is.

Did Terry McMillan actually expect people to like these characters? The way Bernadine was described by the author, her weakness was supposed to be seen as a *spirit of cooperation* in helping her husband build his business. That might not be totally invalid, but you miss an important point if you buy into the characterization one hundred percent.

The other thing that hurt this lady's feelings and demonstrated how indecisive she was about what to do with her life can be gleaned from this passage on page 25:

"Now she looked over at her husband, thinking she had wanted
to be rid of him, had been trying to conjure up the courage, the
nerve, the guts, to tell him to leave, but she didn't have that
much courage."

A couple of sentences later it says:

"But he beat her to the punch."

Bernadine didn't expect her marriage to last forever. She wanted John to leave, but she didn't ask him to because, according to McMillan, she didn't have the guts or courage. But is that really the situation? Did she not have the courage to ask him to leave or did she not have the courage to face the new world that she would have to face if he *did* leave? My feeling is that she feared the latter more than the former, and it was the latter fear that kept her from doing the former. Then he beat her to the punch. He pushed her into a cold pool into which she was thinking about jumping but wasn't prepared for yet. Further on Page 25 it says:

"Not only was he leaving her for another woman. He was
leaving her for a *White* woman. Bernadine hadn't expected this
kind of betrayal, this kind of insult."

Now my question is if two people know that a relationship has run its course, why does it really matter who leaves who or who leaves first if its clear that it is in fact over? If the marriage ever had a good phase, the bad feeling should be about the failure to hold on to those good times, not what the person will be doing with someone new next week. Bernadine was having an ego attack. The very person (John) she counted on to make her who she was now was being taken away in the rudest way and made her feel like a nobody. What was more important, her image or her marriage?

John's leaving was a good thing for Bernadine. I think even she would say that in a calm moment. Her focus should be on how to plan and reconstruct the rest of her life. In other words, dealing with reality, the reality she always knew was coming and the reality that she wanted to make happen herself. But instead of doing that, she focused on "what's John getting, who is John getting, how can I hurt John," rather than how to help herself. If the only way she feels that she can help herself is to hurt John, then that's sad too. But there are a lot of sad sisters out there and many of them who read this book were pulling hard for Bernadine to hurt John as much as she could, because they are just as disturbed as Bernadine is!

Bernadine's first major sick act to hurt John was to pile *all* of his clothes, into the BMW that he had bought *for her* and set the whole thing on fire in front of the house. This is what has been historically described as "Nigga shit". "Nigga shit" is a type of self-destructive, vindictive and completely uncalled for behavior that people act out to "get even" with someone who has hurt them. "Nigga shit" has led to the death of thousands of Black people at the hands of other Black people. Very often, immediate family members have been the killers. No one is suggesting that Bernadine cannot hurt as deeply as some of the poorest sisters from the urban projects. But for her to *act exactly like* the poorest sisters from the urban projects by committing such a violent act says something about the inherent emotionalism of many Black women. If John had been her emotional equal, if his response had mirrored the response of some ignorant, poor brothers from the hood, the character of Bernadine would probably have been *killed* before we got to page one-fifty. You know it and I know it. The burning of John's assets could be seen as a spontaneous emotional act done to vent the rage of marital conflict. One could stretch their imagination and learn to accept that as a semi - reasonable explanation for what happened.

But Bernadine was a bitch with a Capital B. Her next deed, five days later, was to sell even more, much more, of John's assets in a give-away lawn sale. This was nothing but premeditated, unadulterated maliciousness. As proof, note her closing statement on page ninety five:

"Since you want to start a new life, motherfucker, see what
starting from scratch feels like."

Men believe that all things have their consequences. That when you commit the crime, you do the time. That for every action there is an equal and opposite reaction. That what goes around comes around. All this folk wisdom is a way of saying that there is no way under the sun that Bernadine Harris should be allowed to go unpunished for her actions according to the way men view fairness both in the law of the land and the law of the street. It is absolutely beyond the comprehension of most Black men why their women can't, don't, won't see that. How much do Black women think their offended emotional state is worth in dollars and cents?

On page twenty-three, John Harris told his wife that she could have the house. The BMW that she destroyed was her own. He told her she would get money and support for the kids. He had no intentions of having her start over from scratch, materially speaking, anyway. But Bernadine wasn't thinking about that. She just wanted to express the rage, envy and jealousy towards John, a person who knows what he wants and how to get it, in contrast to herself, who doesn't know what she wants and doesn't have a clue how to get it. She wanted him to start from scratch because that's where she felt that she would be starting. John could have been faulted for not coming by with a van and picking up all of his stuff, but maybe he had no reason to believe she was this far out of control and maybe he never even heard about the car fire until days later.

The single most important reason why this book is being written is to demonstrate the role that money plays in defining the nature of the relationships between Black men and Black women. Few situations demonstrate this better than the fight between Bernadine and John Harris as explained by author Terry McMillan. For an entire page or more, beginning on page twenty-nine, Ms. McMillan presents a long list of expensive material things that she wants us to believe mean little or nothing to Bernadine Harris. It includes the beautiful house and its expensive landscaping, the pool and the tennis court. The author names the designer label clothing, the jewelry, the kids toys, the kitchen equipment, and so on. You get the clear impression that riches were unimportant to Bernadine. They didn't make her happy and we're told that "all of this" is John's trip to keep up with White folks. The fact that Bernadine destroyed her own BMW car when she burned the clothes was pretty damn convincing that she had reached a point of feeling disdain toward material things and riches. She certainly could have gotten much more money during her yard sale, right? And she seemed really pissed off with John that he would think money was even a factor with her when he spoke about his desire for a divorce. Instead of assuming that he was trying to assure her of financial security, she thinks he is trying to buy her off. Page 34 shows Bernadine's anger:

" I love my kids," he said, "And I'll make arrangements."

"Arrangements? "

"You'll get money, don't worry."

"Money? " That's what this was really all about. Division.

Dollars. Divvying. He's scared I'm going take his ass to the cleaners. According to McMillan on Page 25:

"All she wanted to do was repossess her life. To feel that sense of relief when the single most contributing factor to her uttermost source of misery was gone."

One day in the twenty-first century, during a routine human genetic research project, a great discovery will be made. Some junior researcher, looking for something else, will discover the gene that causes the *greedy divorce settlement syndrome.* It is disease found mostly in women and it forces them to file divorce papers asking for ridiculous amounts of money *regardless of what their mouths say.* It will be found to be a dominant gene but totally inactive throughout the duration of a marriage. As the marriage comes to an end, a chemical reaction takes place in the blood forcing this inactive gene to activate and grossly effect the functioning of the brain and the mental equilibrium of the female. With this loss of brain function the primary symptom will be a consistent lack of coordination and agreement between what the woman's mouth says and what her divorce papers propose. With this scientific discovery, one of the great puzzling phenomena of all time will be solved. Women lie about money because they can't help it. Its in their genetic make-up. Men have been suspecting this for the last hundred years, but we will have to wait until the next century to have our suspicions scientifically confirmed.

Bernadine, a supposedly non-materialistic, abused spouse, becomes obsessed with getting as much money out of her husband as she can. John has made all kinds of moves, some legal and some illegal, to protect his interests. But he agreed up front to a)give her a home that's more like a palace; b) pay any amount of child support a Judge deems fair; and, c) give Bernadine three-hundred thousand in cash.

Three hundred Thousand dollars would be more than what 99.9% of all single or divorced Black mothers have ever received from their children's fathers in the history of the Planet. But guess what? Three hundred Thousand is not enough for Bernadine, who Terry McMillan said "just wanted to repossess her life and to feel a sense of relief." In her normal yet impressively sophisticated style of communication, Bernadine tells her husband, "My pussy is worth more than Three-hundred-thousand dollars." (Page 131)

For the rest of the book, Bernadine doesn't do much more than a) feel sorry for herself; b)screw married men like her semi-whorish girlfriends, who spend a lot of time complaining about men doing the same thing; and, c) fighting to get as much money, as possible from her ex-husband using, of course, a White female lawyer to do it. I guess she figured her husband is using a White woman against her, so she would use one against him. Finally, there was an agreement reached and Ms. Bernadine's evil, greedy ways paid off in dollars and cents. She received Nine-Hundred and Sixty Four Thousand dollars.

She then proceeded to do what Black people always seem to do when they get money: get rid of it as fast as possible. Bernadine had a list of people and groups in mind and seemed determined to prove herself a good person by giving them all a share of her "hard-earned money." She had a new business idea that she wanted to try, and that was part of her agenda also.

But people like Bernadine will never become good people because weak character has a way of preventing you from doing the right thing on the basis of principle and the right reasons. On the other hand weak character encourages you to do destructive things for the wrong reasons and because of the absence of principles.

After page 338, I felt that Bernadine should be put in an institution and instructed hourly, without sleep, for the next five consecutive years on how to think about someone other than her damn self.

This is what page 338 reveals about Bernadine:

"See what you did, you little bitch!" John junior said.

"You made her cry."

"I did not!"

"You did too."

"I did not."

Bernadine heard John junior slap Onika. "That's for having such a big mouth! You think she's supposed to be happy knowing that White lady is having a baby with our daddy? " She didn't hear Onika respond. She must be in shock, Bernadine thought, and started laughing. Served her ass right. She needed to be slapped. Onika ran her damn mouth too much sometimes. Said the first thing that came to her mind. And he called her a bitch! Now Bernadine was grinning. It was good to know her son was on her side.

"If you go near her room," Bernadine heard him say, "I'll slap you again, only harder."

Bernadine got up, cracked the door, and peeked through it. John Junior was pacing around the couch as if he had a lot on his mind.

"Now sit your little ass down on this couch, and say, I talk too much, five hundred times. And don't even think about getting up until I tell you to!"

Onika started to oblige.

Bernadine covered her mouth to stop from laughing out loud. She had closed the door before Onika made it to fifty-six.

The little girl being slapped is only about six or seven years old. The boy doing the slapping is about eight. Divorce is hard on many aspects of a human being. It hurts egos, health, pocketbooks, self confidence levels, so on and so forth.

But should a human being sink so low as to have her own children act as stand in combatants acting out the hostilities of the divorce in the form of physical violence against each other for the cathartic and amusement benefits of the sick bitch of a mother?

I hope that every Black woman in America who read that passage cringed and wondered as I did, if McMillan had stepped over the line. If we are going to use children like this, then we don't need children, and we don't need marriage, and we don't need to exist on the same planet with other animals because other animals have more decency than that.

Summary on Terry's Girls

Sex and hype have been used to sell everything in America; so the fact that Ms. McMillan's book continues to sell well is not a big shock. This is not in any way a put down of the book or the work or MS. McMillan, because there are many products with sex and hype that do not sell well for any number of reasons. Clearly the secret of the success of this book is the ability of many common folk (mostly women) to identify with both the womens' challenges and characters. I accept at face value the imbalance in the numbers of so-called qualified Black males in proportion to the supposed abundance of available single Black females. It is not something that I have experienced in my personal life in at least the last fifteen years, but I accept it as so.

But I fine it a bit scary to accept the idea that in this book are representative samples of the kinds of personalities and problem people that "free" Black men have to deal with to find marriage partners. As a free Black male, I say none of these women are worth a damn in terms of making a life-long commitment to.

In all fairness, it probably isn't fair to lump Gloria in with the other women. But what we don't know is whether Gloria would be like her friends if she didn't have the weight problem, if men were attracted to her, and if she could rekindle her sexual desires. If the company she keeps is an indication of where her head is, chances are good that she would be like the rest.

Like a molecule represents a bundle of atoms, these women represent merely a bundle of wants. They want and they want and they expect and they are looking for. After four hundred pages, I gained no understanding of what they wanted to *give to any relationship*. The beauty of their relationships were defined strictly in terms of "how he makes me feel," sexually, emotionally and otherwise. The only people they seemed prepared to give to besides themselves was their children and a few Community projects were thrown in. What they have to offer a man or the relationship is a total mystery. Each woman (except Gloria) has a very exaggerated view of the value of their vagina. Bernadine says hers is worth three hundred thousand dollars. Savannah says hers will be much harder to get after her experience with Charles. Robin probably won't share hers as much after the baby is born.

Gloria has to start again from scratch.

On page 327, when they were having their little party, they all pronounced themselves good catches because they were good lays with good hearts. Yeah, if you like larceny in your hearts, they have good hearts indeed.

This is a fiction book, but I kept asking myself, do women approaching 40 actually telephone their female buddies and detail each other's sexual exploits? Do a half-dozen women already know if a men can do it or not before he even gets home and takes a shower? Teenage Black boys fabricate stories of sexual conquests to tell their friends to demonstrate their manhood. But by the time men hit twenty-five you are considered one insecure and immature brother if you still have the need to do a blow by blow sex description to your friends. It's assumed that everybody is laying down with somebody at that age and the manhood challenge has moved on to something else. To think that close girlfriends still relish in detailing their sex lives when they are well into their thirties is surprising and sad. How could any woman think she had a "good heart" if she felt obligated to review the week's sex highlights with their friends? Gloria's salon is the obvious next step in the communication system. In two weeks, a hundred women could know where the wart on your peter is or if you have one. These so-called upwardly mobile professional women are the pits as far as integrity and privacy go. To love one is to put your life story in the street.

It's ironic that on page three-twenty-eight, the group seems to agree that the men don't seem to know what they want when it is painfully obvious that they are the ones so confused about life, men and what they want. It's pathetic. Nobody can out-perform Black women in blaming others, (usually Black men) for what they themselves are most guilty of.

Commit myself to Gloria, Savannah, Bernadine or Robin? What could a Black man commit that would not be taken for granted, consumed, wasted or shared among this pack of self-centered, manipulating wenches? No ladies, I don't think you should wait to exhale before finding the "right brother." If all of them knew what this book says about you, you wouldn't get another chance to breathe again for the next twenty years. At least. Could we see the next group of supposedly deserving women please?

WRESTLING WITH SOLUTIONS

What Has To Be Healed?

There is no part of the Black male-female relationship that can not use some improvement. Even the domination of the Black woman's point of view on male-female relationships during the last fifteen years doesn't change the fact that even this perspective needs further development. The last fifteen years during which today's Black man has heard this critical perspective might seem like a long time, but it's brief compared to how long Black women have been quietly frustrated in America. Most Black men still don't know what pains Black women, or they care too little about what pains them. The work of educating and sensitizing Black men has a long way to go and must continue. Obvious and subtle forms of sexism must be stopped. Having said that however, it is time for Black women to use some of their energy and intellect to understand the Black male also. Hen sessions like that described in *Waiting To Exhale* might do a lot to make sisters feel better temporarily, but it does nothing to increase their understanding of Black men or improve the relationship between the sexes. To the contrary, each participant in a hen session uses the pain of other women to increase the chip she carries on her own shoulder towards all Black men and we all suffer.

This last portion of this book presents concrete steps that men and women can take to try to heal the things that hurt us. Actually the problems discussed thus far contained within them at least a hint of their own solution. For example, if females go astray and lose certain values at fourteen years old by dating older boys, the obvious way to deal with this is for parents to intervene. As a parent, you can advise young daughters to socialize within their own age group. Or you can talk to daughters about the temptations and risks that have been previously mentioned if they have expressed an interest in dating older boys. I make no pretense in offering specific success formulas for a happy relationship. To the contrary, I am convinced that all relationships, like life itself, will create some pain and frustration. All that I can offer are simply ideas that may help in damage *control*, not damage *prevention*.

How Do You Heal?

How do men and women make up after a serious argument or "fight"?

How does a son or daughter get back into the good graces of parents they've angered?

How does a convicted criminal start the process of paying his debt to society?

The common denominator in all three reconciliations is the *admission of wrong doing* and the demonstration of an apologetic attitude even for acts one may have committed unknowingly.

An incredible amount of forgiveness is unleashed when people cast aside their self-righteousness, their pretentious games and their ego and admit to doing wrong. Slates are wiped clean and a new beginning commences when people level with each other and give up their claim to perfection and blamelessness. To the extent that this is true, then the relationships between Black men and women will improve when each party admits to their faults, misunderstandings, and short-comings and tries hard to avoid repeating their mistakes. Only then can a healing process truly begin. If a person is too stubborn to admit to their transgressions, they have, by their behavior and attitude, made a statement which suggests that their ego is more important than the relationship.

For the last fifteen to twenty years, Black men have been accused of every crime, problem, and disruption that has happened in the Black community. In many ways, directly and indirectly, Black men have admitted their crimes. We have confessed to our wives, mothers, girlfriends, police, lawyers, and judges, secret tape recorders and T.V. cameras. And while we await the consequences or serve out our sentences, we wait even longer for the true healing process with our women to begin. But it does not begin. It does not begin because women in general and in this instance, Black women in particular, are not about to admit that they have done *anything* worthy of even criticism, much less apology. Many Black women would have you think that they are blameless and guiltless of any of the chaos going on in the Black community. Think about that for a while. Are we to believe that women, raised in the same deprived ghetto conditions, as men, do not take on negative attitudes, suffer from low self-esteem and participate in some of the same self-destructive behavior as men? What medicine, magic spell or secret potion protects them from falling prey to their environment? Nothing. Women from the inner city do some of the same indefensible acts as men. But they aren't pursued by law enforcement officials anywhere near as forcefully as men. When they are caught, they aren't photographed for the newspapers or television nearly as often as men. It's as if any crime a woman commits is treated as minor.

Improvement in male/female relations will occur as soon as Black women admit to *their* roles in the destruction of our family relationships. Does this statement sound too general and vague? Let me be more specific.

First, women play an important role in the great demand for drugs because a significant portion of them get high. As with many things of value, they often expect to be given the drug, and most of the time it's from a man. Women have never been significantly portrayed as part of the drug trade. Spike Lee did us all a favor in his movie "Jungle Fever" when in at least two instances he showed what significant numbers of sisters are willing to do to get some crack cocaine. John Singleton, in *Boyz In The Hood,* also showed the Black woman's willingness to give oral sex to a stranger in exchange for drugs. It wasn't that we didn't know this before, but it was certainly a powerful reminder that the sisters are contributing to the decadence of our cities.

Another thing that sisters should confess to is the use of children as pawns. Some sisters use kids as pawns for their entire life. They deliberately become pregnant to get a man, and then threaten to separate the kids from the father to extort money from the father. At the same time they are doing all of this, they're claiming to the world that "I raised my son the best way I know how." How many kids in the Black community routinely enter their fatherless homes with thousands of dollars worth of goods and their mothers don't say a word? How many Black mothers silently benefit from the illegal activities of their children, and then when they're arrested claim, "He got mixed up in the wrong crowd" "I didn't know what he was into."

It is not easy for any single parent, even two parents, to raise children properly. We all make mistakes. And single mothers make millions every year. But in their publications, networks, caucuses, sororities, and social circles Black women give themselves so much credit for doing such a good job that it never dawns on them that they are in denial. They are lying to their children, their men, and themselves.

The point here is not to drag sisters down into the mud that many Black men already find themselves in. The point is to fairly distribute the blame for our problems so as to establish honesty in depicting what's really happening in the Black community.

How Do We Stimulate The Healing of Relationships?

The media, so vital in portraying the Black man as a villain and the destroyer of Black families, doesn't appear to be a useful tool for healing Black relationships. An occasional article in Essence Magazine, like the ones by Jill Nelson and LaDonna Mason referred to earlier, will set the record straight momentarily regarding women's mistakes, but it's hardly communicated to the masses of Black men. Women are quite willing to confess all types of dirt and indiscretions to other sisters. Somehow they act as if this cleans their hands.

It's to the *brothers* that these women pretend a holy piousness that makes you want to spit. Communication, that often-used word by the feminine gender, for many Black men begins only when sisters admit to their own screw ups and misdeeds as quickly as they are willing to point-out a brother's. But there is no reason to believe that such behavior will occur on a regular basis without some third-party encouragement. Frankly, it's difficult to imagine what person, event, or set of circumstances could have a significant effect, even temporarily, on the direction that Black male-female relationships are headed. Mothers Day and Fathers Day come and go each year without effect. Movies like *Jungle Fever* can be seen by millions of African Americans and yet I doubt there has been any impact in interracial dating and marriages. The *Bill Cosby Show* depicted the ideal Black family on T.V. during the 1980's and was ranked number one for most of its run, yet sociologists show that the Black family deteriorated more during the 1980's than at any other time in recent history. And for all the popularity of *Waiting To Exhale*, can anyone honestly say that they know of any Black relationships that were positively affected by it? So what vehicle can we use to improve the human dynamics between us? Our community's oldest national communication medium, *Ebony* magazine, ran an article on the healing of Black relationships, by one of our top psychiatrists (Stop The Male Bashing and Infighting, February 1993, Dr. Alvin Poussaint), and its impact was like water running off a duck's backside. Not only does our situation seem to be out of control, but it may now have reached the point where we are unable to *comprehend* what could control the situation, which is even scarier.

Let us imagine for the moment, that we *could* control the destruction of families and relationships. *Exactly how* would we measure our progress in that direction? Would it be:
  a) The decline in the number of Black men marrying White women?
  b) The decline of single Black women?
  c) The decline in the number of children born into fatherless homes?
  d) The increase in income in Black families (since we know that financial problems cause families to break up)?
  e) The decrease in teenage pregnancies?
  f) The decrease in crime?
  g) When the White media stops talking about how bad things are for Black folks?

We know we have a problem in our families and in our relationships. *How* are we to know *when* we are making progress when and if we *do* make progress? What criteria do we measure it by? Who do we count on to do the measuring, ourselves or White "researchers"? If this is the first time you've ever even read these fundamental questions, then you can understand why people give up on even caring after a while and forget about the problems. Which means you can also understand why things seem to get worse rather then better.

Repairs to relationships occur through individual agreements between people, but are significantly affected by many other things occurring in the society at large. The following information should be considered in the establishing of those agreements.

Downplay The Artificial Badges of Superiority

As a teacher, I am constantly looking for people, situations and sources of information that I can learn from. For the past several years I have found that two of the most dependable sources of insight and inspiration came from two very well known, nationally recognized speakers; Les Brown and Tony Robbins. Both of these men share something in common. Although they have people with some of the brightest minds in the country coming *to them* for insight and motivation, and have both become millionaires performing their services, neither of these men have a college education. I have three college degrees. But not for one second do I question if I can learn something from someone who doesn't have a degree. Unfortunately a lot of my brothers and sisters *do* allow the possession of a degree to significantly effect their decisions in personal and business relationships. The college degree is an artificial badge of superiority that some people need to wear constantly to help them believe that they are somebody. If the mere possession of a degree was Black peoples' ticket to salvation, I would be all for it. But most of us, especially those of us who have gone to college, know that it is not. A college degree can represent many different things and, in some instances it *is* important or relevant. But what a degree represents most of the time is a *permission slip*. It is a piece of paper that puts it's owner in a better position to ask permission to get a job so that they can learn the job and get paid. Many college grads know no more about many jobs than non-college grads. But they get a chance to learn the job because they have a degree. Beyond that, many people I think tend to place too much emphasis or importance on a degree.

If Black women insist that because they have one or more college degrees that therefore their Black husband must have one or more also, then they are letting an artificial stamp of approval take over their common sense. As this is being written, Les Brown is engaged to Ms. Gladys Knight (another non college grad). But judging by the artificial standards of some sisters that I know, Les Brown would not have been "good enough" to marry them because he lacked a college degree. In case it has not been made clear before now I will say it again: the Black man's definition of manhood and freedom is not based on absorbing European culture and values (which is what much of college is about), nor is it based on passing the White man's definition of what constitutes education.

Even for the brothers who have graduated college, what they learn is that discrimination practices not only continue but actually increase. Dr. Robert Staples in his book *The Urban Plantation* says on page 81

"A little noted statistic is the fact that as Blacks become more educated,the unemployment rate and income differential between them and their White peers is greater. In 1980 the U.S. census revealed the unemployment rate for Black male college graduates was 5.5 percent. While the rate for similar White males was only 1.6 percent. Data of a Black poll showed that nearly 60 percent of Black college graduates report having experienced racial discrimination in applying for a job, compared to less than a third of Blacks with less than a high school education."

Andrew Hacker in his book *Two Nations* says on page 104

"Moreover, blacks who do stay in school soon learn there is no assured payoff. Those who finish college have a jobless rate 2.24 times that for Whites with diplomas, a even greater gap than that separating black and White high school graduates."

A factor that is not talked about even in these and similar books is Black *underemployment*. It doesn't make a Black person, male or female, feel great when they have their degree and can only get a job that does not require a college education, or one that does not pay a wage that a college grad expects to make. Thus, you have many Black people with degrees, particularly males, who are not on the unemployment lines but who are still very frustrated with their job situation and prospects.

Does this mean that Black women should marry Black men who are dumb and poor? Of course not. But clearly Black women don't appear to be happy the way things are going in their lives now either. When you chase after other peoples' idea of happiness, you often discard your own needs. Ms. Audrey Edwards, for years one of the top writers at Essence Magazine, had this to say in a book she co-authored with Dr. Craig Polite, entitled *Children of The Dream* (page. 162)

"During the seventies, the same decade that marked the economic advance of Black women, the number of divorced black women in 26 reporting states rose from 27,320 to 46,757.

By 1987 it was 49,124. Black female-headed households grew from 716,000 in 1967 to 1,524,000 in 1989, with 46.5 percent of these families below the poverty line. The price of the black female's liberation, it seemed, were deteriorating relationships with her men and economic uncertainty for her children."

I believe that Black women should "measure" men *by what they produce* not by their formal education. Production is what is going to take Black people from where we are now to where we hope to go. Theoretically college degrees are one means to make that happen. But about 98 percent of our college degrees just places most of us back on a nicer, more modern, plantation and most of us simply pretend that that's not the case. *True production* is what you produce for yourself or your people. No other people has to be specifically told that but Black Americans. We so very often get *ourselves* confused with IBM, Xerox, General Foods and General Motors, and we use words like "we" and "us" and "our capability" as if we and these White companies were one big happy family. Apparently it takes some of us longer (a hundred years?) to realize some very basic truths. There's *us* and *them*; it's that simple.

Healing The Black Family

Several themes are consistent throughout this book, and one is the destructive and self-defeating results that emerge when Black men receive mixed messages from Black women. When Black men receive confusing or mixed messages they either; a) ignore the issue altogether because their efforts to understand are not being satisfied; b) believe what they want to believe; c) believe the last thing they heard and forget the rest (realizing that women have this thing about changing their minds; or d) turn rather hostile to the issue itself because it is an added source of unneeded frustration.

The issue of the Black family is one that is riddled with contradictions and mixed- messages. In realizing that the factors in understanding the Black family *are not* simple and that there is indeed a bit of a contradiction in all things, there still seems to be an unnecessary number of contradictions that Black men are being asked to understand. My analysis of the discussions on the Black family show a consistent pattern to protect the image of the Black woman and to consistently "dog" the Black man, all in an effort to generate positive action that would strengthen the Black family. In other words, much of the literature and dialogue seems designed to scold Black men into straightening up and "doing the right thing." This attitude comes across in articles, books and talk show discussions involving Black women who relish these opportunities to publicly express their negative feelings for everyone to hear. Black women in public often act like Black women in private. They act if as the sheer loudness of their tirades, whether it has the proper substance or logic or not, is enough to generate a positive response in their behalf. When Black men don't fall in line, it never occurs to the sisters to question the accuracy and honesty of what they have said. Instead they simply get upset over what they see as the Black mans obvious unwillingness to be cooperative, responsive or sensitive. This pattern seems to be happening in the written dialogue as well.

The crisis of the Black family is too serious an issue for Black men to respond in the normal way we respond to conflicting information. We can't ignore it; we can't believe only what we want to believe; we can't simply give all credence to the latest newsflash, or current issue, and, we can't turn hostile to the overall issue either. Black men must respond, but we must not respond exclusively to that which is thrown at us. Black men must have a say in defining the realities to which they are being asked and expected to respond.

What Do Black Women Actually Want?

It is quite ironic that women, who are generally considered better communicators and more expressive than men, pick the critical times when they are telling men what they want that they fail to get their ideas across. I believe that it's not that women don't know how to say what they want; but that they realize the selfish and contradictory nature of what it is they want. What Black women want is the best of all worlds. But they *don't want to sound* greedy or contradictory in wanting it. This is why women use the popular expression "having it all." No wonder then that the effort to understand women is viewed by men as a laborious, stressful job. Most men want to ask, "What the Hell do you want?"

Do Black Women Want:

a) A return to "the traditional strong Black Family" where all Black men could feel that they were head of the house (even if he made less money).

b) A redefinition of what constitutes a family so that women without husbands would feel that what they have is also "a family."

c) A new concept of Black family that would produce its own values, not necessarily the traditional ones, that would serve women, better.

At any one point or another you can find a spokesperson for Black women advocating any one of the above three options. What Black women have a problem with is *giving up anything as a result of getting any of what they want.* For example, if there was a return to (a) "the traditional Black family," as a lot of people remember it, the Black woman would do "women's work" (take care of children, cook meals from scratch), would be economically dependent on her husband, would not be respected for her brains, and would provide sex for her husband at his request, etc. Few women would want to place themselves back in those stereotypical sex roles. But that's what "the traditional Black family structure" could cost those Black women who advocate its return, but they wouldn't want to pay the price. At the same time, many women know that there is value in the old family structure because many of them grew up in it and have fond memories of their childhoods. They remember what they received from their mothers and they know they are *not passing it on* to their kids.

If sisters want (b) a redefinition of the Black family to include single women with children, they will have to shoulder responsibility in bad times as well as good. Right now if the child of a single parent family (female) does well, the woman will claim all the credit for the *positive development* of her offspring. Nothing is wrong with that if that is the way it actually is. But many times there are good fathers living away from the home who pay child support, buy gifts, attend ceremonies, help with homework and generally support children. But they are still assumed to be a non factor in his child's upbringing. Men have in general grown to expect and accept this role even if it is inaccurate and unfair.

But the response is quite different when the child of a single mother goes astray. From the very time a child is charged with a crime, the police, lawyers, grand juries, probation officers, juries and judges are all made aware that this child is from a "broken home" or "broken family" and therefore should be excused or given special consideration. What are all these people saying? They are saying that the real culprit is the absent father who "allowed" his child to get into trouble. Do you detect a double standard here? Women don't want their family to be considered "broken" if normal development of their children occurs. But when there is a problem with one of the children, then all of a sudden that family is conveniently referred to as "broken" and the only real guilty party is the one that "broke" the family, the man. In other words, the Black man may not receive credit for the good things he does, but he sure as hell will get blamed for the bad things he can be tied to. If Black women want single family parenting units recognized as intact family units, then they have to be prepared to take the responsibility of being at least part of the problem if their children screwup. It should be made clear that *poor parenting* by the custodial parent is significantly responsible for a child going astray.

Apparently that is not the way it is now. Right now the "broken home/absentee father" excuse is universally accepted because it meets everyone's need to shift the blame away from themselves and on to someone who is readily perceived as guilty as charged, the Black man. Its called scape-goating.

The idea of single women with children constituting a complete and legitimate form of family goes even farther than divorced or abandoned women. There are a number of women now who make the specific point that "they don't need a man in their life to feel like a whole person." After centuries of having their personal identity buried beneath the identity and status of their husbands, more woman are convinced that they can only be seen as a whole person without the presence of a man. That working on your own compels society to deal with you directly and not assume that your accomplishments are attributable to a more capable male partner. It is not important here to analyze how they arrived at this philosophical position, but only to say that quite a few women subscribe to this position, and they are not necessarily "man- haters" or lesbians. Many of these women adopt children rather than conceive their own, and that constitutes their family.

In addition to not wanting to need a man, there are some sisters who are not comfortable with a man needing them. Black women are quick to point to their history of being used sexually and financially by men. Given the fact that more Black women today are financially independent, they interestingly enough want to *make sure* that they are *not* viewed in a way that they find unacceptable (as a meal ticket, a free ride, a paycheck). Thus some women who have money and are in a position to actually share resources (because she's got something to actually share) are often the *very* women who do not share their money with boyfriends and mates. Why? Because she wants to be "treated like a woman" in the traditional sense, which means being catered to, wined, dined, and presented with gifts, all courtesy of the gentlemen in her life. I can understand how psychologically a sister reaches this point. She doesn't want her career success to deprive her of the routine benefits and the ego gratification that her less successful female friends and relatives enjoy all the time. Although it is understandable, it just undermines the foundation of what men understood the women's movement to be about. It says that, when all is said and done, women want to be treated as women of yesterday were treated, particularly when it suits their pocketbook. They want their cake and want to eat it too.

Dr. Warren Farrell has done a lot to work to cut through the double talk that women freely offer. Although I am aware that his studies focus on White American lifestyles, I am also aware that these are the same lifestyles that influence sisters. In this passage from page 359 of his book *Why Men Are The Way They Are*, he explains the fine line that men have to walk for women to feel comfortable in their relationship.

.... in contrast women have received a conflicted message in their attitude toward men: they want men to need them yet feel neediness is unmanly. They "turn off" to a man they feel they must "mother" -so only a little leeway is allowed between his showing neediness and being "too needy". This also creates a dilemma for men: he looks bad if he lets himself feel needy and looks bad if he doesn't let himself feel needy.

How do many women satisfy this basic human need to feel special to someone by feeling needed? By letting children need them. So one incentive for women to have children is for women to get part of their "power" of feeling needed from the "appropriate" outlet of children rather than from the inappropriate outlet of a needy man.

A needy man creates a fundamental void for a woman: he does not confirm her specialness as a woman to her peers, to her parents, or to herself; he does not confirm that she is able to attract a hero man."

In Mr. Farrell's explanation, you can understand how women can find contentment in a family unit comprised of just themselves and their children. They receive everything they need to support both their ideological and emotional needs. Ideologically they can say assert that "they don't need no man" and that they can take care of themselves. They can say that they also aren't so desperate for a man that they would "buy one" or allow any of them to spend her hard-earned money. On the other hand, she can meet her own material needs and also satisfy her desire to feel needed and important by smothering her children from her reservoir of love that has been placed off-limits to males. What we don't know often is whether sisters like this are truly happy or are just trying to convince themselves that they are happy. Are they happy for a long period of time or does the contentment wear thin after a while? And like Gloria in *Waiting To Exhale*, what do you do when the children are grown and you begin the next phase of your life? Do men start to look better, sound better or feel better? Do you adopt a new set of kids? Do you wait to be the fully involved grandmother? What's next?

For Black women who choose c) a new style of Black family that would create its own values, they are usually uncomfortable with that decision because it represents the unknown. Many Black women are uncomfortable with their new found freedom to be all that they can be because they don't want to fail in their professional efforts, and they also have a strong need to feel they are taking care of business at home. Black women are aware that "the job" has disconnected them from old friends, extended family members and family affairs. So Black women, a significant number of them at least, either don't know what they want or are uncomfortable with their selection of a home life style. That is understandable. This generation of Black workers is making the transition from the traditional roles to new lifestyles for the next century. It's quite understandable to admit confusion if the circumstances are confusing. But that's not what usually happens a lot of the time. Black women seldom admit that they are wrong or confused about such things. What they do well, however, is *place blame*. The husband or boyfriend will find themselves on the receiving end of an argument that is caused by the *internal contradictions and confusion of the lifestyle she is trying to design as she goes along*. The message that brothers read into this is: "She doesn't know what she wants", or "She wants too much", or "She can't pull off what she thinks she can pull off, and needs someone to blame when it all doesn't come together." It's a typical situation Black men find themselves in; while you are being sent mixed messages about what your lady supposedly wants or doesn't want, you are in the middle of a dammed if you do and damned if you don't situation.

If Black women are serious about healing the institution of marriage in the Black community, they have to do a much better job at identifying the most preferred workable lifestyle and realize there will always be trade-offs. Obviously each couple will iron out specifics as they develop in their relationship. But right now many Black men can't be complementary in a relationship because they aren't sure what they are suppose to complement. Ideally there should be some kind of national debate or discussion going on between Black men and women around this issue of lifestyle and values. But a lot of the 1960's emphasis on *unity* is gone. Black men and women at least tried back then to show a united front to the rest of the world, even if there were unresolved issues between us. Today, in the 1990's, the pendulum has swung all the way to the other side. It is popular for Black women today to seek the advice and guidance of a White (male or female) "mentor" on the job site. This White mentor's job is suppose to be to guide the sister over the hills and valleys that must be traveled to be successful in the work place. In advising how to navigate the pathways to success at work, this White mentor is also suggesting many specific practices that may conflict with success in the home. Thus, it's not enough for a brother's wife or girlfriend to be dictated to by a White supervisor, now these women seek other "unofficial bosses" called mentors to see where and how they can put in more time to get more brownie points for the next promotion or pay raise. So the lifestyle at home is in a sense being determined less by what the husband and child want or need and instead moves to the beat of the wants and advice of the wife's bosses and mentors at work.

Another development that mushroomed greatly during the eighties was the great increase in the number of Black women's organizations, and their need to put forth a specific Black woman's agenda. Because of the sheer number and variety of Black women's organizations today, there is a greater sense of division between the sexes. For example, as difficult as it is to get a Black person elected to an influential position, is it really in the best interest of Black *people* to have a local Black women's political caucus? And is it possible that that caucus might find themselves supporting a White female "progressive" candidate over a Black male candidate one day? The point being made here is that today, to show how *unrestricted*, how *free*, how *self determined* and *independent* she is, some Black women have a need to consult every one on important matters *except* the Black man. Some women feel that to discuss female issues with Black men is politically incorrect. It's viewed as caving in to stereotypical traditions and placing yourself back in the subservient position that the women's movement helped free them from. Some Black women experience a sense of power in being able to offer Black males "take it or leave it" propositions. It seems clear that it shouldn't have to be this way.

Marriage And The Black Economy

There is an African proverb which says "no matter how great an image, it must stand on something." This means that all things must have a foundation or a base on which to stand. Black marriages and Black families could possibly reach a point where all major problems were worked out (communication, fidelity, values etc.) and those relationships would still fall apart without a solid foundation. The foundation on which all families must rest is that which provides the basic needs of food, clothing, shelter, utilities (gas, heat, electric), health care and transportation. Without these basic needs being met, people can not maintain a normal life. And when they can not maintain a normal life, they will usually leave the situation where these basic needs are not being met and look for a situation where they can be provided. The need to live a normal life is usually stronger than the need to stay in a relationship where one can not live normally. Thus, when all is said and done, economics plays a paramount role in maintaining the structure of Black relationships.

The Black Family will not and can not be reconstructed without a much stronger economic foundation which Black people themselves largely control. Any idea that family stability can be based on jobs from White folks has to be erroneous if the job itself is not stable. Today even the dumbest among us realize that jobs are, by their nature, temporary. Thus we must discuss some of the requirements for this new Black economy.

The best way to begin conceptualizing a stronger Black economy is to see where we are now and where we should be. One of the best books on this topic is *Black Economics-Solutions for Economic and Community Empowerment* by Dr. Jawanza Kunjufu. Dr. Kunjufu's book gives a good analysis of Black economics, including our historical economic development and the current situation of "foreigners" owning stores in our community. One of the first things he notes is the frequency of various groups going into business versus the frequency of Black Americans going into business. On page 25 of Dr. Kunjufu's book the following figures are quoted:

"The business ownership ratio per thousand is 107 (Lebanese),93 (Syrians), 89 (Koreans), 65 (Japanese) 64 (whites), 60 (Chinese) 30 (Colombians) 21 (Jamaicans) 17 (Hispanics), and 9 for African Americans."

Black Americans go into business only half the time of the second lowest group measured. Black Americans should be playing catchup in terms of economic development. To catch up with anyone you must travel at a *faster rate of progress* for an extended period of time if one is to ever catch up.

While new Black enterprises are very important, it means very little if African Americans do not support such businesses. According to figures offered by Tony Brown and Black Enterprise Magazine, Black people only spend six percent of their income with African-American-owned businesses. This means that ninety four percent of their money is spent outside of the community. This six percent figure needs to be multiplied many times if Black businesses are to have a chance at surviving. One of the ways that this new support can come about is for African American businesses to do a better job at advertising their companies to our communities. Exchanging business cards at "networking sessions" is not nearly enough. Dr. Kunjufu cites the sad picture currently in Black advertising in two popular magazines.

"In one of the latest issues of Essence, there were 48 full page ads and only two of them were from African American companies. They were both hair care companies ... In one of the current issues (1991) of Ebony, there were 76 full page ads and only one was an African American company ... This is an unofficial qualitive look at the state of Black advertising and the interest in the ninth richest market in the world." (page 7)

Black people constitute about twelve percent of the American population. We take in about eight percent of its total income (about 300 billion dollars or more). But our total number of businesses account for a little over one percent. The total amount of money received by those businesses is less than one percent of all the money received by all businesses in the U.S. and this is after "tremendous growth in Black businesses" during the 1980's." These two statistics reinforce the previous point about how you must grow faster than your competition in order to register any significant advancement. Had Black people not had tremendous growth but merely stayed at pre 1980 numbers, we would have less than one half of one percent of the business receipts.

With all due respect to African American women, I do not envision them to be the driving force for the development of a stronger Black business community. While it is true that Black women as a group have or control the spending of more money than Black men, I do not see the sisters leading the way. While Black women, being more verbal than Black men, may be better salespeople than brothers, I still do not see sisters leading the business boom. The reason for this has been explained earlier. Women by nature are security-conscious and shun obvious risks. There is probably nothing as risky as trying to start a successful Black business. Thus, if Black businesses are to greatly multiply, it seems to me that it will have to be up to Black men to take the lead.

Money alone however will not save Black marriages. Black people's respect will rise in America and around the world as our ability to produce and control things increases. As other people respect Black people more, we will respect ourselves more. And it is from that self respect and self love, along *with* increased finances and a better understanding of how to manage those finances, that our families and communities will grow stronger. I really don't see it happening any other way.

Each couple has its own capacity for business success, but success costs. It is not simply a matter of two people deciding to go into business and just doing it. They must be fairly clear about the boundaries and limits within which they agree to operate to reach the success they seek. Are the goals and the costs to reach those goals agreeable to both parties so that other family responsibilities can be met as well? One thing that the media has made sure that people of this generation understand is that success, like any other "high", can be addictive. The relentless pursuit of success can destroy relationships just as completely as alcohol or drugs, and the last thing that the Black family needs is to have the success of its members destroy the unit itself.

Redirecting Black Male Sexuality

Black men seem to pressure Black women for sex in inappropriate situations and places. Many Black women tell stories of the Black males preoccupation with sex. Because she is the recipient of all the advances, remarks, suggestions and aggressions of Black men, the Black woman is a bona fide "expert" on Black male sexuality. Let us say for the sake of argument, that? Black men *are* too concerned about sex, sexual conquests, sexual performances and sexual images. Furthermore let us say that a significant degree of improved relations between sisters and brothers will not happen until this sexual pressure is toned down. A major question would naturally be how do we do that. Obviously women would have to done down a lot of their dress. Men seeing them on the street should see them as people first rather than as sets of breasts or pairs of legs or sculptured behinds, things that many women overly display at present.

But the key ingredient to this transformation in Black relationships can be found in the greatest self help book of all time, *Think and Grow Rich* by Napoleon Hill. This classic, originally written in 1937, has a chapter on *The Mystery of Sex Transmutation*, chapter eleven of the book. Dr. Hill, says the following:

> "Sex transmutation is simple and easily explained. It means the switching of the mind from thoughts of physical expression, to thoughts of some other nature. Sex desire is the most powerful of human desires. When driven by this desire, men develop keenness of imagination, courage, will-power, persistence, and creative ability unknown to them at other times. So strong and compelling is the desire for sexual contact that men freely run the risk of life and reputation to indulge it. When harnessed, and redirected along other lines, this motivating force maintains all of its attributes of keenness of imagination, courage, etc., which may be used as powerful creative forces in literature, art, or in any other profession or calling, including, of course the accumulation of riches. The transmutation of sex energy calls for the exercise of will-power, to be sure, but the reward is worth the effort." (Think and Grow Rich, Napoleon Hill, 1937, p. 176)

According to Dr. Hill, the men of greatest achievement are men with highly developed sexual natures who have learned how to transmute their sexual energy. The people that Dr. Hill interviewed for his book were all successful White males with the advantages that being a White male in the early part of this century provided. It is unlikely that Dr. Hill took those factors into account when chronicling their "success." Many of these men have been alternatively referred to as geniuses or robber barons. The question then is how much of what Dr. Hill talks about can be considered as universal principles of human nature. Or were they simply characteristics observed in White men? How much of the "success principles" are really part of a racist class system that allows thousands of people to work low wages to make a single owner super rich?

Money, sales and success have for decades been closely related in the White business world. Thus, one area in which Dr. Hill saw sexual transmutation being very effective was in the field of sales.

"A teacher, who has trained and directed the efforts of more than 30,000 salespeople, made the astounding discovery that highly sexed men are the most efficient salesmen. The explanation is that the factor of personality known as "personal magnetism" is nothing more nor less than sex energy. Highly-sexed people always have a plentiful supply of magnetism. Through cultivation and understanding, this vital force may be drawn upon and used to great advantage in the relationships between people. This energy may be communicated to others...." (Page 187)

As a writer of Black business books, I have often commented on Black people's failure to respect the field of sales as a great area through which we can "catch up" to the rest of America economically. According to Dr. Hill's studies that same field, sales, is also a beneficial one for people who have "highly sexed natures." Thus, the Black man can make progress both in his relationships with women as well as improve his financial position (which will no doubt also improve his relationship with women) simply by redirecting his sexual energy away from sex and towards something more financially beneficial.

If the stereotypical image of the poor Black man with a continuous erection has any basis in reality, the following quote, from page 188 of Dr. Hill's book, seems to have been written precisely for him:

"The salesman who knows how to take his mind off the subject of sex, and direct it in sales effort with as much enthusiasm and determination as he would apply to its original purpose, has acquired the art of sex transmutation, whether he knows it or not. The majority of salesmen who transmute their sex energy do so without being in the least aware of what they are doing, or how they are doing it.

Transmutation of sex energy calls for more will-power than the average person cares to use for this purpose. Those who find it difficult to summon will-power sufficient for transmutation may gradually acquire this ability. Though this requires will-power, the reward for the practice is more than worth the effort."

If it is generally true that the White woman has always perceived the Black man as sexy (and yet forbidden), then the implementation of Dr. Hill's idea by Black men holds incredible economic opportunities for Black people. White women are greater in number than any other group in America. They spend an astronomical amount of money. If Black men could position themselves to sell to White women, Black salesmen, have the potential to be very successful. Black men can turn on their sexual energy during sales transactions with White women and the Black community inturn would reap the benefit.

The nationally known motivational speaker and writer Og Mandino *(The Greatest Salesman In The World)* was once quoted as saying that the most beat up underlined copy of *Think and Grow Rich* that he ever saw was held in the hand of Michael Jackson. Think about that for a moment. Out of two hundred fifty million people in America, I can't think of anyone who has transmuted his sexual urges from sex to his work more than Michael Jackson. Michael Jackson's voice has a quality most people would consider only "fair", yet he is the biggest star in the history of music. Why? Could it be that he has transformed virtually all of his sexual energy into the music. The "real" Michael Jackson comes off as virtually sexless. Never before has an international sex symbol had to "make up" girlfriends and relationships in order to seem normal.

Interestingly, Dr. Hill also has his own view about why men seek money, wealth and greatness. On page 195 he says:

"Man has the same desire to please woman that he had before the dawn of civilization. The only thing that has changed is his method of pleasing. Men who accumulate large fortunes, and attain to great heights of power and fame, do so, mainly, to satisfy their *desire to please* women. Take women out of their lives, and great wealth would be useless to most men. It is this inherent desire of man to please woman which gives woman the power to make or break a man.

The woman who understands a man's nature and tactfully caters to it need have no fear of competition from other women."

In summary, I believe the following comments make a great deal of sense. The relationships between Black men and women would improve if Black men did not direct all of their sexual energy toward Black women, but instead saw Black women as something other than sexual objects. Some of this sexual energy could be "transmuted" to other areas of life where the Black man could develop a greater degree of excellence. One such area could be the area of sales where sex appeal is a key ingredient for success. Success in sales would result in bringing other people's money into the Black community, which would unquestionably be an economic improvement for our community.

If this idea sounds rather far-fetched, think about two things. Isn't sex now used in almost every commercial and advertisement to sell everything from tooth paste to fifty thousand dollar cars? And if this is true, then why aren't the people assumed to be the most sexy (Black people) using their sex appeal to increase their incomes rather than making many more babies that they can't afford to take care of? Think about it!

CONCLUDING REMARKS

Black men and women must take specific and concrete actions to narrow the gaps and heal the wounds that have caused them to go in opposite directions in the last twenty years. To not do so and merely complain about each other on the sidelines is to risk having an already bad situation in Black family development get worse. At the very least each gender has to consider the following ideas:

A. They must understand that they have been operating as individuals and as couples within a climate of financial ignorance. This ignorance has led to rampant material consumption leaving the average Black household without many tangible assets or much in savings. Nor has this spending enriched many Black businesses since better than ninety percent of Black money goes immediately back to White retailers. Thus Black people operate not only without economic sense but also without an economic base. Without an economic base on which to stand, many improvements that could be made in our relationships would last only temporarily as would anything that lacked a foundation.

B. Both males and females must understand the fact that Black people have been very successful in the last forty years in adding many more roles and options to Black life. A man and woman of African descent have many choices of how they can live their lives, either as individuals or as a couple, than they had forty years ago. But these new options require a lot more understanding, respect and communication between males and females if either is to take maximum advantage of their new choices. Even though these new choices offer more opportunities for variety in Black lives, they also offer many more opportunities for bad decisions and mistakes to be made. This is just a simple mathematical reality, the more keys you have to open more doors, the easier it is to grab the wrong key for any particular door. What this means in practical terms in family life is that there is a greater chance that problems can occur in life and sometimes it is not particularly any persons "fault".

With so many options about many aspects of family life, there is a stronger need for coordination and communication, otherwise honest mistakes can be made much more easily. For people understanding this concept, there should be less need to have to place blame or fault for every problem that arises.

C. Within the efforts at communication between the sexes, both Black men and women have to understand the long term disincentives that Black males have had to verbalize their feelings. Both sides must be patient in working thru this communication and try not to force all communication *to be verbalized.*

D. With respect to Black men leaving the marital home, Black women must understand that they must assume some, if not half, of the responsibility for brothers leaving. Black women must reflect and honestly critique their own behavior and attitudes and never assume that wedding vows, family ro religious traditions, laws or children will ever guarantee that the Black man will always be around. The Black man has participated in a four hundred year search for freedom. This freedom has not been within his power to grasp. But he is aware of ways and means of escaping restrictions to his current level of freedom. Thus the very efforts that some women employ to "trap" a man are the very efforts that make him feel trapped. And he will usually make great efforts to escape the feeling of being trapped. Thus when marriage or commitment more closely resembles a restriction on freedom than a shared cooperative relationship, many Black men will move on. There is a thin line that separates normal levels of responsiblity from that which constitutes uncomfortable restrictions on freedom. No single definition holds true for all men, it will be determined differently from man to man. Each couple has to work out their ideas to their mutual satisfaction. The woman in the relationship must be fully aware of her power in how she makes a man feel. She can make him feel like he is the captain of *their* castle or like he is a captive in her dungeon. To the extent that she can avoid the latter, she improves her chances of a stable household.

While it is clear that a happy marriage has to be worked at by both husband and wife, it may be incorrect to assume that they have to work on the same things. Men usually have to work on being responsible since it is so easy it seems, for them to hesitate or decline taking responsiblity for duties, expenses and obligations. Women it seems, have to work on being more restrained since it appears that it is so easy for them to be demanding in their language, their material requirements, their level of expectations, etc. When both parties notice the other working on their weaknesses, it usually helps them to better
appreciate each other.

E. Black men must agree on a definition of manhood that shuts
down the excessive use of their energies doing nonsensical things to prove this manhood. Black men should see manhood defined today primarily in terms of their ability to create and produce goods and services of value to our community and the rest of the world. In order for Black men to truly feel a part of the rest of the world, the rest of the world must see the value of and be willing to pay for the goods and services they produce. Black people certainly buy from the rest of the world. When his creations are as valued by other people as Black men now value the goods of others, he will truly feel equal.

326

Relationships between Black men and women cannot be totally normalized until the Black man truly feels like a man. And try as she may, the Black woman usually cannot by herself, make an insecure Black man feel like a man. He has to <u>do</u> things that make him feel empowered. But all efforts must be made to stop his present tendency to feel his empowerment from his ability to destroy, kill, scare and threaten others. This is particularly true when those killed and threatened bear little resemblance to his true and historical enemy, but bear a striking resemblance to the people of his own community. Empowerment must be directed to provide things that everyone wants and is willing to pay for and Blacks become the people in control. African Americans have watched Whites, Koreans, Japanese, Chinese, Arabs and others develope their economy. And we called it power when we saw the ability to produce and get paid was in their hands.

We cannot complain about our lack of access to capital while watching three hundred billion dollars of "above ground" money and perhaps billions more in "underground" money pass thru our hands every year. The Black woman must support these businesses as the ultimate spender of dollars in our community. She cannot do this if she continues to buy Calvin Klein and Ann Kleins. Until she veiws her people as capable of providing products as good or better than the designer labels she usually craves, Black economic development may die a still birth.

F. Black women and men should learn to accept the fact that a certain percentage of us will continue to be fascinated with, date and marry others outside of our race. And as much as it may appear to be on the rise, all national statistics state that it is occurring a good deal less than ten percent of the time. Thus after over four hundred years of racist programming thru all means and media, there is still better than a ninety percent chance that a Black man will marry a Black woman when he marries. To dwell on the six or seven percent of Blacks who do not find an ideal African American mate is counter productive for all who participate in the moaning and groaning.

G. Black women are aware of the lackluster record of Black men as husbands, fathers, providers and protectors. They should be made aware however, that both the laws and practices of this land as it relates to welfare, divorce, division of property and child custody all encourage Black men to hesitate in making the full commitment of marriage. Poor to mediocre husbands and providers emerge from unsuccessful marriages fairly intact financially. But conscientious and hard working husbands seeking a divorce are required to continue much the same sacrifice that they willingly submitted to in the marriage. This seems unquestionably unfair.

H. As parents, Black men and women need to do a better job at getting their children off on the right foot regarding relationships with the opposite sex. They must start by respecting the importance of their children's feelings about the opposite sex instead of suggesting that they are too young to think or feel about boys or girls. In a society as sexually oriented as America is, it would be impossible not to think about the opposite sex from an early age.

Parents should also do more to instill in their children a responsiblity to support Black businesses. Many habits learned in childhood are carried forward into adulthood. Perhaps more Black adults would support Black businesses if they began to do so under the encouragement of their parents as kids. Besides, its very contradictory to try to establish Black pride and self esteem in young people by telling them how great and capable Black people are and yet boycott all Black businesses at every opportunity. Don't think that children don't notice the contradiction.

The greatest responsibility of parents to their children is to encourage them to reach their full potential. Few people of sound mind and body believe Black people can reach their full potential by working for White people all their lives. Yet few parents encourage or even suggest to their children that they are capable of working for themselves. It should be easy then to see how then our cycle of human under achievement and under develeopment is perpetuated. Degrees and corporate titles have very little to do with the direct improvement of the Black community and the people who live there.

I. Present day reality finds a significant number of Black women making very substantial salaries in a wide range of occupations and fields. Economic differences and lifestyle choices are a significant consideration in judging the potential for long term compatibility between men and women. Black women should consider the true significance of the work of their potential mate as measured in value returned to the Black community and not just in gross dollars earned per year. A hard working but underpaid social worker, coach, boys club leader, minister, teacher, guidance counselor etc. can have a long lasting positive effect on an entire community. Such a person would certainly merit the same level of respect and admiration (if not more) as a person who gets paid handsomely to help White folks make more money.

J. The word education is an overused but misunderstood concept in the Black community. Usually the word education is used to mean only the obtaining of a formal degree from a college or university. And in using the word mostly in that sense, it can be a divisive instrument that limits Black people's ability to understand each others potentials and true value.

This game is a particular turn off to a broad range of Black men. And it would appear that those persons waiting to see a dramatic rise in the number of Black males entering college are in for a long wait. Black women will continue to dominate the college scene because in a sense it is easier for them to do that than what some Black men are trying to do, which is to make a world for themselves in America that *reflects their own image*. When Black men *have* succeeded in doing that, they have been very successful and the accomplishments have been recognized not just in America but worldwide.

K. As important as it is to develop an economic foundation for the Black community, there are other reasons for the Black man in particular to get involved in business. Business provides opportunities for Black people to express their creativity. This creativity is not valued in normal educational institutions where memorization and rote learning is employed. By using businesses as places to cultivate creativity, businesses become a legitimate alternative (and/or complement) to the campus as a place where intellect and talent are developed, recognized and made functional.

Business can be a primary place where the Black man can re-channel his sexual impulses and energy which have often been an unsettling factor in the balance and harmony of the Black community. Sex is in part a symbolic act to express energy, passion, and creativity. On another level, these same needs and urges can be satisfied in the world of business. Thus business can help our community not only because its valuable in itself, but because it can also re-channel something (sex) that sometimes has been negative when present in excess.

Finally Black male success in business can also help balance some of the conflict in some relationships. If Black women continue to shine on the campus and continue to "fit in" in corporate America, she will continue to be in a better position to obtain the best or higher paying jobs. This challenges Black men to identify the source of their income and stability. Because when all the talk is done, there is a good portion of both the males and females in the Black community that are still uncomfortable with the female making more money than the male in a relationship. Business success for Black males can offer an opportunity for those couples looking for a more traditional income balance. Money issues in Black male female relationships are endless or seemingly so. This volume has tried to address a few so that those looking for a resolution of conflicts can find some answers.

REFERENCES

The World of Black Singles, by Robert Staples
Published by Greenwood Press, Westport, Conn. 1981

The Black Male In America, by Doris Y. Wilkinson and Ronald L.
Taylor Published by Nelson - Hall, Chicago 1977

The Black Woman An Anthology, edited by Toni Cade
Published by Signet Classics, The New America Library, 1970, New
York, New York

The Black Family - Essays and Studies, edited by Robert
Staples Published by Wadworth Publishing Company, Belmont, California
1991

Children of The Dream - The Psychology of Black Success, by
Audrey Edwards and Dr. Craig K. Polite Published by Doubleday
Publishing, New York, N.Y. 1992

David Walkers Appeal, edited by Charles M. Wiltse
Published by Hill and Wang, America Century Series, New York, N.Y. 1965

The Minority Executives Handbook, by Randolph W. Cameron
Published by Warner Books an Amistad Book - New York, N.Y. 1989

The Black Woman In America, by Robert Staples
Published by Nelson Hall Publishers, Chicago 1973

The Urban Plantation, by, Robert Staples
Published by Black Scholar Press, Oakland, California 1987

Two Nations, by Andrew Hacker
Published by Ballantine Books, New York 1993

Think and Grow Rich, by Napoleon Hill
Published by Fawcett Crest, New York, N.Y. 1960

Black Masculinity, by Robert Staples
Published by Black Scholar Press, Oakland, California 1982

330

Manhandled Black Females, by Victoria King
Published by Winston-Derek Publishers, Nashville, Tenn. 1992

Why Men Are The Way They Are, by Warren Farrell
Published by Berkley Books, New York, N.Y. 1988

Certain People, by Stephen Birmingham
Published by Little, Brown and Company, Boston, Mass. 1977

Black Men: Obsolete, Single, Dangerous? by Haki R. Madhubuti,
Published by Third World Press, Chicago, Ill. 1990

Waiting To Exhale, by Terry McMillian
Published by the Penguin Group, Viking Press, New York,N.Y. 1992

Stallone! A Hero's Story, by Jeff Rovin
Published by Pocket Books, New York, N.Y. 1985

Black Macho and the Myth of the Super Woman, by Michelle
Wallace Published by Dial Press, N.Y.,N.Y. 1978

Successful Women, Angry Men, by Bebe Moore Campbell
Published by Random House, New York, N.Y. 1986

A Biographical History of Blacks In America Since 1528, by Edgar
A. Toppin, Published by David McKay Co. Inc. New York, N.Y. 1971

Black Economics, by Jawanza Kunjufu
Published by African American Images, Chicago Ill. 1991

Magazines

Ebony Magazine
Published by Johnson Publications, Chicago Ill.
February 1993 issue

Essence Magazine
Published by Essence Communications, Inc. New York, N.Y.
Essence issue of November 1992, April 1993

Money Magazine
December 1989 issue

Secondary Material

The following materials were read and used to broaden the perspective of this volume but were never directly quoted.

The Black Family Past, Present and Future edited by Lee N. June Published by Zondernan Publishing House Grand Rapids, Michigan 1991

Mad At Miles, by Pearl Cleage Published by The Cleage Group, Inc. Southfield, Michigan 1990

Crisis in Black Sexual Politics, by Nathan Hare and Julia   Hare Published by Black Think Tank, San Franciso, California 1989

Can The Black Family Be Saved? by H. Malcolm Newton Published by African American Evangelical Press, Monterey, California 1988

Confusion By Any Other Name, edited by Haki Madhubuti Published by Third World Press, Chicago, Ill. 1990

Sexual Racism, by Charles Hebert Stember Published by Harper and Row, New York, N.Y. 1976

The Blackman's Guide To Understanding the Black Woman, by Shahrazad Ali, Published by Civilized Publications, Philadelphia, Pa. 1989

In Search of Goodpussy, by Don Spears, New Orleans, La. 1991 Printed by Wendell Printing

Makes Me Wanna Holler, by Nathan McCall Published by Random House, New York, N.Y. 1994

Distributor Opportunity

Very Serious Business Enterprises is a company with one primary goal. To develop, distribute and sell books and materials specifically designed to educate Black Americans about business and/or economic advancement. We have found that the best means of getting our products to the people they were designed for is through a network of individual distributors. Our distributors, like ourselves, have gained fair profits, interesting and supportive contacts and the satisfaction of helping people improve their financial circumstances. Any person, business, organization or group can become a distributor of our material. By simply purchasing a minimum number of books (ten) a distributor is entitled to the wholesale rates.

PHOTOCOPY THIS PAGE - and fill in the information below, Send it to.

VERY SERIOUS BUSINESS ENTERPRISES
P.O. Box 356
Newark, N.J. 07101
(609)641-0776

☐   Add my name to your mailing list. I'd like a chance to examine any opportunity you wish to share with your readers. I am under no obligation to buy or sell anything.

☐   I'd like to order copies of these books. Enclosed is a check or money order for each copy I am requesting.

			Retail	Wholesale
☐	1.	GETTING BLACK FOLKS TO SELL	$14.00	$8.40
☐	2.	BLACK FOLKS GUIDE TO MAKING BIG MONEY IN AMERICA	$12.95	$7.75
☐	3.	BLACK FOLKS GUIDE TO BUSINESS SUCCESS	$12.95	$7.75
☐	4.	MONEY ISSUES IN BLACK MALE AND FEMALE RELATIONSHIPS	$15.95	$9.25
☐	5.	GETTING BLACK FOLKS TO SELL CASSETTE TAPE	$49.95	$30.00

			Retail	Wholesale
☐	6.	MIS EDUCATION OF THE NEGRO	$30.00	$18.00

You must order at least ten books in total to get the wholesale rate.

You must order at least 5 cassette tape packages to get the wholesale rate.

If ordering a wholesale book order you can order 3 tape packages and get the wholesale rate.

Name_____

Address_____

City_____   State_____ Date_____

Telephone_____   Occupation_____

GETTING BLACK FOLKS TO SELL - AUDIO TAPES

A new 1994 audio tape version of Getting Black Folks To Sell is now available. It includes six 90 minute cassette tapes for nearly 9 hours of information and inspiration. Includes live lecture presentations, informative radio interviews and challenging question and answer sessions from sharp professionals. Interviews from Black Network Marketing Professionals also included. This package contains new information not included in the original 1988 volume. Cassettes are enclosed in an attractive six pocket vinyl jacket case.

A REAL BARGAIN AT $49.95 $30.00 WHOLESALE